POSTCOLONIAL SUBJECTS

POSTCOLONIAL SUBJECTS

Francophone Women Writers

MARY JEAN GREEN
KAREN GOULD
MICHELINE RICE-MAXIMIN
KEITH L. WALKER
JACK A. YEAGER

EDITORS

UNIVERSITY OF MINNESOTA PRESS
Minneapolis / London

Grateful acknowledgment is made for permission to reprint excerpts from
the following: Antonine Maillet, *Pélagie-la-charrette* (Montreal: Leméac, 1979);
Marie Laberge, *Jocelyne Trudelle trouvée morte dans ses larmes.*

Chapter 3 first appeared in *Research in African Literatures,* 25, no. 2 (1994), reprinted
by permission of Indiana University Press; the original French version of chapter 14
was published in *Violence, Théorie, Surréalisme,* ed. J. Chenieux-Gendron and
T. Mathews (Paris: Collection Pleine Marge, Lachenal & Ritter, 1994),
copyright 1994 Association des Amis de Pleine Marge, translated into English
by permission of the editors; chapter 19 first appeared in *College Literature* 19.3/20.1
(1992/1993), reprinted by permission.

Published by the University of Minnesota Press
111 Third Avenue South, Suite 290, Minneapolis, MN 55401-2520
Printed in the United States of America on acid-free paper

Library of Congress Cataloging-in-Publication Data

Postcolonial subjects : francophone women writers / Mary Jean Green
... [et al.], editors.
p.   cm.
Includes index.
ISBN 0-8166-2628-6 (hc)
ISBN 0-8166-2629-4 (pbk.)
1. French literature — Women authors — History and criticism.
2. French literature — French-speaking countries — History and
criticism.   3. Women and literature — French-speaking countries.
I. Green, Mary Jean Matthews.
PQ149.P57   1996
840.9'9287 — dc20
95-43890

Contents

Part II. Border Crossings

Part III. Engendering the Postcolonial Subject

Introduction

Women Writing beyond the Hexagon

Beyond Hexagonocentrism

Postcolonial Subjects is a collective project centered on questions of language, identity, and voice as they engage issues of gender, race, ethnicity, culture, and nation. The critical essays presented here focus on the literary contributions of contemporary women writing in French whose cultural ties, ethnic identities, and historical roots lie beyond the Hexagon, beyond the six-sided map of France.[1] Their writings emanate from the cultures of Africa and the Indian Ocean, the Middle East, the Caribbean, Southeast Asia, and Quebec and other French-speaking regions of Canada. In their use of French as a language of literary expression, the women writers discussed in this volume have acknowledged and often consciously written against the literary traditions, linguistic constraints, and cultural heritage of France and French letters. In so doing, they have produced a variety of creative works that participate in the subversion of European literary traditions and in various forms of cultural and linguistic *métissage*.[2] They have also generated new artistic currents.

The editors of and contributors to *Postcolonial Subjects* share an interest in the study of francophone literatures — literatures written in French in various parts of the world. Turning the spotlight outward — beyond France and Western Europe—our collection highlights the works of women writers who, while distanced from the French literary establishment and from French traditions by geography, culture, and ideological perspectives, nevertheless continue to be influenced by the adapted use of French in their respective regions and cultures and, in many instances, by the vestiges of French colonialism.

Francophonie/s

In its purest and most "objective" reading, the term *francophone* means "in the French language," a phrase that generally evokes France and its cultural and literary traditions, thereby subsuming all other texts "in French" under that rubric. In practice, however, the word *francophone* carries with it multiple meanings and connotations. One of the earliest proponents of *la francophonie,* the Senegalese president and poet Léopold Sédar Senghor envisioned the concept as an acknowledgment of identification with the history, culture, and civilization of France through a common use of the French language: "beyond language and French civilization, *francophonie* is more precisely the spirit of that civilization, that is to say French culture."[3]

In his book *Mission to Civilize: The French Way,* Mort Rosenblum argues that France has used this centralizing concept of the French language and culture to maintain its former colonial hegemony in what is commonly designated as a "postcolonial" era. Now with some 200 million French speakers on five continents, who share not only a language but many of the cultural practices and attitudes it expresses, Rosenblum contends that "a subtly structured empire, as rewarding as any in history, maintains France as a world power, perhaps the only cultural superpower, one that is based firmly and squarely on illusion. Freed of its colonies, it is master."[4] The hegemonic perils of the singularized term *francophonie* have been discussed at length by numerous critics, including Michel Tétu, who has warned against "cultural neoimperialism" in the act of linguistic appropriation.[5] Clearly, the overdetermined notion of francophonie tends to minimize and may even ignore differences of history, race, ethnicity, and culture within a broad and constantly shifting linguistic field.

For many people today, however, the referent for the word francophone often lies outside of France, paradoxically evoking differences of race and ethnicity as well as language and culture. In American academic circles, in particular, the term often suggests noncanonical literary manifestations; it commonly refers to peoples and cultures outside France whose relations and contacts with France, both cultural and linguistic, vary widely in degree and intensity. In works as diverse as the regions and cultures that have inspired them, the flavors of Creole, the rhythms of the Montreal plateau, and the vocabularies of Southeast Asian communities expand the sonorities of *la Touraine*, stretch the patterns of "standard" metropolitan French, and modify traditions inscribed in it. The remarkable variance of these voices in French undermines attempts to unite francophone manifestations and even to make sweeping statements about them. At the very least, then, it would seem that a pluralization of the term francophonie would allow us to begin to resist neat definitions that homogenize francophone authors and their cultural specificities.

Yet, despite the differences of linguistic situation and cultural background that distinguish francophone women writers from one another, it has been our fundamental understanding as editors that there are common issues linking writers who struggle to work within and against the same language. For a language is not a mere collection of words with commonly accepted meanings; it is also intimately tied to the culture that has given it form. As Frantz Fanon has pointed out on behalf of those writing outside of France, "[t]o speak means to be in a position to use a certain syntax, to grasp the morphology of this or that language, but it means above all to assume a culture, to support the weight of a civilization."[6] To write in French is, in one sense, to engage in dialogue with Racine and Voltaire, Proust and Descartes. For a woman writer from Guadeloupe, New Brunswick, or Algeria, the act of writing in French is, of necessity, an attempt to make a place for herself in that elite, male-dominated, white European literary tradition. Moreover, for many francophone writers, French is a second or even third language, and one imposed by a colonizing power. The Algerian writer Assia Djebar admits that for her, the use of French inevitably evokes the hostile interrogation of the colonizer rather than the loving words she learned as a child in her mother's house. Indeed, for many francophone writers, the French language has itself been a site of struggle, not only against colonization but against the more subtle imperialistic forces at work in postcolonial situations.

At the center of critical concern in any discussion of francophone literatures and the differences among and within them must be an examination of this problematic relationship of the writer to the language/s of literary creation. In the 1950s and 1960s, as former French colonies in Africa gained independence and as North American minority cultures such as those of Quebec and Acadian New Brunswick sought to affirm the distinctiveness of their French-speaking cultures and histories, issues of language and questions of nationhood, cultural survival, and collective identity became inevitably intertwined. In the case of francophone Africa, for instance, many writers have explored their own ambivalent relationship to the French language. Often, they have sought to examine the multiple implications of writing in the colonizer's language, of embracing Eurocentric and Hexagonocentric literary structures and aesthetics, and of turning away from their own heritage. Implicit in all these problematics of language choice has been the question of audience and the implied reader. Since the 1950s, emerging nationalisms have cast these issues in high relief as the traditions of colonized cultures have been rediscovered and valorized in the various struggles for independence and cultural reaffirmation.

In Quebec, where the language of the "colonizer" is English and where the word francophone signifies a native speaker of French, the use of the French language has been promoted as an assertion of cultural identity; writing in French has been viewed as a weapon in the struggle to give meaning to a distinctly "québécois" identity. Yet even in North America, where the use of French has coincided with a desire for cultural and political affirmation, difficult linguistic questions remain, particularly regarding language legislation and efforts to legitimate forms of Québécois and Acadian French — witness the controversy that erupted over the recent *Robert* dictionary of Québécois French. And although the historical relationship to France has developed quite differently in Martinique and Guadeloupe, similar issues have arisen in Caribbean francophone writing, where the presence of spoken Creole in literary texts has worked to expand and subvert the grammatical, lexical, and syntactic patterns of the dominant language.

In the women's writings examined in this collection, the overlay of gender exposes, intensifies, and reinforces moments of linguistic rupture to reveal new angles of vision, which, in turn, recast old questions and highlight additional problems. The inscription of oral forms, for example, has become a useful strategy in francophone women's writings for representing historical traditions in which women have had little access to the written word. Storytelling by women, the process of transmitting a cultural heritage from woman to woman, and from one generation to the next, has been foregrounded in texts by the Acadian Antonine Maillet and the Guadeloupean Simone Schwarz-Bart. As they have sought to affirm their identity through writing, the Algerian Assia Djebar and the Eurasian Kim Lefèvre have had to adopt the language of the former colonizers. Ironically, then, their means of self-expression and access to the written word have occurred at the expense of their respective "maternal" languages, ethnic origins, and precolonial cultural histories.

The now plural question of "language(s)" remains central to the field of francophone literary studies, and although problematic, it is indispensable to an understanding of the cultural specificity of texts written in French by francophone women. Through the use of various kinds of French, contemporary francophone women writers are developing other modes of exploration and other ways of responding to the transitional social and political realities of contemporary francophone cultures with which they identify. For the editors of *Postcolonial Subjects,* it is not a shifting alliance of political states that constitutes the meaning of the word francophone but rather a common literary project of engaging, and often resisting, the language, culture, and history of France from perspectives that are culturally, ethnically, and ideologically distinct. However, although this engagement in a common struggle with the language and cultural heritage of France provides an overarching framework for the study of specific texts, the essays in this collection reflect a cautious and at times critical stance with respect to the idea and even the concept of francophonie.

Francophone Women Writers

The enterprise of framing a collection of essays on women writing in French from various regions of the world offers an opportunity for bringing together texts of an intriguing heterogeneity. But the decision to center a study of writers from many different cultures around the term "women" is not an innocent one. Indeed, it involves the implicit assumption that gender is a meaningful category of analysis of textual and cultural production. The use of the concept of gender itself has particularly preoccupied Western feminist critics, who have frequently attempted to trace the outlines of women's writings in broad strokes. Their scholarship has often aligned women's literary production across historical, cultural, and material differences by privileging the contexts of contemporary feminist themes, politics, and aesthetics. In her study of feminist literary history, Janet Todd has argued that, for the most part, American feminist criticism has been more interested in gender than in issues of class or race, focusing primarily on white, middle-class literary politics — a current she juxtaposes with British feminist work on the impact of class and capitalist ideology.[7]

Recognizing the inadequacy of a limited focus on gender, critics with an eye to the diversity of women's psychosexual, ethnic, racial, cultural, and national identities have challenged the homogenizing trends in earlier critical discussions of women's writings. Today, a growing number of critics, such as Gayatri Spivak, Paul Lauter, Barbara Christian, Paula Gunn Allen, Bonnie Zimmerman, and Susan Willis, are engaged in *specifying* the various differences that have distinctly marked women's lives and their writings. Scholars like Judith Butler and Eve Kosofsky Sedgwick have extended their critiques to the problematics of gender construction itself. Our essay collection seeks to affirm the significance of these recent directions in "Western" critical approaches to the examination of women's writings.

A further, equally serious question is raised by the inevitable positioning of this project in a world in which political, economic, and ideological power is unevenly distributed among "Western" nations and the various nations and cultures associated with a vaguely defined "third world."[8] Many of the writers discussed in *Postcolonial Subjects* have participated in the struggles against colonialism and are now deeply enmeshed in situations of economic marginalization and fights for cultural survival. Does the very project of analyzing the textual production of these women in the terms of Western scholarship — whether feminist or not — risk participation in what Chandra Mohanty has called "discursive colonization"? To use "women" as a category of analysis, Mohanty argues, has far-reaching implications: "The assumption of women as an already constituted, coherent group with identical interests and desires, regardless of class, ethnic or racial location, or contradictions, implies a notion of gender or sexual difference or even patriarchy which can be applied universally and cross-culturally."[9] Such a cross-cultural notion of gender risks substituting itself for "the material and historical heterogeneities of the lives of women in the third world,"[10] thus providing yet another instance of a colonizing, hegemonic Western discourse.

By assembling studies that consider the interconnectedness of gender, nation, history, ethnicity, language, and cultural identity in a broad range of works and across genres, we seek to interrogate what Elizabeth Meese has called "the complex interlocked nexus of multiple oppression"[11] that links the various literary projects and divergent political outlooks of the francophone women writers discussed here. At the same time, a number of critical studies in our volume suggest that some francophone women writers also seek to affirm their subjectivity by resisting Western notions of women's subordination and victimization. By placing together studies of women writers from different countries, continents, ethnic backgrounds, and cultural traditions, we are encouraging readers to recognize both the cultural specificity of the perspectives presented in these texts and the extent to which the writers examined here speak to one another across differences. We are not interested in promoting a reductionist, composite, female francophone "Other" that would deny distinctions among these writers and their various cultural, historical, ethnic, and racial identities, nor do we want to obfuscate the material differences that mark their lives.

It is, of course, impossible to avoid the difficulties inherent in a project undertaken by a group of editors and contributors who — despite their own differences in national origin, race, ethnicity, gender, and sexual orientation — participate in a common universe of American and European academic discourses. Perhaps at best, as Mohanty suggests, we can remain aware of the fact that our own discourses, as well as those of the women writers whom we have chosen to study, are positioned within various systems of power and domination. The organization of *Postcolonial Subjects* is designed to highlight different modes of analysis and to avoid the production of a monolithic critical voice. Rather than attempt to define a single, common framework within which the works of these diverse women writers can be placed, we have tried to create an expanded space in which divergent voices, those of writers and critical readers, may establish grounds for dialogue, a space in which the commonalities and differences of history, culture, ideology, and daily life may be acknowledged and interrogated.

Margins, Center, and Canon Formation

Within the context of the traditional French literary canon, selecting as a basis of study women who write in French and whose cultural identities and ethnic roots lie outside France is an inclusive gesture that acknowledges the continuing marginalization of francophone literary production and of francophone women writers in particular. It is thus a doubly decanonical impulse inasmuch as the writings of francophone women are often marginalized within their own cultures as well as in relation to the literature of France. Given the growing interest in postcolonial writing, and given the generally scant attention critics in France have accorded francophone women writers, it is our hope that *Postcolonial Subjects* will generate further studies of francophone women writers individually and in dialogue with one another.

When compared to the long tradition of women writing in other, industrialized cultures, the "coming to writing" (as Hélène Cixous would put it) of women who write in French outside Europe, especially in "third world" countries, is a relatively recent development. Even within particular francophone literary traditions, texts by male writers usually appear much earlier than those of women, a frequent consequence of women's more limited access to education and their more circumscribed cultural space. In Quebec, where the francophone novelistic tradition dates back to the early nineteenth century, the first published novel by a woman appeared only in 1881. In other francophone cultures, women's writing emerged later still. The first francophone text by a single female writer in Viet Nam was published in 1962, nearly five decades after the publication of the first francophone text by a Vietnamese man. In Africa, women's literary production in French began as late as 1976, with the first novel of Aminata Sow Fall.

Canons are created by critics, editors, and existing literary establishments. As editors, our intention is not to reaffirm existing francophone canons nor to create an alternative one but instead to give a sense of the richness and diversity of works written by women from various francophone regions and cultures. Not all of the creative writers whose works are examined in this volume are equally well known. Indeed, we have intentionally assembled studies of well-known and lesser-known women writers in order to acknowledge and to challenge the politics and economics of canon formation, a process of legitimation that often occurs outside the country of origin in the discourse of Western critics. We agree with Valerie Smith that it is crucial to recognize "the literary activity of those who have written despite political, cultural, economic, and social marginalization and oppression."[12] Therefore, some essays in *Postcolonial Subjects* treat internationally recognized writers, such as Antonine Maillet, Anne Hébert, Marie-Claire Blais, Mariama Bâ, Simone Schwarz-Bart, and Maryse Condé—writers whose works are already widely disseminated and taught in many North American academic settings. Other essays analyze newly emergent literary voices, such as Kim Lefèvre, Marie-Thérèse Humbert, Marie Chauvet, and Monique LaRue. Our aim is not to present an exhaustive panorama of francophone women's writings nor to confer major or minor status upon a particular writer but rather to examine the urgency and complexity of each writer's statements within the contexts of her own position in language, culture, and history.

Organization and Methodological Approaches

We have organized our volume into three parts whose topics complement and frequently overlap one another. While suggesting a number of cross-cultural and transcultural stances, the essays contained in each of these sections raise issues of positionality, plurality, and place that resist the homogenization of francophone women's writings and of francophone cultures in general. In addition, many of our contributors consider questions of literary convention and innovation in their examination of the traditional and countertraditional literary practices of francophone women writers.

Virtually all of the women writers discussed in *Postcolonial Subjects* have had to come to terms with the past on a personal as well as cultural level. And because the socialization of women as gendered, racial, ethnic, and cultural subjects has differed greatly over time and across continents as well as within countries, diverse views of individualism, interdependence, community, and nation also surface in many of the essays contained in this volume.

Part I, which is devoted to studies that situate the francophone female subject in "history, rememory, and story," presents essays that address a number of the historical and cultural preconditions for francophone women's writing. Like the cultures previously colonized by France, whose peoples have worked to retrieve a past long obscured by the colonial discourse of "nos ancêtres les Gaulois," women's lives have often remained in an obscurity to which they have been relegated by their exclusion from the written word. Positioning women in history—familial, social, and political—becomes a way of illuminating women's experience over time.

If female subjects are discursively constituted through history, they are also reconstituted through women's forms of remembrance and through the stories women write or rewrite about themselves and their foremothers. A number of the essays assembled in part I discuss the strategies francophone women writers employ to reinscribe women in history. When retelling past stories, the reexamination of cultural myths may serve to reinsert the modern female self into history, thereby rendering "history" itself meaningful to the contemporary mind.

Eloise Brière reads the Acadian writer Antonine Maillet as a postcolonial writer whose narratives thread together and reintegrate Acadian history and identity on the North American continent, thus reversing a tradition of inscribed female passivity in the Acadian oral tradition. Centering her analysis on the enigmatic, indigenous figure of Erzulie, who has embodied the ambiguities of cultural experience in a mythic yet personal form, Joan Dayan demonstrates how the personal trajectories of individual female subjects are interwoven with the historical realities and cultural mythologies of Haiti. Working in the same context as Dayan, Kitzie McKinney makes reference to a body of literary criticism grounded in the cultural history and folkloric traditions of the Afro-Caribbean people and of Guadeloupe, suggesting ways in which the reconveying of oral genres enables the characters of Simone Schwarz-Bart to affirm their own voice and reclaim the power of the word.

While grounding their analyses in specific historical contexts, other critics nevertheless approach their subject through the lens of contemporary feminist theory. Using American feminist psychological theory as a critical framework for her study, Mary Jean Green examines the ways in which Quebec women writers such as Marie-Claire Blais have narrated the double conflict of the daughter's struggle with her mother and a culture's struggle with its own tradition-bound past. Complementing Green's historical perspective on Quebec women novelists, Jane Moss situates the dramatic concerns of playwright Marie Laberge within a double framework, examining both the psychological dimensions of familial politics in Laberge's plays and the evolution of women's theatre in Quebec. Finally, in a close reading of Aminata Sow Fall's *L'Ex-père de la nation*, Mary-Kay Miller employs recent feminist theories of autobiography to decode strategies of fictionalized autobiographical writing, describing Sow Fall's work as a writing that questions and displaces Western notions of autobiography and political literature.

A number of essays in this collection venture beyond the bounds of a single culture and geographical space in an attempt to use engagement with the French language and culture as well as encounters with other cultures as bases for cross-cultural comparisons and for critique. The essays assembled in part II examine sites of convergence and resistance in francophone women's writings across national and continental boundaries, cultural spaces, ethnic groups, and racial identities.

Christiane Makward offers a panoramic perspective on women writing in French, including European francophone women writers outside France. In their works, Makward identifies a series of perspectives on and responses to what she views as a common situation of patriarchal oppression. Moving beyond national, cultural, and racial differences, Elisabeth Mudimbe-Boyi's essay focuses on the numerous parallels in women's experiences and in the conveying of life stories that structure *Kamouraska* by Anne Hébert from Quebec and *Juletane* by Myriam Warner-Vieyra from Guadeloupe. As is the case with any critical construct, such cross-cultural comparisons invariably entail the privileging of one aspect of a writer's work over another—in this case, gender—but they also create the possibility of rich intercultural dialogues.

The cultural interplay that results from such border crossings may take place within a specific geographical region as well when differences of language, ethnicity, and race inhabit the same national territory. In the context of North Africa and the Middle East, sites of intersecting francophone and arabophone cultures, Miriam Cooke approaches issues of language use, cultural ties, and identity formation by juxtaposing works written by women of the same culture but in different languages, French and Arabic. Although Cooke emphasizes commonalities among women, as does Makward, she nevertheless suggests that the cultural perspectives involved in the use of a particular language may shape the ways in which gendered experience is perceived and communicated. In her study of the Ivory Coast writer Véronique Tadjo, Micheline Rice-Maximin considers innovations in formal composition and narrative rhythm that give a distinctly modern character to Tadjo's work while also evoking the orality of more traditional forms of African cultural expression. Exploring the paradoxical representation of Africa in the work of Maryse Condé, Christopher Miller examines the Afro-Caribbean writer's preoccupation with the nostalgic impulse to idealize the African past, underscoring the significance of Condé's evolving vision of an Africa demystified and reconsidered from a number of Afro-Caribbean perspectives.

Although nostalgia for the continent of their cultural and ethnic roots inspires Afro-Caribbean writers such as Condé and Warner-Vieyra, a number of contemporary Quebec women writers are looking south to the United States to locate the North Americanness of their own cultural identity. Focusing on recent critiques of violence and American materialist culture, Karen Gould highlights the strategies that Madeleine Monette, Nicole Brossard, and Monique LaRue employ to inscribe women's experience in a broadened cultural context.

Border crossings need not involve physical displacement. Indeed, the space of cultural exchange may at times be located within the female body itself, a site of literal métissage for the blending of race. Jack Yeager's essay looks at multiple forms of métissage in Kim Lefèvre's autobiographical narrative *Métisse blanche* and indicates how this Eurasian writer overturns the Western concept of *métis/se,* with its point of reference in Western, white, dominant culture.

A growing number of works by francophone women writers look beyond colonialism and patriarchal oppression toward the engendering of postcolonial subjects. Many of these texts point to a subject no longer defined in the terms, categories, and codes of the colonizer, no longer characterized by monolithic national identities that may in fact deny intracultural differences. Emerging postcolonial subjects, as they are represented in the works of various francophone women writers today, resist patriarchal and colonialist definitions of women in culture — definitions that have worked to exclude women's voices and experiences from the history and literary production of colonized peoples. Part III includes essays that engage colonial and postcolonial issues — violence and domination, cultural suppression and the retrieval of traditions, revolt and liberation, transcultural identities, and the struggle to forge a culturally distinct future.

Outlining Marie Chauvet's compelling indictment of Duvalier's repressive Haitian regime, Ronnie Scharfman explores how violence and resistance are replicated textually by implicating the reader in a world of rape, torture, and murder. Establishing an intriguing analogy between the biological transition of menopause and Africa's transition from colonized to postcolonial continent in Mariama Bâ's *Une si longue lettre,* Keith Walker seeks to foreground race, ethnicity, gender, the sociopolitical, literariness, and textuality so as to destabilize the centrality of any one of these issues. In her study of the Cameroonian writer Werewere Liking, Irène d'Almeida points to the way in which Liking's novels create a vast intertextual space, deconstructing and revising the discourse of negritude and feminism in order to effect a transformation in both her text and African society. Lori Saint-Martin's essay focuses on the work of a new generation of "metafeminist" Quebec women writers who, although concerned with recognizably feminist issues, nevertheless present individual stories largely devoid of complex theoretical frameworks and experimental writing forms. In Assia Djebar's *L'Amour, la fantasia,* John Erickson finds cross-cultural tensions that are characteristic of Maghrebian writing. Probing the function of language and the speechlessness of Algerian women in Djebar's text, Erickson suggests that Djebar's own writing becomes a contradictory way of revoicing the muted aspects of women's experience in the language of the colonizer.

In an essay that concludes part III, Françoise Lionnet discusses the concepts of métissage, cultural appropriation, and transculturation as a point of departure for her investigation of works by writers from Guadeloupe, Mauritius, Algeria, and Arab immigrant communities in France — women writing from "the border zones" of culture. Uncovering the interrelations of cultures in a postcolonial context, Lionnet points out the emergence of new tensions between the individual and the collective, autobiography and history, writing and orality.

The various critical perspectives articulated in *Postcolonial Subjects* indicate some of the important differences as well as the interconnections between culturally specific texts by women writing in French from various parts of the francophone world. The methods of reading presented in this volume differ, of course, according to the cultural, historical, psychosexual, and social theories of subjectivity employed by these critics. Some critics rely heavily on culturally indigenous critical concepts, whereas others do not. Yet even when "Western" theoretical frameworks are privileged, the contributors assembled here acknowledge and investigate the cultural differences that lie at the core of their particular subject of study. As critics, we are all, in some sense, cultural translators of the works we read and discuss because the interpretive act is, by nature, one of displacement as well as repetition.

Contemporary debates over the politics and cultural impact of essentialism, sexism, homophobia, racism, classism, and Western ideological and discursive domination have not been laid to rest here. Nor have the essays collected in this volume resolved urgent political questions about the connections and points of resistance among feminisms, nationalisms, and struggles to assert ethnic identities. Indeed, these interrogations continue through the critical voices in this collection.

It is our recognition of the positive value of difference — in critical reading and in writing — that has marked our editorial project since its inception. By incorporating a multiplicity of vantage points and critical modes of analysis, we hope to suggest the necessity of expanding the interpretive field in which the works of francophone women writers can be read. We realize, however, that the critical perspectives offered here are by no means exhaustive. Rather, they indicate some of the directions that can be fruitfully taken; others have been charted elsewhere or remain as yet unmapped.

Notes

We would like to offer special thanks to the Guthrie fund of the Department of French and Italian at Dartmouth College for its sponsorship of a workshop that brought the editors togehter and helped to launch this project. We also thank Annie Dycus, Kristin Johansen, and Jill Albrecht for their help in the preparation of this manuscript. We have enjoyed working with our editor, Biodun Iginla, Elizabeth Stomberg, and the many other people at the University of Minnesota Press who have made this project possible. And finally, we would like to thank our spouses and partners for their many contributions to this project, both intellectual and culinary, and for their unfailing support.

1. As all students of French know, *l'hexagone* is a metaphorical term that refers to the geographical shape of France, a country with roughly six sides. French children learn early that "la civilisation" radiated outward from the Hexagon during the colonial period.

2. According to the *Robert* dictionary, the French word *métissage* means the mixing of races. It may also signify zoological or botanical hybridization. In the francophone world, the concept of *métissage* extends beyond these primary meanings to include the blending of cultures, ethnicities, languages, and so forth. When considering French colonial situations, this blending commonly refers to the combining of French characteristics with those of indigenous colonized peoples. The term's meaning in current critical discourse is shifting, unstable, and problematic, as Françoise Lionnet points out in her contribution to this volume.

3. Léopold Sédar Senghor, "La francophonie comme culture," *Etudes littéraires* 1, no. 1 (1968): 131. Our translation.

4. Mort Rosenblum, *Mission to Civilize: The French Way* (New York: Doubleday/Anchor, 1988), 4. This statement was previously cited by Jack Yeager in his essay "Bach Mai's Francophone Eurasian Voice: Remapping Margin and Center," *Québec Studies* 14 (spring/summer 1992): 53.

5. Michel Tétu, "Langue française, civilisations et littératures d'expression française," in *Guide culturel: Civilisations et littératures d'expression française,* ed. André Reboullet and Michel Tétu (Paris: Hachette, 1977), 37.

6. Frantz Fanon, *Black Skin, White Masks,* trans. Charles Lam Markmann (New York: Grove, 1967), 17–18.

7. Janet Todd, *Feminist Literary History* (New York: Routledge, 1988).

8. For a thoughtful discussion of gender, Western critical discourse, and the writing of "third-world" women, see Sidonie Smith and Julia Watson's introduction to their critical anthology *De/Colonizing the Subject: The Politics of Gender in Women's Autobiography* (Minneapolis: University of Minnesota Press, 1992). See also Gayatri Chakravorty Spivak, *In Other Worlds: Essays in Cultural Politics* (New York and London: Routledge, 1988).

9. Chandra Talpade Mohanty, "Under Western Eyes: Feminist Scholarship and Colonial Discourses," *Feminist Review* 30 (autumn 1988): 55.

10. Ibid., 53.

11. Elisabeth Meese, *(EX)TENSIONS: Re-Figuring Feminist Criticism* (Urbana: University of Illinois Press, 1990), 107.

12. Valerie Smith, "Black Feminist Theory and the Representation of the 'Other,'" in *Changing Our Own Words: Essays on Criticism, Theory, and Writing by Black Women,* ed. Cheryl A. Wall (New Brunswick and London: Rutgers University Press, 1989), 43.

PART I

Situating the Self:
History, Rememory, Story

CHAPTER ONE

Antonine Maillet and
the Construction of Acadian Identity

ELOISE A. BRIÈRE

Although North American historical and literary discourse has spoken about Acadians, only in this century have Acadians begun to speak about themselves, in their mother tongue. The silencing of Acadians is a project that began with the Treaty of Utrecht in 1713. With its signing, Acadie became Nova Scotia, ushering in attempts to eradicate the French presence in the colony. French-speaking Acadians would be assimilated by the British colonizer; failing that, they would be deported. The novels of Antonine Maillet are part of a project by the French of North America to construct a language-based identity that defines their New World experience. No longer silent objects of discourse, Maillet's Acadian characters become speaking subjects. Moreover, Antonine Maillet has created not only a linguistic homeland for Acadians but a space for the emergence of feminine discourse, contesting genealogies of gender on which supremacy has rested. Thus, with Maillet's works a new space of cultural significance opens up within the Canadian national discourse.

Antonine Maillet's novels generally exhibit traits rooted in Acadian oral culture; none, however, so clearly attempts to recreate that culture and the gender-based dynamics of its transmission as does *Pélagie-la-charrette*.[1] Recreating the time when word, raconteur, and audience were one, Maillet's novel affirms primal Acadian culture while it contests the hegemony of

North American Anglo culture.[2] In depicting her people's baptism of fire, Maillet creates an American epic that establishes the Acadian people's claim to North American history. Now written down, the Acadian vernacular and the story of the "Grand Dérangement" become tools for the decolonization of Acadian historical and literary discourse. In a radio interview in 1985 Maillet reminded the audience of the epistemological shift that her works represent: "Don't forget that I'm the first one in history to have written down the Acadian language in books that were sold outside of Acadia . . . which means that it's about fifteen years ago."[3]

Maillet's book is based on a collective epic generated at different moments by different authors/tellers who, through the generations, were unaware of each other's retellings. Until her novel, the Grand Dérangement story was the work of the entire community, a collective form of orature, produced through the binding force of the vernacular. Acadian French played a key role in this collective production, providing the affective link between the audience and its history of resistance to the British attempt to annihilate Acadie.

True or false, original or copy, the story has been the basis for a shared feeling of community among the Acadian diaspora of North America (the Canadian Maritime Provinces, Louisiana, and New England) from 1755 to modern times. Its significance lies in the collective death and rebirth it embodied. A communal experience that sealed the bond between language and collective emotion, the retellings of the Grand Dérangement provided a basis for Acadian identity. The Grand Dérangement thus predetermined the way each member of the community conferred significance on the Acadian past and interpreted the Acadian encounter with the British colonizer.

As Acadian society changed, the relationship between tellers of tales and their audience lost the intimacy of shared ancestry and known bloodlines. Modern means of communication widened the rift between author and audience, transforming the latter into an anonymous group of readers. As a result, the modern writer would be quite incapable of reciting the genealogy of any one of her readers, whereas the Acadian teller of tales would most probably have known the lineage of each listener sitting around the hearth. In turn, each of the listeners would probably already have heard at least one version of the Grand Dérangement story, the expulsion of Acadians by the British having been, up until Maillet's book, collectively generated.

As the Canadian nation took shape after the 1867 confederation, francophone minorities of the Canadian Maritime Provinces were educated into the written English tradition and moved into employment where French was not used. As a result, Acadian national legends and myths were no longer functional in structuring the nascent Canadian national identity. Although collective orature would be practiced well into the twentieth century, it could no longer give significance to the larger Canadian national history.[4] Thus, the textual authority of written English and historiography replaced collective oral history in French; the new language and written tradition were pressed into service to spawn a Canadian national identity that perpetuated British colonial objectives. Such a strategy inevitably led to the deconstruction of Acadian identity. Forgetting—a common strategy in the forging of national identities—is implicit in the use of the English language and the British imperial perspective.[5] Longfellow's *Evangeline* conveniently filled the void left by the forgetting, distancing Acadians still farther from their past and their culture.[6]

Thus in the case of Maillet, writing not only rescues the Acadian language from oblivion but also nurtures and shields the revived Acadian identity from the "othering" implicit in the British control of Acadie. The effects of alienation from othering were clearly shown in *La Sagouine,* Maillet's first work in the Acadian vernacular. The protagonist knows she is Acadian, yet she discovers that there is no "national" context into which this survival of early French colonial America will fit. Based on what the government census taker tells her, she concludes that Acadie is not a country nor is Acadian a nationality, because nothing has been written about it in "Joe Graphy's books."[7] In order to qualify as reality, existence must be grounded in written texts. Because Acadian identity had no such guarantee, Acadians were denied the comfort of social belonging, the powers of political affiliation, and a clear sense of social order.[8] *La Sagouine* thus defines the problem of the postcolonial subject in a nation whose discourse—like an ill-fitting garment—is a constant reminder of the subject's otherness. As in much of the colonial and postcolonial literature, the congruence between identity and national discourse will remain elusive for la Sagouine.[9]

Maillet's writing down of the Acadian language is, however, more than an attempt to counter the voices that deny Acadian claims to culture, language, and justice. Not only is her novel a form of resistance to British and North American Anglo hegemonic discourse, but it aims to give voice to those who have had the least access to such discourse: Acadian women. *Pélagie* is unique in its attempt to create a space in North American French writing for Acadian women. It is, then, a program that aims to counter three centuries of silence, which in Acadie were punctuated only by birthing screams or the soft, sweet sound of convent voices, raised in prayer, to His everlasting power. *Pélagie-la-charrette* is an attempt to confer power on women's voices by erasing the boundaries relegating Acadian women outside the margins of the North American nation-space as determined by male British/ North American Anglo narratives. Maillet's epic narrative restores Acadian women to history.

Gynocentric history has not always figured so prominently on Maillet's agenda, however. Years before the novel's publication, she made it clear that she had no intention of telling the story of the Grand Dérangement. No need to tell a story already told by men, a story written down in history books:

> Mais ne vous énervez pas; je ne vous raconterai pas l'histoire de la Déportation. Il existe bien trop de gros livres sur la question. Tous plus savants les uns que les autres. On a tout dit, épuisé le sujet, épuisé raide mort.[10]

> [Don't worry; I'm not going to tell you the story of the Deportation. There are too many fat books about it, each more authoritative than the other. Everything has been said, the subject has been exhausted, exhausted to death.]

Here the writer is clearly defining her turf. No, she will not touch the monument to the Acadian holocaust; men have said all that need ever be said about the expulsion and its sequels. The Grand Dérangement is surely not the theater Maillet will use for the Acadian woman to recover her voice, for — as we shall see — writing about the expulsion is where the "anxiety of influence" weighs most heavily.[11]

Thus for twenty years, Maillet remained within the boundaries of the kitchen, so to speak, writing about girlhood, schoolteachers, charwomen, nuns, prostitutes, and religious bigots, maintaining a respectful distance from the "fat history books" and their account of the Grand Dérangement. Why then did Maillet suddenly take leave of the kitchen in 1979? Perhaps this was, as the narrator of *Cent ans dans les bois* states, a time for unearthing the past: "Le temps était venu pour défricher."[12]

In Acadian, "défricher" means not only unearthing, clearing the land, but also examining bloodlines, determining one's genealogy, one's ancestry. If women are to be a part of contemporary Acadie, female genealogy must be made clear. It can best be clarified through a reexamination of the moment when the identity of Acadian woman — like Acadie itself — was ripped apart by English rule. In deporting Acadians from their land, families were split, with women becoming pawns in the imperialistic conflict between France and England. The successful rape of Acadie by the British plunged the land and its people into silence; hegemonic discourse would henceforth be in the King's English.

Pélagie-la-charrette is not the account of events as one would find them in history books: it is a return to an epic moment in the Acadian past. A common New World attempt, the journey back to the kernel of national origins, by laying claim to the past, is a means of reclaiming the foundation on which identity will be (re)built. It is only when this knowledge is whole that the poet's words can envision the future.

Maillet views history with some suspicion because none of the "fat history books" have succeeded in stoking the fires of Acadie's soul. Her view is typical of those about whom historiography has spoken, but who have been unable themselves to articulate the written record of their own past: women, minorities, and the colonized. Her suspicion is evident in the opening chapter of *Cent ans dans les bois*:

> La différence entre le menteur et le menteux, dans mon pays, est la même qu'entre l'historien et le conteur: le premier raconte ce qu il veut; l'autre, ce que vous voulez. Mais au bout d'un siècle, tout cela devient de la bonne pâte à vérité. (13)

> [The difference between the liar and the fibber, in my country, is the same as between the historian and the teller of tales: the first one recounts what he will and the other tells you what you want to hear. But after a century or so, it all becomes fodder for truth.]

What Maillet is interested in is not official archival history but the mechanism that makes a people create oral epics from their history and how the production of orature is related to their survival. The seeds of such concern can be seen in Maillet's early work *Par derrière chez mon père* (1972), where she states that at a time when it was forgotten by history itself, Acadie was forging its own new soul, so filled with vitality that historiography would be quite incapable of containing it. It is precisely out of this vital legendary period, pregnant with life, that Maillet will forge Acadie's epic: *Pélagie-la-charrette*.

Reclaiming the Mother Tongue

Language, especially the affirmation of mother tongue, is at the epicenter of Maillet's novel. No one will deny Maillet's pride, delight, and skill in exploring the resources of her language as she uses it to shape a North American legend.[13] Although Maillet was schooled in standard English and later learned to write standard French, neither of these is her first language. Both are far removed from the speech of the people she writes about. At the risk of being unintelligible to the reading majority, Maillet has rejected European languages for her mother tongue: the Acadian variant of New World French.[14]

Such a choice is highly significant: the expulsion from Acadie and subsequent exile caused the vernacular to become the "carrier" of *Acadiénitude,* for as Vossler has stated: "If a man is robbed of his earthly home he finds a spiritual home in his mother tongue, which is everywhere and always present to his senses, and can, therefore, at some time again become concrete and have an earthly 'home.' "[15]

Reclaiming the mother tongue is much more than reproducing a dialect or marshaling archaic vocabulary; it is an allegory of national rebirth, a strategy for finally producing congruence between language, geographic space, and time.[16]

Through the use of the sounds of Acadie and the rich oral tradition in which women have participated, Maillet makes *Acadiénitude* palpable. Acadians now have a crystal through which the culture can be refracted. It is through linguistic consciousness that the writer can gather up the dispersed pieces of Acadie's past to create an epic, just as Pélagie fills her wagon with exiles who will form a new Acadian nation. The following statement from *Pélagie-la-charrette,* often repeated by the narrator's informant, exemplifies the stirrings of ethnic consciousness that precede national rebirth:

> Les gens du pays se reconnaissent sans s'être jamais vus, à de tout petits signes: la voix rauque, l'odeur de sel sous la peau, les yeux bleus et creux qui regardent par en dedans comme par en dehors, le rire enfin, qui vient de si loin qu'il a l'air de dégringoler de quelques cieux perdus. (90)

> [Our countrymen could recognize one another without ever having met before, by certain small signs: a hoarseness in the voice, the smell of salt under the skin, the hollow blue eyes that look inside as well as out, and last but not least the laugh that comes from so far away it seems to have tumbled down from some seventh heaven. (60)]

Small details perhaps, but the rebuilding of ethnic identity rests also on the recognition of such common traits.

Thus, Maillet has chosen to exploit a historical theme not for its content but for the opportunity it offers her as a crafter of words to use Acadian French, and to introduce Acadian otherness within the Canadian national dialogue. Such a stance signals that Acadian culture has clearly entered a postcolonial phase, questioning the old British cultural hegemony, adding its voice to the Canadian national cultural dialogue. Maillet's attitude toward language is an indication of this newfound stance: she is no longer bound, as she was, by standard Euro-French, the only French once recognized by Anglo-Canadians. Maillet has used Acadian syntax and vocabulary since the production of her highly successful radio play *La Sagouine* in 1971. Such a shift must be considered against the backdrop of Quebec's Quiet Revolution and the subsequent experiments among writers with the use of "joual" as a medium of literary expression and national self-affirmation.

There is more, however, that motivates the creation of Pélagie against the backdrop of the Grand Dérangement, for any number of heroines/heroes from the past could have been created for the purpose of demonstrating the renaissance and viability of Acadian culture and language. Maillet chose the story of Pélagie because, as she says, "J'ai grandi avec ce bouchon dans la gorge: un compte à régler avec mes premiers parents" (I grew up with this lump in my throat: a need to get even with my ancestors).[17]

This "bouchon," or primordial lump in the writer's throat, impedes self-expression and comes from a score she feels she must settle with her ancestors. They are responsible for the pervasive existential anguish that prevented her from finding her true voice. It is clear, though, that at least part of the lump in Maillet's throat is due less to existential malaise than to the particular ordering of her gender and history that has been imposed from without—from the United States, and in a foreign tongue besides. Writing is therefore Maillet's way of setting things aright, of reordering the world, and of getting even with her forebears, who were unable to ensure that Acadian genealogy was inscribed in history.

Evangeline: The Anxiety of Influence

By the time Maillet was old enough to read, an American myth at the root of such dispossession had firmly taken hold in the popular culture of the Maritime Provinces, where she spent her childhood. From the patriotic song "Evangeline," performed at most school and religious functions to the name of the province's daily newspaper, *Evangeline,* the presence of Longfellow's saintly submissive—and silent—heroine was pervasive.[18]

Published in 1846, Henry W. Longfellow's cantos in hexameter met with immediate acclaim; within a century there had been over 270 different editions and at least 130 translations of *Evangeline.*[19] Maillet settled on the story of the Grand Dérangement and chose to develop a legendary female protagonist as part of a strategy not only to repatriate Acadian discourse but also to reshape the perennial evangelinian myth that glorifies patriarchal values. If Longfellow's poem transformed living, acting Acadian women into "objects," mere reflections of an already written history, Maillet's work would regenerate them as performers in a national story.

John Nickrosz noted some time ago that all of Acadian literature is written in reaction to the Evangeline myth.[20] Although such a sweeping generalization may be difficult to maintain today, it does apply to Maillet's work: there is an ongoing dialectic between Longfellow's heroine and the women characters Maillet has developed, most notably in *Pélagie-la-charrette* and *Evangeline deusse.*

In Maillet's early novel *Pointe-aux-coques* (1958) Evangeline is no more than a reference to the name of the Acadian daily newspaper. In *L'Acadie pour quasiment rien*, however, her nonfiction book on Acadie from the same period, we see Maillet's first attempt at replacing the Longfellow myth with a homegrown version:

> Et au lieu d'Evangeline Bellefontaine, assise au bord du puits, vous verrez passer une femme qui s'en va éteindre avec son seau l'incendie de l'église; et au lieu de Gabriel, l'angélique, vous verrez le capitaine maîtriser l'équipage anglais. (31)

> [And instead of Evangeline Bellefontaine, sitting on the edge of the well, you would see a woman with her bucket, going to put out the fire of the burning church; and instead of Gabriel, the angelic one, you would see captain Belliveau gain control of the English crew.]

The passage demonstrates an obvious desire to replace the passive acceptance of calamity with energetic resistance. This short paragraph contains the seeds of Maillet's revolt against the Longfellow myth, a revolt which in *Pélagie-la-charrette* will produce an energetic foil for the meek Evangeline and one for Gabriel as well: the sea captain Broussard, dit Beausoleil. In the quoted passage, Belliveau's overpowering of the English crew signals not only the writer's first attempt at rewriting Longfellow but also her wish to counter English language domination as well.

Given Maillet's own experience of being forced to use English as a schoolgirl in New Brunswick, linguistic domination is no doubt also part of the lump in the writer's throat, propelling her to reorder the world. In *Pélagie-la-charrette*, the name change of the British ship, the *Pembroke*, can be seen as a figure for linguistic decolonization. Pélagie's male counterpart, the sea captain Beausoleil-Broussard is captured by an English navy commander near Charleston during the Revolutionary War. Expecting to discover American rebels on board, the British captor is stunned to find that what had been a British ship twenty years before had become a French vessel.

Beausoleil-Broussard glibly explains that the British crew became French after having lost its ability to speak because of the extreme cold in the northern seas. The crew sailed in total silence for six months; it regained the power of speech during a hailstorm, as it was pelted by the frozen French words it has been using since. The British *Pembroke* now bears the appropriately rabelaisian name "La Grand' Goule." It is precisely through his own "grande gueule" that Beausoleil-Broussard fabricates the story that extricates him from difficulty.

Beausoleil's decolonization of the *Pembroke* is the equivalent of "merde au Roi d'Angleterre," the blithe refrain from a traditional French folksong that punctuates all of *Pélagie*. The use of words to outsmart the British tormentor is not a futile exercise, for as the narrator states, at the bottom the plight of the Acadians was really a matter of words:

> Une parole est une parole; et son peuple avait déjà payé assez cher une parole donnée au roi d'Angleterre qui, sur une clause controversée d'un serment d'allégéance, l'expédiat à la mer sans plus de cérémonie. (94)

> [A man's word is his word, and Beausoleil's people had already paid dear enough for the word they gave the King of England who, over a controversial clause in the oath of allegiance, had packed them all off to sea without standing on ceremony. (63)]

The renaming of the *Pembroke* is then part of the scheme for national rebirth. Exactly as the British had erased the French name of the province and its villages from the map, the writer removes the British name from the ship that captain Beausoleil will use to repatriate countless numbers of Acadians.

The linguistic revenge implicit in the ship's renaming is essential to Maillet's program. The metaphor is based on knowledge that no real emotional integration of identity — of *Acadiénitude* — is possible as long as those in charge of administration, law enforcement, business, and industry communicate in a language that the Acadian masses do not share. Such linguistic alienation began to change in New Brunswick with the election of the Acadian Prime Minister Louis Robichaud in 1960 and the province's subsequent adoption of official bilingualism in 1969; thus the stranglehold of English in New Brunswick began to wane.

Maillet's vernacular Acadian French is primal cultural self-affirmation. For the rebuilding of identity to be effective, however, not only must language domination end but so must the hegemony of the older debilitating Evangeline myth. Maillet sensed that Evangeline had to be replaced by a character that could energize Acadie. Such energy was waiting to be exploited in the myth of death and rebirth contained in the Grand Dérangement. It could be said that in this respect *Pélagie-la-charrette* exemplifies Fanon's thesis on the creation of a national culture:

> La culture nationale est l'ensemble des efforts faits par un peuple sur le plan de la pensée pour décrire, justifier et chanter l'action à travers laquelle le peuple s'est constitué et s'est maintenu.[21]

> [National culture is constituted by all of the conceptual efforts made by a people to describe, justify, and celebrate the actions through which it became and maintained itself as a people.]

Women, Words, and Rebirth

Evangeline's foil is quite a different character from other feminine protagonists in Maillet's works. La Sagouine, Mariaagelas, la Bessoune, and even Evangeline deusse are all clearly socially determined. Their strong nature and aspiration for a more just social order are in a dialectical relationship to Acadian society's prescriptions for women in the twentieth century. Although we know that Pélagie has worked alongside black slaves in cotton fields, this detail has little import in determining the character herself. In *La Sagouine,* on the other hand, exploitation of the main character as a "fille de joie," then as a charwoman are significant elements in her social determination, making it impossible for her to heed the inner voice of rebellion, too faint to spur her to action.

Pélagie is a character freed from the societal constraints that govern Maillet's earlier female characters. She has already fulfilled the requirements prescribed for her gender: motherhood and marriage. With Pélagie's husband dead and her children grown, Maillet sets the scene for the development of a protagonist who is not at odds with society and who is at the same time free to embody a new myth. As Carolyn Waterson has stated, "Pélagie embodies the most important individual myth Maillet has been striving to generate in the majority of her works . . . the myth of the heroic Acadian woman."[22]

Thus it is this liberated woman who will lead her people along the freedom trail, through the obstacles of exile to rebirth. Although the rebirth quest or journey is commonplace in literature, in women's fiction it is an expression of women's awakening to selfhood. Quest in this novel, however, is not that of individual rebirth: it is intended to encompass a collective phenomenon. As Colin Partridge has explained, "The narrative device of journeying bridges the enormous gap between the internal socio-historical phenomena that shaped the culture and the artist's inward vision seeking to encompass new proportions."[23]

These new proportions bear the distinctive trait of women's culture; Pélagie, a powerful, integrative mother figure, is assisted in the rebirth journey by Celina the midwife. The narrator of *Pélagie-la-charrette* conflates Celina's skill at delivering babies with her mastery of oral history. The theme of the interplay between verbal creativity and cultural survival is emphasized as the midwife — "sage-femme" — becomes the saga woman, a "défricheteuse" or teller of tales.

Celina knows everyone's genealogy. Her own ancestry is significant because it is the very embodiment of the new society being created in North America. With the arrival of the Europeans, races that had never before met began to blend. With a father who was a Micmac Indian and a French mother, "coureuse des bois" and part sorceress, Celina's genealogy certainly fits no typical evangelinian pattern of Acadian femininity or racial "purity."

The blending of races, and the attendant verbal transmission of Native American lore and medicine, contributes to the revival of the Acadians in exile. Celina presides over this renaissance, bringing countless numbers of babies into the world. Significantly, the first of these births on the trek engages Celina as no other had before. Not only does she deliver the baby, but she feels the birth physically as if she herself were the mother: "Une crampe l'envahissait, une crampe retenue durant trente ans, trente ans de sa vie de femme délaissée" (159). ("A cramp invaded her body, a cramp held back for thirty years, thirty years of her life as a neglected woman" [111].)

The birth is clearly part of the attempt to rewrite history, to revise the evangelinian myth that had frozen Acadian women in time. Unfreezing past history, the women characters have decided to give birth without the help of their men. The best of them, an aging chronicler enthralled with the past, is clearly not a comrade with whom to build the future. Thus the female characters in *Pélagie* unite in a fierce rebirthing of Acadie that the men can only witness but not participate in.

Significantly, the first birth on the trek back to Acadie turns out to be a girl. Her naming takes on special significance: the first Acadian ever to bear the American name of Virginie, she will start a new lineage. The women borrow the name itself, Virginia, from the American state where the birth occurs. It suggests a new virgin beginning where all is possible because old myths are wiped away to make room for new dynamic ones. At the same time the name calls to mind manly strength ("vir") borne by a woman ("gyn"). The fundamental act of naming, as Partridge states, responds to a basic need in a new culture: "the first need is to name: ... the bestowal of names is comparable to the axe-blow of the pioneer in the silent forest."[24]

Narration

Narration in *Pélagie-la-charrette* is Maillet's strategy for encompassing continental space and immemorial time. The verbal equivalent of a pioneering axe-blow, narration will enable the writer to retrace a history that was to have left no trace. Thus, in *Pélagie-la-charrette* the reader sees the origins of the oral tradition that stretches from the characters who participated in the Grand Dérangement — modern Acadie's founding myth — to the contemporary narrator who retells the story. Narration clearly shows how the common thread binding one generation to the other was initially spun in 1780, several years after deportation. From such emanations of popular culture, the Acadian ethnic group will be reborn.

In the penultimate chapter of *Pélagie-la-charrette,* as the ragged band of exiles at last reaches Acadie, it meets its other half: a group of Acadians who avoided deportation by hiding in the woods. Both groups are of common stock, yet their history, their past, has diverged over the course of an entire generation. Now reunited, they are are faced with the task of building bridges between the history of those who were exiled and those who sought refuge in the woods.

Their reunion echoes an encounter that occurred ten years before, reuniting the passengers of Pélagie's carts and the crew of Beausoleil-Broussard's ship, la Grand' Goule. At this earlier reunion, family members eagerly sought information about the missing. We do not yet see, however, the formal emergence of a "story" that allows the deportees to make sense of the holocaust. An oral history of the deportation will emerge later, through the consciousness of Belonie-the-younger, grandson of Belonie, the chronicler of the carts. At this juncture, however, it is too soon to sift through the events, to reorder them into a unified chronology.

The reordering of history occurs at the journey's end when the two halves of Acadie begin to fill the void that has separated them. As they reconstitute their existence as a whole people, the reader sees how a common discourse about an epic event emerges in an "oral" setting. The novel details the initiation of Belonie-the-younger — grandson of the Belonie who made the journey in Pélagie's cart — into the art of telling oral history, as he recounts, for the benefit of those who had remained in the woods, the story of the carts. His counterpart from the woods, Bonaventure dit Bellefontaine, then takes up the young tale-teller's verbal thread to spin the parallel story of those whose clandestine existence was concealed from the British by the woods of the territory that had lost its French name to become Nova Scotia.

We thus have Maillet's account of how an oral epic tradition is born. As the two tale-tellers mend the rent in the whole cloth of the Acadian past, each supplying a different version of the cataclysmic event, the reader composes the scene of rebirth not through the sound of the teller's voice but by means of a solitary reading of the printed word.

Thus the immediacy and the intensity of the act performed by the teller of tales recede. We no longer hear the modulation of the teller's voice, see the dramatic gestures of his hands, the contortions of his face as he mimics pain, terror, joy, and sorrow. Writing represses the immediacy of this experience into the unconscious layers of *Pélagie-la-charrette,* constituting its oral subtext. No longer is group solidarity reinforced by the sharing of an aesthetic experience.

Despite this, Maillet deliberately reconstitutes certain paradigms of such an experience, which is why *Pélagie* acts as a catalyst that reconstitutes the sentimental links between Acadians today and their counterparts in epic time. Thus the reader has the distinct impression of witnessing the gathering of fragmented Acadian collective consciousness. As Edward Saïd has remarked about such texts, Maillet "deliberately conceives the text as supported by a discursive situation involving speaker and audience; the designed interplay between speech and reception, between verbality and textuality, *is* the text's situation, its placing of itself in the world."[25]

The most typical device to this end is the "placing" of the audience around the "macoune," the hearth of la Gribouille's kitchen, which is periodically repeated throughout the novel. The narrative strategy in *Pélagie-la-charrette* functions in a way that recreates the illusion of the moment in time when word, raconteur, and audience were one. In another admirable example of this, the reader "sees" Belonie's audience come out from under the tale-teller's spell:

> Toutes les têtes sortent du conte l'une après l'autre, laissant le conteur Belonie ralentir ses phrases, freiner, puis semer dans l'air du temps trois ou quatre points de suspension, avant de baisser les yeux sur son auditoire qui déjà s'affaire et court aux quatre horizons. (77)

> [One by one the heads pull out of the tale, leaving storyteller Belonie to slow down his phrases, brake, then cast three or four points of suspension out into the waiting air, before lowering his eyes to his audience who are already busily dashing hither and thither. (50)]

Not only does Maillet tie the otherwise silent text to the world of orality, but *Pélagie-la-charrette* contains several variants of the Grand Dérangement oral tradition. As the two halves of Acadie are reunited in 1780, each has a different story to tell the other. Not only do the different parts of Acadie carry on a synchronic dialogue, but the different Acadies through time pursue diachronic dialogue in the narrative symphony Maillet develops in *Pélagie-la-charrette*. Such a strategy allows the reader to see the Grand Dérangement story from multiple perspectives and along several time lines. The reader sees the story take root as a formal oral performance in Belonie-the-younger's initial telling in 1880. His is not the only version of the story, however, because the narrative strategy Maillet develops gives the illusion of hearing subsequent retellings, each a century apart from the other.[26]

The first of these occurs in 1880, a date considered to be a watershed in Acadie's rebirth, because this is when Acadians began to speak for themselves, ending what Maillet has called elsewhere "a century of silence and incubation."[27] At the end of this period, several Acadians were invited to participate in Quebec's Société St Jean-Baptiste congress in 1880. In a deliberate attempt to create a unified vision and group ideology, Acadians held a series of similar "national" conventions before the turn of the century.[28] Like the Acadians who participated in these "national" conferences, the narrators Maillet places in 1880 begin the tentative process of conscious reflection on the past, melding multiple points of view to create a national history.

The second retelling of Pélagie's return from exile occurs in 1979, the year the novel was completed; this time the teller is the narrator/writer's cousin, Louis à Belonie. The three renditions of the cart story — 1780, 1880, and 1979 — are not sequential nor chronological but rather woven as a tapestry, with the threads of one story interrupting those of the other as they pass through the narrative focal point provided by the "je/I" narrator-writer of 1979. The latter and his informant share bloodlines with previous tellers of the tale, signaling the durable nature of the cart story, reaching the reader via the narrator who is genealogically linked to the oral source of the first telling. Such a device is the narrator's guarantee of authenticity required for the reader's willing suspension of disbelief, and for the creation of a founding myth.

The narrator's voice is heard throughout, interrupting the diegesis to sum up, make a point, or ensure that the reader has grasped the causal relationship between the oral tradition and cultural survival. For instance, Belonie's tale of the quest of the golden ring leading the protagonists through the innards of a white whale parallels the cart people's escape from the bowels of the Charleston jail. The narrator of the 1880 retelling concludes his story in this way: "Et c'est comme ça que je sons encore en vie, nous autres les exilés, par rapport que j'ons consenti à sortir d'exil et rentrer au pays par le cul d'une baleine" (84) ("And that's why we're still alive today, those of us who were exiled, because we ended our exile and returned home through the arse end of a whale" [55]). We then hear the narrator of 1979, who tells us how the white whale story was added to Acadie's repertoire of tales, passed down in front of the hearth.

As this example illustrates, the diachronic narrative voices do not exist as separate entities, but they speak in counterpoint with each other across the centuries, completing each other as the modern narrator provides information not available to the 1880 narrator. In addition, the narrator provides the contemporary reader with information that establishes yet another type of dialogue, this one being synchronic.

When a name must be chosen for the baby girl born in Virginia, for instance, the group considers the name Frédérique; then the narrator adds the following comment enclosed within dashes: "pas Frédérique, mais non, en 1773 personne n'aurait songé à confondre les sexes à ce point-là" (161) ("not Frédérique, why of course not, in 1773 no one would have dreamed of confounding the sexes to that extent" [112]). Such a comment implies that the reader has participated in the protagonists' debate over the name and has supplied the inappropriately modern "Frédérique," thus causing the narrator to intervene for the sake of historical authenticity!

In view of the fact that *Pélagie-la-charrette* is Maillet's attempt to create a "feminine epic" that would recover the voices of Acadian women occulted by patriarchy and the evangelinian myth, questions arise about narrative choices made by the writer. Pélagie's story is filtered through the male voices of the Belonie line of tale-tellers, clearly highlighting the generative powers of male discourse. Moreover, the narrator in the prologue to *Pélagie-la-charrette* states that were it not for male chroniclers, History would have died long ago. This narrative seems to stand in conflict with what Maillet herself has stated about her novel. She sees it as a tribute to the generative powers of women rather than to the masculine forces of destruction common in male-generated epics of conquest.[29]

Adding to the contradiction, the narrator of 1979 continually reminds the reader of the weighty patriarchal voice s/he is transmitting, and that s/he is merely relating the words of Belonie-the-younger, as they have come down through the centuries. This narrative strategy is a rhetorical triumph over silencing by death and the passage of time for it produces multiple layers of imagined listeners, metaphors for the durability of the Acadian nation through time. However, does it not show storytelling and the attendant cultural regeneration to be men's work? Does this narrative device not perpetuate the kind of situation Maillet has risen up against in her desire to blaze an empowering new path? Like the Acadians silenced by Longfellow's account of their history, women in the novel must first pass through male consciousness before they can exist, rather than speaking for themselves as the principal actors in the Grand Dérangement story.

Such attention is not accepted calmly by Pélagie's descendant, Pélagie-la-Gribouille, however; throughout the novel this contemporary of Belonie (the 1880 tale-teller) contests his version of her ancestress's story. Belonie cannot take seriously la Gribouille's repeated attempts at telling Pélagie's story on the cold wintry nights when listeners gather round the hearth. These are times—the narrator tells us—when Belonie laughs at la Gribouille's amateurish attempts to recreate the past. He is in effect deauthorizing her story, sending the putative verbal artist back to her kitchen and proper women's work. The constant joshing of la Gribouille and her vain attempts to produce her own version of Acadian women's history illustrates the fact that although women may have been important actors in the central Acadian epic, they could not be entrusted with its telling, at least not in 1880.

La Gribouille's numerous protests nonetheless contain the suggestion that despite the existence of several male versions of the story, hers is the "correct," yet unheard, one. Her conviction is such that she swears to the scoffers sitting in front of her hearth that she will write the story of her family herself, just to set the record right. Her intention is an ironic reminder that the making of the narrative, as constructed by the reader through Belonie's account, is still man's work. Does Pélagie's descendant's powerlessness before male narrators indicate that Maillet—a student of folklore herself—has fallen into the trap that has plagued folklorists who traditionally have ignored women as the producers of oral literature and history?[30]

Perhaps the male narrative voice simply illustrates the point where Maillet's revisionism in *Pélagie-la-charrette* falls short, opting instead to reflect the patriarchal aspects of Acadian reality. Or is she telling us something else? Is she implying that women are the true builders of society (pel-agi/*agir* = to act) whereas men are the passive spinners of yarns; does she want us to read "baloney" into Belonie? After all, when the reader follows the thread handed to him by *Pélagie-la-charrette's* narrators, the thread that enables him to weave his way back through the meanderings of the path already taken, whose powers do we admire? The man who tells tales or the woman who weaves the living threads of Acadie back together?[31]

The information the narrator tells us would have been inscribed on Belonie's tomb provides a key to the enigma of the male narrative voices in *Pélagie*. The fictional inscription would have stated that Belonie was the "son of Antoine Maillet," making it at last clear that the Belonie and Maillet lines are one and the same. Thus, like Antonine Maillet herself, the 1979 narrator is a direct descendant of this Maillet as is her informant and cousin Louis-à-Belonie. Because of this genealogical information, the 1979 narrator can thus be conceived of as Antonine Maillet's "double": a woman.

The strictures of dominant mores in 1880 defeated Pélagie-la-Gribouille's attempts to tell Pélagie's story; control of narration could not yet be wrested from Belonie. A century later, however, Maillet seems to be saying women need no longer accept such hegemony. The female narrator of 1979 is invested with all of the power inherent in the verbal creativity formerly held by the Belonie line. Thus not only does Maillet create a dynamic protagonist, but she places a woman at the helm of the story's telling. In so doing, Maillet subverts Acadian male oral creativity as represented by the Belonie "tradition." Moreover, Maillet has reversed the terms of Longfellow's poem, in which male discourse framed feminine action, creating the myth of Acadian submissiveness. Maillet's double, recycling myth and transposing gender, reverses the evangelinian tradition of female passivity inscribed in the dominant scripts of the Acadian legacy.[32] *Pélagie* then counters the cultural displacement inherent in Longfellow's powerful narrative, which had so conveniently slipped into the void created by British colonial discourse after the Grand Dérangement.

Through this skillful representation of the recuperation of narration, Maillet has succeeded in giving the Acadian past and women's history cultural significance within the context of Canadian national identity. Recognition of the Acadian past and women's creation of history is not just a substitution of terms: Acadian for Anglo, Acadian French for Canadian English, female narrators for male narrators. The new strategies for identity, language, myth, and narration produce forms of meaning from an Acadian feminine perspective, something North America had not heard before Antonine Maillet.

Notes

1. Antonine Maillet, *Pélagie-la-charrette* (Montreal: Leméac, 1979). *Pélagie*, trans. Philip Stratford (New York and Toronto: Doubleday, 1982). Page numbers will appear in parentheses.

2. No longer one of the village folk telling tales as they sat around the "macoune" (hearth), today's Acadian raconteur is a highly educated spokesperson for an entire people. Often writing in the vernacular French of Acadie, s/he provides the masses with the emotionalized link between language and nationalism that has always existed for elites at the level of ideological and intellectual program. For a discussion of the latter points, see Joshua Fishman, *Language and Ethnicity* (Philadelphia: Multilingual Matters, 1989), 283.

3. Maillet tells of her role in creating public awareness of the Acadian variety of North American French: "I had to explain on TV to the French that I was an Acadian, a true Acadian, a pure breed... and there I was living in New Brunswick, Nova Scotia, Prince Edward Island, which is today's Acadie, that I was still speaking French and that I was writing in French my books, and that the French that I was bringing back to them belonged to them because they had given it to me three centuries ago." Interview: Antonine Maillet with Brin Quell, WAMC Radio, Albany, New York, April 1985.

4. Jacques Derrida, in *De la Grammatologie* (Paris: Edition de Minuit, 1967, 43), states: "L'historicité elle-même est liée à la possibilité de l'écriture... l'écriture ouvre le champ de l'histoire du devenir historique" (Historicity itself is linked to the possibility of writing... writing opens the field of history—of historical evolution). Derrida goes on to say that the use of writing has most often been linked to what he calls "l'inquiétude généalogique" or to a people's concern with establishing their origins.

5. Homi K. Bhabha places this type of forgetting at the beginning of a nation's narrative. See *Nation and Narration* (London: Routledge, 1990), 316.

6. My interpretation of the Acadian shift from orature to historiography was inspired by Edward Saïd's concept of filiation versus affiliation as discussed in *The World, the Text, and the Critic* (Cambridge, Mass.: Harvard University Press, 1983), 16–30 and 116–25. The Kenyan writer and thinker Ngugi wa Thiong'o calls the shift from original culture and language to the colonizer's the "culture bomb," which annihilates a people's belief in their names, in their languages, in their environment, in their heritage of struggle, in their unity,... and ultimately in themselves" (*Decolonising the Mind*, [Portsmouth, N.H.: Heinemann, 1986]), 3.

7. Antonine Maillet, *La Sagouine* (Montreal: Leméac, 1973), 135.

8. Bhabha discusses similar points in *Nation and Narration*, 2.

9. The négritude movement, under Léopold Sédar Senghor and Aimé Césaire, illustrates the use to which the past is put in the creation of "national" belonging.

10. Antonine Maillet, *L'Acadie pour quasiment rien* (Montreal: Leméac, 1973), 30. Unless otherwise indicated, all translations are mine.

11. I am applying Harold Bloom's term to the Acadian woman writer's situation. She must break free from a doubly weighty cultural hegemony that is male and anglophone (*The Anxiety of Influence: A Theory of Poetry* [New York: Oxford University Press, 1973]).

12. Antonine Maillet, *Cent ans dans les bois* (Montreal: Leméac, 1981), 15.

13. In his work on the typology of new cultures, echoing the work of Frantz Fanon on the development of national cultures among formerly colonized people, the Canadian Colin Partridge indicates that "the final stage in establishing a new culture, which often coincides with the shaping of home-made legends, is acceptance of—and pride in—the resource of local language" (*The Making of New Cultures* [Amsterdam: Rodopi, 1982]), 21.

14. Reed Way Dasenbrook has shown unintelligibility to be a necessary and productive feature of "multicultural texts." "Intelligibility and Meaningfulness in Multicultural Literature in English," *PMLA* 102 (1987): 10–19.

15. Karl Vossler, *The Spirit of Language in Civilization* (London: Routledge, 1932), 123, cited in Joshua A. Fishman, *Language and Ethnicity in Minority Sociolinguistic Perspective* (Cleveland and Philadelphia: Multilingual Mattters, 1989), 286.

16. Concerning the politics of language in neocolonial literature, Ngugi wa Thiong'o sees it as part of "the search for a liberating perspective within which to see ourselves clearly in re-

lationship to ourselves and to other selves in the universe." He calls this "a quest for relevance" (*Decolonising the Mind*, 87).

17. Antonine Maillet, *Le Huitième Jour* (Montreal: Leméac, 1986), 10.

18. George Arsenault gives a good idea of the Evangeline phenomenon in "Chanter son Acadie" in *L'Emigrant Acadien vers les Etats-unis 1842–1950*, ed. Claire Quintal (Quebec: CVFA, 1984), 100.

19. Gerard J. Brault, *The French-Canadian Heritage in New England* (Hanover and London: University Press of New England; Kingston and Montreal: McGill-Queen's University Press, 1986), 123.

20. John Nickrosz, "Les Origines populaires de la littérature acadienne contemporaine en prose," *Présence Francophone* 13 (fall 1976): 90.

21. Frantz Fanon, *Les Damnés de la terre* (Paris: Maspéro, 1968), 163.

22. Carolyn Waterson, "The Mythical Dimension of *Pélagie-la-charrette*," in *Francophone Literatures of the New World*, ed. James Gilroy (Denver: Department of Foreign Languages and Literatures, University of Denver, Occasional Papers no. 2, 1982), 54.

23. Partridge, *Making of New Cultures*, 79.

24. Ibid., 18.

25. Saïd, *The World, the Text, and the Critic*, 40.

26. This was first pointed out by Kathryn J. Crecelius in her thoughtful article "L'Histoire et son double dans *Pélagie-la-charrette*," *Studies in Canadian Literature*, 6:2 (1981): 212–20.

27. Antonine Maillet, *Rabelais et les Traditions populaires en Acadie* (Quebec: Laval University Press, 1980), 8: "Ce siècle de silence et d'incubation qui se situe entre 1780 et 1880 ... pendant un siècle les Acadiens renaissants ont eu tout le loisir de se rappeler leurs traditions orales et d'en vivre" (That century of silence and incubation between 1780 and 1880 ... for a century the regenerating Acadians had the leisure to remember their oral traditions and to find sustenance in them).

28. Jean-Claude Vernex, *Les Acadiens* (Paris: Editions Entente, 1979), 63.

29. Notes from lecture by Antonine Maillet on *Pélagie-la-charrette* April 11, 1985, State University of New York at Albany, French Visitor Program.

30. Claire Farrer points to this oversight, telling us that when collectors of folklore had a choice between a story as told by a man or as told by a woman, the man's version was chosen. "Women and Folklore: Introduction," in *Women and Folklore* (Austin: University of Texas Press, 1975).

31. I am indebted to Nancy K. Miller's discussion of the interpretation and reappropriation of a story as it relates to gender, power, and identity in "Arachnologies," in *The Poetics of Gender*, ed. N. K. Miller (New York: Columbia University Press, 1986), 270–95.

32. For a discussion of the relationship between narrative control and female passivity, see Françoise Lionnet, *Autobiographical Voices: Race, Gender, Self-Portraiture* (Ithaca: Cornell University Press, 1989), 25.

CHAPTER TWO

Memory, Voice, and Metaphor in the Works of Simone Schwarz-Bart

KITZIE McKINNEY

Among the narrative genres represented in the literary works of Guadeloupean writer Simone Schwarz-Bart, those most closely associated with Caribbean, African, and European oral traditions play a privileged role. Proverb and song, folktale, story and fable, initiation story, and epic provide a way of structuring and translating literally and figuratively the particular cultural realities about which the author writes, as she creates her own narrative métissage of Creole and French, oral and written sources, sound and image, history and myth.[1] Varied in nature, eluding categorization by conventional genre, her texts focus on the experience of black protagonists marginalized and silenced because of their race, gender, or social class. In one way or another, all of her works begin and end with the island of Guadeloupe; moreover, all her works present themselves, in whole or in part, as the narratives of women who are characters within the fiction and, often, fictionalized creators as well. Through the diverse stories told by these women, whether they be *récits* about their community or myths and imaginative tales, Schwarz-Bart's texts challenge many of the assumptions and conventions of "heroic" genres and affirm the voices of black women who bind together, through memory, voice, and metaphor, the quotidian detail of community life, moral and spiritual insight, and the profoundly personal. My aim in this essay is to consider some of these stories and the ways in which the narrators' act and art of telling them illumine Schwarz-Bart's first three works of fiction and latest text of history and homage, help shape their aesthetic and moral character, and recenter traditional oral genres so that the voice "which 'speaks' them is no longer heard as 'other.'"[2]

Coauthored with her husband André in 1967, Simone Schwarz-Bart's first published work, *Un Plat de porc aux bananes vertes,* was introduced by the authors as the initial volume of a seven-part epic, titled *La Mulâtresse Solitude,* which was to evoke the experience of black peoples from precolonial Africa to contemporary Europe and the Americas.[3] When viewed in its historical context, *Un Plat de porc* is a groundbreaking text in West Indian letters. Its liminal quotes and textual allusions shift the focus of Guadeloupean history and epic away from the male ancestor Louis Delgrès and onto female figures: the pregnant *métisse* Solitude and her descendents. Furthermore, the novel explores contemporary issues of alienation and exile from the point of view of Solitude's (fictional) great-granddaughter Mariotte, an elderly Martinican confined to a Parisian hospice for the aged. Mariotte's efforts to reclaim her identity and remember her childhood require her to uncover and face ambivalent and emotionally painful questions of affiliation, internalized oppression, and resistance, questions that are as much part of her present, as the only person of color in a doubly alienating environment, as they were in her and her ancestors' past.

One of the many ways in which these questions are presented and addressed in the text is through Mariotte's memory of a *récit* told by Madame Tété, a family friend, to Mariotte's presumed father, Raymoninque, a rebel imprisoned for attacking a plantation foreman. Madame Tété's narrative describes a "local event": the brief adventure of "Marcello-Barrique" ("Marcello-the-rum-cask"), a neighbor from "behind the ravine" of the village, who suddenly decides to hang himself.[4] He persuades the local Middle Eastern merchant to sell him six sous's worth of rope and lend him the rest. Although Marcello changes his mind as soon as he has rope in hand, he visits in turn four of his neighbors to communicate his intention. To his discomfiture and vexation, his announcement is met each time with tongue-in-cheek dissuasion. The last interlocutor snatches away the rope and dashes off to make the rounds, repeating the story to one and all. The now gleeful neighbors make it a point to come by to tease Marcello: "So, you want to hang yourself... ah my dear fellow, what a life!" (132).

Madame Tété's story functions on three levels. In its description of the interaction between Marcello and his neighbors, it illustrates cultural sanctions that have to do with language and community. Marcello's neighbors

recognize the power of the word to take on a life of its own after it is pronounced, and they caution him against giving voice to idle threats, lest the
devil arrive to slip the knot of the noose. At the same time, their words of
advice and dissuasion remind him of his ties with the community. The
teasing that follows when he is disarmed conveys relief that the threat of
suicide has been averted, understanding of the oppression and underlying
despair that inspired it, and ridicule meant to deter him from the grand
but self-destructive gesture.

On the narrative level, the story repeats this lesson of connection of self
and other. Struggling to contain her own laughter, Madame Tété brings
the tale to Raymoninque as a gift; it is the verbal equivalent of the special
pork and plantain stew that Mariotte and her mother present to the imprisoned man in a gesture of remembrance and communion. As she speaks,
Madame Tété continues the narrative chain of voices by remembering neighbors' words, while she also produces her own version of the tale, "comme
une accouchée" (130) ("like a woman giving birth"). Her intent is to nour-
ish Raymoninque, through the pleasures of verbal creation, through the
memory of particular voices and Creole turns of phrase, which are signs of
a community that holds its own against despair, and through Rabelaisian
laughter that marks life's triumph over death.

When Raymoninque interrupts, asking why Marcello wanted to hang
himself, the annoyed Madame Tété draws another revealing parallel: "Il y a
en a des qui demandent pourquoi se pendre, au lieu de tendre l'oreille à un
bon-petit-joyeux-conte: mais y donnent des coups de sabre pour la même-
raison-pareille!" (126) (There are some people who ask why hang himself,
instead of pricking up their ears to hear a funny little story; but yet they
slash away with a machete for the very same reason!). Both Marcello and
Raymoninque are driven to action by feelings of anger, impotence, and entrapment; integral to Madame Tété's laughter and the Marcello story, con-
substantial with them, is a long history of black slaves' suffering, anger, despair, and rebellion by suicide as well as by armed revolt. Raymoninque
identifies with this history in its heroic aspects, while rejecting his neighbors' manifestations of weakness and self-doubt. Living in isolation from
others in his community, he honors the memory of Mariotte's great-grandmother, the rebel Solitude; his own acts of resistance echo hers in their overt,
direct, and violent nature.

Madame Tété's "funny little story" refuses to follow the dichotomy that,
in theory, separates heroic gesture from comic absurdity, fear, and abjection,
and that places the rebel up in the solitary hills ("mornes") rather than down

in the community "ravine."[5] Angered at Raymoninque's interruption and demand for an explanation, Madame Tété unleashes a proverbial insult ("Sing for a mule and you get turds") that subversively reduces the space between him (as "Raymoninque-bourrique") and "Marcello-the-rum-cask" ("Barrique") to the punning slip of a vowel. Refusing to let her story become matter for heroic elaboration — and refusing to relinquish her new-found narrative authority, insight, and power — Madame Tété metaphorically returns both men to what Mikhail Bakhtin calls "the lower material body stratum."[6] They are brought back to their physical selves and to the neighbors who surround them — a domain from which Madame Tété herself refuses to depart. Her act of resistance has nothing to do with seizing a machete or a rope; rather, she makes another gesture as she begins to speak, marking her accession to narration: "attrapant ses énormes seins, auxquels elle devait son surnom, elle s'est mise à pouffer de rire" (124) (taking hold of her huge breasts, from which she got her nickname [tété], she burst out laughing).

At its third level, this story implicates and engages Mariotte herself. Simultaneously a child who witnesses the prison scene and an old woman who becomes its ultimate scribe, Mariotte will also compose her own story of being saved from the living death of exile by compelling voices and powerful, sensual images from her childhood, of which Madame Tété's story is a part. Her own search for identity entails finding place and terms for memory and metaphor: to acknowledge her desire not only to emulate the heroic resistance of her great-grandmother Solitude and Raymoninque but also to understand the misdirected anger, powerlessness, and maternal fear embedded in her grandmother's submissiveness and scorn for those of her own race.

She does so through memory and metaphor by appropriating Madame Tété's strategies of narration within her own story. Mariotte recreates voices from her childhood and affirms her own authority though the redemptive power of language and laughter, which she has learned from her Martinican neighbors and develops in herself. From her grandmother's negative, alienating image of Antilleans as a naive netful of teeming, unsavory fish, Raymoninque's personal song of irreducible defiance ("*Je ne suis pas un poisson / Qui se laissera hacher*" (117) [I'm not a fish / That will let itself be chopped up]), and her mother's subtle, teasing expressions of surprise and ironic amusement at "le comique profond qu'elle voyait dans toutes les formes antillaises de l'insubordination" (113) (the deeply comic essence that she perceived in all Antillean forms of insubordination), Mariotte finds her way back to her native land through metaphorical transformation: a "vision drôlatique" of herself as a "small, crazy black fish" who swims her way back to Martinique, "à petits coups de nageoires véloces qui remuaient par brasses toute l'eau fangeuse contenue dans [s]on crâne" (83) (with tiny, rapid finning movements which stirred up, with each stroke, all the muddy water contained in [her] head).[7]

In the closing pages of the novel, the dying Mariotte remembers the metaphors of the prison scene and Madame Tété's story. Having escaped from the hospice in search of a last "taste of home," she stops short of entering Rosina Soleil's Antillean restaurant, preferring to imagine the welcome she would find there. What she envisions is the comforting maternal presence, the voice, laughter, and physical abundance of the proprietress; the equally maternal sounds and fragrance of Creole language, music, and food; traditional gestures of respect for the aged; and the scent, beauty, and colors of home. Infused with sensual metaphor, memory is carried in the same special pork and plantain dish that was once offered both to her dying grandmother and to Raymoninque in prison. These opposite figures from her past are brought together again, as they were in the prison scene, by nourishment both real and symbolic: the image of the pork and plantain dish transcends empty exoticism and evokes instead a family's sacrifice, physical pleasure, a gesture of respect and affection for even the most opposite of characters (Raymoninque and the dying Man Louise), and a community's thought for each of its members.

Within her fiction, Mariotte dies alone in a white French culture that sees and hears none of her story and that imposes its alienating linguistic structures on her writing, and its racist stereotypes on her person.[8] Her work remains hidden, equally inaccessible to the illiterate, Creole-speaking family ghosts who would understand its spirit but not its written letter, to the one or two sympathetic but senile French women in the hospice, and to the Parisian public that dismisses her as an insignificant black woman. It is only the extratextual reader who sees and "hears" Mariotte's story and who, at the end of it, is left to reflect on its places of insight and understanding, its many points of suspension and silence, and the Creole words with which Mariotte expresses her most profound sense of self.[9] A testament to the pain and loneliness of the diaspora as well as to the construction of memory through a metaphorical network of voices, all of whom bear witness to her past, Mariotte's writing also serves in turn (as) a will and a voice that, like those of Marcello and Madame Tété, persist in wanting to be heard, acknowledged by one's neighbors, and thereby kept alive.

In *Pluie et vent sur Télumée Miracle*, (*The Bridge of Beyond*), Simone Schwarz-Bart's first singly authored work, the narrative also begins and ends as an elderly black woman's life comes full circle and she reflects on its meaning. But unlike Mariotte, whose memory is fragmented in time and place and who is cut off from her people, Télumée Lougandor lives out her life in the same isolated area of rural Guadeloupe. In her narrative, the link between voice and memory is not broken by personal exile; her story is interwoven with that of the rural black communities in which she lives. Instead of being the marginal "Other" in this text, Télumée is at its center, and her voice controls the narrative from beginning to end. It is the francophone "outsider" reading this fictional autobiography who needs to learn to "hear" the voices and the cultural context celebrated by the text. As Ronnie Scharfman notes, *Pluie et vent* is a work which "generously allows us to identify with the plenitude of its experience, to incorporate it and assimilate the [positive, nurturing female] bonding mirrored in the act of reading."[10] As Télumée articulates her growing understanding of herself, her community, and her culture, the reader is given the opportunity to be formed — and transformed — through the metaphors in the proverbs, songs, and stories that are the narrative's principal vehicles of education and initiation, both within Télumée's fictional world and for the reader as well.

As a young girl, Télumée goes to live with her grandmother Toussine, herself a legendary figure known as "Reine sans Nom" ("the Queen-who-cannot-be-named"). Every Thursday night, Toussine tells five stories to her granddaughter and the neighbor's son Elie. The last tale is always the same: that of "the Man who tried to live on scent." Toussine begins with two precepts that illustrate her view of human nature and responsibility: "la façon dont le coeur de l'homme est monté dans sa poitrine, c'est la façon dont il regarde la vie" (76–77) (the way in which man's heart is set into his body determines the way in which he looks at life); "Tout ce qu'il possède: les sentiments de son coeur..." (77) (All that man possesses: the feelings in his heart).[11] She then relates a creation story that describes two contrasting paths of human development. At the beginning, there were persons "of human lineage" whose hearts remained as their Creator intended, able to perceive beauty as they toiled in the world, alternating between tears and laughter. Others, however, became so possessed by vice that they turned (in)to allegory ("l'avarice même, la méchanceté même, la profitation même") (77), simultaneously losing their human form.

Into this world of metamorphoses by designs and desires of the heart, Toussine introduces the story of Wvabor Longlegs, a handsome, green-haired cavalier who saw only the wickedness of men. He grew so disheartened that he abandoned his material possessions and set off in despair, letting his mare "My Two Eyes" carry him where she willed. Unable to take delight in the beauty of the world, reluctant to dismount and immerse himself in existence, Wvabor wandered, always keeping the physical world at arm's length, partaking only of the essence or "scent" of life. One day he glimpsed a woman, with whom he fell in love. But it was too late. He discovered that he could not dismount or control his horse: "La bête était devenue son maître" (78) (the animal had become his master).

Toussine's fable illustrates by counterexample her earlier explanation to Télumée of "good" and "bad" ways to live: "trois sentiers sont mauvais pour l'homme: voir la beauté du monde, et dire qu'il est laid, se lever de grand matin pour faire ce dont on est incapable, et donner libre cours à ses songes, sans se surveiller, car qui songe devient victime de son propre songe..." (51) (three paths are bad for man: to see the world's beauty and to say that it is ugly; to get up early for that which one is incapable of doing; to give free rein to one's dreams without keeping oneself in check, for the dreamer falls prey to his own dream). Preferring an abstract world of essence to the complexity of bodily existence, substituting one dimension of human nature for its entirety, Wvabor reduces human pleasure, ambivalence, multiplicity, and nuance to identical terms of the Same ("wickedness"), thereby destroying all sense of difference, including his own. The mare provides him with a way to avoid contact with the earth and with humanity, enabling him to "live on scent," rather than with a sense of human reality. He becomes an (anti-)Quixotic cavalier who seeks impossible metaphysical perfection, the antidote to equally abstract wickedness, and finds only the reflected image of his own despair. At the same time, Wvabor relinquishes first his vision, then his will, to the creature who carries him; in so doing, he loses both his autonomy and his voice. Toussine's fable of origins thus ends with images of loss, exile, and regression. Through a false quest for transcendence, the "handsome cavalier" Wvabor loses control and disappears, having become a silent, passive object subject to the whims and the will of an omnipotent other.

As Toussine finishes her story, Elie takes flight, fearing Wvabor's return as an apparition. Confused, Télumée "écoutai[t] sans comprendre" (79) (listened without understanding). For her, Toussine retells Wvabor's story, revising it through a reversal. She empowers her granddaughter by putting her astride the horse, giving her control of the reins and of metaphor itself, and encouraging her to live with the fullness of vision, sense of ambiva-

lence, and power to control that Wvabor lacked: "ma petite braise . . . si tu
enfourches un cheval, garde ses brides bien en main, afin qu'il ne te con-
duise pas. . . . derrière une peine il y a une autre peine, la misère est une
vague sans fin, mais le cheval ne doit pas te conduire, c'est toi qui dois
conduire le cheval" (79) (my little ember . . . if you ever get on a horse, hold
on tight to the reins so that it's not the horse that rides you . . . behind one
source of pain is another . . . misery is a wave without end. But the horse
must not ride you, you must ride it).

Scharfman's commentary on this passage illumines many of the important ways in which Toussine's "gift of metaphor" influences Télumée's subsequent growth and accession to integrity as a black woman and as a narrator:

> It is a myth about internal enslavement, and its meaning is articulated as a
> struggle for control . . . [Reine sans Nom] is proffering the moral which lays
> the foundation for intelligibility in the discourse of autobiography, the key
> to the defense against alienation by the Symbolic . . . It is a truth learned
> through metaphor, on grandmother's knee. Whether the horse be a figure
> for sensual love, for madness, for narrative, the structure of the dynamic is
> the same. In all instances, the question is one of struggling against the
> forces of domination, without getting carried away or broken.[12]

Télumée will remember and repeat this metaphor in situations where she
risks losing her identity and becoming "alienated by the symbolic": that is,
letting herself become defined as an object, whether it be through the paternalistic, racist discourse of her white French employers, the abuse and
loss of self-esteem she suffers at the hands of Elie, or, later in her life, the
struggle for survival in the cane fields. She also draws upon the literal details of Wvabor's story to explain, both to herself and to her reader, Elie's
progressive alienation as he loses his means of making a living, succumbs
to anger and despair, and disappears from his community.

But the presymbolic setting of the metaphor is equally important to the
structure and intelligibility of Télumée's narrative. Toussine gives her young
granddaughter no additional explanation of either her creation story or
the warning not to "live on scent." She does so indirectly, however, in her
gestures of living, over their many years together. Télumée, too, indirectly
demonstrates her understanding of the personal, social, and political implications of Toussine's lesson by the way in which she "recollects" her grandmother's voice and composes her own narrative. Pluie et vent both begins
and ends with references to the relationship between Télumée's disposition
of heart and her sense of who she is and where she belongs. The first part,
Télumée's "presentation of my people," as well as the longer narration of

her own story, celebrates four generations of Lougandor women who refuse to "live on scent." Like their mythical ancestors "of human lineage," they accept the changing vicissitudes and pleasures of existence and see themselves as part of creation. Télumée and Toussine also revise Wvabor's story not just by affirming their will and celebrating the physical aspects of existence but also by acknowledging the human relationships that connect them to others. Both women gain mythic and political status in their communities not just because they prove themselves as exemplary figures of moral strength and integrity, but also because they remain active forces in the lives of others. Both of them teach others how to live; at the same time, they derive support and strength from the "invisible threads" that link them to each other and to their neighbors.

In this context, *Pluie et vent* raises interesting questions of genre and gender. The general structures of this work clearly reflect those of the traditional European and African epic and the initiation story: genealogy of the protagonist, childhood education, trials and exploits, recognition and consecration by the community. But Schwarz-Bart's work alters the generic codes that traditionally valorize the protagonist's noble origins and male gender, as well as the implicit, reassuring presence of a transcendent order and/or grand political scheme revealed or affirmed by an omniscient narrator.[13] Télumée and her grandmother are poor, black, and female; the society in which they live is alienated and fragmented by the trauma of slavery and the lack of collective memory. The reassurance of "authority" and "transcendent" revelation is demystified as the "symbolic" subterfuge of a falsely benevolent master who continues to enslave the oppressed: "C'est depuis longtemps que pour nous libérer Dieu habite le ciel, et que pour nous cravacher il habite la maison des blancs, à Belle-Feuille" (61) (For a long time now, God has been living in heaven in order to free us and, in order to whip us, he's been living in the white people's house at Belle-Feuille). Télumée's narrative, like Toussine's story of Wvabor, rejects the quest for "quintessential" transcendence, the privileging of mind over body, and the passive resignation of the initiate awaiting revealed truth.[14]

Instead, Télumée evokes modes of action, insight, and knowledge based on a language of immanence and the detail of everyday life. Hers is the untold epic of the "ordinary people" Wvabor left behind, an epic in which she, an illiterate woman, holds the narrative reins. Like Madame Tété, she translates the past into the present, expressing memory as voice, pride, and pleasure in her particular reality and in that of her community. Schwarz-Bart's written text fully reflects and supports Télumée's act by "remembering" and reflecting its heroine's maternal language (Creole) as a source of voice and metaphor and by inviting the reader, creolophone or not, to share in the same practice of empathy as Toussine taught Télumée.[15] To do so means to "hear" and understand metaphor not as a mechanism that alienates, either through simplistic "reduction to sameness" or, on the contrary, through isolated, voiceless noncommunicability, but rather as a complicated but at least partially communicable sign of immanence, integrity, and difference, a "carrier" that moves back and forth in a different kind of initiatory journey, one that begins and ends with a specific place, an engaged voice that speaks, and a heart grounded in Guadeloupe that listens, remembers, and acts.[16] Given the criticisms leveled at *Pluie et vent* for its lack of an explicit political message and its self-indulgent (women's) "intimism," the possibility of reading the Wvabor tale as a political allegory of dependent Guadeloupe surrendering its will and voice to France, a figure in turn "unseated" by Télumée's version of engaged grassroots epic, is interesting indeed.

Questions of heart and heroism, memory and voice raised in both *Plat de porc* and *Pluie et vent* are also central to *Ti Jean L'horizon*, the most complex of Schwarz-Bart's works. This surrealistic fable of initiation follows a circular itinerary that twice reverses the trajectory of the Middle Passage from Africa to the Antilles. Swallowed by a huge, cowlike beast, thereby plunged into a world of dream, fantasy, and science fiction, the protagonist, Ti Jean, journeys from Guadeloupe to Africa and the legendary Kingdom of the Dead, then to Europe, and back to Guadeloupe. After a return to Africa, during which he is twice killed by his ancestors, he wanders for "eternities" in the Kingdom of the Dead, in a vain search for the reflected image of his native island.[17] In the most remote part of the underworld, Ti Jean meets an unnamed woman, "the most lost of the lost ones," a grotesque figure whose lips are distended into a ducklike bill.[18] The stories that she tells and hears enable Ti Jean not only to depart from the Kingdom of the Dead but also, concomitantly, to break the narrative impasse of male heroic myth by revising his (own) story.

The woman's story is briefly related by the omniscient narrator, who serves as the reader's guide. Mutilated by her own people to deter pillaging neighbors from enslaving her, the woman throws herself into a river, seeking to lose her disfigurement in death. But the beak remains, as does the laughter of others at her disfigurement. Simultaneously taking masochistic pleasure in the laughter and wishing to flee the gaze of others, the woman withdraws from the legendary cycle of death and rebirth, isolates herself, and waits, withdrawn but not entirely disenchanted.

This narrative puts into question the heroic assumptions and the gendered omissions that have characterized Ti Jean's adventures until this point. Taught from childhood by his grandfather Wademba to idealize Africa, admire the violent legend of black heroes who died with spear in hand, and acquire the power of men able to leave their bodies and transform themselves into totemic animal spirits, Ti Jean becomes a hunter who goes off to the forests in the hills. He searches for the personal story that Wademba has promised him, a story that Ti Jean imagines as a warrior's glorious rise and meteoric fall ("une course dans l'ombre, et une chute, un foudroiement" [89]). Like Raymoninque in *Plat de porc*, he roams the hills and forests alone, leaving behind him the community "ravine." Seduced by Wademba's intransigent glorification of heroism, war, and male power, Ti Jean is particularly oblivious to the voice and experience of his mother, Awa, to the presence of his fiancée, Egée, and to the prosaic detail of everyday life in his village, signaled by the narrator as sources of hidden mystery and meaning:

> Il avait cru marcher sur un chemin qui a du coeur.... Mais peut-être avait-il perdu son temps sur les crêtes, petit garçon qui avait pris le monde pour la surface d'une table, alors que bien des couches s'étageaient par en dessous, jusque-là insoupçonnées. (80)

> [He had thought that he had taken the path of courage and done battle in his own way... But perhaps he had wasted his time on those mountain crests, a little boy who had thought that the world was the surface of a table, whereas so many layers were laid out in tiers beneath it, layers that, until then, had gone unsuspected.]

The duck-woman's story puts into question the animistic, heroic universe of male power by presenting conquest, war, and the disfiguration(s) inflicted by "culture" from the point of view of a powerless victim. From birth, the woman is seen and treated as an object, property to be desired and plundered. Her body is stretched to the limits of humanness, until metaphoric resemblance is forced out of its figurative domain, brought closer to the literalness of flesh become a duck's bill. Her disfigurement is the antithesis of the men's active, purposeful self-transformation into totemic animals, a sign of their mastery of ancient knowledge and their desire to become like gods. At the same time, her deformity reminds the reader of the part of Awa's story that the narrator has revealed but that Ti Jean does not know: the way in which his mother's sexual "lips" were also stretched by Wademba prior to his incest with her. In both cases, neither woman tells these stories directly; their memory of their own body is conveyed through a voice that is not theirs.

At the end of the third-person narrative, however, sentence structure shifts to approximate direct quotes, and the duck-woman moves closer to her own words as she explains to Ti Jean that she has chosen to endure the laughter of others without entirely giving up her sense of life's mystery and hope of renewal, to be "withdrawn" from the cycle of life but not "entirely disenchanted." Her nuanced, thoughtful affirmation of choice and engagement also reflects that of Ti Jean's mother and his fiancée, Egée; her example brings to Ti Jean's consciousness, for the first time in the fable, an image of heroism that does not celebrate the violent gesture of the warrior, but, rather, affirms the deliberate moral choice to overcome despair by retaining one's attachment to, and engagement in, life's creative cycle. If there is a lesson to the fable, a hidden source of wisdom that motivates Ti Jean's immense quest, it is already here, implicit in a "dead" figure, delaying but still awaiting her turn for rebirth. The duck-woman's tenacity and courage become more striking when one compares her "figure" in the underworld with that of Wademba, who chooses never to narrate his shame of being rejected and killed by his own people because he had been a slave in the New World; like Wvabor in Toussine's story, Wademba loses his voice and disappears, the prey of his own heroic obsession.

Ti Jean listens to the duck-woman's story, as she will then listen to him, "avec intérêt, honneur et respect, sans manifester la moindre surprise" (203) (with interest, honor, and respect, without showing the least bit of surprise). This is the first instance where Ti Jean stops to listen to a woman's story in this way; perhaps he begins to discover the serious reciprocity that underlies the real hearing and telling of stories. Pleased that he has been the first to hear her story through to the end, the duck-woman relates, this time in her own voice, a folktale told to her in childhood about a beast that swallowed the sun and about Losiko-Siko, the young hero who killed the beast and freed the sun and the creatures within it. This tale uncannily doubles the fantastic adventure that Ti Jean has just narrated to the duck-woman (and that the narrator has been "telling" the reader), including the exact coincidence of the two protagonists' "hidden" name ("He-who-says-yes-to-death"). What is more, the folktale that both contains and is contained by Ti Jean's own story has an end. As he cuts his way out of the beast, Losiko-Siko hears the cry of the thousands of creatures entrapped with him: "prends garde, tu nous déchires" (204) (be careful, you're tearing us apart!). The seemingly fortuitous metonymical relationship of devouring beast and devoured victim, container and contained, evil and innocence, is, in fact, metaphorical; the boundaries between self and other cannot so easily be taken for granted or defined by the hero's knife.

A gift of memory and association through similarity, the duck-woman's childhood tale unblocks the present by projecting the past into the future in a way that will profoundly influence Ti Jean and transform his story. The folktale of Losiko-Siko does not exclude heroism, but it does teach the protagonist that there is no such thing as a solitary gesture. Its lesson is one of empathy: a call to perceive and act on the invisible relationships that bind even apparent opposites, a refusal to split experience into mutually exclusive, binary poles that can be kept/cut apart. This lesson is crucial. It holds the power to mend the multiple schisms that have made Ti Jean's quest for identity so difficult: between the proud, rebellious "old ancestors" living with an idealized memory of Africa and the "new generation" of Guadeloupeans trying to forget the past and adopt European culture; between the intransigent heroism of his grandfather and the vaguely perceived healing gestures of his mother, who already bridged both worlds with her body, even if she did not do so in words.

Just as Toussine's tale of Wvabor teaches about and gradually inspires psychological — and narrative — control through the exercise of human will, so do the duck-woman's stories give Ti Jean an understanding of control through the exercise of empathy. Each stage of Ti Jean's return journey will repeat this lesson and deepen his insight. The duck-woman directs Ti Jean to the hidden home of another legendary "incarnation" of folktale, the "Queen-with-long-breasts," who knows the way out of the underworld. Before she uses her powers to free Ti Jean, the Queen, like the duck-woman, sharpens the vision of Ti Jean's "eyes on the inside of his head," which perceive hidden unity beneath surface antithesis: he will come to "see" that the old hag and the young beauty are one and the same woman. The lesson will be repeated once again by Eusebius the Ancient, one of Wademba's peers and friends, as Ti Jean lies dying in Europe, having been drained of his will to live and transformed into a creature more animal than human. This time, the story of empathy that saves him from death and that "reorients" his spirit in life-giving ways is itself set free from the limits of gender. The character who offers Ti Jean the blood of his heart and lays out symbols and vials of healing (as did Awa for her neighbors in Guadeloupe), who reveals the secret of the Beast and then knowingly sets off on an impossible search for his friend, the disgraced Wademba, is male. Ti Jean's childhood sensitivity to "la face cachée des choses, ... l'univers invisible et grandiose qu'il avait toujours pressenti sous le masque" (58) (the hidden face of things ... the invisible, grandiose world that he had always intuited under the mask) and his epic quest for "le chemin qui a du coeur" (80) (the path of courage) are thus complemented by equally necessary versions of "heart" taught to him through the metaphors of others of both genders: courage, determination to keep a sense of life's mystery, and active care for others.[19]

Ti Jean is guided to the Beast not by Wademba's magical belt of strength but rather by his grandfather's bracelet of wisdom, which "speaks" to him for the first time after his return to Guadeloupe. After he shoots the Beast and is about to bring down his machete on the dead creature, Ti Jean remembers the tale of Losiko-Siko, stops in midblow, and then proceeds with care and with conscience to free the worlds and peoples held captive inside. His gesture, simultaneously an act of memory, revision, and symbolic rebirth, is a manifestation of the insight and the empathy he has gained. As voices and stories overlap and old memory emerges in a new context, Ti Jean brings an end to the feeling of being exiled in one's own country, as well as, perhaps, in one's own constructions of gender. When Eusebius asks him for a "small word" to take to Wademba in the underworld, Ti Jean retells his grandfather's story of the African diaspora through images of grounding, renewal, and fruition: "Dites-lui ... que nous sommes peut-être la branche coupée de l'arbre, une branche emportée par le vent, oubliée; mais tout cela aurait bien fini par envoyer des racines un jour, et puis un tronc et de nouvelles branches avec des feuilles, des fruits ..., des fruits qui ne ressembleraient à personne, dites-lui ..." (248) (Tell him ... that we're perhaps the branch cut off from the tree, a branch carried off by the wind and forgotten; but all that could well end up sending out roots one day, and then a trunk and new branches, with leaves and fruit ... fruit that would resemble no one else, tell him ...). His words evoke the future, with promising metaphors of Antillean creation yet to come. But they also evoke stories of the past, both those that were given voice and others kept silent, "cut off from the tree" and "carried off by the wind," their figures "withdrawn but not entirely disenchanted." Ti Jean's wisdom is to know, to hear, and to remember them, their shapes a palimpsest at the end of his fable.[20]

In the author's foreword to her most recently published work, the six-volume *Hommage à la femme noire*, Schwarz-Bart expresses her desire to honor black women whose voices and memory are excluded not just from "the" high canon of Western literature but often from other canons, other literatures, and other narratives of history as well: "For the first time in any language, a work evokes the history of the black woman in its continuity, from the beginning of time until the present, thus ending a thousand years of silence . . ."[21] Created for the general public, her text appears as a striking mosaic that is visual as well as verbal: photographs, prints, and paintings of black women are interspersed with eighty-five short biographies of women from ancient and modern Africa, the Americas, and the Caribbean, and passages from fiction and autobiography written by and about women. The margins of the main text contain poems, proverbs, and excerpts from scholarly and general works offering sociocultural background related to the biographies and visual pieces. This unusual text, with its abundant, often seemingly fragmentary array of formal elements, focuses more directly on many of the issues concerning the voice and memory of black women that were implicit in Schwarz-Bart's earlier fiction: the text challenges the boundaries of cultural canons, values, and aesthetic assumptions that exclude black women, defies traditional notions of genre, and asks its reader to participate in the construction of new narratives that also "remember" forgotten figures.

In the first biography of the collection, titled "Black Eve," the author/narrator returns to the origins of both story and history, the creation of the human race. She fuses the language of mythical beginnings with data from recent archaeological and genetic reseach, not just to demystify one of the first assumptions of male precedence and power but also to destroy all subsequent claims to hierarchical ethnic or racial superiority:

> Thus we come full circle: the narrative of science overlaps with the old story of creation . . . the first man is a woman . . . More recent verifications attest to it: Lucy, the small African woman, is our common grandmother, Black and White, Yellow, Red, peoples of the sea and inhabitants of the steppes, those who know the warmth of the sun or the polar cold, she is the sole womb from which came all of humanity. (1:15–16)

The African stories of creation, in which God is both male and female, and the Haitian paintings of "Black Eve" in Eden that surround Schwarz-Bart's text remind the reader of the multiple stories, the ambiguities of gender, and the underlying sense of common origins in woman's body that are excluded from traditional Judeo-Christian representations of God as a white male creator, of the serpent as a symbol of evil, of Eve as a disobedient temptress rather than as a source of life and curiosity about what is not yet known, and of Adam as the dominant male, the guardian and perpetuator of language, law, and power.

This founding story of remembering and restitution is at the heart of *Hommage* as a whole, as it is of Schwarz-Bart's entire literary enterprise.

Hommage contains striking images, both visual and literary, of the consequences suffered by black women when the culturally dominant male "particular" is written, imposed, and accepted as false "totality": fragments of
crumbled bone buried in layers of history; repressed memory of wives, con-
sorts, and mothers whose unrecorded words of counsel and inspiration have
little or no place alongside the epic deeds of "great men"; queens excluded
from the chronicles of ancient Africa because their kingdoms had no history of war; psychological strictures applied to women whose intelligence
was too obvious and too threatening to men; and obstacles past and present
based on sexism, racism, and class differences and meant to silence women.
Hommage explores these painful places of loss, where black women's voices
and memories have been erased and alienating images have been imposed
in their place by those whose desire for domination and power — cultural,
political, sexual, or otherwise — have led them to represent difference only
in their own terms. The apparent fragmentation of this work and its visual
laying out of many pieces and images of black women are reminders that
women have often been represented through the rhetorical figure of synecdoche as a collection of fragments, an aesthetics of parts. For besides mediating the false substitution of male "part" for human whole, synecdoche
invites dismemberment and dominance, not just as woman's body is trivi-
alized, isolated, and pulled apart as a physical object but also as that body
is emptied of self-possessed voice and memory and transformed into a pre-
text for male subjective fantasies, an echo chamber used by him to find his
voice and vision.[22]

What *Hommage* does, on every level of its functioning, is to re/member
black women through synecdoche, the very figure traditionally used to exclude and dismember the female body. As black women overcome obstacles
blocking their aspirations, affirm their presence, and reclaim their integrity,
memory, and voice, synecdoche is rehabilitated as a creative principle. In
the individual biographies, the author does not include detailed "surface"
chronology, nor an exhaustive summary of the life of her subject. Rather,
she focuses on a limited number of episodes that seem to her to illumine
essential traits of her subject's character. In this way, particular details are
transformed into powerful — that is, "competent" — signs. Synecdoche is
made to work conjunctively, rather than disjunctively, linking part to whole,
outer circumstance to inner reality, the vicissitudes of the present to a vision of one's past, and everyday life to heroic acts that emerge from it. Epic
no longer belongs to the privileged (male) few; beauty is no longer made

into a transcendent abstraction and isolated from functional reality. Women's voices and images affirm power as difference, resistance, endurance, and courage and make that power available to others as a living inheritance.

To be sure, this transformation depends not just on women's acts but also on the author's own work of memory and interpretation. It is she who restores women's words and presence through quotes and visual images woven into her narrative. It is she who reconstructs the voice of forgotten women so that the act of hearing and telling remains a communicative triangle, where the object of homage, like her fictional characters in earlier works, gains voice as a subject in the text. She is also the contemporary *griot* who transposes the Creole turns of phrase, the repetitions, the parallelisms, and the techniques of direct address of oral tradition in a written and visual text, thereby continuing to remember the affective relationship linking the singer of tales, the object of praise, and the audience, even as she transfers the visual power usually reserved for the living storyteller to the images of the women in her texts. Schwarz-Bart is the first to admit that her choices — both of figures and her illumination of them — are subjective "coups de coeur."[23] But in *Hommage,* as in her fiction, those "coups de coeur" have a design and an aesthetic raison d'être.

And it is here that one final remark must be added about what Schwarz-Bart's works contribute to the sense of memory, voice, and metaphor that arises as her female figures tell stories. It is tempting to classify her texts as a founding countercanon that celebrates the "voice of the black woman" in a world that still often ignores that voice. But to read Schwarz-Bart's fiction in an exclusive — and exclusionary — way would be to miss its point. For her works, like the stories of the women within them, are both part and whole, texts that valorize the coexistence and the conjunction of both the particular and the universal. Even as they celebrate black women, they refuse the isolation of parts, the prison of binary reversals. Even as they embody the voice and memory of black women through the medium of images, through quotes, and through the empowering presence of a female narrator in the text, Schwarz-Bart's works are also inspired by the voices of both genders from other races, religions, and cultures. Writers such as Anton Chekhov, Nikolai Leskov, Isaac Singer, and André Schwarz-Bart were important influences in her early fiction. Passages of Aimé Césaire's *Cahier d'un retour au pays natal* serve as liminal quotes in *Un Plat de porc* and in all six volumes of *Hommage. Hommage* includes texts by Césaire, Winnie Mandela, Frederick Douglass, Baba de Karo, Angelo Maliki, twenty contemporary black American women, as well as excerpts from *Pluie et vent,* while it also draws on a variety of literary intertexts that, along with the documents retrieved from archives and taped interviews from living sources, lend form and spirit to the work: for example, Erskine Caldwell's fiction, James Agee's portrait of sharecroppers in *Let Us Now Praise Famous Men,* Thomas Morfolo's *Chaka,* and a collection of ancient Chinese biographies, *Biographie des regrets éternels,* written to capture the "essence" of both great and lowly persons through the writer's selection and development of significant details.[24]

In many ways, Schwarz-Bart's fiction asks its reader to practice an ideal pedagogy, and it does so through the gesture of storytelling, especially as it is practiced by women. It encourages us to negotiate a difficult, delicate, and endless process of initiation, both acknowledging difference and appreciating shared experience, of renouncing power as dominance and envisioning it instead as competence and empathy, and of listening for and understanding the "music" of other voices in what they offer that is both particular and universal, as they teach us about the limits and the relativity, as well as the range and the resonance, of our own.

Notes

Portions of this study have been developed from material initially presented at the 1988 and 1989 meetings of the Modern Language Association and in my article "Antillean Versions of the Quest in Two Novels by Simone Schwarz-Bart," *French Review* 62, no. 4 (March 1989): 650–60. Because this essay focuses on the reconstruction of voice and memory through the creation of text, Simone Schwarz-Bart's play *Ton beau capitaine* is not included. I have written about it in "Vers une poétique de l'exil: les sortilèges de l'absence dans *Ton beau capitaine* de Simone Schwarz-Bart," *French Review* 65, no. 3 (Feb. 1992): 449–60. I would like to express my appreciation to Peter S. McKinney and Eileen Julien for their critical reading of the manuscript and to the Bentley College administration and Faculty Affairs Committee for a sabbatical leave, a summer grant, and travel support for this project.

1. The notion of multilinguistic, multicultural métissage as a positive, egalitarian force in Caribbean artistic creation was introduced by Edouard Glissant in *Le Discours antillais* (Paris: Editions du Seuil, 1981), 462–63. Françoise Lionnet further explores and develops this idea in *Autobiographical Voices: Race, Gender, Self-Portraiture* (Ithaca and London: Cornell University Press, 1989).

2. The "different voice" of women and their concerns about the sense of moral commitment and relatedness to others are the subject of Carol Gilligan's *In a Different Voice: Psychological Theory and Women's Development* (Cambridge, Mass. and London: Harvard University Press, 1982) and *Mapping the Moral Domain* (Cambridge, Mass. and London: Harvard University Press, 1988).

3. The Schwarz-Barts did not pursue their collaborative project, at least as the series was initially described, beyond *Un Plat de porc.* Yet the idea of epic would remain important for both of them and would eventually be realized in other forms. André Schwarz-Bart continued the original series with a second, historically oriented novel about Guadeloupe's national heroine, *La Mulâtresse Solitude* (Paris: Editions du Seuil, 1972). Simone Schwarz-Bart took what might be called a Chekhovian approach to epic, redefining it through the detail of everyday reality and the figures of black women who appear in her works. The Schwarz-Barts again joined forces to produce *Hommage à la femme noire,* a six-volume work that combines

portraits of eighty-five black women written by Simone and sociocultural, pictorial, and historical material gathered and edited by André. In its scope and effect, this contribution returns to — and fulfills — the couple's initial desire to create an epic focusing on the experience of black peoples.

4. Simone and André Schwarz-Bart, *Un Plat de porc aux bananes vertes* (Paris: Editions du Seuil, 1967), 125. Page references are given in parentheses. Translations are my own.

5. For discussion of the heroic symbols associated with the Caribbean hills ("mornes"), see J. Michael Dash, "Le Cri du morne: La Poétique du paysage césairien et la littérature antillaise," in *Soleil éclaté: Mélanges offerts à Aimé Césaire à l'occasion de son soixante-dixième anniversaire par une équipe internationale d'artistes et de chercheurs.* (Tubingen: Gunter Narr Verlag, 1984); and Micheline Rice-Maximin, "*Koko sek toujou ni dlo*: Contribution à l'étude des caractères spécifiques de la littérature guadeloupéenne," *Dissertation Abstracts International* 49, no. 10 (April 1989): 3023A; and "The Maroon in Guadeloupean Literature," *West Virginia University Philological Papers* 32 (1986–87): 15–20.

6. Mikhail Bakhtin, *Rabelais and His World,* trans. Helene Iswolsky (Cambridge, Mass.: MIT Press, 1968). This is the domain of the lower body parts, sites of excretion and procreation, reminders of humanity and the inseparable copresence of life and death.

7. Mariotte's "vision drôlatique" of herself as a fish swimming back to Martinique is, in and of itself, a liberating image of play and pleasure. It frees her not only from her sordid surroundings and feelings of alienation but also from her crippled body. At the same time, her metaphor suggests a parody of Aimé Césaire's solemn "return to [his] native land" (*Cahier d'un retour au pays natal*).

8. Mariotte begins the first of her seven personal "notebooks," which constitute the "chapters" of this novel, with a struggle to find the "right" French word to describe her thoughts and feelings. The only black woman in the hospice, she is seen by "caretakers" and peers as an exotic object, a sexually compliant "doudou," a sorceress, a cannibal, and a creature who can understand only pidgin French.

9. "Et j'ai dit à la Martinique, dans ma langue maternelle: 'Zotte ki d'l'autre côté d' l'eau, miré moin, couté ti brin . . . Cé moin, cé moin même ki là: moin la Mariotte, la Marie Bel Chiveux, la Marie Diab', la Marie à Grands-Fonds, la Marie à Morne Pichevin et toutes ces montagnes vertes à nous-là-ça! . . . Zott ka tann'? . . . " (138) (And I said to Martinique, in my mother tongue: "You who are over there, on the other side of the water, look at me, listen to me a little . . . It's I, it's I myself who am here, I Mariotte, Marie with the beautiful hair, the little devil Marie, Marie from Grands-Fonds, Marie from Pichevin Hill and all those green mountains that are ours! Do you hear me? . . . ") This declaration of identity is not accompanied in the text by the usual parentheses or footnote containing a French translation.

10. Ronnie Scharfman, "Mirroring and Mothering in Simone Schwarz-Bart's *Pluie et vent sur Télumée Miracle* and Jean Rhys's *Wide Sargasso Sea*," *Yale French Studies* 62 (1981): 106.

11. Simone Schwarz-Bart, *Pluie et vent sur Télumée Miracle* (Paris: Editions du Seuil, 1972), 76. Page references are given in parentheses. Translations are my own.

12. Scharfman, "Mirroring and Mothering," 95. Scharfman also discusses the ways in which Toussine's positive mothering empowers Télumée.

13. For a study of the characteristics and modes of traditional (oral) genres and their imaginative adaptation, through parody and imitation, to meet and express aesthetic, cultural, and social needs in the African novel, see Eileen Julien, *Unknotting the Thread: African Novels and the Question of Orality* (Bloomington: Indiana University Press, 1992).

14. Caribbean cultural context and socioeconomic circumstances place Télumée and Toussine in an environment radically different from that experienced by the passive, repressed (white bourgeois) heroines of the European *bildungsroman* for women, fictions of development characterized by "a moment of simultaneous awakening to inner aspirations and social

limitations." (See *The Voyage In: Fictions of Female Development,* ed. Elizabeth Abel, Marianne Hirsch, and Elizabeth Langland (Hanover and London: University Press of New England, 1983), 15.

15. See Jean Bernabé, "Le Travail de l'écriture chez Simone Schwarz-Bart: Contribution à l'étude de la diglossie littéraire créole-français," *Présence africaine* 121–22 (1982): 166–79. Bernabé's study helps the non-creolophone reader appreciate the skill and subtlety with which Simone Schwarz-Bart practices linguistic métissage, weaving together French and Creole to make a new language.

16. There is a Guadeloupean proverb often quoted by the old (with stories to tell) to the young: "Reté kouté, / Kouté pou tann, / Tann pou komprann" (Stay to listen, / Listen to hear, / Hear to understand). During a 1979 interview, Simone Schwarz-Bart explains that *Pluie et vent* was written in memory of an elderly friend, Stéphanie Priccin ("Fanotte"), who felt that the story of her life held special meaning and who feared that no one would hear and remember her words ("Elle se sentait incomprise par la jeunesse, en dehors de son temps, en dehors de cette jeunesse sans dons qui n'avait pas d'oreilles pour les vieux. Elle voulait leur raconter son expérience . . . "). Schwarz-Bart "stayed to listen" to her friend, as she has since done for many others. *Pluie et vent* is "a collection of privileged moments [from her life] . . . a sort of memory that I tried to restore." Héliane and Roger Toumson, "Interview avec Simone et André Schwarz-Bart: sur les pas de Fanotte," *Textes, Etudes et Documents 2: Pluie et vent sur Télumée Miracle* (Centre Universitaire Antilles-Guyane, Guadeloupe: Editions Caribéennes, 1979), 15.

17. For commentary on the mythical elements of this Antillean quest for identity, see Bernadette Cailler, "*Ti Jean L'horizon* de Simone Schwarz-Bart, ou la leçon du royaume des morts," *Stanford French Review* 6, nos. 2–3 (fall–winter 1982): 283–97; Fanta Toureh, *L'Imaginaire dans l'oeuvre de Simone Schwarz-Bart: Approche d'une mythologie antillaise* (Paris: L'Harmattan, 1987).

18. Simone Schwarz-Bart. *Ti Jean L'horizon* (Paris: Editions du Seuil, 1979), 202. Translations are my own.

19. See McKinney, "Antillean Versions of the Quest in Two Novels by Simone Schwarz-Bart."

20. Borrowing the closing chapter title from Jacques Roumain's *The Masters of the Dew* ("The End and the Beginning"), Schwarz-Bart ends by saluting her Haitian predecessor's celebration of renewal through community solidarity and the "freeing of waters" through one man's vision and love for his people. At the end of her own fable, in which Ti Jean restores to Guadeloupeans a vision of the past able to blossom into "new fruit," mythical and metaphorical "waters" also circulate: a life-giving liquor flows from the breast of the slain beast, just as blood flows from Eusebius's heart and a song of hope from Egée's lips.

21. Simone Schwarz-Bart, *Hommage à la femme noire,* 6 vols. (Belgium: Editions Consulaires, 1988–89), 1:5. Translations are my own.

22. For a study of the fragmentation of women as "poetic objects," see Nancy J. Vickers, "Diana Described: Scattered Woman and Scattered Rhyme," *Critical Inquiry* 8 (1991): 265–79.

23. Interview with Françoise Simon, "Le tour du monde en six volumes," *Afrique-Elite* 36 (1989).

24. Simone Schwarz-Bart, discussion with author, Goyave, Guadeloupe, June 1990.

CHAPTER THREE

Erzulie

A Women's History of Haiti?

JOAN DAYAN

> They burned all the documents, Ursa, but they didn't burn what they put in
> their minds. We got to burn out what they put in our minds, like you burn
> out a wound. Except we got to keep what we need to bear witness. That scar
> that's left to bear witness. We got to keep it visible as our blood.
> Gayle Jones, *Corregidora*

Gods born out of blood. Scars that do not die, making visible again and
again, whenever they visit their faithful, those times that might be forgotten. Phantoms stored in the minds of a people, residues of the past, lands
fat with the blood of memory. As Toni Morrison writes in *Beloved*, "If it is
still there, WAITING, that must mean that Nothing ever dies."[1] There are
some things we know that are better dead. But that is not part of this history.
That is not part of the lessons these gods teach, and these gods do not die.

If it is the traces of African religion that, as the historian and poet Kamau
Brathwaite writes, form "the kernel or core" of culture in the New World,
those fragments of rituals and recollected or reexperienced gods are the
mark of savagery for most historians (and other ideologues of "progress"
or "civilization"). But for the majority of people, these folk or local religions not only gave collective strength but preserved the histories ignored,
denigrated, or exoticized by the standard "imperial" histories. It was the

survival of these customs and these gods that provided continuity for the dispossessed. This continuum leaped across or superseded the European-imposed periodicities of such categories as colonial and postcolonial.

Erzulie, the goddess, spirit, or loa of love in vodoun, tells a history of women's lives that has not been told. A goddess was born on the soil of Haiti who has no precedent in Yoruba or Dahomey. In her various incarnations, her many faces, she bears the extremes of colonial history. Whether the pale and elegant Erzulie-Fréda or the coldhearted, savage Erzulie-gé-rouge, she dramatizes a specific historiography of women's experiences in Haiti and throughout the Caribbean.[2]

In describing Erzulie most writers have turned to analogy. She is Venus. She is the Virgin. What if we decided to forgo such external impositions — and dichotomies such as pure and impure, evil or beneficent — and instead tried to talk about the continuing presence of Erzulie through those relationships and events particular to women in Haiti, whether black, mulatto, or white? Although most ethnographers, whether Haitian or foreign, present her three emanations (Erzulie-Fréda, the lady of luxury and love; Erzulie-Dantor, the black woman of passion identified in Catholic chromolithographs with the mater Salvatoris, her heart pierced with a dagger; and Erzulie-gé-rouge, the red-eyed militant of fury and vengeance), Erzulie bears witness to a far more complicated lineage. Indeed, in ritual practice there are slippages and uneasy alliances between these apparently antagonistic gods.

Unlike Western religions that depend on dualisms such as matter and spirit, body and soul, for their perpetuation and power, vodoun unsettles and subverts such apparent oppositions. That subversion becomes most evident when we turn to the question of gender distinction and color division. Maîtresse Erzulie-Fréda, the *mulâtresse blanche,* is the lover of Ogoun, a very black god of war, often identified with Papa Dessalines. But she also wears the rings of Damballah, the white snakegod of the sweet waters, and Agoué-Taroyo, the god of the sea who is figured as white. Although a woman, Erzulie vacillates between her attraction for the two sexes. She holds her servitors in between two irreconcilables. What Frantz Fanon in *The Wretched of the Earth* has called that "zone of occult instability" becomes in the practices of Erzulie a suspension between the supposedly antithetical constructions of masculinity and femininity.[3] She is not androgynous, for she deliberately encases herself in the trappings of what has been constituted in a social world (especially that of the Frenchified elites) as femininity. Erzulie thus goes beyond false dichotomizing, as she prescribes and responds to multiple and apparently incoherent directives. She takes on the garb of femininity—and even speaks excellent French—in order to confound and discard the culturally defined roles of men and women.

If vodoun remains a locus of feminine strength—with women and men equal in practice—it can be so only because it ever reconstitutes specifically gendered stereotypes. Erzulie demands of her servitors abstention from sex on her sacred days. But Erzulie "marries" women as well as men. Everything written about Erzulie can be contradicted. She is, some will tell you, the loa of lust most often prayed to by prostitutes. A goddess served by the Haitian elite or young virgins, Erzulie is also sought after by those with homosexual tendencies.[4] The indeterminacy of the goddess, whose libido wanders between women and men, enacts a fantasy of *l'amoureuse*, a play that is ever determined by precise sociocultural models.

Many accounts of Erzulie concentrate on what she does to men and how they must serve her. One *houngan* told me, "Every woman is an emanation of Erzulie." And a "feminist" scholar in the United States warned: "To be Erzulie is to be imagined and perceived by men." Can we go beyond these divisive engenderings? How can we as writers de-exoticize what might remain a pretty icon? More precisely, in dealing with any image, how can I avoid turning daily practice—a rigorous dialogue of thought and memory—into something transcendent, or more serious still, a trope that gives me a language that fascinates but distorts or annihilates the very realities it attempts to describe?

Michael Taussig in *Shamanism, Colonialism, and the Wild Man* wonders, as he writes about iconic virgins in the southwest of Colombia, "what sort of historiography the image sustains and puts into speech."[5] Images of women have coerced us into silence, have either praised us as icons of purity or damned us as proofs of pollution. In either case we are liberated from history, and thereby petrified in those idealizations that deny our freedom.

How do the rituals associated with Erzulie, and the often contradictory images she evokes, reenact for a community not granted a voice a knowledge of the past? How does Erzulie help us to work through and reconstruct a history of women that is simultaneously an inquiry into the language of conquest and a revelation of the terms of mastery?

A Goddess Is Born

Ireneus tells us how Simon Magus of Samaria, "from whom all sorts of heresies derive their origin," freed a woman from slavery in Tyre, a Phoenician city. He called her Helen, made her his escort, and introduced her to the multitudes as the thought of God and the mother of men. She had descended to earth, Simon says, and there was detained and thwarted by the very angels and powers that emanated from her. The story is one of loss, jealousy, and degradation: "she was even enclosed in human flesh and migrated for centuries as from vessel to vessel into different female bodies. . . . Thus, she was also that Helen about whom the Trojan war was fought, and in this manner Greeks and barbarians beheld a phantasm of the truth. Migrating from body to body, suffering abuse in each, she at last became a whore in a brothel." She makes a journey from the head of God to the body of man, from high thought to the depths of lust.

It is no wonder that the church, with its son of God, so suffering yet so immaculate, would be threatened by this fable of a God-woman betrayed but never purified of her defeat at the hands of men. Instead of rising to heaven in apotheosis, this fallen Sophia remained on earth, a terrible reminder of submission and defilement. This relic of endurance has many faces: Défilée, the madwoman and ex-mistress of Dessalines who gathered up the pieces of his mutilated body; Baudelaire's "Beauté," his "ange gardienne" and "nymphe macabre," with her glance infernal and divine; Carl Brouard's Erzulie, the cannibal of delight; or René Depestre's virginal Hadriana, "the ideal of French beauty," violated and turned into a zombi on Haitian soil; and the amazing Marie Laveau, the "Voodoo Queen of New Orleans": "To some she was a saint, to others the devil incarnate."[6]

I begin with this cult of mystification — the familiar splitting of women into objects to be desired or abhorred — and its complications in the Caribbean imagination in order to get at the domination such a celebration of difference allows. An ideal woman, pure of stain, fixed on her pedestal, is only possible in the male imaginary because of the invention of a dark, debased sister. The presence of Jane Eyre in Rochester's narrative reconstructions allows him to hate Bertha absolutely: the forced coordination of the "fiery West Indian night" and the English "Eden," like the dark and light lady, are oppositions against which he can make himself whole.

The sublime is a production of excess in the minds of men. And nowhere is that production more evident than in the cultivation of this compelling dualism: the urgent split between what can be allowed and what must be forbidden. The spiritualized and desexualized images of white women depended on the prostitution or violation of the dark women in their midsts. In the history of the Caribbean, where a slave, a piece of property, became an object of "love," this controlling spectacle of difference would, nevertheless, be derailed and dismantled.

If the masters claimed civilization on the backs of those they called polluted or bestial — claims ever threatened by the evidences of a terrible brutality — the spectacle of vodoun replays, repeats, and exposes the mechanisms of that lying ideology. We get the story from the supposed victims, and instead of loss and passivity (the lie of the film *Mississippi Burning*), they produce a more demanding history. Haitian historian Thomas Madiou wrote in 1847: "If the Spanish and French, in possessing the Queen of the Antilles, left there the bloody traces of their domination, they also left their languages, their mores, their customs, ultimately the germs of this 'new civilization.' "[7]

Erzulie-Fréda possesses her servitor (known in vodoun, as "mounting" her "horse"), the pale lady gets into the head of the black peasant, and *they* turn history around. They speak again the perfect French, bringing it forth, now as goddess and servitor, in the middle of a ceremony of Creole rhythms and languages. In vodoun's respeaking the memory of a particular colonial power relation, the *mulâtresse* "whom passion has worn" — to recast Yeats's epitaph for the white woman of his *Wind among the Reeds* — and her horse together work through the rites of *possession*, belying an intimacy that remembers servitude, while resisting the haunts of resignation.

Whether white, mulatto, or black Creole, to be colonial is to be indeterminate. The forced intimacy of what Pierre de Vassière, writing of St. Domingue as it was from 1629 to 1789, called "a very strange familiarity" between those who called themselves masters and those who found themselves slaves made the old practices of idealization unworkable. Citing from Moreau de Saint-Méry's *Notes historiques*, he substantiates this promiscuity: "These white women live with their domestics under the weight of the most bizarre intimacy. Nearly every young white Creole owns a young mulâtresse or quarteronne, and sometimes even a young négresse, whom they make their *cocotte*. The cocotte is the confidant of all the thoughts of the mistress (and this reliance is sometimes reciprocal), the confidant of all her loves."[8] (Note that the word *cocotte* means both "darling" and "tart.") In plantation isolation, the extremes of difference were blurred in an odd promiscuity, where those who were supposedly indisputably inferior were absolutely necessary to those who imagined themselves superior.

Erzulie and the rituals associated with her store and reinterpret the past: the confusions and vociferous identities of colonial St. Domingue, its passage into independence, and its ongoing crisis of neocolonialism. As she retells these histories in ceremonies and songs, she does something extraordinary to the way we think about the Caribbean. For if the colonizer exercised privilege by distorting or annihilating the African past, vodoun — the religion that kept alive the lives and deaths of the ancestors — reimaged a unique relation to a brutal institution. Gods were born in the memories of those who served, and they took on not only the traits or dispositions of their servitors but also those attitudes and languages of the masters and mistresses from long ago, tough revenants carried in the memories of the descendants of slaves.

Remembering St. Domingue

They lived amid a commotion of rites.
Michelle Cliff, *Abeng*

Rites of love and pleasures of the toilette, ceremonies of consumption, betrayal, and revolt. If we try to understand Erzulie's attributes by looking to Africa or to Europe, Oshun, Yemanja, Oya, the Virgin Mary, or Venus, or as the Haitian Louis Maximilien has argued, to Helen, or as Emmanuel Paul adds, to "Ishtar of ancient Babylon" (venerated as "she who gives herself to every one"), we cannot account for her particularities.[9]

Something else has happened to this pressure of love, this image of the erotic impulse, what some have called the "eternal feminine" or the "maternal libido" on the soil of Haiti. Instead of starting with an analogy, finding her complement in another religious system or legend, I treat her as a god specific to Haiti, whose strangest attributes delineate a history of women during slavery — whether white or mulatto mistresses, negro servants or mulatto concubines, in their vexed class and color connections.

Erzulie continues to articulate and embody a memory of slavery, intimacy, and revenge. She survives as the record of and habitation for women's experiences in the New World. As motive, then, for a specific kind of Caribbean history, she emerges at a time when men and women, black and white, were linked in the throes of power and domination. What the slave who practiced vodoun saw in the house of the white planter could have contributed to producing a loa who is both caring and tender, indifferent and savage. In her words and gestures the goddess replays this slippage between opposites: she both demands and obeys, gains and loses, loves and hates.

Given the recorded intimacy between domestic and mistress, it is less surprising that Erzulie moves in Maya Deren's description in *Divine Horse-*

men from the "Goddess of Love," who "protests that she is not loved enough," to "that combined rage and despair which is Erzulie-Gé-Rouge."[10] In a world of reciprocal demoralizations, we cannot limit our interpretation to generalities of good and evil, love and hate. For when the slaves channeled, localized, and materialized what they saw and whom they served in their communal religious practices, they made a history — and an ethics — that we will not find in books.

What many see as the surprising, incomprehensible weeping of Erzulie ("this weeping is so inaccessible to reason," as Deren puts it) has perhaps a too reasonable cause in the exercises of enslavement: in the cries of those whose children were taken from them, those who were raped by their masters and used and tortured by their mistresses. Such tears cannot be generalized out of history as the tears of the Virgin Mary or the Mater Dolorosa, for if Erzulie is a "Mother of Sorrows," she is also "Une soeur de Solitude," "born out of this violence with a green eye and a black eye, heartless, who one day took up arms."[11]

In the story of Sor Rose, or Sister Rose, mother of all Haitians, the claim of generative reproduction depends on her violation. This cosmology begins with rape, as the Haitian historian Timoléon Brutus retells the story: "Haiti has its origins in the flancs of a black woman brutally fertilized by a slave in heat or a drunken white, a criminal escaped from Cayenne [the French colonial prison]; or a degenerate from feudal nobility in quest of riches throughout the continent."[12] How, then, do we begin to understand Erzulie, her rites of love and abandon, when we remember the determinant and constraining conditions, the "facts" of the history that undergird her ritual emanations?

The colonized are not necessarily, as Albert Memmi has written, "outside of the game,"[13] victimized into incomprehension. They are not swallowed up by the coercions and productions of the colonizer, but bend and adapt these facts to their own uses. Vodoun testifies to that labor of resistance and change, comprehending multiple histories in what Roger Bastide has argued to be a syncretism that defies "the logic of Western thought, which is based on the principle of identity and noncontradiction."[14]

Imagine for a moment the slave watching a world that, in the words of Madiou, had "all the luxuries and pleasures of Europe" but also demonstrated the most extraordinary cruelties displayed before avid spectators, a world where grace and "the charm of evenings on the Faubourg St.-Germain" (as the Haitian Madiou wrote) coexisted with "a nearly absolute lack of sensibility and even a certain native cruelty resulting from the harsh and brutal way that they [the planters] treated their slaves" (as the French-man de Vassière wrote). The only escape from the experience of such brute extremes was during the night, when slaves initiated into the mysteries of vodoun reconceived and interpreted the experiences of the day.

One of the most fascinating accounts of colonial St. Domingue, which is also the first written record of vodoun, is Moreau de Saint-Méry's *Description topographique, physique, civile, politique et historique de la partie française de l'Isle Saint-Domingue* (1797). He was astonished by the opulence, excess, and tyranny of the senses exhibited by the white and mulatto Creoles of St. Domingue, where men lose control in a tumult of passion and women burn themselves out in quest of love, victims of jealousy and greed. Writing of "the sensibility" of the New World mistress, he concludes, "their temperament makes them unable to live without love."[15] The business of love and the fact of abandon did not so much characterize Haitians from Africa as those who descended from France, who seemed to "exist only for *les jouissances voluptueuses*": "even among honorable women themselves, the frequency of second marriages attests to the imperious necessity of love. Second marriage? I should say third, fourth, fifth, sixth, seventh. . . ."[16]

I want to suggest that the loa themselves were born out of the slaves' awareness of the demands and accoutrements of their masters. And the presence of Erzulie repeats, perpetuates, and subverts the experiences of this colonial relation. Whether recalled in her garb of grace as Erzulie-Fréda or in the alternating fury and lust of her other incarnations, she is not so much a "dream of luxury," as Deren writes, as a mimicry of excess.

Erzulie sustains that curious feeling of attachment to what is most feared, and she is both more and less Western than we might assume. There are as many loa of love as there are experiences of love in the New World. Yet Erzulie always holds the idea of love in suspension, for those who *serve* are after recollections of those experiences that must defeat or question that love. Deren responds to Erzulie's contradictions by explaining: "She who has been loved by all the major loa . . . is convinced, by some curious inversion, that they have each betrayed her. . . . She, who is the wealthiest of the loa, the most frequently gifted with luxurious accoutrement, suffers for not being 'served' enough. She, who is the most complimented . . . — she who is Goddess of Love — protests that she is not loved enough."[17]

Yet this lady of the impossible demand should not be romanticized. Obviously, her elaborate toilette and preference for all kinds of sweets and desserts mark her as that locus of recall for what was, and still is *not* possessed. For Haiti's poor in the urban ghetto or the countryside, Erzulie demands an exuberant devotion that plays itself out as a surfeit of matter. Those who do not have are possessed by the spirit of those who did.

What has been represented as a devilish or savage god, and a jealous if somehow all-too-loving god, finds explanation in the attributes of those who enslaved. But Erzulie also carries on the dialogue — a talk not possible either in the colony or in contemporary Haiti — between those who rule and those who do not. She continues her interrogation of those who were nourished by "chocolate, candies, and café au lait above all," those white Creole women whose alternating indulgences and fury apparently knew no bounds: "Nothing equals the anger of a creole woman who punishes the slave that her husband has perhaps forced to dirty the nuptial bed. In her jealous fury she doesn't know what to invent in order to satisfy her vengeance."[18] What some ethnographers have described as fantasies of luxury, the misconceptions evidenced by those who serve Erzulie, might well be the blunt recording of what those who were violated, first by the master and then by the mistress, had come to know.

Yet Erzulie's exquisite, if sometimes delirious femininity also draws women together in a history that was not always of their own making. When Erzulie as mulatto conforms to what we deem to be signs of the lady of pleasure — decked out in the lace, jewels, powders, and perfumes that recall most colonial descriptions of the mulâtresse, those "filles de joie" — such embellishments betray a commodification (and subjugation) that affected *all* women. Even Zora Neale Hurston's "ideal of the love bed" (her description of Erzulie in *Tell My Horse*)[19] might well describe a cult defined by men, though always put forth as *what a woman wants*.

When we consider a historian like Moreau de Saint-Méry's characterization of the mulatta, we are struck by the way his description resembles those of Bryan Edwards or Edward Long writing about Jamaica. For no matter the place, the indeterminacy captured by the idea of the mulatta depends for its force on the same iteration of value, luxury, and excess. In Moreau de Saint-Méry's words: "The entire being of a Mulâtresse is given up to pleasure, the fire of this Goddess burns in her heart only to be extinguished with her life. This cult is her law, her every wish, her every happiness... To charm all her senses, to surrender to the most delicious ecstasy, to be surprised by the most seductive ravishing, that is her unique study."[20]

Whether called whore or virgin, women seem always to find themselves in the hands of the definers. When we read that Erzulie is Virgin and Venus, and served by prostitutes (who are considered her children) as well as virgins, we should always try to think about the possibilities and constraints of her ceremonial articulations. What does it mean to serve Erzulie? For whom does she act out her rites of love? At once a celebration and ironization of the costliness and ambiguities of naming, Erzulie confounds the terms of praise and damnation, as she slides out of luxury into the militant poverty of Erzulie-gé-rouge or the sombre care of old Grande Erzulie.

Women and the Gods

> Love, this need, or rather this tyrant of the sensitive soul,
> reigns over that of the Creole.
> Moreau de Saint-Méry

Vodoun remains a religion of worldly life. Concerned with the processes of thought and memory in a community, its gods can discredit what those who dominated had constituted as desirable. Erzulie can be said to defy the very love she represents. Indeed, she desensitizes herself through her extremes, through emotion exercised to the breaking point, finally — according to many accounts — collapsing in tears at the end of the ceremony. She has as many temperaments as the recollections of those who serve her. Erzulie recalls and replays all the uses, pleasures, and violations of women in Haiti, from colonial St. Domingue to post-Duvalier Haiti, whether they be slaves, free coloreds, or white Creoles (divisions still operating today in obvious, if changed ways).

Her range of colors figures the experience of color division in Haiti and the confusions of origins so powerfully suggested in Erna Brodber's text of intimacy and imitation *Jane and Louisa Will Soon Come Home*. Again, I want to emphasize that the multiple emanations of Erzulie resist the splitting so necessary to turning what lives into an icon of someone else's dream or fantasy of desire. Erzulie and her devotees dramatize the temptations of lactification (the whitening that both Frantz Fanon and Derek Walcott recognize as the hexed desire of the Caribbean Creole), as well as the ironization of that very desire. Could she also conjure a closeness between women, who in their intimacies — whether cruel or affectionate — from colonial times to the present momentarily experience a place without color? What some had put forth as the easy division between "lady" and "savage" was of course made impossible by the planters' wives and daughters, who could move from a lengthy tête-à-tête with their servants to flogging and spitting. This goddess who oscillates between the extremes of grace and brutality is thus no mere perpetuation of Christian notions of Virgin or Temptress, nor of masculine projections of Venus or Hag, but more exactly, a dramatization of how black women saw, reacted to, and survived the experience of slavery and the realities of colonialism.

The survivor, the servitor, knows that the claims of color are nothing more than a sometime masquerade, depending on who wields power when. In Haiti, a place where terms and ideologies change faster than they can be recorded (where the word *négritude* masks a totalitarian ethos as authoritative as the racial theories of Joseph Arthur de Gobineau), where writers and politicians keep producing texts, the Haitian peasant alone gives their loa the right to cross color lines, and to thereby subvert the artificial divisions of the church and the hegemonic exploitations of the state. Not only did the vodoun adepts practice the mélange so horrifying to church purists — praying to their gods while putting them in saint's clothes — but they brought secret lives out into the open, playing with the forbidden and voicing what had been silenced.

I have often wondered, when reading Fanon's assertion that "the black soul — *l'âme noire* — is a white man's artifact," how we as writers, critics, and teachers might begin to talk about *la femme noire*. Whose artifact is she? Religious practices and the return to the "Gods of the Middle Passage" evidenced in the writings of Marie Chauvet, Mayotte Capécia, Paule Marshall, Michelle Cliff, Erna Brodber, Gayle Jones, and Toni Morrison, to name just a few of those new historians, take the images others have made of women, of blacks — of anyone who does not conform to the demands of domination and assimilation — and voice a revelation that depends for its power on their writing again about that place where the old terms for good and bad, pretty and ugly, love and hate are ever dissolving. That place might be the habitat of the outsider, the slave, the courtesan, the conjure-woman, the lady who had to be all things for all people.

We hear the "Riddym Ravings" of Erzulie, of Jean Binta Breeze's "Madwoman's Song"; we read about Erzulie with her "jewels and gossamer veils" in the love-bed of Avey Johnson in Marshall's *Praise Song for the Widow* until she loses her memory of that place where the Ibo walked out over the waters. Morrison's Sula becomes suspect as sorceress and love-bait when she makes her way in the world and with her best friend's man. And in her incredible retelling of Charlotte Brontë and Jean Rhys, Brodber gives us all the blacks, whites, and mulattoes who fight it out in the head of a storyteller who tells the epic of the diaspora, the song of métissage. Nellie inherits the debris of history but converts that waste into words, making something new and unexpected, as do all the Erzulies, on that sliding scale of experience and recall.

Fictions of Erzulie

Ezili o! pa Ezili sa!
[Erzulie, oh! that's not Erzulie!]
A song of Erzulie

Haitian history has been written by men, whether colonizers who distort or negate the past, or the colonized who attempt to reclaim or reimage what has been lost or denied. Where are women in the conquistador's tale, in the hero's epic? What is the name of the *mambo* or vodoun priestess who assisted the *houngan* Boukman Dutly in the legendary ceremony that began the Haitian Revolution in 1791 in the Caiman woods? According to some stories, the *mambo* began the attack: "As the history tells it she made the conspirators drink the blood of the animal she had slaughtered, while persuading them that therein lay the proof of their future invincibility in battle."[21] Unlike the Black Jacobins (the monumental triad Toussaint L'Ouverture, Henri Christophe, and Jean-Jacques Dessalines), women left no records: "They have remained nameless except for Sanite Belair, Marie-Jeanne Lamartinière for Saint-Domingue and the mulatta Solitude in Guadeloupe."[22] When women are mentioned in the early histories of Haiti, those of Thomas Madiou or Beaubrun Ardouin, for example, their stories are something of an interlude in the business of making history. Bracketed off from the descriptions of significant loss or triumph, the *blanches* raped and butchered, or the *noires* ardent and fearless, become symbols for *la bonté, la férocité, la faiblesse.*

Images of women help to make a glorified, if ambiguous past palpable and definitive. Consider the madwoman Dédée Bazile, known as "Défilée," who, according to some accounts, carried the bloody remnants of the assassinated Dessalines to the city cemetery. The historian Windsor Bellegarde asks all Haitians to remember "Défilée-La Folle who on the sad day of October 17, 1806 . . . saw the Founder of Independence fall under Haitian bullets; and when the people of Port-au-Prince suddenly seemed to go mad, she gave to everyone an eloquent lesson of reason, wisdom, and patriotic piety."[23]

How does the explicit use of Erzulie as image help us to understand the fictions necessary to the myth of a Haitian nation? Vodoun has to a large extent been preserved in the so-called peasant novel with ethnographic precision, represented as a complex system of ritual practices with a variety of spirits who have highly developed, clearly defined characters. Originally used by the Fon tribe in Dahomey, vodoun means not only "spirit" or "god" but also "image." Further, if the *crise de loa*, or "possession" (when the spirit mounts, haunts, or inhabits his/her human envelope), is a spiritual idiom that can only articulate itself as image, what does it mean when a writer takes Erzulie as motive for characterization? Because Erzulie remains the most heavily textualized (and romanticized) of vodoun spirits, her representation tells us much about the risky collaborations of romance and race.

What happens when an oral tradition of lived history becomes the basis for aesthetic representation? Can the gods be conceived in the literary? There is a history told in the novels of Jacques Roumain, Jacques Stephen Alexis, and Marie Chauvet, especially. That history is inseparable from the pulse of the gods in the text. The constitution of a self, of a particularly Haitian subject, depends on the call to vodoun, on the way history relates to the grammar of religious experience. Whether we turn to the dust of Roumain's *Gouverneurs de la rosée*, the scorched earth of his *La Montagne ensorcelée*, the enforced deforestation in Alexis's *Les Arbres musiciens*, or Chauvet's cursed world of beggars, torturers, cripples, and martyrs, the gods remain.

I have argued that Erzulie and her presence in ceremonial reenactments fix an erotic impulse into image (considered either illicit or excessive by elite or Christian), while she destabilizes the categorical imperatives of race and gender. Yet when we consider the Haitian novel and the centrality of women (as goddess, ripe fruit, treasured landscape, blasted earth, or rotten whore), we must ask certain contextual questions: How does the image of Erzulie as idealized love, unbridled erotics, or unrelenting suffering help constitute what some like to call a "national literature"? Further, can a particular representation of Erzulie support the elaborate and often covert metaphorizing of a necessarily masculine rhetoric of defeat, conquest, or victimization?

From Jean-Baptiste Cinéas (in *Le Drame de la terre, La Vengeance de la terre* and *L'Héritage sacré*) to Roumain, Alexis, and Chauvet, certain rituals of nationalism and loss are repeated, almost formulaic in their intensity. The land has been mistreated, the trees have been cut down, the sun blasts the barren earth, while the peasants remain ignorant, oppressed, and miserable. In these scenes of poverty and injustice, there remains one image that carries the heaviest weight, a figure that bears the burden of Haiti's history. "[L]a terre est comme une bonne femme, à force de la maltraiter, elle se révolte" (The earth is like a good woman, if you mistreat her, she revolts), Roumain writes in *Gouverneurs de la rosée*.[24] In *Fonds des Nègres* the most radical presentation of vodoun in any novel, Chauvet takes up the trope of land as violated woman and carries that representation to its extreme. Her problematic vodoun priest, Papa Beauville, begins the novel with words that place it quite squarely in the tradition Chauvet intends to subvert: "Pour la sonder, cette terre, pas grand'chose à faire, ses os sont aussi visibles que ceux d'une femme maigre et elle agonise comme une poitrinaire à ses derniers moments" (It's not such a difficult thing to probe this earth, its bones are as visible as those of a skinny woman, and she is dying like a consumptive in her last moments).[25]

What happens when a woman writer turns to *le peuple* who have been so heavily metaphorized by the men who preceded her? When Chauvet wrote *Fille d'Haiti,* her mulatto heroine, Lotus, carried on the tradition of women standing by their men that Roumain and Alexis had established. But in *Fonds des Nègres* Chauvet's mulatto Marie-Ange (yet another surrogate for Erzulie-Fréda) remains recalcitrant, both in her relationships with men and with the gods. Arriving from Port-au-Prince to visit her grandmother and conjure-woman Soeur Ga ("la femme sage"), her real quest has less to do with courting the various men in her midst — though she plays the game of seduction — than with the gods, and with what remains for her their most compelling articulation, the houngan Beauville.

Chauvet writes a love story that undoes the idea of love. How can love be expressed amid crumbling rites, resistant and angry gods, and resigned mortals? The eroticism of the gods, the service they demand in sterile, wasted lands amid death and starvation, permeates the story of Marie-Ange and Papa Beauville. No matter how we look at it or try to avoid it, the business of possession, initiation, and service is suffused with sex, or more precisely, with the idea of submission. Yet Chauvet prods her readers to reinterpret what it means to submit. Neither Marie-Ange nor Beauville acts in ways that reconcile easily with assumptions of mastery or servitude. Marie-Ange is no servile *hounsi* (spouse of god), and Beauville is as easily "taken" by Marie-Ange as she is possessed by him.

To understand the uniqueness of Chauvet's ambiguous tale, the complicated roles of gods and humans, and the total reversal of claims of progress or enlightenment, we need to reconsider Roumain's *Gouverneurs de la Rosée.*

In Roumain's book hope returns with the arrival of Manuel, the worker, to his native land, where the peasants who have no "esprit," and who do not know will be redeemed by the intellectual who knows. Although that possible renewal is fraught with ambiguity (the competing claims of traditional gods and new ideology), Manuel dies a hero. In *Fonds des Nègres,* the promise embodied in the dreams of Papa Beauville comes with the visit of Marie-Ange to a land in which she has no intention of remaining. The story of why she does finally remain undermines any claim to heroics.

What must be stressed here is that Chauvet's use of the vodoun gods, whether Ogoun (the warrior god who loves alcohol, politics, and women, identified with Papa Beauville) or Erzulie (identified with Marie-Ange, "la griffonne habillée en bourgeoisie"), does not depend for its effect on the vodoun backdrop. Nowhere do we get a full description of possession by Erzulie or Ogoun. Instead they make their presence known through the behavior, words, and thoughts of a most unlikely pair: old *houngan* Beauville and young bourgeoise Marie-Ange. In this novel no idealization of love or elevation of the Haitian heterosexual couple, for example, the rebel and his "négresse," is possible.

Chauvet does not mention vodoun in her preface. She relegates the term to a *notez bien* at the bottom of the page: "N.B. — The vodoun ceremonies have been drawn from the study of Dr. Louis Maximilien: *Le vodou haitien.*"[26] Although a wrong lead, this derailing of what remains unique about her project is significant. Chauvet will not claim (or let her readers assume) that she knows or has experienced vodoun. She cannily delimits her expertise to a text, thus disavowing at the outset what she will reclaim in the course of her novel: the gods in her blood, the irreversible if unreconstructable past in Guinea.

Chauvet's bourgeois readers are set up for an unexpected revelation. No doubt they have read Maximilien's classic 1945 study, which attempted to recuperate vodoun for an elite audience. He draws on Western religion and pagan practice, quoting from Lucien Lévy-Bruhl, Hippolyte Taine, and Leo Frobenius in order to explicate and defend vodoun. Whereas Maximilien expounds on vodoun as a system of beliefs and forms of worship, Chauvet details the pressing needs of abject lives. This difficult pragmatism leaves little room for anything so sacrosanct as worship, so abstract as belief. She refuses to idealize what remains for the impoverished Haitian of the hills a costly and constant attention to the spirits. Instead of providing an inventory of ritual, a catalog of divinities or ceremonial symbols, Chauvet questions how the gods can be served — how they can be fed — when those who serve them can barely survive.

Further, vodoun no longer provides a space for what remains pure in a place of greed and betrayal. Nor is it the mark of barbarism. The spirits and those who serve them resist idealization. Like Marie-Ange, the wayward yet generous visitant to Fonds des Nègres, the spirits subvert categories like "femininity" and "masculinity." Chauvet shows how spirit possession, or a believer's testimony about the life of the spirit (those spirits bearing down), does something to the way we think about gender classifications.

The story of Marie-Ange is nothing less than her transformation into a god-possessed soul. Although identified with Erzulie, Marie-Ange is not divinized or made more glorious. Something happens to her that approaches what it means to be possessed, to act out the contradictory drives of Erzulie. Into this abode of the dead and the dying, Marie-Ange brings her old communion garb, recalling the precious lace demanded by Erzulie. The starving children who surround her are thrilled "at the sight of her communion dress, embellished with flounces and lace." When she arrives, like the proud and extravagant Erzulie, she demands a fork, desires a bed, a plate and a glass, and reminds Soeur Ga that she has grown up with "la propreté" and "l'instruction." Marie-Ange teases Doce and turns toward and away from Facius (both men are her suitors), yet Beauville/Ogoun both fascinates and threatens her. It is he who reclaims her: " 'Je t'ai vue cent fois dans mes rêves. Erzulie te tenait la main, et tu marchais à ses côtés. Pour moi ça a une grosse signification' " (126) ("I have seen you one hundred times in my dreams. Erzulie held your hand, and you walked by her side. For me that has great significance").

Chauvet's footnote to Erzulie is simply "femme d'Ogoun." As Marie-Ange becomes attached to the land and to Beauville's inexplicable force, she gives up the material trappings of Erzulie in order to apprehend more fully what it means to desire. Erzulie might be her "mait-tete" (the loa in her head), yet she remains no mere metaphor. Beauville appreciates the intelligence of Marie-Ange; he longs for her flesh and promises to give her the "points" (powers) of Ogoun. Obsessed with his dream of saving the earth, he urges her to barter her sex for the land: " 'As-tu oublié ta promesse de m'aider?' lui répondit-il fermement. 'Cherisme est un homme et toi une femme. Comme les pêcheurs, jette la ligne et attrape-moi des hommes' " (140) ("Have you forgotten your promise to help me?" he asked firmly. "Cherisme is a man and you are a woman. Like a fisherman, throw out your line and catch me some men"). Marie-Ange has not forgotten anything that has passed between her and Beauville, but she will help in a way that even he could not have expected.

In *Les Damnés de la terre*, Fanon urged a return to that "occult zone of instability where an authentic upheaval can be born."[27] Chauvet goes further. For the first time in any literary text, she examines what it means to serve, shows us how possession works on those who believe. Erzulie's meaning, like that of the other spirits, depends on all kinds of contingencies: relationships are destroyed or healed, decisions made and unmade. Alexis's *houngan* Bois-d'Orme in *Les Arbres musiciens* praised "these gods in the image of men," but Chauvet wants her readers to apprehend how that image constitutes itself. Like Beauville, Marie-Ange does violence to any belief that could be imagined as incorruptible or certain. Understanding, like belief, is provisional.

Chauvet's *Folie*, the story of four mad poets locked in a stinking room, pursued by "devils," focuses on the inexplicable power of the objects of vodoun, the heritage packed up in a trunk and left René by his black mother. Chauvet knows that no claims to modernity or progress can destroy the call of the past, the pull of blood. In *Fonds des Nègres* fear of the gods and paranoia about evil-working neighbors stalk the minds of all the characters, no matter how educated or how rich. Chauvet offers no alternative.

The Djablesse

I conclude with a story about a ghost. In Haiti it is no good to be a virgin, no matter what the priests, nuns, or prospective partners tell you. One of the most feared ghosts is the *djablesse*.[28] Haitians will tell you that she wanders in forests and cities, condemned to walk for a number of years for the sin of having died a virgin. The nuns taught that virgins would go to heaven, but instead they end up wandering around looking for what they missed, or scaring the hell out of those who have it. What is a woman to do? If you believe in the church, then you must remain chaste until marriage, but if you listen to the gods, you must be physically possessed in order to rest in peace. Erzulie might well be telling us that you do not have to choose.

The ideal of virginity, like the curse of promiscuity, is always something imposed from the outside. As Chauvet's Rose, ridden by the one simply called the "gorilla" in *Colère*, reminds us: "Etais-je vierge? Complice? Ne suis-je pas en train de m'y habituer, d'y chercher mon plaisir?" (Am I a virgin? Accomplice? Am I not getting used to him for my pleasure?)[29] To be possessed by Erzulie might demand that we become fully virgin and whore until the words do not mean. To serve Erzulie might mean experiencing all the possibilities of command and surrender until those word-merchants and their wares no longer have the power to divide and conquer.

Notes

A version of this paper was presented at the "Caribbean Women's Writers Conference" in Trinidad in April 1990. I am grateful to Lizabeth Paravisini and Betty Wilson for their responses, which helped in the early formulation of this project. Another version of this essay appeared in *Research in African Literatures* 25, no. 2 (summer 1994): 5–33.

1. Toni Morrison, *Beloved* (New York: New American Library, 1987), 36.

2. There are many Erzulies, either regarded as members of the same family or as different manifestations of the same deity. Depending on region, ritual, *hounfort* (temple surround), or even individual servitor, the attributes and expressions of Erzulie vary. She has many names: Grande Erzulie, Erzulie Taureau, Erzulie Fréda, Erzulie-gé-rouge, Erzulie Mapian, Erzulie-dos-bas, Erzulie Zandor, Erzulie-severine-belle-femme, Erzulie Dantor, Erzulie-coeur noir, Erzulie-kokobe (Erzulie the shriveled), Erzulie-batala.

3. As I have argued elsewhere, in her persistent negotiations between extremes, Erzulie reconstitutes specifically gendered stereotypes. See "Caribbean Cannibals and Whores," *Raritan* (fall 1989): 45–67; and "Reading Women in the Caribbean: Marie Chauvet's *Amour, Colère et Folie*," in *Displacements: Women, Tradition, Literatures in French*, ed. Nancy K. Miller and Joan DeJean (Baltimore: Johns Hopkins University Press, 1991), 228–53.

4. In *Panorama du Folklore Haitien* (Port-au-Prince: Imprimerie de l'Etat, 1962), 274–76, Emmanuel Paul describes how Erzulie can alternately hinder and promote consummation. Stressing her homosexuality, he explains that her punishment for failed sexual abstinence on those days consecrated to her (Tuesday, Thursday, or Saturday) is "impotence" for men and "frigidity" for women. All translations, except where otherwise indicated, are my own.

5. Michael Taussig, *Shamanism, Colonialism, and the Wild Man* (Chicago and London: University of Chicago Press, 1987), 97.

6. Raymond J. Martinez, *Mysterious Marie Laveau: Voodoo Queen* (New Orleans: Hope Publications, 1956), 3.

7. Thomas Madiou, *Histoire d'Haïti*, 3d. ed. (Port-au-Prince: Editions Henri Deschamps, 1989), vol. 1, iii.

8. Pierre de Vassière, *Saint-Domingue (1629–1789): La Société et la vie créoles sous l'Ancien Régime* (Paris: Perrin et Cie, Libraires-Editeurs, 1909), 280–81.

9. According to Paul in *Panorama du Folklore Haitien*, she does not recall Africa except by her name, because "in Dahomey, there is an Azilie who is associated with the river of Oeme and Freda could be a deformation of Frieda, the river people of the lac Athieme" (273). Robert Thompson in *Flash of the Spirit* (New York: Random House, 1983) identifies Erzulie with the river goddesses Oshun (Yoruba name) and Aziri (Fon name).

10. Maya Deren, *Divine Horsemen: Voodoo Gods of Haiti* (New York: Chelsea House, 1970), 140, 143.

11. See Arlette Gautier, *Les Soeurs de Solitude: La condition féminine dans l'esclavage aux Antilles du XVII au XIX siècle* (Paris: Editions Caribéennes, 1985), 7. See also the meditation—constructed, it is said, out of the oral histories retold by his wife, Simone Schwarz-Bart—of André Schwarz-Bart, *La Mulâtresse Solitude* (Paris: Editions du Seuil, 1972).

12. Timoléon Brutus, *L'Homme d'Airain* (Port-au-Prince: Imprimerie N.A. Théodore, 1946), 120–21.

13. Albert Memmi, *Portrait du colonisé* (Paris: Bucher/Chastel, Corréa, 1957), 91–92.

14. Roger Bastide, *The African Religions of Brazil: Toward a Sociology of the Interpenetration of Civilizations,* trans. Helen Sebba (Baltimore and London: Johns Hopkins University Press, 1978), 271.

15. Médéric Louis Elie Moreau de Saint-Méry, *Description topographique, physique, civile, politique et historique de la partie française de l'Isle Saint-Domingue,* 2 vols. (Philadelphia: chez l'auteur, 1797–98; reprint, Paris: Société de l'Histoire des Colonies Françaises, 1959), 19.

16. de Vassière, 311.

17. Deren, *Divine Horsemen,* 143.

18. Moreau de Saint-Méry, *Description topographique,* 42–43.

19. Zora Neale Hurston, *Tell My Horse: Voodoo and Life in Haiti and Jamaica* (1938; reprint, New York: Harper and Row, 1990), 121.

20. Moreau de Saint-Méry, *Description topographique,* 104.

21. J. B. Romain, *Quelques moeurs et coutumes des paysans Haitiens* (Port-au-Prince: Imprimerie de l'Etat, 1959), 59.

22. Gautier, *Les Soeurs de Solitude,* 221. Gautier reflects that many writers, including Edouard Glissant, have assumed that women accepted slavery — as lovers of the masters or protectors of their children — while men became the *marrons* (fugitives). Three significant books that consider the forms that women's resistance took are Lucille Mathurin, *The Rebel Woman in the British West Indies During Slavery* (Kingston: Institute of Jamaica for the African-Caribbean Institute of Jamaica, 1975); Barbara Bush, *Slave Women in Caribbean Society: 1650–1838* (Kingston: Heinemann Caribbean; Bloomington: Indiana University Press, 1990); and Marietta Morrissey, *Slave Women in the New World: Gender Stratification in the Caribbean* (Lawrence: University Press of Kansas, 1989).

23. Windsor Bellegarde, "Les Héroïnes de Notre Histoire," *Ecrivains Haïtiens: Notices biographiques et pages choisies* (Port-au-Prince: Societe d'Editions et de Librairie, 1947), 218–19. See also the ambiguous ending of Aimé Césaire's *Cahier d'un retour au pays natal,* when he celebrates the perfect apotheosis of freedom as that négritude "standing/and/free/standing and no longer a poor madwoman in/her freedom and her maritime destitution gyrating/in perfect drift."

24. Jacques Roumain, *Gouverneurs de la rosée* (1946; Paris: Messidor, 1988), 37.

25. Marie Chauvet, *Fonds des Nègres* (Port-au-Prince: Imprimerie Deschamps, 1961), 3.

26. Louis Maximilien, *Le Vodou Haitien: Rite Radas-Canzo* (Port-au-Prince: Imprimerie de l'Etat, 1945). Only one loa has a chapter devoted to her: Erzulie Fréda Dahomey.

27. Frantz Fanon, *Les Damnés de la terre* (Paris: Maspero, 1961); *The Wretched of the Earth,* trans. Constance Farrington (New York: Grove Press, 1968), 227.

28. The djablesse is known in the English West Indies as "jablesse," and in Martinique and Guadeloupe as "guiablesse" or "diablesse." In most accounts, she is beautiful and can be seen near a bridge or river. Men, especially, are warned that if they follow a gorgeous woman, they might disappear, never to be seen again. As far as I know, the return of the unsatisfied virgin is a peculiarly Haitian phenomenon.

29. Marie Chauvet, *Amour, Colère et Folie* (Paris: Gallimard, 1968), 289.

CHAPTER FOUR

The Past Our Mother

Marie-Claire Blais and the Question of Women in the Quebec Canon

MARY JEAN GREEN

In 1975, at an international colloquium on women and writing, the Quebec feminist writer Nicole Brossard gave voice to a question central to the understanding of women writers in Quebec: "il faudra bien s'expliquer une bonne fois comment il se fait que les femmes aient joué un rôle si important dans notre littérature: Gabrielle Roy, Anne Hébert, Germaine Guèvremont, Marie-Claire Blais. Comment il se fait surtout que leurs oeuvres aient su toucher une vaste partie du public québécois? Sur quelle schizophrénie collective leurs fantasmes ont-ils eu prise? Sur quelle oppression ont-ils fait le jour?" ("How is it that women have played such an important part in our literature: Gabrielle Roy, Anne Hébert, Germaine Guèvremont, Marie-Claire Blais. How come, in particular, that their works were able to reach a wide section of the Quebec public? With what collective schizophrenia did their own phantasms connect? On what oppression did they throw light?")[1]

It is not merely coincidental that Christiane Makward used these words of Brossard to introduce Quebec women's writing to American readers in her pioneering 1979 article in *Women and Literature*. I have found myself repeating them in my own work, and the question so lucidly articulated by Brossard has been a force motivating my exploration of the writing of Quebec women. For American feminist readers, the fact that women writers have been part of the Quebec literary mainstream, at least since the publication of Gabrielle Roy's *Bonheur d'occasion* in 1945, has been a source of amazement. Feminists engaged in locating women writers in the literary canon of France can easily share this amazement. As Brossard has speculated, the anomalously canonical status of a certain number of women writers in Quebec suggests that their works have spoken not only to women but to the culture as a whole. And yet, in the texts of the writers to whom Brossard refers — Gabrielle Roy, Anne Hébert, Germaine Guèvremont, Marie-Claire Blais — experience unique to women, if it is not the central focus, nevertheless plays an important role. I would like to suggest that these writers' inscription of women's experience may bear an important relationship to certain moments of perceived change in Quebec culture. In particular, I would like to explore the idea that one form of women's experience repeatedly portrayed in texts written by Quebec women — the relationship of mothers and children, and especially mothers and daughters — enacts issues at stake in evolving concepts of Quebec identity in the post–World War II era when women writers were accepted as important cultural voices.

It was in this postwar period, and particularly during the era in the 1960s known as the *Révolution tranquille,* that the concept of francophone Canadian identity in Quebec underwent a radical transformation, marked by the displacement of the very concept of "French Canadian" by the term Québécois. A sense of continuity with the past, of fidelity to French origins, had long been central to the formation of a collective Quebec. The American social scientist Seymour Martin Lipset has suggested, in fact, that a certain sense of continuity with the past is uniquely characteristic of Canadians, in both Quebec and English Canada. Canadians' positive relationship with history stands in contrast to the attitudes of their American neighbors, whose cultural values trace their origins to a revolutionary break with the past.[2] Nevertheless, especially during the period of the Révolution tranquille, the nature of this relationship with the past was profoundly questioned in Quebec. In one sense, the central gesture of the Révolution tranquille can be seen as the rejection of an outmoded tradition based on rural life and a resolute commitment to the values of modernization and secularization. In another sense, however, it may be interpreted as a renegotiation of a relationship with the past, the search for new sources of connection with a collective history even as certain elements of tradition, long privileged by the dominant ideology, were being set aside. Quebec intellectuals of the 1960s were deeply engaged in forging new links with their own history, as the independence-minded editors of the journal *Liberté,* for example, found new "ancestors" in the heroes of the unsuccessful Patriots Rebellion of 1837–38, which had been erased by Quebec's clerically dominated official history.[3] The sense of continuity with history that persists throughout the Révolution tranquille is signaled by the proud inscription on automobile license plates of the old Quebec motto, "Je me souviens" (I remember). The need for a new understanding of their own history was also deeply felt by Quebec women: one of the major emphases of the Quebec feminist movement that followed closely on the heels of the Révolution tranquille has been a search for forgotten foremothers and a rewriting of Quebec history to include the experience of women's lives.[4]

An article by Pierre Maheu, which appeared at the height of the Révolution tranquille, suggests a possible relationship between the conflicts between mothers and daughters that appear so frequently in works written by Quebec women and the struggle of an entire culture to redefine a collective relationship to the past. In an article titled "L'Oedipe colonial," which appeared in a special issue of the radical journal *Parti pris*, Maheu reframed the relationship of the "colonized" people of Quebec to their own tradition in the terms of the Freudian family romance. As Patricia Smart has observed, this analysis bears special significance for the position of women in Quebec literature of the time,[5] because Maheu sees the struggle with a certain concept of the past not as an Oedipal rivalry between father and son but, rather, as an engulfing relationship with a mother:

> Authority threatens not to strike us but to swallow us; it is a tradition: not a set of precise rules, but a presence of vague and obscure prohibitions, an all-encompassing, maternal presence. Our mythology is an affirmation of the world of the Mother; it is the universe of moral Values, of the intemporal, of the interiorized; opposed to the world of *action*, it is a world of *being*, of immutable nature, it is the frozen dream of our traditionalism. And the concrete role of the mother within the family corresponds to these structures: she is above all the guardian of the home, the faith, and the language.[6]

Maheu's Freudian analysis of the Quebec cultural dilemma has implications for the acts of violence against women that are frequently found in masculine texts of the 1960s, as Smart has convincingly argued. It also, I think, bears an important relationship to women's writing, where the tortuous process of rejection and reconciliation, of separation and continuity, which characterizes the mother-daughter bond in the work of Freud and many contemporary feminist theorists, becomes the expression of an equally complex and ambivalent relationship with tradition.

My analysis here focuses particularly on the fiction of Marie-Claire Blais, whose work I have chosen to privilege for two reasons. First, her very extensive fictional production provides a working out of this mother-daughter relationship in its various dimensions. Second, her writing covers a crucial period for the evolution of Quebec literature, and particularly for the writing of women: she began publishing in 1959, just before the Révolution tranquille, and she has continued to produce a steady stream of novels and plays throughout the succeeding decades. Her work can thus serve as a framework within which similar representations in the work of other major women writers can be seen and understood.

I have said that the mother seems to be a dominant figure, certainly the dominant parental figure in modern Quebec fiction, at least since World War II. To make my case quickly, I have only to refer to Roy's Rose-Anna Lacasse in *Bonheur d'occasion*, Madame Plouffe in Roger Lemelin's *Les Plouffe*, Claudine Perrault in Hébert's "Le Torrent," and the many unforgettable maternal figures created by Blais herself, most vividly Grand-Mère Antoinette in *Une Saison dans la vie d'Emmanuel*. Blais's novelistic career, in fact, begins with *La Belle Bête*, the symbolic story of a daughter who murders her mother by setting fire to the family house, an act Margaret Atwood has seen as emblematic of a certain moment in Quebec literature as a whole.[7]

The mother in much of modern Quebec fiction is meant to be seen as more than an individual woman; she is clearly endowed with symbolic dimensions. In general, the mother could be said to represent tradition,[8] and in their analysis of individual texts, various critics have corroborated this interpretation. In Quebec, tradition is not a vague term, but one that was, for a long time, susceptible to rather precise definition, in terms of a quasi-official ideology that dominated the province in the period extending from 1840 until about the time of World War II. In a sense, the mother would seem to be a particularly appropriate representative of this tradition, because it was very much rooted in the large rural family of *la revanche des berceaux* (the revenge of the cradle), in which the mother obviously played an essential role. As Maheu has reiterated, the mother was also the one responsible for transmitting to new generations the central element of the tradition, as it was defined by nineteenth-century ideologues: the *langue maternelle*, the mother tongue, and its associated religious faith.[9] In the novels I have mentioned, the maternal figure is clearly identified with this traditional society, as has been recognized by numerous critics. Lucien Goldmann, in his well-known analysis of Blais's *La Belle Bête* and *Une Saison dans la vie d'Emmanuel*, sees both novels as allegorical representations of

the rebellion of a new generation of Quebec intellectuals against the traditional society, which he identifies with the mother figure. In a common interpretation of *Bonheur d'occasion,* the fate of Rose-Anna Lacasse illustrates
the defeat of the old Quebec rural values in the modern urban environment,
and Hébert's Claudine Perrault in "Le Torrent" is immediately recognized
as a particularly harsh caricature of the traditional clerical ideology.

The mother has, in reality, always had an important role to play in the
functioning of traditional Quebec society.[10] She has not always been seen,
however, as its appropriate symbolic representative. In official expressions
of the nineteenth-century ideology, this central place was always reserved
for the man, the father, the patriarch — the earthly representative of a naturally hierarchical order that culminated in a masculine Pope representing
a masculine God. Mgr. François-Louis Laflèche, a major contributor to the
definition of the ideology that came to dominate Quebec in the nineteenth
century, writes, for example, "In the family, the person endowed with authority is called Father; in the State, this person is called Emperor, King, President . . . in the Church, this person is named Sovereign Pontiff or Pope. Thus,
when you speak of family, state, church, you are at the same time saying Father, King, Pope."[11] When the Quebec historian Lionel Groulx sought to per-
sonify tradition, he repeated this androcentric vision in his famous phrase,
"notre maître, le passé," the past our master.

This recognition of the man as the appropriate bearer of tradition is
honored in literature as well. In the *roman du terroir* (the rural novel), a
dominant literary genre in nineteenth- and early twentieth-century Quebec, a primary drama is the passing on of the land from father to son, as
Janine Boynard-Frot has convincingly documented.[12] The land is, to quote
the title of an early Quebec novel, *la terre paternelle,* the paternal land: it
can properly be dominated and possessed only by the father. Quebec rural
novels from *La Terre paternelle* in 1846 right through Ringuet's *Trente Arpents* in 1938 stress the continuation of tradition through the male line, although, as Philippe Garigue points out, this mode of inheritance was not
always the practice in real life.[13] As an alternative to this drama of apparently
unending fascination, traditional Quebec fiction has described the foundation of a new patriarchy, as in the nineteenth-century Jean Rivard novels
of Antoine Gérin-Lajoie.

In either fictional scenario, however, the woman does not play an active
role, and the mother, in particular, is almost completely effaced. In fact,
Boynard-Frot offers striking statistical data to show that marriage and motherhood in the roman du terroir have the effect of totally suppressing female

characters. Women play a role in the roman du terroir as long as they are maidens waiting to be married; once this single goal is accomplished, they commonly fade out of sight, often physically dying off, like Maria Chapdelaine's mother or Alphonsine Moisan in *Trente Arpents*.[14] Readers of Blais will recognize the extent to which she has parodied this effacement of women in the roman du terroir in *Une Saison dans la vie d'Emmanuel*. The cowlike mother in that novel does not even have a name, and her string of indistinguishable daughters are known only as the big As and the little As. Even in the work of early Quebec women writers, mothers are not really prominent. In 1881, Quebec's first woman novelist, Laure Conan, killed off her heroine's mother in *Angéline de Montbrun* before the novel even began, freeing Angéline to concentrate exclusively on her father: Laure Conan, at least, had a clear understanding of the cultural priorities.

The centrality of the father as bearer of the cultural tradition is again illustrated, at the very end of the series of romans du terroir, by Guèvremont's metaphorical depiction of the end of the old order in her novels *Le Survenant* and *Marie-Didace*.[15] She describes the decline and death of the male patriarch, Didace Beauchemin, and the abdication of the men eligible to replace him. In the end, the Beauchemin heritage falls to a female, Didace's infant granddaughter, Marie-Didace. Interestingly, and hardly coincidentally, it is at about the time Guèvremont was registering her vision of change in Quebec society — near the end of World War II — that the mother begins to replace the father as the important figure in Quebec fiction. The immediate postwar years see the appearance of both Roy's *Bonheur d'occasion* and Lemelin's *Au pied de la pente douce,* considered Quebec's first urban novels. In these postwar realist texts, women are clearly the dominant figures in the family, for better or worse. The end of the 1940s also witnesses the appearance of more allegorical tradition-figures as well: Hébert's Claudine Perrault and the hideously repressive mother, a mother also embittered by the father's abandonment, in Françoise Loranger's novel *Mathieu*. It is the latter character, in particular, who prompts Suzanne Paradis, in her study of feminine figures in Quebec fiction, to lament that at the very moment when the character of the mother finally begins to display a certain strength, she moves in the direction of the horrible.[16]

Why, at this particular time in Quebec's literary history does the figure who incarnates tradition change from father to mother? Why, too, does this figure often appear as repressive and, at the same time, strangely powerless, defeated by her environment? One explanation for the predominance of mothers in postwar literature may be that, really for the first time, in the immediate postwar years, women were attaining the status of major writers. It is possible that in speaking from their own experience — their experience as, among other things, women — these writers were able to say something that struck a responsive chord in their readers, male and female alike. In their process of "thinking back through their mothers," as Virginia Woolf has put it — in seeing the past as embodied in a woman — these writers were able to give form to an altered vision of the relationship to tradition, a vision that seemed to evoke recognition by the society as a whole. I am suggesting that a central reality of Quebec's collective experience since World War II has been given expression in the struggle of fictional charcters, often female, to work out a tormented and ambivalent relationship with a mother figure.

The meaning of this changed vision of the traditional culture is most clearly and vividly expressed by Guèvremont: the central figure of the traditional culture is no longer viewed as a strong and active man, capable of mastering the means of economic production. The traditional father figure was able to found and maintain a family by serving as intermediary between the enclosed space of the home, which was the proper sphere of women, and the world outside it. When the male figure is shown as no longer able to act effectively on the world outside the home, when the maintenance of the culture is seen as dependent on women, what is being said is that the sphere of effectiveness of traditional values has been greatly reduced. Like the mother figures who serve as its embodiment, the tradition retains a certain vigor and, in the view of some writers at least — certainly Roy — the values connected with it retain their importance. But the extent of its power is limited. Roy's Rose-Anna Lacasse and Blais's Grand-Mère Antoinette are heroic women, but their powers fall far short of those possessed by earlier male figures like Jean Rivard, Samuel Chapdelaine, and even the ultimately dispossessed Euchariste Moisan of *Trente Arpents*. The decadence and gradual disappearance of strong male figures from the postwar Quebec novel has, in fact, been an almost universal subject of lamentation among critics.[17]

The shift from the father to the mother as the fictional incarnation of tradition, then, seems to express at least two aspects of the view of tradition in the postwar era. The shift from an active man to a strong but ineffectual woman suggests that the tradition is being perceived as debased, that it appears lacking in power to affect the world. Indeed, this constituted a major source of the criticism leveled against the traditional Quebec ideology at this time, namely, that its values had rendered the Québécois unable to cope with the twentieth-century industrial economy. The traditional ideology emphasized an outmoded rural existence and was opposed to commercial activity and material acquisition — not attitudes designed to insure one's success in the modern world. In addition, the incarnation of tradition in a mother also gives rise to ambivalent attitudes on the part of the fictional protagonist, attitudes that must have corresponded to what many Québécois were feeling at that time. On the one hand, the mother is both humiliating and oppressive and must be escaped; on the other, however, she is a haunting presence, with whom identification can never be fully denied, on pain of denial of self.

These features closely parallel the response to the mother developed in the Freudian scenario by the child, and particularly by the daughter. Very late in his career, in the 1920s and 1930s, Freud was forced to deal directly with what he called "the riddle of the nature of femininity."[18] By this time Freud had already worked out the Oedipus complex, in which the male child attempts to compete with his father for possession of the mother. The female child would, correspondingly, compete with her mother for possession of the father, in an exact mirror image of male development. Eventually, however, Freud came to realize that there was, in fact, a lack of symmetry between the sexes, because both male and female infants experience their mother as their original love-object. In order even to enter the Oedipal phase, the girl first has to switch her affections from her mother to her father, a shift unnecessary in the case of the boy. In seeking to explain why a girl turns away from her mother, Freud cites allegations of inadequate nurturance and sexual repression. But both these factors are also present for the boy. The principle Freud finds determinative for the girl, in the end, is the famous concept of "penis envy": the girl discovers that her mother, like herself, is without a penis and thus humiliated and debased. Filled with hostility toward her mother, who is not only herself humiliated but also responsible for humiliating her daughter by sending her out into the world "insufficiently equipped," the girl turns to her father and ultimately to heterosexual love-objects in order to obtain the penis denied her by her mother.

Freud's analysis of the process seems rather crudely anatomical — indeed, one of his essays on the subject is titled "Some Psychical Consequences of the Anatomical Distinctions between the Sexes" — and it has frequently inspired criticism or even ridicule at the hands of women analysts and feminist thinkers alike. Later theorists, like Simone de Beauvoir and Nancy Chodorow, have, however, attempted to redefine Freud's basic insight by explaining the girl's devaluation of the mother in more symbolic terms. In Beauvoir's interpretation, for example, the girl recognizes that power in the family, and in the world beyond, resides with men, and she turns toward the father in an effort to gain justification in his eyes.[19]

In the Freudian scenario, the boy also realizes that the mother has been castrated, but this does not cause him to feel hostility toward her: his identity, after all, is not in question. He can easily take the path of identification with his father, often developing in the process what Freud calls "a triumphant contempt" for women.[20] But such a conflict-free resolution is not possible for girls, who have no way to dismiss their own fundamental similarity with the mother. Even though the daughter is initially overcome by hostility, she can never fully abandon her very strong feelings of attachment and continuity with the mother. In his essays on femininity, Freud comes belatedly to recognize the importance of the close "preoedipal" relationship between the daughter and her mother and the way in which this relationship follows her throughout her life, even, Freud speculates, determining her mode of interaction with her husband. The girl thus exhibits a psychic complexity unknown to the boy, who enters easily into the Oedipal period and experiences its definitive, if violent, resolution.

In *The Reproduction of Mothering* Chodorow sees the persistence of the preoedipal bond between mother and daughter as determinative of feminine identity, characterized by fluid ego boundaries, a sense of continuity with others, as opposed to masculine autonomy.[21] Freud observed that some of the problems of feminine development may be resolved when the woman becomes a mother herself, making possible the woman's identification with her own mother. As Chodorow elaborates, motherhood permits the woman to re-create and reexperience the closeness of the original mother-daughter bond.

This summary of the Freudian scenario may suggest some reasons for the importance accorded mother-daughter interaction in fiction in the ideological context of Quebec. According to Freud, the daughter is jolted out of a harmonious relationship with her mother because of her sudden realization that this hitherto all-powerful figure is, in fact, powerless. Disillusioned and resentful of the way in which the maternal impotence has also determined her own being, the girl turns elsewhere for a source of identity. Despite her attempts, however, she can never succeed in fully breaking away, and her conflicts seem ultimately resolved only when she can accept her continuity with her mother as she becomes a mother herself. The Freudian scenario provides a context for the tormented and often violent relationship with the mother seen in Quebec fiction in the period immediately preceding the Révolution tranquille. In addition, it provides a vision of a potential reconciliation made possible by the daughter's attainment of maturity and self-acceptance.

In Blais's first published novel, *La Belle Bête,* the daughter actually acts out her feelings of hostility toward her mother by setting fire to the family house, with her mother inside. The drama in *La Belle Bête* is one of continuity and repetition, which is also a very powerful dynamic in Quebec's traditional ideology. The ugly daughter in the novel, Isabelle-Marie, consciously rejects her mother's valorization of superficial beauty, but the relationship she has with her blind husband is essentially an effort to repeat her mother's life as a beautiful and desired woman and to measure up to her mother's expectations. Because this attempt is based on a lie, a falsification of her own reality, it is obviously doomed to failure.

There is much concern with mirrors in the short novel, as the characters see their self-image in the eyes of others. In the case of mothers and daughters, this is a negative process, passed on from generation to generation. The mother rejects Isabelle-Marie because she is not a mirror in which she wants to see a reflection of herself, and Isabelle-Marie rejects her own daughter because she sees in her daughter the being her mother has already rejected in herself: "Mais c'est à Isabelle-Marie que l'enfant ressemblait. Dès sa naissance, Isabelle l'avait trouvée plus monstrueuse qu'elle-même et ce visage d'enfant, affligé de la même laideur, porteur de son sang et de ses traits labourés, la révoltait" (101–2) ("But she looked like Isabelle-Marie. From the day of her birth Isabelle-Marie had found the baby even more hideous than herself, and the tiny face, afflicted by the same ugliness, bearing her blood and the same tortured features, repelled her" [81]).[22]

Blais plays consciously with the mother-daughter motifs prevalent in fairy tales. In her obsession with the image in her mirror, the mother resembles the wicked queen of Snow White. But unlike the fairy tale heroine, Isabelle-Marie is not the "fairest of them all," and cannot invoke a superior beauty to triumph over the older woman. It is rather the mother who succeeds in destroying both of them with the poisoned apple of her rejection. As Jennifer Waelti-Walters has shown,[23] Blais also rewrites the story of Cinderella — another victim of a cruel stepmother — by creating a Prince Charming who turns away in horror once the magical illusion of beauty has been dispelled.

Torn between the need to separate and the inability to break the attachment to her mother, Isabelle-Marie is incapable of resolving her conflict except in a violent outburst that ultimately destroys her psychologically as it destroys the mother. As I have said, Lucien Goldmann[24] has interpreted this work as an allegory for the struggle of young Québécois to break free from an outmoded traditional ideology in the late 1950s. This is a struggle for which the complex and tormented mother-daughter relationship provides a more appropriate model, I believe, than the more commonly cited alternative scenario, the clear-cut conflict and definitive resolution of the Oedipal situation.

The grim playing out of the mother-child relationship in *La Belle Bête* is not far removed from the drama enacted in Hébert's "Le Torrent" by an adolescent protagonist — a boy in this case — equally torn between rejection and attachment to an overpowering mother. In his case, too, the mother's violent death, for which the son is responsible, is not sufficient to free him. There is a similar struggle in another work of the late 1940s, Loranger's *Mathieu,* where a young protagonist does succeed in wrenching himself free of an oppressive mother. A number of works of the early 1960s also show adolescents, in this case, generally girls, who act out a similar revolt against their mothers. As Paradis comments, such rebellious adolescent heroines seem to proliferate in the Quebec novel of the early 1960s; this phenomenon was surely not coincidental in the early years of the Révolution tranquille.

But in these novels of the early 1960s, a change has taken place in the portrayal of the mother, in contrast to earlier works like "Le Torrent" and *Mathieu.* Hébert's Claudine Perrault is a powerful and oversized figure who can be destroyed only by a rampaging stallion. The mother in *La Belle Bête,* however, is already dying of cancer by the time her daughter gets around to burning down the house.

It is the progressive weakening of the mother — corresponding chronologically to a perceived weakening of the hold of the dominant ideology — that seems eventually to permit a tempering of the daughter's hostility. In Blais's *Une Saison dans la vie d'Emmanuel* the mother herself is too exhausted by farmwork and an unending series of maternities to have any existence at all for her children. The real maternal figure in this novel is the grandmother, Grand-Mère Antoinette. This, in itself, is an interesting phenomenon. Blais again seems to have chosen a form of representation — the transfer of maternal qualities to the grandmother — that recurs in a number of other works of the same era, including Claire Martin's *Dans un gant de fer* and Jovette Marchessault's *La Mère des herbes.* As the daughters described in the psychoanalytic literature tend to split off the positive and negative aspects of the mother, often separating her positive features from the mother herself, the grandmother figure in literature seems an attempt on the part of the writer to split off the nurturant qualities of the mother from

the aspects that call forth the protagonist's rejection. Martin's autobiographical persona, for example, cannot repress a word of resentment against the
weakness of her mother, even though she feels sorry for her, but she views
her grandmother with unmixed affection, although she is equally powerless to help her.

Grand-Mère Antoinette, however, remains an extremely difficult and ambiguous figure, possessing a richness that accounts, in large part, for the continuing fascination of *Une Saison dans la vie d'Emmanuel*. This richness is
apparent in the striking opening page of the novel, which describes the
grandmother from the point of view of the newborn Emmanuel:

> Les pieds de Grand-Mère Antoinette dominaient la chambre. Ils étaient là,
> tranquilles et sournois comme deux bêtes couchées, frémissant à peine dans
> leurs bottines noires, toujours prêts à se lever: c'étaient des pieds meurtris
> par de longues années de travail aux champs (lui qui ouvrait les yeux pour
> la première fois dans la poussière du matin ne les voyait pas encore, il ne
> connaissait pas encore la blessure secrète à la jambe, sous le bas de laine, la
> cheville gonflée sous la prison de lacets et de cuir . . .) des pieds nobles et
> pieux (n'allaient-ils pas à l'église chaque matin en hiver?) des pieds vivants
> qui gravaient pour toujours dans la mémoire de ceux qui les voyaient une
> seule fois — l'image sombre de l'autorité et de la patience. (7)

> [Grand-mère Antoinette's feet dominated the room. They lay there like two
> quiet, watchful animals, scarcely twitching at all inside their black boots,
> always ready to spring into action; two feet bruised by long years of work in
> the fields (opening his eyes for the first time in the dusty morning light, he
> couldn't see them yet, was not yet aware of the hidden wound in the leg,
> beneath the woolen stocking, of the ankles swollen within their prisons of
> leather and laces . . .), two noble and pious feet (did they not make the
> journey to church once every morning, even in winter?), two feet brimming
> with life, and etching forever in the memories of those who saw them, even
> only once, their somber image of authority and patience. (3–4)][25]

As she herself has been confined by her environment, the grandmother
exerts a somewhat repressive influence on the children, particularly in the
domain of sexuality: she censors Jean-le-Maigre's manuscripts and ultimately
forces Héloïse to seek sexual expression in a brothel. Blais's critique is evident in the opening scene, where the monologue in which Grand-Mère
Antoinette presents her philosophy of life is punctuated by the cries of the
infant Emmanuel demanding his mother's breast. But this nourishment is
denied him, as is the physical warmth he so desperately seeks from his grandmother. Refusing him contact with her body, Grand-Mère Antoinette offers
him only baths in icy water, the symbolic equivalent of her austere philoso-

phy of life. In this trait, she clearly embodies one of the accusations leveled against the mother by the Freudian daughter. Even so, Grand-Mère Antoinette does not inspire in her grandchildren the hostility felt by Isabelle-Marie in *La Belle Bête,* and her courage and nurturant qualities are stressed: she cuddles the infants, fights for the older children's education, and conserves the writings of the poet-grandson. Yet, ironically, the grandchildren can save themselves only by leaving her and her stifling world — even then they are not very successful — and no ultimate mode of reconciliation is suggested.

The possibility of a more positive relationship with the mother begins to appear in Blais's trilogy of the late 1960s, *Manuscrits de Pauline Archange.* Here again, the mother is a weakened figure, debilitated by some unidentified disease. Pauline Archange rebels against her mother's repressive authority, but she also recognizes her victimization as a woman and feels pity for her more strongly than hostility. Nevertheless, she is determined to avoid repeating her mother's life, and she even consciously rejects the invitation to identify with her as a woman: "craignant, plus que tout, de rompre notre fragile lien de pudeur et de silence, par ce geste de consolation qu'elle attendait de moi, lui confirmait ainsi que nous n'appartenions pas à la même race meurtrie" (25) (Afraid, more than anything else, of breaking our fragile bond of modesty and silence by this gesture of consolation that she awaited from me, thus confirming that we did not belong to the same ravaged race [translation mine]). The relationship of Pauline Archange with her mother recalls that of Florentine and Rose-Anna Lacasse in *Bonheur d'occasion.* Florentine is equally committed to escaping her mother's fate, but, like Pauline in the end, she is finally able to reach out to her in what could be called a maternal gesture, when she invites Rose-Anna to share her new and more prosperous home.[26]

Pauline Archange, too, eventually finds a way of combining nurturance and independence in her work as an artist. Whereas she had previously defended herself against a threatening identification with society's victims, she can now express her natural empathy with them in her art. She sees that through her writing, she will even be able to reach out to her mother: "Et ma mère, qui avait toujours eu si peu d'existence pour elle-même, ne vivant toujours que pour les autres, sortait de l'ombre comme un portrait inachevé et l'absence de ses traits effrayés semblait me dire: 'Achève cette brève image de moi'" (96). ("And my mother, who had always had so little existence in her own eyes, never having lived except for others, my mother emerged from the shadow like an unfinished portrait and the void where her frightened features should have been seemed to be saying, 'Finish this brief sketch of me' " [78]).[27]

Blais's fiction of the 1970s and 1980s develops this more positive view of the maternal figure and works out a mode of reconciliation between mothers and daughters. Her 1978 novel, *Les Nuits de l'Underground,* is set in the lesbian bars of Montreal and Paris, perhaps not the expected background of a mother-daughter scenario. Yet the network of relationships that structures the fiction is explicitly based on a model of "moral maternity" summed up for the narrator by a Rodin sculpture. Through an initial relationship with a woman doctor, the narrator herself becomes able to nurture an older woman whom she saves from despair. The mother-daughter relationships thus become mutual and reciprocal, echoing the vision of mother-daughter reconciliation expressed by the American feminist theorist Adrienne Rich: "[I]t is a timidity of the imagination which urges that we can be 'daughters' — therefore free spirits — rather than 'mothers' — defined as eternal givers. . . . To accept and integrate and strengthen both the mother and the daughter in ourselves is no easy matter, . . . But any radical vision of sisterhood demands that we reintegrate them."[28]

In Blais's subsequent novel, *Le Sourd dans la ville,* this pattern of a younger woman mothering an older one is repeated in the relationship of Judith Lange, a young philosophy professor, and Florence, a depressed middle-aged housewife. And, for the first time in Blais's work, there appears an exuberantly positive version of the traditional Quebec mother of many children. Gloria is a striptease artist and proprietor of a sleazy hotel, seemingly a far cry from Rose-Anna Lacasse, but she provides the same loving care to her many children, who include a dying son (if *Une Saison dans la vie d'Emmanuel* is a negative rewriting of the roman du terroir, perhaps *Le Sourd dans la ville* is a modern version of *Bonheur d'occasion*). Blais's Gloria is, symbolically, a feminine deity, a female creator. She also possesses an exuberant sexuality, both in her work as a stripper and in the generosity she shows in providing sexual solace to the various men in her life. A new vision of the Quebec mother, Gloria reintegrates female creativity and sexuality with the caring maternal figure.

In *Le Sourd dans la ville* Blais also extends her appreciation of the power of maternal nurturance beyond the care of biological children. In this new vision, feminine caring becomes a force capable of responding to and perhaps even combating the many forms of suffering in the world. Judith Lange sensitizes her students to all forms of human suffering, from the Nazi concentration camps to the homeless wanderers of contemporary urban society. In *Visions d'Anna*, Blais's 1982 novel, the adolescent Anna is tormented by visions of nuclear destruction, while her friend contemplates ecological disaster. And in Blais's 1989 *L'Ange de la solitude,* the characters witness the ravages of AIDS.

Consistently opposed to all these forms of suffering and violence is the vision of maternal care that in *Visions d'Anna*, at least, is able to overcome the separation between real mothers and daughters. The novel is structured around two sets of mothers and daughters who repeat the entire cycle of filial rejection and return. Throughout the course of their flight into a hippie drug culture, it is the thread of attachment to their mothers that enables the daughters to survive and that eventually brings them back. Although they do not themselves become mothers, the daughters are ultimately able to assume an understanding and quasi-maternal attitude toward their mothers, affirming their identification with them. *Visions d'Anna* can be seen as one of the most powerful statements of the positive force of the mother-daughter relationship in modern literature.

In Blais's work, then, the portrayal of the mother-daughter relationship has come full circle, moving through hostility and rejection of the mother to a reaffirmation of mother-daughter continuity. The more recent mother figures in Blais's work are not as clearly allegorical representatives of traditional society as was Grand-Mère Antoinette. Yet, as mothers, they embody many of the concerns that lay behind particular expressions of traditional values — for instance, an affirmation of concern for children and personal relationships in opposition to an anonymous and materialistic world. Perhaps these are the elements of tradition that, once separated from their association with sexual repression and religious guilt, now appear to be most enduring.

A similar reaffirmation of the maternal can be seen in the work of other important women writers as well. In Hébert's *Les Enfants du Sabbat* the mother is a witch, seen as a strong and heroic figure who is the model for her daughter's successful rebellion against the repressive world of the convent. When she confronts the exorcist, Hébert's protagonist proudly traces her ancestors through the maternal line, producing them for him one from inside the other, like Russian dolls. In *Les Fous de Bassan,* the spirit of the murdered Olivia finds solace in the company of her dead mothers. And, more recently, in *Le Premier Jardin* Hébert's sympathetic protagonist is herself a mother, and her quest to be reunited with her daughter becomes interwoven with her rediscovery of the lives of her Québécois foremothers and her encounter with suppressed memories of her own traumatic child-hood. The search to identify through imagination with her foremothers seems, in fact, to have long been a part of Hébert's writing project: like her protagonist in *Kamouraska*, the woman who plants "the first garden" in Quebec City—Marie Rollet, wife of Quebec's first official settler, Louis Hébert—is herself one of Hébert's ancestors. This positive evaluation of the role of mother appears late in Hébert's work; it is only in *Le Premier Jardin* that the various attributes of motherhood are joined in a real and sympathetic human being and embedded in a historical continuity capable of linking past and future.

The personal past is often associated with a mother, and a cultural tradition can easily be conceived of one as well: it has a potential for nurturance but can also become a source of both humiliation and oppression and thus a target of resentment. But for Quebec protagonists, at least, the tradition cannot be viewed with contempt without entailing devaluation of the self. Personal growth and creativity seem possible for these protagonists only through a turning back toward the mother, an acceptance of a certain identification with her. For writers in Quebec, the relationship with the cultural heritage seems to be a difficult and tortuous one, a relationship that finds an appropriate equivalent in the ambivalent feelings of a daughter toward her mother. If the mother-daughter relationship is a central literary representation of the Québécois attitude toward the past, this may go some way toward explaining why women writers in recent years have played such an important role in Quebec literature and have been able to give form to a reality that is recognized by their readers not as exclusively feminine but, rather, as essentially Québécois.

Notes

1. Brossard's remarks were reprinted in *Liberté* 18, no. 4 (July–Oct. 1976): 13. Christiane Makward, whose translation is used here, quotes Brossard's statement in her article, "Quebec Women Writers," *Women and Literature* 7, no. 1 (winter 1979): 3.

2. Seymour Martin Lipset, "Revolution and Counterrevolution: The United States and Canada," in *Revolution and Counterrevolution* rev. ed. (Garden City, N.Y.: Anchor Books, 1970), and "Canada and the United States: The Cultural Dimension," in *Canada and the United States*, ed. Charles F. Doran and John H. Sigler (Englewood Cliffs, N.J., and Scarborough, Ont.: Prentice-Hall, 1985).

3. *Liberté* 7, nos. 1–2 (Jan.–April 1965). See especially the article by André Major, "Chénier, mon ancêtre," 94–95.

4. This historical emphasis has produced texts far too numerous for mention here, but it is evident, for example, in the work of the Collectif Clio, *L'Histoire des femmes au Québec* (Montreal: Les Quinze, 1982).

5. Patricia Smart, *Ecrire dans la maison du père* (Montreal: Québec/Amérique, 1988), 241.

6. Pierre Maheu, "L'Oedipe colonial," *Parti pris* 1 (9–11): 19–29, translation mine.

7. Margaret Atwood, "Quebec: Burning Mansions," in *Survival: A Thematic Guide to Canadian Literature* (Toronto: Anansi, 1972), 215–31.

8. This interpretation of the significance of the mother figure coincides with that of Soeur Sainte-Marie Eleuthère in *La Mère dans le roman canadien-français* (Quebec: Presses de l'Université Laval, 1964), in which she studies novels published in the period 1930–60: "The maternal image encompasses everything we have inherited with life itself: our faith, language, traditions and also prejudices, conformism, a certain narrowness of spirit" (127, translation mine).

9. See, for example, the description offered by Sainte-Marie Eleuthère, 3.

10. Philippe Garigue's 1958 study of Quebec family life, ("La Famille canadienne-française dans la société contemporaine," *Revue Dominicaine*, April 1958: 151) corroborates the importance of the mother's role: "Normally the father is the symbol of authority as head of household, but it is normally the mother who is the center of family life" (151, cited by Sainte-Marie Eleuthère, translation mine). See also Garigue's *La Vie familiale des Canadiens français* (Montreal: Presses de l'Université de Montréal, 1962).

11. François-Louis Laflèche (Mgr.), *Quelques considérations sur les rapports de la Société civile avec la religion et la famille* (Montreal: Eusèbe Sénécal, 1866), 85, translation mine.

12. Janine Boynard-Frot, *Un Matriarcat en procès* (Montreal: Les Presses de l'Université de Montréal, 1982), 59.

13. Garigue, "La Famille canadienne-française," 23.

14. Boynard-Frot, *Un Matriarcat en procès*, 99.

15. For a more complete analysis of Guèvremont's work, see my articles, "The Novel in Québec: The Family Plot and the Personal Voice," in *Studies on Canadian Literature: Introductory and Critical Essays*, ed. Arnold E. Davidson (New York: Modern Language Association of America, 1990); and "Gabrielle Roy and Germaine Guèvremont: Quebec's Daughters Face a Changing World," *Journal of Women's Studies in Literature*, summer 1979, 243–57.

16. Suzanne Paradis, *Femme fictive, femme réelle* (Ottawa: Garneau, 1966), 65.

17. Jean-Charles Falardeau discusses the disappearance of the exemplary hero in the Quebec novel around the time of World War II; he cites *Menaud maître-draveur* as the last incarnation of the hero preoccupied with an ideal model (*Imaginaire social et littéraire* [Montreal: Hurtubise HMH, 1974], 36). Paradis, too, comments: "if Didace Beauchemin imposes the myth — which is now, unfortunately, losing force — of the strong, authoritarian male, head of the dynasty and conqueror of the land, the presence of the hard-working, constructive man, a sort of fortress of authority, is slowly disappearing" (103, translation mine).

18. See Sigmund Freud's essays "Femininity," in *New Introductory Lectures on Psychoanalysis*, ed. James Strachey (New York and London: W. W. Norton and Co., 1965); and "Female Sexuality" and "Some Psychical Consequences of the Anatomical Distinctions between the Sexes" in *The Standard Edition of the Complete Works of Sigmund Freud*, ed. James Strachey (London: Hogarth Press, 1961), 21: 252.

19. Simone de Beauvoir, *Le Deuxième Sexe*, vol. 2 (Paris: Gallimard, 1949).

20. Freud, "Some Psychical Consequences," 252.

21. Nancy Chodorow, *The Reproduction of Mothering* (Berkeley: University of California Press, 1978). I am indebted to discussions with my colleague Marianne Hirsch for my understanding of the importance of Chodorow's work. See her book, *The Mother/Daughter Plot* (Bloomington and Indianapolis: Indiana University Press, 1989).

22. Marie-Claire Blais, *La Belle Bête* (1959; Montreal: Pierre Tisseyre, 1977); *Mad Shadows*, trans. Merloyd Lawrence (Toronto: McClelland & Stewart, 1986).

23. Jennifer Waelti-Walters, "Cinderella and *Mad Shadows* (Blais)," in *Fairy Tales and the Female Imagination* (Montreal: Eden Press, 1982), 45–57.

24. Lucien Goldmann, "Note sur deux romans de Marie-Claire Blais," in *Structures mentales et création culturelle* (Paris: Editions Anthropos, 1970).

25. Marie-Claire Blais, *Une Saison dans la vie d'Emmanuel* (Editions Quinze, 1978); *A Season in the Life of Emmanuel,* trans. Derek Coltman (New York: Farrar, Straus & Giroux, 1980).

26. For a more extensive analysis of this relationship, see my articles, "The Novel in Québec" and "Gabrielle Roy and Germaine Guèvremont."

27. *Manuscrits de Pauline Archange* (Montreal: Jour, 1968); *The Manuscripts of Pauline Archange,* trans. Derek Coltman (Toronto: McClelland & Stewart, 1982).

28. Adrienne Rich, *Of Woman Born: Motherhood as Experience and Institution* (New York: Bantam, 1981), 257.

CHAPTER FIVE

Family Histories

Marie Laberge and Women's Theater in Quebec

JANE MOSS

From the late 1970s through the early 1990s, the plays of Marie Laberge have dramatized the changing role of the family in Quebec society. From domestic melodramas depicting the failure of the traditional Quebec family to cathartic plays that suggest the possibility of redefining the family, Laberge's theater has reflected the feminist critique of gender roles within patriarchal institutions. Just as the nationalist politics of the independence movement inspired the *nouveau théâtre québécois* beginning in the late 1960s, so the sexual politics of the feminist movement gave rise to a distinctive Quebec *théâtre de femmes* in the mid-1970s.[1] Feminist activists used the stage to dramatize economic and sexual exploitation of women, to denounce repressive virgin-mother-whore stereotypes, to exorcise fears that reduce women to silence or madness, and to create an empowering female discourse. An outgrowth of the alternative theater movement, women's theater initially depended on improvisation techniques and collective creation. Written, produced, and performed by women for women spectators, it sought to represent female subjectivity and to specularize the female body freed from the fetishizing male gaze. In its early stages, feminist drama by groups such as Montreal's Théâtre des Cuisines presented a radical critique of conservative Quebec society to deconstruct the traditional family by taking up issues such as abortion, child care, single parenting, lesbianism, and the feminine mystique. In pursuing the political goal of denouncing the oppression of women, the collective creations known as *spectacles de femmes* rejected the conventions of bourgeois realist theater by using monologues, poetry, sketches, songs, masks, cross-dressing, and other Brechtian techniques.

Professional writers and actresses also began to use the stage in the mid-1970s to explore the possibilities of creating a specifically female dramatic universe with its own discourse of the female body. In 1974, three members of the Grand Cirque Ordinaire, Paule Baillargeon, Suzanne Garceau, and Luce Guilbeault, examined women's personal relationships and the sexual stereotypes presented in children's tales in a work provocatively titled *Un Prince, mon jour viendra.* Two years later came the first major event in Quebec women's theater, the successful run of *La Nef des sorcières* at Le Théâtre du Nouveau Monde.[2] *La Nef* is composed of eight monologues by seven well-known actresses and writers: Luce Guilbeault, Marthe Blackburn, France Théoret, Odette Gagnon, Marie-Claire Blais, Pol Pelletier, and Nicole Brossard. All of the monologues express the alienation of women in patriarchal society, and the need for independence and liberated sexuality. The main message of the play is that women must create a language of their own, an empowering discourse of the body that will allow for the expression of both heterosexual and lesbian desire. Denise Boucher's *Les Fées ont soif* presented a similar message, blaming misogynistic Catholic dogma for sexual repression and calling on women to reclaim their sexuality. Rebellion against stereotypes and a determination to redefine women's roles also motivated the work of the Théâtre Expérimental des Femmes, which from the late 1970s through the early 1980s was a center for feminist creation in Montreal.

Meanwhile in Quebec City, a group of actresses founded the Centre d'essai des femmes (1977), which became the Commune à Marie (1978) and then the Théâtre de la Commune. The group produced a number of collective creations dealing with issues such as sexual violence against women, and it staged some early works by Quebec City native Marie Laberge. Since 1980, an amateur feminist theater group amusingly named Les Folles Alliées has performed a variety of collective creations that use playful satiric humor, musical comedy numbers, and gender-confusing cross-dressing to make its feminist message more entertaining.

The energy and enthusiasm driving collective feminist theater groups led to works that stressed the common experience of women and the need for solidarity in order to improve their condition. These *spectacles de femmes* were composite, nonlinear or loosely plotted works structured around cer-

tain themes or scenic metaphors. Interestingly, the other dramatic form privileged by women playwrights was the monologue. Theoretical and practical reasons explain the importance of the theatrical monologue or one-
woman show in the development of women's theater. Actress and director
Michelle Rossignol called it "notre première forme d'expression" (our first
form of expression), a first step toward self-affirmation for women who have
been denied or diminished for so long.[3] France Théoret and Nicole Brossard
insisted that it conveyed the alienating isolation of women and helped them
to develop a discourse of subjectivity.[4] The monologue encouraged women
to write from personal experience and made staging their work easier because one-woman shows were less costly to produce. Although the vogue
of collective creations has virtually disappeared, the monologue continues
to flourish for practical reasons.

By the mid-1980s, critics were quick to declare women's theater "dé-
passé," pointing to the fact that of the ten feminist theater groups active in
1980 only one professional and two amateur groups survived in 1985.[5] Although it is true that women's theater seemed to turn away from the collective approach to social, political, and ideological issues that had galva-
nized it in the 1970s, it had redirected its energies toward personal and
family issues. Perhaps this change reflected the apolitical post-referendum
climate of the province or the fact that the baby-boom generation of feminists had reached middle age and was reexamining priorities. The three subjects that drew the most attention were "la vie du couple," mother-daughter
relationships, and maternity. In other words, women continued to examine how liberation could be achieved within redefined family structures.
The exploration of female eroticism continued to be an important aspect of
the more *intimiste* women's theater of the 1980s, with sexuality often presented as part of problematic mother-daughter or male-female relationships.

With attention focused on women's issues and the family, Marie Laberge
emerged as a leading figure in Quebec theater during the 1980s. Her steady
stream of staged and published plays has earned her an international reputation. *L'Homme gris* (1984) has had successful runs at the Bobigny and Ma-
rigny theaters in Paris and a reading of the English translation at New York's
Ubu Repertory. *Oublier* (1987) was staged by the Théâtre National de Bel-
gique just before it opened in Montreal. Moving from stage to screen, she has
written film scenarios for director Jean-Claude Labrecque and has directed
her own feature film, *Les Heures précieuses*. She has published three novels,
Juillet (1989), *Quelques Adieux* (1992), and *Le Poids des ombres* (1994). Today,

Marie Laberge's importance in Quebec theater history is firmly established, and her *C'était avant la guerre à l'Anse à Gilles* (1981) has found a permanent place in the national theater repertory.

Laberge's early work bears the imprint of the nationalist political and social ideas that dominated all aspects of Quebec life during the 1970s. Like the advocates of the *nouveau théâtre québécois*, she made a deliberate choice to write in Québécois rather than international French, and she frequently blamed the unholy alliance of clergy, politicians, and Anglo-American capitalists for the economic and psychological oppression of the Quebec working class. Two of her early plays, *Ils étaient venus pour...* (1981) and *C'était avant la guerre à l'Anse à Gilles*, take real and imagined episodes from rural Quebec history as the basis for stinging critiques of the exploitive capitalist system and the repressive conservative ideology that dominated the province up until the sweeping reforms of the Quiet Revolution in the 1960s. Liberal reform sentiments also inspired Laberge to write *Le Bourreau* (1980), an allegorical play condemning capital punishment. Never performed and still unpublished, *Le Bourreau* convinced Laberge that she was, as she puts it, "une auteure sensible plutôt qu'une auteure intelligente" (a sensitive rather than an intellectual writer).[6] In this self-deprecating comment, the playwright displays not only an honest assessment of her talents but also a wariness about writing ideologically motivated thesis plays with easy answers to complex questions.

Perhaps it is this wariness of ideology and facile political solutions to personal problems that differentiates Laberge's work from feminist theater that often seems didactic and utopian. In an interview after the premiere of her first works, she insisted "Ce ne sont pas des textes à messages mais des textes d'inquiétude avec beaucoup de nuances. Bien que mes personnages soient des femmes, j'aimerais qu'on comprenne que j'ai voulu aborder là des questions avant tout humaines" (These are not texts with messages but rather texts that express anxiety with lots of nuances. Although my characters are women, I would like people to understand that above all I am addressing human questions).[7] Laberge thus reveals the key preoccupation of her theater: a constant questioning of the human condition, which she sees as characterized by anguish and lack of emotional fulfillment. Her theater is often dominated by a dark, tragic vision of life. There is existential solitude, despair, and death in a world devoid of religious reassurance.

What Laberge does offer her protagonists is her humanistic faith in the essential goodness of people, in their courage and will to survive. She also offers them her belief in the cathartic value of tears and suffering. In a newspaper interview given to promote her play on suicide, *Jocelyne Trudelle trouvée morte dans ses larmes* (1981), Laberge expressed an almost classical Greek view of theater:

> C'est libérant de crier qu'on a mal. Si on crie on va arrêter de se tuer.... L'émotion n'exclut pas la réflexion... Je ne veux ni moraliser ni conseiller le spectateur, je veux le toucher. S'il pleure ou s'il rit, c'est qu'il se reconnaît en ce qui se passe devant lui.... C'est par l'émotion qui émane de la scène que le spectateur se purge de ses propres émotions.
>
> [It is liberating to cry out when one feels pain. If people cry out they will stop killing themselves.... Emotion doesn't preclude reflection... I don't want to moralize or give advice to the spectator, I want to touch him. If he cries or laughs, that is because he recognizes himself in what is happening on stage.... It is through the emotion that emanates from the stage that the spectator purges himself of his own emotions.][8]

Her stated preference for emotional existential humanism over feminism notwithstanding, Laberge owes much to women's theater. In her lucid dramatization of women's experience in Quebec, she uses the stage to talk about how the dominant conservative ideology of Quebec through its institutions (church, school, family) conditioned women to subordinate personal needs to familial duties, to repress sexuality, to accept maternity as their vocation, to endure all suffering in silence. Like other women playwrights, Laberge places women center stage and lets them talk about lives filled with solitude, alienation, fear, madness, anger, and despair. And she lets them talk about the female body and the right to sexual pleasure without shame or guilt. Laberge focuses particularly on women's roles within the family, that is, on maternity, mother-daughter relationships, and father-daughter relationships, and on how they affect women's behavior in the context of the couple. Her dramatic universe includes women from Quebec's past and present, from rural towns and urban centers, and from all social classes. They are young and old; single, married, divorced, and widowed; whores, housewives, teachers, and doctors; and anorexic and obese. Despite their different circumstances, most of Laberge's female protagonists are trying to balance personal and sexual needs with familial responsibilities. Unfortunately, their quests for independence, love, and fulfillment often end in failure because of the negative forces of society and family. Laberge may resist the label "feminist playwright," but she clearly identifies with the goals of the women's movement and her twenty-odd plays deal with the key themes of women's theater.

The family often appears to be the root of suffering in the bourgeois realist world of Laberge. Her plays are filled with dysfunctional families and
failed parent-child relationships. Because her female protagonists define
themselves by their roles as daughters, they find it difficult to escape the
emotional and psychological damage inflicted by fathers who may be alcoholic, abusive, and incestuous or passive, weak, and withdrawn. Laberge's
daughters are equally damaged by mothers who are fearful, submissive martyrs or cold, selfish, and unloving. The lack of good role models leads naturally to marital failure or avoidance. Sometimes, delving into family history
uncovers past sins, original sins that have corrupted the family paradise.
Although the death of a parent has the potential to liberate the adult child,
it does not always have this effect. The only female characters with any real
chance at independence and happiness are those who leave the patriarchal
or matriarchal family, reject marriage and motherhood, and redefine themselves as sisters. In the plays that end on hopeful notes, the protagonists succeed in turning their backs on the past, leaving the ancestral home, and finding new places to rebuild their lives. These few positive Labergian women
question socially constructed gender roles and accepted notions of femininity in their quest for personal fulfillment.

Laberge has stated her belief in the necessity of reinventing the family.
In her view, the father is "un être en voie de disparition" (a vanishing breed),
and the idealized mother is "un mirage impossible" (an impossible mirage).
The traditional family structure is outmoded because it is based on authority, and all power relationships imply victims. It is also rooted in a collective past that is harmful to individuals. According to Laberge, the family
must be reconstituted on the principles of mutual respect and love between
equals. Until that happens, there can be no truly satisfying male-female
relationships.[9]

After trying out her skills in the short pieces and the historical, musical
epic *Ils étaient venus pour...*,[10] Laberge was ready to write the three plays
she calls her second cycle: *Avec l'hiver qui s'en vient* (1980), *Jocelyne Trudelle
trouvée morte dans ses larmes* (1981), and *C'était avant la guerre à l'Anse à
Gilles* (1981).[11] The first two reflect her preoccupation with the disguised
violence of family relations, the self-destructive games people play, the failure of communication, stifling gender roles, and the inability to love. They
are family-triangle plays in which mother, father, and daughter are locked
in death struggles. Debilitated by past familial relations and lacking inner
resources, Laberge's protagonists seem powerless and pathetic. No longer
willing to deal with emotional violence and lack of love, Jocelyne Trudelle

and Maurice Gingras (the father in *Avec l'hiver qui s'en vient*) choose death. In so doing, they are also choosing mutism and silence, rejecting the everyday language of their lives, which is a constant stream of vulgarity, banality, complaint, reproach, and clichés.

Avec l'hiver qui s'en vient centers around Maurice Gingras, who, after retiring from his job as a bookkeeper, has fallen into a state of mutism and total apathy. In contrast to the realism of the language and setting, Laberge uses flashbacks and interior monologues, signaled by lighting changes and an area of the stage called "le coin du passé" (the corner of the past), to explain the psychological trauma that has induced this rejection of life. As Maurice looks back on his life, he sees a meaningless job, a passionless marriage, and years of boring, senseless chatter. The sole bright spot is his memory of childhood summers spent in the country with his Tante Félicie, the only person who ever loved him freely without making demands on him. Since her death, he has felt abandoned and unloved. Now that he has done his duty as husband and father, he sees no reason to go on, so he lapses into dementia. His wife, Cécile, like many Labergian mothers, is an ambiguous mother figure described in the cast list as "Mère de famille qui n'a plus de famille à élever, mais qui a gardé le réflexe du frottage" (Mother of the family who no longer has a family to raise, but who still has the scrubbing reflex).[12] As she goes about her cleaning, she never stops talking, and her speech is an endless stream of complaints about her children, husband, and housework. What hurts her most is that Maurice was never interested in her sexually and made her ashamed of her sexual desire.

There is sad irony in the parallel but separate monologues at the end of the first act in which both husband and wife say they have spent their lives fulfilling familial duties without ever feeling loved, cared for, or understood. Maurice's lament echoes Cécile's: "Ma vie est ben âcre, à soir. J'ai de la misère à l'envaler" (My life is acrid tonight. I have to swallow the misery).[13] As is often the case in Laberge's plays, the daughter is caught between her parents. Perhaps sensing the impending family tragedy, Hélène has left home to be on her own at age twenty. Although she still feels sympathy and love for her parents, good relations and dialogue are impossible. Cécile resents the fact that Hélène loves Maurice even though he is so lost in his reveries of Félicie, the lost mother figure, that he hardly takes notice of his daughter. The play ends with husband and wife both calling for help, "Viens m'charcher... sors-moé d'icitte... viens..." (Come get me... let me out of here... come...),[14] but there is no exit from the Gingras family prison of solitude. Although Maurice and Cécile are unable to overcome an unhappy past conditioned by a repressive society that offered no meaningful experience, there is still hope for Hélène.

The daughter of *Jocelyne Trudelle trouvée morte dans ses larmes* is less fortunate than Hélène: she commits suicide to escape what drama critic Pierre Lavoie called the "trio infernal" or the "maudite trinité" of the Labergian family.[15] In interviews, Laberge has admitted to an obsession with death and stated that *Jocelyne Trudelle*, written to exorcise some personal demons, is her favorite play.[16] The action of this musical drama takes place in a hospital where twenty-one-year-old Jocelyne lingers comatose after shooting a bullet into her head. The emergency room nurse charged with caring for the patient becomes the motor of the play as she questions family and friends in an effort to understand the suicide. It does not take long to establish the fact that Jocelyne's family life was hellish. Her mother, a negative figure whom Laberge refuses to dignify with a name, is a pathetic, fearful, domestic slave more concerned with her husband's dinner than her daughter's death. The father inspires revulsion; he is a vulgar, macho, sexist, violent brute.

Forced out of the house at eighteen, Jocelyne lived on unemployment compensation, filling the empty hours by drinking excessively and listening to music. Despite the parents' denials, her friend Carole reveals the depression, loneliness, and desperation that led Jocelyne to see suicide as an acceptable solution to her problems. Within this starkly realistic dramatic situation, Laberge employs an antirealistic technique to allow Jocelyne to explain herself. The actress playing Jocelyne (or her spirit) wanders about the stage, from her bed in the intensive-care ward to the waiting room where her parents and friends converse to the third part of the stage, which represents death and nothingness. This third space is filled by a grand piano played by a suave man who incarnates the seductive attraction of death. Silenced by emotional and psychological violence during her life, Jocelyne sings poetic songs that become more and more sensual as she approaches death. Echoing the feminist collective plays of the 1970s, Jocelyne finally names her fears, her solitary despair, sexual desire, and need to escape from sexual violence. Failing to find human love or carnal satisfaction, she now welcomes death in a final song of seduction:

> Les yeux avides, le ventre ouvert
> Le sexe offert, je tremble d'elle
> Je n'ai plus d'air, qu'un immense frisson
> Et la certitude de ses mains
> Je cambre, m'écartèle, m'ouvre

Tout entière donnée
Tout entière aspirée par elle
Fascinée, enfin reconnue
Elle me boit, me prend
Et je lui tends mon âme entière
Vibrante, délirante dans son souffle . . .

[Eyes eager, belly uncovered
Sex offered, I tremble before Death
My only breath an immense shiver
And the certainty of her hands
I arch my back, spread and open myself
Completely given
Completely drawn to her
Fascinated, finally acknowledged
She drinks me in, takes me
And I present my soul to her completely
Vibrating, delirious in her breath . . .][17]

Jocelyne dies, ignoring her friend's plea to reject her family and live for the sake of their friendship. And, as if to stress the point that when Jocelyne uses the first-person plural pronoun "nous," she speaks for a generation of females, a Voice announces at the end of the play that Carole killed herself the next day in Jocelyne's apartment.

The bleak vision of *Avec l'hiver qui s'en vient* and *Jocelyne Trudelle* is somewhat relieved by *C'était avant la guerre à l'Anse à Gilles,* in which Laberge's most feminist protagonist, Marianna, refuses to be a victim. Winner of the Governor General's award, this play established Marie Laberge as an important Quebec playwright. In returning to Quebec's past, she was seeking the origins of modern feminism and making a strong statement about the need to reject the conservative ideology that dominated the province for three hundred years. The play's action takes place in the kitchen of Marianna Bédard, a twenty-nine-year-old widow who seems content to live alone in her own home, taking in laundry to earn money. Marianna's circle of friends includes Rosalie, a naive nineteen-year-old orphan who works as a maid for a rich lawyer; Honoré, a gardener-handyman in love with Marianna; and Tante Mina, a narrow-minded widow who finds fault with everyone except the parish priest. In the first part of the play, Laberge re-creates the atmosphere of a rural village in 1936 through the conversation of her characters. Beneath the gentle humor and caricatural portraits, however, Laberge subtly accuses the church and the state of social injustice, political inequality, anti-Semitism, and xenophobia. In the political debate at the beginning of the second part, Marianna horrifies Tante Mina by saying she would like the right to vote. Mina repeats the church's antisuffrage, anti-communist, antiprogress, and pro-Duplessis opinions.[18]

The nostalgic comic tone changes dramatically halfway through the second part of the play when a distraught Rosalie seeks refuge at Marianna's after being raped by her employer. When the village bourgeoisie covers up the rape and accuses the orphan maid of theft and promiscuity, Marianna decides she must leave l'Anse à Gilles for the city, taking Rosalie with her. Toward the end of the play, Marianna explains this decision to her rejected suitor, Honoré, by reading the famous passage from the classic Quebec "ro-man de la terre" *Maria Chapdelaine* in which three voices tell Maria that she must stay on the land because nothing must change in Quebec. Whereas Honoré finds the passage beautiful, Marianna is enraged. In rejecting the traditionalist thinking that led Louis Hémon's heroine to marry a boring clod out of duty, Laberge's heroine, Marianna, rejects marriage, motherhood, martyrdom, hypocrisy, and the past:

> Chus tannée du passé, Honoré, chus tannée de t'nir le flambeau pis de trimer pour des croyances que j'ai pas: j'pense que queque chose meure, moé, j'pense que nous aut' les femmes, on meurt dans l'silence pis l'ordinaire. On porte not' passé comme un étole de fourrure, collé dans l'cou, la face enterrée d'dans, pis on voit pus rien. J'veux pas élever des enfants dans un passé qui dit qu'monsieur peut battre pis violer sa sarvante sans s'inquiéter; j'veux pus voir des Rosalie défaites pis brisées pour toujours parce que c'est la loi du désir pis d'l'homme, j'veux pas continuer l'règne de l'ennuyance, l'règne du temps égrené entre la misére pis nos marées, pis les lavages, pis les silences pis les chapelets. J'veux pas rester dans une place oùsqu'on veut que rien change, parce que j'ai pour mon dire qu'on a droit à plusse qu'une robe de georgette rose pis des fleurs plein l'église le jour de nos noces, pis l'jour d'la levée du corps. Pis c'est pour çà que j'm'en vas, Honoré. Pis j'amène Rosalie. P'tête ben que c'est pareil ailleurs, p'tête ben que l'silence pis la prière mènent partout dans l'monde, mais au moins je l'saurai parce que je l'aurai vu ...

> [I am tired of the past, Honoré, I am tired of keeping the torch burning and slaving away for beliefs that I don't have: me, I think something is dying, I think that we women are dying in silence and banality. We carry our past like a fur stole, wrapped around our throats, face buried within, and we don't see anything anymore. I don't want to raise children in a past that says a man can beat and rape his maid without worrying; I don't want to see any more Rosalies defeated and broken forever because that is the law of desire and of man, I don't want to carry on the rule of boredom, the rule of time stuck between misery and the tides, between washings, and silences and rosaries. I don't want to stay in a place where people want nothing to change,

because I say we have a right to more than a pink georgette dress and a
church full of flowers the day of our wedding, and the day of our burial.
And that's why I am leaving, Honoré. And I'm taking Rosalie with me.
Maybe it's the same everywhere, maybe silence and prayer rule everywhere
in the world, but at least I'll know because I will have seen it . . .][19]

This angry rejection of the past inspires confidence in Marianna's future,
but Laberge cautions against an overly optimistic feminist interpretation
of the play. In an interview with the theater journal *Jeu* she said, "Pour
moi, Marianna s'en va vers une défaite. . . . Son seul courage est d'aller voir"
(In my view, Marianna is headed for defeat. . . . She wins only by seeking
something else).[20]

The urgent need to explore the difficulty daughters face in achieving independence and happiness as women and wives inspired Laberge to write
two plays in 1982: *Deux tangos pour toute une vie* and *L'Homme gris*.[21] Ironically, the well-educated protagonist daughter in *Deux tangos* fails to escape the stifling family enclosure despite her lucid analysis of it, whereas
her less articulate counterpart in *L'Homme gris* intuitively breaks with the
family past. *Deux tangos* focuses on Suzanne Langlais Casgrain, a thirty-
three-year-old woman temporarily on leave from her job as a gynecological
nurse because she is suffering from severe depression. Suzanne has reached
a crisis point in her life and marriage: she must decide whether she will
stay with her sympathetic but vapid husband, Pierre, and whether to have
a baby. Her recently widowed mother, Martine, preaches duty and resignation, scolding Suzanne for asking too much out of married life. The midlife
crisis is further complicated by a passionate affair with Pierre's office colleague Gilles, which proves to Suzanne that her body is not dead to sexual
desire and pleasure. The two tangos mentioned in the title refer to the two
times Suzanne and Gilles made love, accompanied by sensual Latin music.
As her leave runs out, Suzanne gives in to her mother's arguments and decides to be "raisonnable"; she will stifle the violence within her and give up
the quest for romantic love. The epilogue shows us a pregnant Suzanne
several months later. Having abandoned her struggle for personal happiness,
she expresses her hope that her child will make his or her own choices in
life, that is, to tango or not to tango.

At first glance, *Deux tangos* appears to be a love-triangle story, but the
marital and adulterous relationships deflect attention from the true subject of the play: the mother-daughter relationship. Laberge has said that the
play is about a daughter trying to live according to her mother's wishes.[22]
Suzanne has always been a dutiful daughter, conforming to the traditional

bourgeois values preached by Martine. But she is also a passionate woman who as a child suffered from the lack of parental affection as she now suffers from the lack of sexual passion. At a moment when nothing in Suzanne's life seems worthwhile, Gilles awakens her to the possibilities of passion, but she is not sure she has the right to her own desire. There can be no compromise in the conflict between the mother's vision of women's social roles as wife and mother and Suzanne's romantic vision of personal happiness. The educated, articulate Suzanne may talk of leaving and dream of liberation from roles that deny her own needs, but she does not have the courage or strength to act. The mother wins the debate between duty and desire, needs and emotions, pragmatism and romanticism, self-sacrifice and self-fulfillment. Because of her fears, guilt, and insecurity, Suzanne accepts what she had angrily denounced as "la loi de Pierre. La loi du silence. La loi du 'dis-pas-un-mot-ça-va-aller-mieux' " (Pierre's law. The law of silence. The law of "don't-say-a-word-and-everything-will-be-better").[23] This law of silence is, of course, the Law of the Father, the patriarchal authority that, in league with martyr mothers, reduces women to silence in order to domesticate them. For the feminist critic, Suzanne represents a giant step backward from Marianna, the independent protofeminist of *C'était avant la guerre à l'Anse à Gilles.* It is disturbing that fifty years after Marianna found the courage to seek happiness and personal fulfillment outside the patriarchal system, Suzanne gives in to familial pressures and remains in what feminist critic Patricia Smart has called the "Father's house."[24]

The daughter of *L'Homme gris* does escape from the family-marriage trap, but she does so with tragic violence. Translated into six languages, this play has established Laberge's international reputation. It presents a twenty-one-year-old woman, Christine Fréchette, who has been "rescued" from an abusive husband by her father. The text describes Christine as "L'anxiété incarnée mais profondément intériorisée" (Anxiety incarnated, but profoundly interiorized);[25] she is anorexic and on the rare occasions she speaks, she stutters on the letter *p* (as in "père").

On the way back to the family home, father and daughter stop to spend the night at a cheap motel. As the evening wears on and Roland Fréchette consumes a bottle of gin, it becomes clear that Christine's problems are rooted in her dysfunctional family. In his rambling monologues, Roland reminisces, revealing that he still mourns the death of the stillborn son that occurred a year before Christine's birth and that he was sexually attracted to her at age eleven when she reached puberty. Her anorexia is a response to her father's incestuous attention; it is her perverse and self-destructive way of taking control over her body, of refusing sexuality and the maternal model. Her stuttering and mutism are the result of a patriarchal, bourgeois society that denies women subjectivity and reduces them to silence. The climax of the play comes when the desperately unhappy Christine looks at herself in the mirror and realizes she has two choices: to die or to save herself by killing her father. Repeating the cry "J'veux pas m'tuer" (I don't want to kill myself) and then "Tu veux m'tuer" (You want to kill me), Christine kills Roland with a broken gin bottle.

Returning to the familiar ground of the bourgeois family drama, Laberge focused on the difficult mother-daughter relationship in her 1987 work, *Oublier*.[26] In this play, four daughters gather in their childhood home to determine a course of action for dealing with their mother, who has been reduced to infantile dependency by Alzheimer's disease. As the discussion stretches on into the snowy December night, the ghosts of the past come back to haunt the family home. The mother, Juliette Tessier, was a strong-willed, egotistical woman married to a weak man. She took over his position as head of family in many ways: usurping the right to name her daughters (all but the youngest, who is illegitimate, have names beginning, like hers, with a *J*) and the right to take a lover. Ironically, Juliette Tessier's failure to be a model mother did not make her daughters love her less, even though she kept them at arm's length and made them feel inadequate, betrayed, or abandoned.

The daughters, now middle-aged, have chosen silence, alcoholism, self-exile, and amnesia as ways of dealing with their unhappy childhood experiences. Jacqueline is trying to be the perfect mother Juliette never was, devoting herself totally to her family. Judith has chosen to live abroad in cynical self-indulgence in order to forget the disillusionment and guilt she felt because of her complicity in her mother's adultery. Joanne, deeply wounded by her mother's lack of maternal affection, drinks to forget the emotional insecurities that are destroying her marriage and medical career. The illegitimate daughter, Micheline, who has lived with the fear that her mother would abandon her the way she abandoned her lover, suffers from amnesia brought on by her mother's admission that she wanted to abort her.

Oublier dramatizes the failed ideal of motherhood. Juliette Tessier fell far short of the model, and because her daughters idealized and loved her excessively, her failure to love them in return left them all emotionally scarred. Perhaps the point here is that all mother-daughter relations based on emotional dependency are doomed to fail. Early in the play, Judith asks, "C'est quoi être une mère?" (What is it to be a mother?), and Micheline responds (in English), "Take care."[27] Before it was up to Juliette to take care of her daughters; now that the situation is reversed, the three younger daughters refuse responsibility for her. Even the staging of the play emphasizes the estrangement between mother and daughters: the senile woman remains in an upstairs bathroom (unseen but heard flushing the toilet) while three sisters refuse to confront her directly. Judith suggests a nursing home and returns to New York; Joanne, the doctor, mentions euthanasia; Micheline leaves after recovering her memory. Only the oldest sister, Jacqueline, remains to live up to the old maternal ideal; she will be the silent, submissive, self-effacing martyr who devotes herself to taking care of others.

Labergian daughters need to confront and overcome the past with lucidity before they can leave the ancestral home, be it patriarchal or matriarchal. To survive the emotional and psychological traumas of childhood, they must have the strength to reject the family as it has been consecrated by Quebec social tradition. Literally or figuratively, they must kill the parent to achieve adulthood and independence. Only an event as fundamental as the death of a parent can liberate them because as long as they are defined as daughters, they will be unhappy. Because there are few positive parental role models to emulate, Labergian daughters must reinvent motherhood and reconstitute the family. In a sense, this is the topic of *Aurélie, ma soeur* (1988).[28]

This play marks an important change in Laberge's theater, a change signaled immediately by the decor and the two female protagonists as described in the published text. Leaving behind the dreary kitchens, seedy motels, sordid bars, sterile sickrooms, and stifling salons of earlier plays, Laberge calls the solarium setting of *Aurélie* a "lieu privilégié" (a privileged place), a place filled with love and well-being where Aurélie "fait pousser ce qu'elle veut" (grows what she wants to).[29] Aurélie herself, forty-five at the beginning of the play, is characterized in emotional terms: "une femme remarquable d'humanité, de lucidité et de compassion" (a woman remarkable for her humanity, lucidity, and compassion).[30] The other protagonist is La Chatte, twenty-three in the first of the five "Nuits" or acts. She has all the other qualities that Laberge admires: "Vive et passionnée, elle n'entretient pas des rapports serrés avec la compromission et l'abnégation. Pas de demi-mesure avec elle, la vie doit être vécue dans son plus fort et son plus vibrant. C'est beaucoup plus qu'une jolie fille, c'est une femme habitée d'une profonde beauté, follement attachée à la vie" (Lively and passionate, she refuses all compromise and self-denial. No half-measures with her, life must be lived to the fullest. She is much more than a pretty girl, she is a woman filled with deep beauty, madly attached to life).[31] In Aurélie and La Chatte, Laberge has created two wonderfully independent, intelligent, articulate, generous, feminine characters. For once, Labergian daughters survive the pains of family trauma and romantic disillusionment and become stronger for it. By defining themselves as sisters, as the title suggests, and by exorcising the painful memories of their parents, Aurélie and La Chatte manage to reconstruct a familial unit based on mutual respect and love between equals. Laberge's stage directions specify: "On devrait éviter un ton 'mère-fille' et privilégier la complicité et la tendresse" (One should avoid a mother-daughter tone and stress complicity and tenderness).[32] This new family of women, jokingly termed "une belle race d'orphelines" (a fine race of orphans) by Aurélie, seems to be matrilineal, but the mothers are chosen surrogates rather than biological mothers. Aurélie, whom La Chatte calls "ma mère choisie" (my chosen mother), combines the mother-sister-aunt roles and bases the relationship on honesty, lucidity, and demonstrations of affection.

In five conversations that take place at night in Aurélie's solarium over a two and a half-year period, the sisters talk about everything in their lives: the shared past, passions and romantic failures, career goals, joys and pains. Eavesdropping on their intimate conversations, the audience follows two main plot threads — a family tragedy and a romantic melodrama. The family tragedy, hinted at in the first half of the play, is fully revealed in the fourth night when Aurélie and La Chatte return from their father's funeral. Having just buried the father she adored as a child, Aurélie finds it difficult to mourn his death because he sexually abused her younger sister, Charlotte. After giving birth to La Chatte, the product of this incestuous relationship, Charlotte left for Italy, where she has remained for over twenty years, working as a sculptress in virtual silence. Before leaving, Charlotte gave the baby to Aurélie, knowing full well that her sister was better equipped emotionally if not biologically for motherhood. La Chatte has never seen her birth mother, but following the death of the father she never knew, she feels compelled to go to Italy to meet her. What she finds is a hard, rude woman who lets her sculpture speak for her. Charlotte's art is an expression of her deep psychic pain, her inability to come to terms with her family history. On the other hand, confronting the truth about her father and mother frees La Chatte to hate them and to make a life for herself without them.

The second plot thread, the romantic melodrama, follows La Chatte's passionate love affair with her former film professor, Pierre Louis, a married man in his thirties. From the first date, through the broken promises to leave his wife, to the final breakup, the audience watches the spectacle of La Chatte's sexual desire, passion, jealousy, and anger. In striking contrast to previous Labergian women who did not believe they had the right to sexual desire, La Chatte speaks of hers with unembarrassed enthusiasm. The story of Aurélie's marriage and divorce ironically parallels La Chatte's tale of sentimental disappointment, underscoring the sexual liberation of Quebec women since the 1970s. Aurélie married young in order to leave home, and like that other Labergian heroine Marianna, her conjugal sex life was spoiled by ignorance and guilt, the legacies of a Catholic upbringing in Quebec. She could not have children, and eventually her husband left her for his pregnant mistress. Despite their disappointments in love, Laberge's women express pity for men. As are the men in *Avec l'hiver qui s'en vient, Deux tangos,* and *La Réparation,* the three men absent but discussed in *Aurélie, ma soeur* (father, husband, lover) are incapable of real love and commitment because of their own fears and insecurities. Speaking for Laberge, Aurélie explains this inability to love by saying that people who do not love and accept themselves as they are cannot love another human being.

Aurélie, ma soeur* is a cathartic, healing play about "toutes les formes de l'amour" and "tout ce que l'amour peut faire" (all forms of love and all that love can do).[33] Finally, Laberge balances her tragic vision with her faith in essential human goodness and inner strength. Her sisters escape the family-marriage traps; they survive betrayal, scandal, and loss; they move confidently toward personal and professional fulfillment without compromising their integrity. What is remarkable about this Labergian family tragedy is that these victims survive, stronger for the experience. Exorcising parental demons gives La Chatte a sense of identity and a capacity to love as deeply as she hates. During the fifth night of *Aurélie, ma soeur,* Laberge gives us a beautiful, emotional illustration of motherhood reinvented. Before La Chatte goes to Italy, she and Aurélie read together copies of the letters that Aurélie has written to Charlotte chronicling the twenty-five years of the young woman's life. The letters are a hymn to the power of love, that is, Aurélie's maternal-sororal love for La Chatte and Charlotte.

Aurélie and La Chatte may have been disappointed in their love affairs, but this does not diminish their capacity to love in other ways: to love each other, their careers (Aurélie teaches emotionally disturbed children), and life in general. The conversational and physical intimacy of *Aurélie, ma soeur* makes it possible for these two female characters to avoid the lack of communication, tenderness, and love that emotionally crippled so many other

Labergian protagonists. Words (spoken and written), love, and tears seem to have helped Laberge as well as her characters work through the apprenticeship of pain that her theater represents.

Indeed, the two plays written after *Aurélie, ma soeur* also dramatize the triumph of the human spirit over tragedy. In spite of Laberge's announcement that she will no longer write plays,[34] it seems premature to draw final conclusions about her theater. What we can say now is that she has been working to break down the walls of the "Father's house" in Quebec and to break the silence that reigned within. In giving voice to women's fears, anger, violence, love, and desire, Laberge participates in the larger enterprise of the feminist theater movement. She contributes to the creation of a female dramatic discourse that expresses the reality of women's lives in Quebec. She reminds us that social and economic changes may improve the material circumstances of women's lives, but that true liberation must take place within the family. Until women are able to express themselves emotionally and physically, until they have the right to their anger, violence, and personal goals, there can be no happy endings.

Notes

1. On the subject of feminist theater in Quebec, see the dossiers "Théâtre-femmes" in *Jeu* 16 (1980) and *Jeu* 66 (1993) as well as my "Women's Theater in Québec," in *Traditionalism, Nationalism, and Feminism: Women Writers of Quebec*, ed. Paula Gilbert Lewis (Westport, Conn.: Greenwood Press, 1985), 241–54; "Les Folles du Québec: The Theme of Madness in Quebec Women's Theater," *French Review* 57, 5 (1984): 617–24; "Creation Reenacted: The Woman Artist as Dramatic Figure," *American Review of Canadian Studies* 15, 3 (1985): 263–72; "The Body as Spectacle: Women's Theatre in Quebec," *Women & Performance: A Journal of Feminist Theory* 3, 1 (1986): 56–64; "Filial (Im)pieties: Mothers and Daughters in Quebec Women's Theater," *American Review of Canadian Studies* 19, 2 (1989): 177–85; "'All in the Family': Quebec Family Drama in the 80s," *Journal of Canadian Studies* 27, 2 (1992): 97–106; "Women, History, and Theater in Quebec," *French Review* 67, 6 (1994): 974–84; "Hysterical Pregnancies and Post-Partum Blues: Staging the Maternal Body in Recent Quebec Theater," in *Essays on Quebec Canadian Theater*, eds. Joseph Donohoe and Jonathan Weiss (East Lansing: Michigan State University Press, 1995), 47–59. See also Lorraine Camerlain's chronology of women's theater in "En de scènes multiples," *Canadian Theatre Review* 43 (1985): 73–90.

2. Nicole Brossard et al., *La Nef des sorcières* (Montreal: Quinze, 1976).

3. Michelle Rossignol, "Table Ronde: L'image de la femme dans le théâtre québécois," *Revue de l'Université d'Ottawa* 50, 1 (1980): 151.

4. France Théoret and Nicole Brossard, preface to *La Nef des sorcières*, 7–13.

5. Lorraine Camerlain and Carole Fréchette. "Le Théâtre expérimental des femmes: essai en trois mouvements," *Jeu* 36 (1985): 59–66.

6. Marie Laberge made these comments during the SUNY-Plattsburgh Winter Seminar, 4 March 1989, at Saint-Marc sur Richelieu.

7. Laberge in an interview with Ginette Stanton, "Deux Jeunes Femmes de Théâtre: Marie Laberge et Nicole Marie Rhéault," *Le Devoir*, 13 January 1979. The translation is my own as are all translations from French texts unless otherwise indicated.

8. Laberge in *Le Soleil*, 4 October 1986.

9. Laberge in comments made at SUNY-Plattsburgh Winter Seminar, 4 March 1989.

10. *Ils étaient venus pour...* was written in the spring of 1976 for a class Laberge taught at the Université du Québec à Chicoutimi. It was given two public readings (1979, 1980) before it was performed by Quebec City's Théâtre du Bois de Coulonge in July 1981. It has also been given public readings in France and Switzerland.

11. *Avec l'hiver qui s'en vient* premiered at the Théâtre du Vieux Québec in September 1980 with Marie Laberge directing the Commune à Marie production. The grim subject of *Jocelyne Trudelle trouvée morte dans ses larmes* discouraged potential producers, and although the work had two public readings in Montreal and Quebec City in 1981, it was not staged until October 1986, by the playwright with Quebec City's Théâtre de la Commune. First performed in January 1981 by Montreal's Nouvelle Compagnie Théâtrale, *C'était avant la guerre à l'Anse à Gilles* has been translated into English for a Toronto production and restaged in Montreal.

12. Marie Laberge, *Jocelyne Trudelle trouvée morte dans ses larmes* (Montreal: VLB éditeur, 1983), 10.

13. Ibid., 57–58.

14. Ibid., 104.

15. Pierre Lavoie, "Le Trio infernal ou l'impossibilité d'aimer," in *Marie Laberge, dramaturge: Actes du Colloque international,* ed. André Smith (Montreal: VLB éditeur, 1989), 119–21.

16. Marie Laberge in interview with Gilbert David and Pierre Lavoie, *Jeu* 21 (1983): 62.

17. Ibid., 124. Note that the word for death is feminine in French.

18. Maurice Duplessis was premier of Quebec from 1936 until 1939, and then again from 1944 until his death in 1959. He was a reactionary nationalist who preached isolationism, anticommunism, and rural values. His Union Nationale Party aligned itself with the Catholic Church. With the end of the Duplessis era (often called "Quebec's Dark Ages") came the progressive reform period known as the Quiet Revolution.

19. Marie Laberge, *C'était avant la guerre à l'Anse à Gilles* (Montreal: VLB éditeur, 1981), 116.

20. Laberge's comments in *Jeu* 21 (1983): 60–61.

21. *Deux tangos pour toute une vie* was first performed in November of 1984 at the Théâtre du Petit Champlain in Quebec City by the Commune à Marie with the dramatist herself in the lead role. *L'Homme gris* premiered at the Salle Fred-Barry in Montreal in September 1984 and soon after was performed in Brussels, Paris, and Quebec City.

22. Comment at SUNY Plattsburgh Winter Seminar, 4 March 1989.

23. Marie Laberge, *Deux tangos pour toute une vie* (Montreal: VLB éditeur, 1985), 146.

24. Patricia Smart uses the term "the Father's house" as a symbol of the patriarchal institutions and conservative ideology that dominated Quebec for centuries. She won the Governor General's Award for her analysis of Quebec women's writing, *Ecrire dans la maison du père: L'émergence du féminin dans la tradition littéraire du Québec* (Montreal: Québec/Amérique, 1988).

25. Marie Laberge, *L'Homme gris suivi de Eva et Evelyne* (Montreal: VLB éditeur, 1985), 12. The play has also been published in its original form and in a French adaptation by Jacques de Decker in *Avant-Scène, Théâtre* 785 (1986). There is also an English translation, *Night,* trans. Rina Fratricelli (New York: Methuen, 1988). The play has also been translated into German, Italian, Dutch, and Latvian.

26. *Oublier* premiered in Brussels (in an International French version) before opening in Montreal. This production was a clear sign of Marie Laberge's status in Quebec theater; she directed an all-star cast of the Compagnie Jean Duceppe at the Théâtre Port-Royal of the Place des Arts.

27. Marie Laberge, *Oublier* (Montreal: VLB éditeur, 1987), 45.

28. With the playwright directing the Théâtre du Trident production, *Aurélie, ma soeur* premiered at Quebec City's Grand Théâtre in November 1988 and was reprised at the Café de la Place at Montreal's Place des Arts in January 1989.

29. Marie Laberge, *Aurélie, ma soeur* (Montreal: VLB éditeur, 1988), 12.

30. Ibid., 13.

31. Ibid. During a discussion following a reading at the American Association of Teachers of French conference in Quebec City in July 1994, Laberge stated that La Chatte is the one character in her theater whom she would like to use in another work.

32. Ibid.

33. Laberge made this comment at the SUNY-Plattsburgh Seminar, 4 March 1989.

34. Laberge declared her intention to leave the theater during a CBC radio interview, 17 July 1994.

CHAPTER SIX

Aminata Sow Fall's
L'Ex-père de la nation

Subversive Subtexts and the Return of the Maternal

MARY-KAY MILLER

When Aminata Sow Fall wrote *Le Revenant* in 1976, she simultaneously wrote herself into history, for her novel would be the first published in French by a West African woman.[1] Because of her unique position, the circumstances of her writing command almost as much attention as the writing itself. As a Senegalese woman, Sow Fall finds herself doubly marginalized: first, as a West African author writing against the backdrop of French literary tradition, and second, as a woman writing within the predominantly male Senegalese literary tradition. From these margins, Sow Fall rereads and rewrites boundaries drawn between male and female, colonizer and colonized, autobiography and fiction.

These conflictual relationships subtend Sow Fall's, *L'Ex-père de la nation*, which is the fictional autobiography of the former head of state of an imaginary African nation.[2] Sow Fall manipulates autobiographical structures in such a way as to discourage readings of her corpus as a mere representation of her personal experience. To read her texts in this way would be to invest them with a reproductive function, that is, to see in them only a continuation and extension of the biological and social reproductive roles traditionally assigned to women. Such a reading is at cross-purposes with the development of a female literary subject and voice, a development found in several of Sow Fall's texts, and especially in *L'Ex-père de la nation*.

There exists in Sow Fall's work a tension between reproduction and production that plays itself out in terms of gender, colonialism, and genre. One
sees gender concerns manifested in a female character's rejection of a biologically reproductive role in favor of a maternal role that paradoxically
excludes the reproductive, yet ultimately redefines it. In the context of colonialism, reproduction and production take on Marxist connotations as Sow
Fall's text works to dismantle colonial and capitalist systems of production
and reproduction that perpetuate dependent relationships between former colonies and colonial powers, thereby reproducing ad infinitum certain patterns of domination. Finally, Sow Fall's text problematizes the relationship between autobiography and fiction. Autobiography has historically
been considered a "reproductive" genre, that is, a genre that is often reduced to an "accurate" representation or reproduction of events exterior
to the text. Although more and more Western critics are reading and theorizing autobiography as fiction, women's relationship to it as writers is still
highly problematic, due in part, I believe, to their traditional place within
the reproductive or private sphere.[3] Furthermore, African critics seem far
less convinced than Westerners about the fictional nature of autobiography,
making questions of autobiography as reproduction of particular concern
to a writer such as Sow Fall.[4]

Many feminist critics have argued that the problem does not lie in the
genre of autobiography itself but rather in a tendency to read *everything*
that women write as autobiographical. Domna Stanton remarks:

> How could that void [unavailability of autobiographies by women] be
> reconciled with the age-old, pervasive decoding of all female writing as
> autobiographical? One answer ... was that "autobiographical" constituted
> a positive term when applied to Augustine and Montaigne ... but that it
> had negative connotations when imposed on women's texts. It had been
> used ... to affirm that women could not transcend, but only record, the
> concerns of the private self; thus, it had effectively served to devalue
> their writing.[5]

Stanton indicates two problems that are germane to my study: first, that
women's writing is systematically misread as autobiography, and second,
that autobiography written by women is devalued because it is said to reproduce and record rather than transcend the personal. These notions of
personal experience and transcendence are linchpins in any discussion of
the peculiar relationship between gender and autobiography.

Autobiography, I would contend, is not a question of transcending personal experience, which I would define as the extratextual narrative that con-

stitutes the author's life, but of creating a literary narrative that picks up pieces from and sometimes parallels this extratextual personal narrative. In such a text, the existences of the narrating and the narrated self or selves are inextricably bound up with one another. Autobiography is simultaneously an act of renarration, narration, and creation, as much for Aoua Kéita and Ken Bugul[6] as for Rousseau and Montaigne. This view of male and female autobiography has often been obscured, however, by the perception of women as "agents" of reproduction in all areas of life: sexual, social, and economic. Although such a perception is clearly erroneous, the fact of circumscribing women and women's voices within a reproductive sphere has, of course, forged certain relationships between women and the processes of reproduction. These links have, in turn, sometimes structured, or otherwise influenced, women's writings. The differences between male and female autobiographical voices that I consider among the most compelling are found in the relationship of those narratives to the processes of reproduction and maternity.

As already stated, I am concerned not only with gender but with colonialism as well, two forces that serve to doubly marginalize Sow Fall's texts. Autobiography, traditionally defined as a narrative explication of the self and its evolution, has been labeled by some scholars as a quintessentially Western genre, and thus a potentially colonizing one.[7] Hence, Sow Fall's redefining and rewriting of autobiography not only disturb the constellation of gender, reproduction, and autobiography but also dilute autobiography's power as a colonial tool for reproducing a Western image of the self in a non-Western narrative.

I would like to look now at the involvement of *L'Ex-père de la nation* in autobiographical projects and strategies. Sow Fall commented, during an interview in June 1989, that she welcomed the opportunity to write in the first person with impunity, knowing that no one would try to attribute to her the thoughts and deeds of a character so unlike her.[8] Yet despite her disavowal of any autobiographical intentions, the delight she expresses at writing in the first person invites closer scrutiny. A theory advanced by Julia Watson in an essay titled "Shadowed Presence: Modern Women Writers' Autobiographies and the Other" encourages us to look for the presence of autobiographical projects in seemingly unlikely places:

> The metonymy implicit in women autobiographers' strategy of
> otherness — presenting the "I" through the models of others — is in fact
> less a substitution, more a constitution, of the autobiographical "I" in texts

where an external other seems to loom largest as the apparent subject of life-writing. Yet the reader's experience of an autonomous voice narrating a life may be strongest where the self is apparently suppressed, suggesting that for the woman writer, the tactic of writing in the shadow of an Other can be an act of liberation from the constraints of conventional accounts of female lives.[9]

Watson refers specifically in this essay to texts such as *The Autobiography of Alice B. Toklas,* actually written by Gertrude Stein, but her theory can be fruitfully applied to Sow Fall's text as well. I do not wish to suggest that *L'Ex-père de la nation* recounts the life of Sow Fall but merely to point out the resonance between Watson's reference to the use of another's autobiography for the purpose of liberation and Sow Fall's expressed pleasure at having the freedom to write in the first person without necessarily implicating herself in the text. Moreover, one's first impression of *L'Ex-père de la nation* as recounting anything but a female writer's experience as writing subject is radically questioned by Watson's call for "a reconsideration of the metaphysical imposition by which autobiography is restricted to the history of the lived life rather than that internal history of the subject's writing,"[10] as well as by Françoise Lionnet's redefinition of female autobiography, stated in the following terms:

> To read a narrative that depicts the journey of a female self striving to become the subject of her own discourse, the narrator of her own story, is to witness the unfolding of an autobiographical project. To raise the question of referentiality and ask whether the text points to an individual existence beyond the pages of the book is to distort the picture.[11]

Lionnet's readings are based on a concept of métissage, the weaving together of multiple voices, perspectives, and cultures in such a way that they are allowed to coexist rather than be hierarchized or collapsed into one another. Therefore, clear distinctions between autobiography and fiction are false according to this theory, as might be more recent distinctions between canonized "male" autobiography and women's autobiography.

By writing a kind of "anti-autobiography," Sow Fall signals her distance from autobiographies written by women such as Nafissatou Diallo, Aoua Kéita, and even Ken Bugul, all francophone African writers whose texts explicitly state their goal as a faithful portrayal of their authors' lives. But before advancing further in this discussion of whose autobiography, or anti-autobiography, is contained in *L'Ex-père de la nation,* we need a clearer idea of the text's manifest subject.

Madiama, a deposed head of state, writes retrospectively of his life from his prison cell. He is a man of caste who becomes a puppet president, controlled by unnamed foreign countries, and who precipitates, albeit somewhat despite himself, the economic ruin of his nation. He fares no better at home, where his ill-chosen second wife alienates his first wife and divides his family. The political component of the plot frequently resembles that of Ousmane Sembene's *Le Dernier de l'empire*, itself loosely based on the 1981 transfer of power in Senegal from Léopold Senghor to Abdou Diouf.[12] In *Le Dernier de l'empire*, the character in line for the presidency is, like Madiama, a man of caste. The conflict and chaos that arise due to this situation, considered unacceptable by many, constitute one of the novel's numerous and pointed critiques of both Senegalese society and neocolonial influences. Sembene's novel is a roman à clef, peopled with figures from Senegalese political life. Sow Fall's text, however, discourages the reader from drawing neat parallels between its events and actual political events in Senegal. A comparison of the two texts indicates that Sow Fall wishes to complicate the questions her text raises by refusing to provide her readers with an unambiguous reference. Rather, it is through the manipulation of autobiographical structures and the introduction of the powerful figure of infanticide that images of colonialism and other power dynamics are constructed and dismantled in *L'Ex-père de la nation*.

Sow Fall's autobiographical moves in *L'Ex-père de la nation* challenge the idea that the use of autobiography by anyone other than a Western man signals the non-Western author's colonization rather than a challenge to white male hegemony. As I have noted earlier, the view of autobiography as a colonizing genre is based on the idea that the very existence of the genre is incumbent on a Western conception of a unique self as origin and center, but it is interesting to note that when autobiography appears as an element in the writings of some non-Western men and women, the position and role of the self often change.[13] If we understand by autobiography a positioning of the narrating self in relation to other selves, a reflection on the development of that self within its own text, if we look at autobiography as an attempt not just to establish subjectivity for one specific individual but to uncover subjects that have long been buried as objects and characters in other people's texts, then autobiography contains great power to resist colonization. In *L'Ex-père de la nation* we find just such an uncovering at work, as a seemingly secondary narrative bubbles up and interrupts the story of the dominant paternal "je."

Family imagery predominates in *L'Ex-père de la nation,* linking its functions as political allegory and feminist fable. Madiama is portrayed alternately as the child and the father of his nation: "Cher enfant de notre cher patrie ... cher fils de notre mère patrie ... Un enfant du pays pour le destin du peuple ..." (12–13) (Dear child of our dear country ... dear child of our motherland ... A native son for the destiny of the people ...).[14] Madiama later becomes known, as the title of the novel indicates, as *"père* de la nation" (father of the nation). Ironically, this title is imposed on him by his manipulative aides, and he accepts it with childlike docility.

Madiama fails to exert his paternal authority successfully in the public sphere. *L'Ex-père de la nation* as political allegory highlights the dangers of one-party rule, the turning of a blind eye to corruption, excessive debt to outside nations, and a whole host of other problems that plague many African nations today. Many passages of *L'Ex-père de la nation* read like dramatizations of the hypotheses of political theorists such as Frantz Fanon in *Les Damnés de la terre* (*The Wretched of the Earth*):[15]

Les masses rurales, dédaignées par les partis politiques, continuent à être tenues à l'écart. (*Damnés,* 92)

[The mass of the country-dwellers, looked down upon by the political parties, continue to be kept at a distance. (*Wretched,* 96)]

Vous [Madiama] ne pouvez plus vous perdre dans la foule. Il faut que le mystère vous entoure et que, progressivement, le peuple vous identifie à un mythe. Mythe de puissance et de gloire. (*L'Ex-père,* 51)

[You (Madiama) can no longer lose yourself in the crowd. It is essential that you be wrapped in mystery, and that, little by little, the people identify you with a myth. A myth of power and glory.]

Les circuits économiques du jeune Etat s'enlisent irréversiblement dans la structure néo-colonialiste. L'économie nationale, autrefois protégée, est aujourd'hui littéralement dirigée. Le budget est alimenté par des prêts et par des dons. Tous les trimestres, les chefs d'Etat eux-mêmes ou les délégations gouvernementales se rendent dans les anciennes métropoles ou ailleurs, à la pêche aux capitaux. (*Damnés,* 125)

[The economic channels of the young state sink back inevitably into neo-colonialist lines. The national economy, formerly protected, is today literally controlled. The budget is balanced through loans and gifts, while every three or four months the chief ministers themselves or else their governmental delegations come to the erstwhile mother countries or elsewhere, fishing for capital. (*Wretched,* 134)]

Je ne pouvais pas me cacher que la banqueroute menaçait le pays ... On avait emprunté et emprunté, pour survivre et aussi pour acheter des armes. Le pays lui-même était devenu une sorte d'objet hypothéqué dans les mains des puissances riches qui nous prêtaient et qui, de ce fait, s'octroyaient tous les droits de me dicter une politique à suivre, des actions à mener, des décisions à prendre. (*L'Ex-père*, 163)

[I could not hide from myself the fact that bankruptcy threatened the country ...We had borrowed and borrowed, to survive and to buy arms. The country itself had become a kind of mortgaged object in the hands of the rich powers who loaned to us and who, because of this, granted themselves the right to dictate to me the policy to follow, the actions to take, the decisions to make.]

Sow Fall fictionalizes political theory within a fictionalized autobiography, consistently choosing production over reproduction as her medium of expression. She does not attempt to "accurately" represent or reproduce details from Senegalese political life, as Sembene often does in *Le Dernier de l'empire*. This difference sets *L'Ex-père de la nation* apart from the dominant masculine mode of literary production represented by *Le Dernier de l'empire* and disturbs the process of its reproduction.

Sow Fall's strategy is also at odds with the call for transparency and truth made by intellectuals such as Fanon and Jean-Paul Sartre in the late 1950s and 1960s. In Sartre's preface to Fanon's *Les Damnés de la terre* (*The Wretched of the Earth*), he states: "in the colonies the truth stood naked, but the citizens of the mother country preferred it with clothes on ... The European elite undertook to manufacture a native elite" (*Wretched*, 7). Perhaps Sow Fall's insistence on "clothing the truth" originates from a desire not to appease the "mother" country but to debunk the myth of the naked native. In other words, the lack of easy, one-to-one correspondences found in her work indicates a refusal of this image of the "naked," "natural" (read uncivilized) "native," who is incapable of dissimulation but also of imagination. Although Sartre's image contrasts sharply with the popular image of the colonized as lazy and deceitful, it smacks nonetheless of a colonizing, though perhaps well-intentioned, representation.

In further opposition to Sartre's "mother" country, hungry for empty and alienated reproductions of itself, stands the father of Sow Fall's fictional nation. Yet if this father figure constitutes an implicit rejection of colonialism and its symbols, it too finds itself negated (l'*ex*-père) even before the beginning of the narrative. Although it seems at first that maternity and reproduction are being rejected and replaced by paternity and fiction, the paternal ultimately gives way to a recuperated maternal force, free of colonial connotations. The boundaries between reproduction and production, autobiography and fiction, become less sharply delineated as these elements are repositioned and redefined.

In the domestic sphere of the novel, Madiama is characterized as a father and a son whose life is directed by his family. Coumba, his mother, plays a critical role in the text, orchestrating and molding Madiama's married life by choosing as his wife Coura, a woman Coumba has raised like a daughter and molded after her own image. The counsel given by Madiama's father determines the course of his son's life, and his influence is preserved even after his death in the person of Madiama's elder brother.

In addition, Madiama is portrayed as having a strong sense of his own paternal identity, particularly at a moment in the text when he considers renouncing his presidency, in part to regain the respect of his family: "J'aurais enfin le sourire affectif de Nafi [his daughter] . . . Nafi serait alors accourue vers moi: 'Papa, je ne t'aurais jamais cru une telle grandeur!' " (116–17). (Finally I would have Nafi's affectionate smile . . . She would run toward me: "Papa, I would never have thought you capable of such a great gesture.") Ironically, this same Nafi, whose aloofness wounds Madiama's paternal ego, becomes a critical factor in his downfall. When she is killed during an antigovernment demonstration, she becomes for both sides the symbol of the other's evil. The opposition party takes as its insignia a picture of Nafi running and laughing with the caption "élan brisé par les balles de son père" (her spirit broken by her father's bullets). Conversely, Madiama is obsessed with her death and cites it as his reason for not resigning his post and for his subsequent tyrannical rule over the populace, whom he holds responsible for Nafi's death.

Madiama is cast as an infanticide; not only is he implicated in the death of his daughter, but his government deprives, oppresses, and threatens to crush the "children" of the nation, justifying the opposition party's depiction of him as a baneful father. One notes with interest that in *L'Ex-père de la nation,* infanticide is a crime committed by the father, not the mother. Madiama, once divested of his paternity and openly accused of "infanticide," allows himself to sink into despotism. Infanticide, as the ultimate breach of faith, is portrayed here as the act that unleashes tyranny, but also revolt, and ultimately change. Although the link is not immediately apparent, I will argue, in the pages that follow, for the existence of an important connection between infanticide and autobiography in this text.

Françoise Lionnet notes that in women's autobiography, "self-writing becomes self-invention."[16] This observation, with which I concur, sets up a very complex relationship between the maternal and the "daughterly" in female autobiography, for the mother is symbolically removed from the scene as the daughter gives birth to herself. Autobiography may constitute the "daughterly"[17] text par excellence, that is, a text in which the mother figure has been eclipsed as a source by the self-inventing daughter. I bring this up on the heels of a reference to infanticide in *L'Ex-père de la nation* because I see a certain tension between autobiography and infanticide, if we read infanticide as a maternal act meant to suppress the daughter or son. Traditional definitions of autobiography associate it with reproduction, whereas the point of infanticide, as I interpret it, is to reject a female reproductive function. Yet thematically infanticide is not a female act in *L'Ex-père de la nation,* and under Sow Fall's pen, autobiography itself works to distance reproduction, making the text a privileged site of mother/daughter conflict, but also, and ultimately, of a certain conflation between the motherly and the daughterly. In a very important move, Sow Fall frees her female characters of the need to commit infanticide by using autobiography first to distance and then to reshape the reproductive.

The figure of the mother in *L'Ex-père de la nation* provides a sharp contrast to the infanticidal father. The characters of Coura and Coumba threaten at each moment in the text to merge into each other, and finally do just that. These women come to wield considerable power; for example, Coumba arranges the marriage of Coura and Madiama, believing that she thus fixes the course of their lives. A second and even more striking example of maternal influence and power in *L'Ex-père de la nation* comes when Madiama announces to Coura his second marriage and she responds in the following manner:

> Je jure au nom de Dieu, que pour toi, je ne serai plus une femme parce que, par ma propre volonté, je me fais dès aujourd'hui la réincarnation de ta mère, ma tante Coumba Dado Sadio. Si tu cherchais en moi la femme, sache que c'est ta mère Coumba Dada Sadio que tu cherches et alors, honte, sacrilège, malheur!... [Madiama narrates] Après avoir lâché la bombe qui m'avait abasourdi, elle avait détaché la bande supérieure du mbottu de Nafi. Elle avait fait gicler le lait de son sein et avait dirigé le jet sur ma bouche encore ouverte. Je m'étais levé avec fougue... prêt à saisir sa main, mais c'est elle qui avait saisi la mienne avec douceur... et elle avait répété avec une maîtrise qui acheva de me désemparer: "Je suis ta mère Coumba Dado Sadio." (58)

> [I swear in the name of God, that for you I will no longer be a woman,[18] because, by my own will, I am making myself, beginning today, the reincarnation of your mother, my aunt Coumba Dado Sadio. If you were to

seek out the woman in me, know that it would be your mother Coumba Dado Sadio that you seek, and then what shame, what sacrilege, what misfortune. (Madiama narrates) After having dropped this bomb that had stunned me, she undid the upper band of the mbottu in which she carried Nafi. She made milk spurt from her breast and directed the stream to my still-open mouth. I leapt to my feet... ready to grab her hand, but it was she who had gently taken hold of mine... and she repeated with a self-control that succeeded in devastating me: "I am your mother Coumba Dado Sadio."]

A sharp distinction is thus drawn between the physically destructive power of the father and the psychologically compelling, and no less potent, power of the mother. Unlike the mother portrayed in Sow Fall's *L'Appel des arènes,* who displays infanticidal tendencies, Coumba and Coura's strength depends in no way on the threat of physical violence directed against their maternity and its products; on the contrary, it derives from their ability to wield their maternity as an arm against the paternal.

A second source of female power in this text lies in the threat of incest, which underlies the entire scene just described between Madiama and Coura. This threat consolidates Coura's power, the mother's milk she squirts into Madiama's mouth instantly forging a relationship between them in which sexuality can no longer play a part. Mariama Bâ's *Une si longue lettre* flirts with this subject as well. Christopher Miller notes that in Bâ's text there is an "over-sameness — just short of incest"[19] in the relationship between petite Nabou and Mawdo, issuing from the fact that petite Nabou has been molded by Mawdo's mother, Nabou, into an exact replica of herself and therefore a "perfect" wife for Mawdo. The relationship between petite Nabou and Nabou is analogous to that of Coura and Coumba. In both cases, by handpicking and forming the women whom their sons will marry, mothers create incestuous relationships, first by making these women sisters to the men in question and ultimately by turning them into younger versions of themselves.

The question of incest is a significant one because of women's rather peculiar role in manipulating this taboo relationship, successfully using it to exert control over the men in their lives. Indeed, these female characters prepare the incestuous situation, then lead their sons and daughters into it, in what can be interpreted as an attempt to prolong their influence and power. As one notes in *L'Ex-père de la nation,* not only does the mother extend her influence beyond her own death, but that influence and a new threat of incest infuse yet another woman, Coura, with strength and freedom of choice that would not ordinarily be available to her: "sache que je ne suis pas malheureuse, au contraire! J'éprouve une joie profonde d'exprimer mon droit à l'existence quand tout apparemment concourait à m'écraser" (59). (Know that I'm not unhappy, quite the contrary! I feel a profound joy in expressing my right to existence when everything was seemingly conspiring to crush me.)

As it is presented in *L'Ex-père de la nation,* incest is analogous to infanticide (as the latter is typically portrayed: a crime committed by the mother) in that it concentrates power in the hands, not simply of women, but specifically of mothers. Although feminist theorists such as Marianne Hirsch might argue that this serves only to reinforce negative stereotypes of the mother figure, I would argue that in this instance, the blame is placed unequivocally on Madiama, with Coura's transformation from wife to mother representing a bid for self-determination and autonomy that relies on the manipulation of identity and taboo rather than on physical violence.

As I have just noted, Coura gains access to power via her position as mother to Madiama; yet, paradoxically, this maternal position frees her from reproduction. After the scene in which Coura assumes Coumba's identity, no further children can issue from her union with Madiama. This subtle reinterpretation and repositioning of the maternal is emblematic of a larger narrative strategy. In many respects Madiama's story is an "anti-autobiography" that serves to bring out the female story in the text, a story of daughters and mothers transforming potentially oppressive situations into opportunities for seizing control over their own lives, for becoming the subjects rather than the objects of this tale. The relationship of Coura and Coumba's embedded narrative to autobiography can best be understood in terms of the oblique moves referred to by Julia Watson, whereby a female voice passes first through an other in order to better constitute and narrate itself.

Because the maternal is affirmed and at the same time separated from the reproductive, one sees a unique conflation of mother and daughter in this text. The initial conflict between autobiography and infanticide is a paternal one: Madiama's "autobiography" begins to unravel and yield to Coura's narrative at the moment he is inculpated in infanticide. Yet the final relationship between autobiography and infanticide in *L'Ex-père de la nation* is the coexistence of two analogous responses to reproduction. In fact, Sow Fall's autobiographical response to reproduction can itself be read as a kind of infanticide in which the reproductive role of the feminine is refused.

L'Ex-père de la nation, a text that calls itself fiction and is written to read like an autobiography, questions and displaces Western readings of autobiography and "political" literature as transparent attempts to translate a world outside the text. Indeed, the potential for an upheaval of sexual, generic, and colonial hegemonies is indicated as early as the title, where the father is crossed out, and as late as the last sentences of the text: "Coura me rend chaque jour une visite, d'une heure environ quand elle m'apporte mon déjeuner.... C'est seulement quand elle me quitte que je prends ma plume pour écrire" (189). (Coura visits me every day for about an hour when she brings me my lunch.... It's only when she leaves me that I take out my pen to write.) Crisis and confinement provoke written narrative, much as the crisis of colonialism underpins the writing of this text.[20] The novel closes on Madiama in prison, while Coura, free, gives shape and direction to his days. Moreover, if writing represents Madiama's only freedom, it is Coura who reveals this freedom to him and grants him access to it. Refusing to accept her "fate" as the first wife in a polygamous marriage, Coura explains:

> "Si de tout l'univers je ne disposais que d'un grain de sable pour asseoir mon corps, je ne laisserais pas l'univers me comprimer sur ce grain de sable . . . "
> [Madiama] "Un grain de sable dans l'univers, c'est petit!"
> [Coura] "Petit, oui. Mais maniable . . . Il n'y a pas de servitude absolue . . . Il faut savoir dénicher la parcelle de liberté cachée au fond de nous . . . Il suffit de le vouloir." (56)

> ["If, in all the universe, I had only a grain of sand on which to seat myself, I wouldn't let the universe confine me to this grain of sand. . ."
> (Madiama) "A grain of sand is very small!"
> (Coura) "Small, yes, but manageable . . . there is no absolute servitude. We must know how to unearth that bit of liberty hidden deep within us . . . We need only to desire it."]

The analogy between Coura's socially dictated subjugation to Madiama and the position of formerly colonized peoples living in the shadow of a colonial past and a neocolonial present becomes explicit in this passage. More importantly perhaps, the strategies proffered by the novel for refusing this position are aligned with the feminine. The roles of Madiama, a seemingly powerful and free man, and of Coura, a female character who appears to have "no choice," have been drastically altered. This narrative of events simultaneously leading to and flowing from masculine confinement reveals itself to be the narration of a feminine progression toward freedom.

The duplicity implied and the confusion generated by a fictional text that "imitates" an autobiography engage with interpretations of autobiography as a colonizing genre. For Madiama has clearly fallen victim to neocolonial forces; he is effectively a colonized product of an ongoing process, altered since Independence but tenaciously and insidiously continuing to shape individuals and governments. Therefore, the process by which a second, embedded narrative reveals itself to be the more compelling and powerful of the two, a process that involves infanticide, reflects a literary shedding of things colonial, including autobiography as an individualistic, isolating, and "reproductive" genre. Thus, in *L'Ex-père de la nation*, Western, traditional, "male" autobiography and the colonization it represents, both in terms of literary models and concepts of the self, are merged with a nontraditional perspective, in the form of an African woman's literary text that strives to confuse and refuse the "laws" of genre.

Notes

1. Aminata Sow Fall, *Le Revenant* (Dakar: Nouvelles Editions Africaines, 1976).

2. Aminata Sow Fall, *L'Ex-père de la nation* (Paris: L'Harmattan, 1986). Page numbers will appear in parentheses. Translations are mine.

3. See, for example, Bella Brodzki and Celeste Schenck, *Life/Lines* (Ithaca: Cornell University Press, 1988).

4. See Samba Gadjigo, *Ecole Blanche/Afrique Noire* (Paris: L'Harmattan, 1990).

5. Domna Stanton, *The Female Autograph* (Chicago: University of Chicago Press, 1987), 4.

6. Aoua Kéita, *Femme d'Afrique* (Paris: Présence Africaine, 1975); and Ken Bugul, *Le Baobab fou* (Dakar: Nouvelles Editions Africaines, 1984). Kéita's text is generally not considered a literary text. She is never, to my knowledge, discussed as part of the group of West African women authors that includes, for example, Mariama Bâ and Aminata Sow Fall. The sociopolitical nature of Kéita's text allows it to be dismissed as a mere recording of the events in the author's life, rather than a creative endeavor. I think this reading is reductive, and I would argue that this text needs to be reconsidered from a literary perspective.

7. Georges Gusdorf, "Conditions and Limits of Autobiography," in *Autobiography*, ed. James Olney (Princeton: Princeton University Press, 1980). Gusdorf argues that "it would seem that autobiography is not to be found outside of our cultural area; one would say that it expresses a concern peculiar to Western *man*, a concern that has been of good use in *his* systematic conquest of the universe and that *he* has communicated to *men* of other cultures; but those *men* will thereby have been annexed by a sort of intellectual colonizing to a mentality that was not their own" (129, my emphasis). Although Gusdorf does not explicitly alienate women from the autobiographical mode, his exclusive use of gender-marked language and male authors, not only in this paragraph but throughout his essay, makes it difficult to argue that Gusdorf's "man" is neuter. Although autobiography may threaten to colonize non-Western men, it poses an even more complex threat for women whose autobiographies, as well as other writings, have not been read as literary texts but rather as sociological, historical, or political documents. This misreading goes a long way toward explaining the absence of women as subjects and objects of critical discourse on autobiography.

8. Aminata Sow Fall, interview by author, Dakar, June 1989.

9. Julia Watson, "Shadowed Presence: Modern Women Writers' Autobiographies and the Other," in *Studies of Autobiography*, ed. James Olney (New York: Oxford University Press, 1988), 182.

10. Ibid.

11. Françoise Lionnet, *Autobiographical Voices* (Ithaca: Cornell University Press, 1989), 91.

12. Ousmane Sembene, *Le Dernier de l'empire* (Paris: L'Harmattan, 1981).

13. Doris Summer broaches a similar topic in "Not Just a Personal Story," (Brodzki and Schenck, *Life/Lines,* 111) and seems to allow for a "subversive" use of autobiography: "Is [autobiography] the model for imperializing the consciousness of colonized peoples, replacing their collective potential for resistance with a cult of individuality and even loneliness. . . . Or is it a medium of resistance and counterdiscourse. . . . " Nellie McKay provides a possible response to this question in another essay from the same collection: "In all aspects of its creation, early black autobiography altered the terms for the production of Western autobiography as they had been defined by the dominant culture" ("Race, Gender, and Cultural Context in Zora Neale Hurston's *Dust Tracks on a Road*" in Brodzki and Schenck, *Life/Lines,* 176). It is important to note here that both feminist critics and scholars of African-American and African literature have remarked that the autobiographies of women, whether or not they have experienced colonization, as well as the autobiographies of colonized men tend to portray a self in its relation to other selves, and emphasize the connection of the individual to his/her community.

14. The term "mère patrie" is interesting because it conjures up images of both the maternal and the paternal. Unfortunately, this complexity is lost in the English translation.

15. Frantz Fanon, *Les Damnés de la terre* (Paris: François Maspero, 1966); *The Wretched of the Earth* (Middlesex: Penguin, 1967). Page numbers will appear in parentheses.

16. Lionnet, *Autobiographical Voices,* 33.

17. See Marianne Hirsch, *The Mother/Daughter Plot* (Bloomington: Indiana University Press, 1980) for a detailed discussion of this concept.

18. In French, the word *femme* also means "wife."

19. Christopher Miller, *Theories of Africans* (Chicago: University of Chicago Press, 1990), 306.

20. See also Mariama Bâ, *Une si longue lettre* (Dakar: Nouvelles Editions Africaines, 1986); and Ken Bugul, *Le Baobab fou,* where, again, the narratives are provoked by analogous crises.

PART II

Border Crossings

CHAPTER SEVEN

Cherchez la Franco-femme

CHRISTIANE P. MAKWARD

> Ranavalona the First, queen of the Merinas: a "xenophobe," she persecutes
> Christian missionaries . . . hence the bombardment of Tamatave.
> Ranavalona II, having forbidden the acquisition of land by foreigners,
> provokes the blockade of the Island of Madagascar . . . she dies two
> months after the fall of Tamatave . . . Ranavalona III having
> shown "evident ill will" in observing treaties, the
> protectorate is established. The Merina Kingdom is
> declared a colony, the queen is deposed and
> deported . . . she dies in Algiers in 1897.
> *Grand Larousse Encyclopédique*
>
> Je pense à vous, ô reines, superbes tigresses
> A vos fronts inondés des éclairs des canons:
> Trois Ranavalona aux marchands dirent non
> Qui prétendaient poudrer l'ébène de leurs tresses.
> [I think of you, o queens, proud tigresses
> Your heads lit by cannon fire:
> Three Ranavalonas said no to the merchants
> Who tried to powder their ebony tresses.][1]
>
> *Métèque*: one who changes houses

Among the three Ranavalonas, they had a sixty-two year reign. Did you
know that? Like so many other extraordinary women and events, they slipped
through the net of history, at least the history that is taught, rethought,

115

reconstructed according to recent developments in the state of knowledge and the disciplines. The history of women is slowly emerging from the obscurity to which the "natural" blinders of men have traditionally relegated them. Strange blind spots in vision that make of the majority of our male companions voyeuristic lovers, myopic grandfathers, nearsighted friends, and the great non-seers of women's history. In the best of faith, Belgians still laugh in your face — perhaps out of embarrassment — when you ask them about Belgian women writers. Of course there is Marguerite Yourcenar; it is not a wasteland, far from it. But there is also Marie Gevers and Marguerite Van de Wiele, Louis Dubrau, and Renée Brock. We would love to hear about their lives and works, their ties to their land, without having to depend on the overburdened literary historians, whose minds are too often incapable of being interested in women's works (Jean Larnac being an exception not totally free from prejudice). So deep and pernicious is the ordinary sexism in which we are immersed, that it makes us more or less unconsciously but systematically (systemically) overvalue the masculine in relation to the feminine. Oppressive but not irreversible, this system of thought is the result of centuries of symbolic "lesser performance": in my opinion, the mother of Catherine of Siena, who died in her eighties after having given birth to twenty-four children, deserves canonization as much as her daughter.

"When the infinite servitude of woman is broken . . ." predicted the child-poet Rimbaud more than a century ago. I particularly like the word "broken," which implies that the change will never be erased or co-opted by the patriarchs, who are themselves on the way out, unless they deprive women of schools and pens. The change takes place at the "school for women," and it happens because of writing and "the path of long study." Christine de Pisan is the most striking literary example of silence, or of a defanged, sugar-coated, euphemized presence, more effective even than an absence, to which they have been able to reduce women's voices and their historical existence. It is only at the beginning of the 1980s and in English (for until recently there has been no current edition in modern French of this dangerous treasure) that we can read: "O my ladies, flee, flee the futile love they urge on you! Flee it, for God's sake, flee! For no good can come to you from it. Rather, rest assured that however deceptive their lures, their end is always to your detriment . . . Flee, flee, my Ladies, and avoid their company."[2]

This lesson was again taught by Marie-Madeleine de La Fayette two and a half centuries later through the character of the Princesse de Clèves (1678), but we had to wait for her "postmodern" and feminist interpreters to be able to hear it. And all the broken hearts in the old "women's literature" or in operas (soap or Italian), which deeply irritate men as much as they do stout-hearted feminists, tell us the same story: "Love's pleasures, etc." Because if you do not flee them (men), you must be ready to imitate Griselda or Violeta, the extreme ideals of a still vigorous patriarchy that wants to have the right of life and death over its subjects, the same principle incarnated by monarchy, and the same dream of absolute power. And if no one questioned their right to call Marie de Sévigné "Lady Creampuff of literature," the great Gustave Lanson could not, after 1970, continue to print his commentary on Christine de Pisan: "The first of this unbearable tradition of women writers able to write anything effortlessly on any subject and who, during the whole life that God gave them, do nothing but multiply the proofs of their inexhaustible facility, equalled only by their universal mediocrity."

Nevertheless, their modern descendants—the academic legislators of literary quality—read only those writers likely to receive a Goncourt or a Nobel, that is, those men (and not men and women) whom the brotherhood has agreed to designate as "good." So, we are left with the "*parole métèque*"—the language of she who has changed houses, she who has gone from the house of the Father not to the mother's house but to her own, the house of now and tomorrow, which must be "without roots" in any specific territory if it wants to remain standing. Too much havoc in human lives still occurs on account of "roots" and territorial claims. This is presented to us in a recent novel of Andrée Chedid. *La Maison sans racines* (The House without roots) gives expression to a silent scream—I am of course not making allusion to the "right to life" film but to the Munch painting, so effectively set against the despair of women and children in the film *Le Sourd dans la ville* (*Deaf to the City*), adapted from the novel of Marie-Claire Blais. In Chedid's novel, there are three generations of women, three temporal layers, three continents, three types of narrative that converge in a staging of the emergence, always sacrificial, of women into the public forum. *La Maison sans racines* (1985, ten years after the explosion of Beirut) is even more depressing to read than *Le Sixième Jour* (1960) (The Sixth Day) because here it is neither God nor the plague that causes the death of a child and the triple murder of peace and life. Here, guns are responsible, and invisible but indicted, so are their bearers and their dealers. This French voice of a woman born in the Middle East, grown to adulthood in France and escaping from time to time to America—*métèque* par excellence—is one of the great poets of the symbolic and living country that is the French language.

As we are often impatient with the label "feminist" when it is applied to us in aggression and reductionist oversimplification, I believe Chedid shrinks from the label "francophone" of which I have sketched out the problematics elsewhere.[3] Barely two out of five French speakers are "French French," as they are still ironically designated in the nonhexagonal literature. Today we are looking for acceptable neologisms to signify these differences without negative connotations. Words inevitably wear out as intellectuals become enlightened and learn to share the power of making themselves heard, as "minorities" produce discourses and words and go so far as to publish independently, as with the Nouvelles Editions Africaines or "des femmes," a publishing house recently rebaptized "Des femmes-Antoinette Fouque."

Women's writing in French is a very recent phenomenon for Africa (if we exclude, as we must, the colonial ladies): it emerged in Algeria during the war with France, and in sub-Saharan Africa ten years after those nations gained their independence in 1960 (Nafissatou Diallo, Mariama Bâ, Aminata Sow Fall, the Nzuji sisters from Zaire, and Werewere Liking and Calixte Beyala, the "rising stars"). Established slightly earlier, and for reasons evidently linked to the history of women's education, which is always behind men's by at least a generation if not several centuries, women's writing in the Antilles (henceforth "franco-Caribbean") becomes important beginning in the fifties (Marie Chauvet, M.-Magdeleine Carbet, Michèle Lacrosil), giving us the present generation of "fully-developed writers," dominated by Maryse Condé and Simone Schwarz-Bart. In North America, the tradition is established much earlier (with Laure Conan in 1884), and even in the seventeenth century if we want to take into account epistolary documents (such as the correspondence of Marie de l'Incarnation, who was born in France). Ironically or inevitably — and we take note of the form chosen by Mariama Bâ for the famous *Une si longue lettre* (*So Long a Letter*) — it is with this same epistolary form and her *Lettres écrites de Lausanne* (Letters written from Lausanne) that Swiss feminist fiction in French was born at the hands of a Dutch immigrant, Belle de Charrière, in 1785.

Beyond the language they use, do these "francophemmes" have anything at all in common? There is certainly a political topography to explore: rare are the contemporary francophone women who are not driven into exile, to preserve their freedom of thought, lifestyling, and writing. The francophone woman writer seeks social anonymity in an exile made necessary by her stifling visibility "at home." As examples, we can point to the various peregrinations of Schwarz-Bart, Carbet, Condé, Antonine Maillet, Anne Hébert, Assia Djebar, Awa Thiam, Pierrette Micheloud, Monique Saint-Hélier, Calixte Beyala, and so on, and even within her own country, the wanderings of Corrina Bille traumatized by the attacks of the local Swiss press, never getting over her timidity as a dutiful daughter and expressing all her considerable daring only through the written word.

Harassed, if not reduced to silence, censured by the press when not by those close to her, too often read "below the belt," to use Christiane Rochefort's expression, the francophone woman writer must also overcome her discomfort with the language "of Racine and Voltaire" (let us add Proust, for good measure). French as it is published, a mythical French, the "good" French of France is, however, marked by local influences. This idea is more and more accepted, thanks to the energetic statements and patient work of the Québécois in particular. Often sacralized because it is the sign of a social and cultural identity (as against English in Quebec, Arabic or English in the Middle East, German in Switzerland, Flemish in Belgium) or valorized because it is the means of access to the Western liberal world, as is the case for Maghrebians, Lebanese, Antilleans (who have no choice in the matter), or Africans, French is the key to a better future, to progress toward greater liberty, but it is also a constraining source of insecurity because, as is particularly the case for Africans, it is never completely a native language. The syndrome of the repressed "native language" is sometimes mythified by poets until it becomes the symbol of the entire problematic of a sociopolitical situation. But we observe every day that bilingualism or multilingualism is not in itself the bearer of psychopathological problems (hysteria, "Antillean madness," etc.)

Along with the more or less difficult relationship to language, the reception of the texts of francophone women constitutes another problem and a potentially common ground. Who, in fact, reads their texts before a media event co-opts them ad nauseam? The public of the francophone woman writer is irremediably composite, heterogeneous. She must be read in Paris and in Lausanne, Montreal, Algiers, Fort-de-France, by the men who do the publicity and the publishing, by the women who assure the greatest share of sales in the last analysis and in the long run, and by the academics and critics who tell people what they must read. And when the potential female public is just about penniless, very often uneducated or illiterate (14 percent of women as against 42 percent of men were able to read in Algeria in 1977), it is a better idea to turn to the audiovisual as a means of communication. That is what tempted Assia Djebar with *La Nouba des femmes du mont Chenoua* (The fete of the women of Mount Chenoue) and *Femmes d'Alger dans leur appartement* (*Women of Algiers in Their Apartment*). But her modern message threatens the patriarchal order, which explains the difficulty of getting herself published or the danger of being published for monetary reasons rather than in the name of art and freethinking.

In the end, all these specific problems of the francophone woman writer, barely outlined here, can be summed up in the vague resistance, the profound indifference, the prejudices (judging before knowing) that are part of the condition of being "other": "other" because francophone and not "native" and "other" because woman and not man. The real public of francophone women writers is perhaps the intercontinental community of women readers, translators, students, and academics, the female "happy few."

Whether it is the illusion or reality of a community in any case symbolic and thus infinitely manipulable, the francophone community—users of a single language—thus finds its greatest reality in the circulation of living words and in the exercise of freedom in literary creation. I will limit myself here to setting forth positive considerations by looking at three gardens—leaving to others the "summits" of the old rhetoric—in the landscape of women writers about whom I am currently preparing a "treasury" (*De Marie de France à Marie NDiaye: A Literary Dictionary,* with Madeleine Hage).

The Caribbean, French-speaking Switzerland, Algeria: Simone Schwarz-Bart, S. Corinna Bille, Assia Djebar—at first glance authors of texts with little in common, lacking a common feminist ideology but nevertheless possessing a gynocentric and constructive vision, a positive feminine identification that short-circuits maternity (not in the lives of the writers but in their fiction). We must think of Colette, a mediocre mother but a daughter whose pen is unmatched when it comes to Sido, never ceasing her dialogue with the mother—the ideal woman, the ultimate security that is cherished in the body of the lover, male or female—in her greatest autobiographical texts. The great creations of these authors deliberately set themselves apart from the morbid victims of the past and the romances on which girls were raised. The heroines are based neither on Griselda (who does not even allow herself the comfort of tears to conform to the ideal of her lord and master) nor Cinderella (who never raises her voice against the harassment and sadism of the father's daughters, and who, ensconcing herself in the hearth, awaits her Prince—is she even really waiting for him?); these archetypes of femininity are no longer features of contemporary francophone women's writing.

Quite the contrary. Our beautiful women writers (fortunately, no one would suspect them of sublimating a lack of beauty in their writing, like Germaine de Staël or Marie-Madeleine de La Fayette) occasionally will stage a man's murder or a physical resistance to masculine aggression. Along with *La Chrysalide* of Aïcha Lemsine, I could mention, as examples of rebellious women, Andrée Chedid and the protagonist of *Le Sommeil délivré* (*Sleep Unbound*) or those in the wonderful short stories of *L'Etroite peau* (Limiting skin): a wife who spends her life plotting the murder of her husband, a mother unleashing the violence of the village on the Moslem holy man because he has wished seven more children on her. Then I would recall the last fight to the death of Télumée Miracle, from which she emerges victorious, using scissors to subdue her former companion, an alcoholic who has just invaded her home. Similarly, Judith, in *La Chemise soufrée* (*A Scent of Sulfur*, a play by Corinna Bille) kills her father who, inspired by the Bible and his hormones, tries to rape her. These are only some of the dramatic situations that provide the common denominator of numerous francophone texts to question or check patriarchal law even if the price is death.

In her story "Femmes d'Alger," Assia Djebar presents two masculine characters, the husband of Sarah, the narrator, and the Islamic scribe, father of many daughters. Both are completely overwhelmed by the feminine characters. The patriarch cannot succeed in arranging a circumcision according to the tradition: it will be done in the hospital, like a common appendectomy. The former hero of the war of liberation sees his son run away from home (from which the narrator gets a certain satisfaction, even though she remains at her husband's side), and (there is no doubt about Djebar's intentions) the son leaves because the father has not "shared his war" with him. An indictment of lack of paternal participation in child-raising: the father refuses to play the hero. The new man will be not heroic or "deheroicized," which means, according to Hélène Cixous, that he will be capable of not forgetting the other, capable of a new economy of attention to the other that would not end in appropriation.[4]

Along with this attempt to put the Father to death or at least into question ("My father the hero"), there is a new strategy of narrative space: the movement toward oral and maternal sources of identity. I have already mentioned *La Nouba des femmes du mont Chenoua*, where this principle is amply illustrated. The narrative space is occupied by women's voices. Djebar sets the stage by attributing to Sarah, narrator of "Femmes d'Alger", the profession of audio archivist. She provides variations on this device with other characters—a Berber translator, a multilingual German woman—and other themes: women singing in the Turkish bath, at home, at work, on the radio. Djebar creates a narrative polyphony that is completely gynocentric and uses it to suggest that salvation—after the subjugation or death of a certain male—is to seek spiritual nourishment with other women.

Simone Schwarz-Bart, for her part, claims to have obtained her admirable narrative from her heroine's own mouth, and it is no small miracle of literary creation to succeed in symbolizing an Antillean identity in which men can recognize themselves if they condescend to read *Pluie et vent sur Télumée Miracle* (along with the failure of the return to Africa, which she discusses subsequently in *Ti Jean L'horizon*). Indeed, there is universal appeal through gender and ethnic identification in the character of Télumée, whose only heroic features are her name ("Miracle"), her very survival, and her integrity: she becomes a healer, but the text remains very discreet on this subject, which borders on the fantastic, to evade the Eurocentric question of "voodoo," which sums up Caribbean identity, Haitian in particular, for whites. Let us remember, however, that Télumée has obtained her knowledge and her identity—her patronymic of Lougandor—from a second grandmother and good witch, Man Cia. And the "miracle" of *Pluie et vent* is, of course, more particularly its wonderful language, which must be seriously analyzed in its relationship to the Caribbean oral tradition and the sociolect of Guadeloupe.

In the case of Corinna Bille, the most important texts focus again on the theme of violence against girls or women and the murder of the man, father or husband. They are also based on the same source of creativity: oral transmission through women (which has also been noted in Mariama Bâ's *Une si longue lettre*), or the development of signs of communication among women. I must mention Théoda, the heroine (in the literary sense) of Corinna Bille's first novel, who is decapitated in the marketplace, as Judith of *La Chemise soufrée* was burned in the marketplace, and like her a real historical person. She loses her head and her life in the end with great fanfare *after* her two accomplices, for having set up the murder of her husband. Although she did not perpetrate the murder, she is judged "the most guilty." If Bille undertook research in the archives of the trial and execution of the criminal trio at Sion, in the middle of the nineteenth century, it is because her mother, Catherine Taffarel, had told her about a distant kinship with "Théoda," and Bille developed a fascination with the historical personage, a truly Durassian fascination with crimes of passion and with the woman, Théoda, who goes unflinchingly to the guillotine. It is from her mother and the housewives of the Valaisan villages (plus an occasional man) that Bille gathers anecdotes, legends, and bits of gossip, from which she weaves her numerous stories. One of the two novellas in *Deux Passions* (Two passions),

"Virginia 1912," is a reconstitution of the romance of her father and mother, based on correspondence between Catherine and her girlfriends in her mountain village when she was working at the home of the painter Edmond Bille. One suspects that Catherine's own words to Corinna helped to fill in the story.

Deeply comparable among these "other" women writers of today (Bille died in 1979), resembling a common or at least parallel project, we find thus, on the one hand, the questioning of the patriarchal principle, the symbolic putting to death of the father or husband, as well as the valorization of oral communication between women. A large number of texts and stories could be cited in support of these remarks, beginning with the other great *métèques* of narrative tradition: the Queen of Sheba, whom we imagine, in the absence of proof to the contrary, as the author of the Song of Songs, and the brilliant Shéhérazade, whom we ought to canonize as the patron saint of storytellers and other "thieves of language."

Notes

1. This is a pastiche of Nerval's quatrain, "je pense à toi Myrtô."

2. Christine de Pizan, *The Book of the City of Ladies*, trans. Earl Jeffrey Richards (New York: Persea Books, 1988), 256, III. 19.6.

3. Christiane P. Makward, "The Others' Others... Francophone Women and Writing," *Yale French Studies* 75, fall 1988, 190–207.

4. Hélène Cixous, "Reaching the Point of Wheat," *New Literary History* 19 (1), autumn 1987.

CHAPTER EIGHT

Narrative "je(ux)" in
Kamouraska by Anne Hébert and
Juletane by Myriam Warner-Vieyra

ELISABETH MUDIMBE-BOYI

> Women have been nameless. They have not been persons. Handed by a
> father to another man, the husband, they have been objects of
> circulation, exchanging one name for another.
> Carolyn Heilbrun, *Writing a Woman's Life*

> When one cannot open one's mouth in public to speak one's mind,
> speaking to God is the safest outlet. God at least,
> is not known to be an informant.
> S. Shannugaratnam, "Seven Days in Jaffe.
> Life under Indian Occupation," *Race and Class*

Elisabeth d'Aulnières in *Kamouraska* and Juletane in *Juletane* tell their stories,
which are so different and yet so similar. What could a French-Canadian
heroine from the nineteenth century of a Catholic bourgeois milieu have
in common with a French Caribbean heroine of the twentieth century who
followed her husband to Africa to find herself involved in a polygamous
marriage? Between Elisabeth and Juletane an intertextual play seems to
point out a similarity of women's condition beyond culture and geography. Despite the cultural, religious, chronological, and geographical distance, the referential *hors-texte* of both novels is shaped by the social matrix
of a patriarchal society in which women's lives are ruled by preestablished

gender roles and definitions of womanhood. In both *Kamouraska* and *Juletane,* marriage and motherhood constitute the yardstick with which to measure a woman's worth and her fulfillment of society's expectations. My reading of the two novels brings to light the ambivalence and the ambiguities of the female characters. On the one hand, their narratives, as an actualization of the act of writing, suggest a reinterpretation of the enclosed space where they live and from which their discourse originates. On the other hand, both narratives develop a feminine discourse that is still muffled, reflecting their characters' entrenchment in repression and a noninternalization of their social roles. Their actions (Elisabeth's love affair, Juletane's rejection of a polygamous marriage) introduce instability in the social order. At the same time, however, the signs of disruption in the social harmony (erotic passion, illness, and madness) are manifestations of their own dissociation from the social milieu.

Juletane's story is told through the diary she writes, confined in the small room where she lives, sharing her husband's house with two co-wives. Hélène, a West Indian woman living in Paris, has discovered the diary, and she is spending the night reading it at the same time the reader does. For Elisabeth, it is in her children's room that she spends most of the time as she unfolds her discontinuous, dreamlike narrative, in which the past and the present cross each other and merge, the past sometimes obliterating the present. People and images, sounds and smells from the past become at times so intense that they create in front of her a complete world, granting it the thickness and the presence of the here and now. Elisabeth's present is the time of Monsieur Jérôme Rolland, her second husband of eighteen years whom she married for "l'honneur" and for whom she bore eight children. Between her first and second marriages, emerges Dr. George Nelson, her lover and the murderer of Antoine Tassy, seigneur de Kamouraska, her first husband.

For both Elisabeth and Juletane, the limits and the enclosure of the room construct a personal space, opening the possibility for dream and evasion from a world from which they feel alienated. The enclosed, marginal space thus transforms itself into a center from which Elisabeth and Juletane constitute themselves as speaking and narrating subjects. For Juletane, the confined space opens a possibility of communication with herself through the diary. For Elisabeth, who has been overwhelmed by the presence of her mother, her three aunts, the servants, and a husband she does not love, the children's room restores intimacy with herself and with her memories. Elisabeth's reveries and memories and Juletane's progressing diary are the ingredients from which the narratives are constructed. The spaces allow the transformation of their enclosure into a source of creativity, generating the new space of the text; they also constitute a place of retreat and refuge in their social, emotional—and in the case of Juletane—cultural exile and solitude.

Let us focus for a moment on Elisabeth as the narrating subject in *Kamouraska*. At the level of the narrative structure, the first chapter constitutes the matrix of the whole novel. The three narrative voices are already present, conveying Elisabeth's life story. Present also is an assessment of the feminine condition in nineteenth-century Quebec: marriage as a wage for respectability, motherhood as a symbol of self-fulfillment. Finally, Elisabeth's rebellion and conflicts with social norms are revealed in the interstices of events, and she voices, at times, her dissatisfaction and frustration with sex, merely a "devoir conjugal," and with marriage in which she is reduced to the status of an instrument for reproduction: "un ventre fidèle, une matrice à faire des enfants"(10) ("a faithful belly, a womb for making babies in" [4]).[1] The events of Elisabeth's life are conveyed through three narrative voices and the fluctuation of the narrative between past and present, in a fragmented structure, without continuity or linearity. *Kamouraska* begins in medias res, setting on stage an extradiegetic and omniscient narrator who introduces with a neutral tone the character of Madame Rolland: serene, impassible, sitting at the bedside of her dying husband:

> L'été passa en entier. Mme Rolland, contre son habitude, ne quitta pas sa maison de la rue du Parloir. Il fit très beau et très chaud. Mais ni Mme Rolland, ni les enfants n'allèrent à la campagne cet été-là.
> Son mari allait mourir et elle éprouvait une grande paix. Cet homme s'en allait tout doucement, sans trop souffrir, avec une discrétion louable. Mme Rolland attendait, soumise et irréprochable. (7)

> [The summer went by from beginning to end. Unlike other years Madame Rolland didn't leave her home on Rue du Parloir. It was very fair, very warm. But neither Madame Rolland nor the children went to the country that summer.
> Her husband was going to die and she felt a great calm. He was just slipping away, ever so gently, hardly suffering at all, and with such admirable good taste. And Madame Rolland waited, dutifully and above reproach. (1)]

This apparent impassibility is almost immediately contradicted by an abrupt transition to a first-person narrator, whose anxiety and anguish are translated in the shifting of grammatical tenses, from the *passé simple* to the historical present, and in the change of sentence rhythm into brief, panting phrases.

La ville n'est pas sûre en ce moment. Plus moyen d'en douter maintenant. On m'observe. On m'épie. On me suit. On me serre de près. On marche derrière moi. (7)

[The city's not safe anymore. No doubt about it now. People are watching. Spying. Following me. They keep coming closer and closer all the time. (1)]

In this context, the use of the indefinite pronoun "on" intensifies a climate of fear and the presence of an anonymous enemy. The changes introduced here already indicate the discrepancy between the external serenity of Elisabeth in her role of Madame Rolland and the intensity of her emotions when she is simply Elisabeth d'Aulnières, still haunted by the memories of a past in which she was a victim of social suspicion as an adulterous woman. A bitter irony summarizes her repressed frustration since her marriage of convenience to Jérôme Rolland:

Jérôme Rolland, mon second mari, l'honneur est rétabli. L'honneur, quel idéal à avoir devant soi, lorsqu'on a perdu l'amour.... Et moi qui emboîte le pas derrière, comme une dinde. C'est cela une honnête femme: une dinde qui marche, fascinée par l'idée qu'elle se fait de son honneur. (9)

[Jérôme, my second husband, and honor is restored. Honor. What an ideal to set yourself when love is what you've lost.... And me, right behind, like a silly little goose. Yes, that's all a virtuous woman is. A gaping fool that struts along, staring at the image of her honor. (3)]

Concurrent voices represent the same Elisabeth: at times a narrator who uses "je," at times a third person, at times a judgmental voice, interpellating and addressing that other person Elisabeth, or another character. There is in the shifting of narrative voices a pathological distinction of the narrator from herself in becoming another person or in creating and projecting another being with whom she does not want to identify, or whose responsibilities she does not want to endorse. Elisabeth is herself when passionately in love with George Nelson. She proclaims:

J'habite la fièvre et la démence, comme mon pays natal. J'aime un autre homme que mon mari. Cet homme je l'appelle de jour et de nuit: Docteur Nelson, docteur Nelson. (115)

[I am living my life in fever and folly, as if they were my native land. I'm in love with a man who is not my husband. This man I keep calling for. Daytime. Nighttime. Doctor Nelson, Doctor Nelson. (112)]

An uninvolved third-person narrator regularly takes over, thus differentiating Madame Rolland or Madame Tassy from the intradiegetic narrator "je": Elisabeth d'Aulnières. Elisabeth at times plays the observer, at times the observee, going back and forth as a "je" and as a third-person narrator. Studying the nature of pronouns in *Problems in General Linguistics,* Emile Benveniste suggests:

> *I* can only be identified by the instance of discourse that contains it and by that alone. It has no value except in the instance in which it is produced. But in the same way, it is also as an instance of form that *I* must be taken; the form of *I* has no linguistic existence except in the act of speaking in which it is uttered. There is thus a combined double instance in this process: the instance of *I* as a referent and the instance of discourse containing *I* as the referee.[2]

He further argues that "it is by identifying himself as a unique person pronouncing I that each speaker sets himself up in turn as the 'subject.'"[3] Benveniste's statements help to explain Elisabeth's attempts to become a speaking subject—and thus assert herself. At the same time, Benveniste explicates the shift in narrative voices and, thus, Elisabeth's splitting of personality and her multiple personae. Echoing Rimbaud's "Je est un autre" (I is another), she clearly acknowledges a situation of *dédoublement* when she declares "Je dis 'je' et je suis une autre" (115). In another chapter, concerning relationship of person in the verb, Benveniste refers to Rimbaud explicitly, in stating that "Rimbaud's 'je est un autre' represents the typical expression of what is properly mental 'alienation,' in which the 'I' is dispossessed of its constitutive identity."[4]

The interplay of narrative voices in *Kamouraska,* as well as the telescoping of grammatical tenses and the fragmentation of the narrative into a nonlinear trajectory, translates Elisabeth's tormented and fragmented personality, her anxiety, and her insecurities. The narrative devices chosen by Hébert embody Elisabeth's inner division, her Self caught between a social identity (Mme Jérôme Rolland, Mme Antoine Tassy), which is only a facade, and her real "je" she is attempting to establish in the self-narrative that pervades *Kamouraska.* Elisabeth's story is indeed a story of dispossession and alienation, of search for an identity. In their possessiveness, the aunts who raise her consider her as nameless: they always refer to her as "la petite." Moreover, through marriage she is granted a new identity in being given someone else's name: Madame Rolland, Madame Tassy. Proclamations of her names at the beginning and at the end of the novel are a revelation about Elisabeth's multiple identities:

> Je suis Elisabeth d'Aulnières, épouse en premières noces d'Antoine Tassy, seigneur assassiné de Kamouraska, épouse en seconde noces de Jérôme Rolland, notaire de Québec. (248)

[I'm Elisabeth d'Aulnières. My first husband was Antoine Tassy, the squire of Kamouraska, the one who was murdered. And my second is Jérôme Rolland, notary in the city of Quebec. (247)]

Or, similarly:

Moi, moi Elisabeth d'Aulnières, veuve d'Antoine Tassy, épouse en seconde noces de Jérôme Rolland. (8)

[Me, Elisabeth d'Aulnières. Widow of Antoine Tassy, wife of Jérôme Rolland. (2)]

In the utterance of "je," Elisabeth is longing for a self-identity erased and stripped from her by marriage. Her desire for a self-ascription becomes a form of resistance tinted with ambiguity. Between her declarations of identity are inscribed Elisabeth's tensions and conflicts. At the same time as she proclaims herself as Elisabeth d'Aulnières, she conjoins her other identities in which irony ("seigneur assassiné de..., épouse en secondes noces de...") mingles with the desire for social respectability encoded in her husbands' social rank and professions ("seigneur de..., notaire de...") she so obviously displays. Elisabeth's life finally evolves as a play. There is in her a hunger for love and passion that leads her to become adulterous. Yet, she renounces her passion and her lover to conform to society's demands and expectations in accepting the role of the perfect wife, knowing inside her that she does not love Jérôme Rolland:

Je n'ai plus qu'à devenir si sage qu'on me prenne au mot. Fixer le *masque* de l'innocence sur les os de ma face. Accepter l'innocence en guise de revanche ou de punition. *Jouer le jeu* cruel, la *comédie* épuisante, jour après jour. Jusqu'à ce que la ressemblance parfaite colle à la peau. (249, emphasis mine)

[Nothing to do now but act so nicely that no one can doubt me. Pull the mask of innocence over my face. Against the bones. Accept it like some kind of vengeance, some kind of punishment. Playing the cruel game, the tedious comedy, day after day. Until the perfect resemblance sticks to my skin. (248)]

When Elisabeth recalls her wedding, it is with the distant unconcern of an outside spectator, voicing in this muffled manner her refusal to be that bride:

Penser à soi à la troisième personne. *Feindre* le détachement. Ne pas s'identifier à la jeune mariée, toute habillée de velours bleue.
    Voici la mariée qui bouge, poupée mécanique, appuyée au bras du mari, elle grimpe dans la voiture.
    La mariée embrasse à nouveau sa mère, ses tantes et toute la noce. (71, emphasis mine)

[Seeing yourself as someone else. Pretending to be objective. Not feeling that you and that young bride dressed in blue velvet are one and the same.
    And now the bride begins to move. Little mechanical doll, clinging to her husband's arm, climbing into the carriage.
    Again the bride gives her mother a kiss. And her aunts, and all the guests. (67)]

Or, as she states elsewhere,

C'est le moment où il faut se dédoubler franchement. Accepter cette division définitive de tout mon être. J'explore à fond le plaisir singulier de faire semblant d'être là. (196)

[The time has come now to split in two. Accept this total, sharp division of my being... Deep as I can, I probe the pleasure I feel. This rare delight, pretending I'm really here. (194)]

Elisabeth's life is an inauthentic one, in the Sartrian sense: she is oscillating between several identities, alienated from herself. Her words "Je suis une autre," or "jouer le jeu," or "fixer le masque" reveal her life as a comedy and herself as an actress, just playing a role. Between the "je" who proclaims to be Elisabeth d'Aulnières and the third-person narrator who says, "Foulée aux pieds la défroque de Mme Rolland" (115) ("Off with the venerable garb of Madame Rolland! Trampled underfoot" [112]) is inserted a second person interpellated and lectured at times by a judgmental voice. Beside Elisabeth, sitting next to her dying husband, emerges the past, unfolding Nelson's image as the murderer of Antoine Tassy, and Elisabeth's own responsibility as accomplice. To escape this responsibility and social ostracism, Elisabeth wraps herself in her new status of respectability, thus distancing herself from that Elisabeth of passion and love. Addressing the phantoms of her reveries, she summons them, condemning them and proclaiming her own innocence:

Laissez-moi passer. Je ne puis vivre ainsi dans une aussi forte terreur. Face à une action aussi abominable. Laissez-moi m'en aller. Devenir Mme Rolland à jamais. M'exclure de ce jeu de mort entre Antoine et toi. Innocente! Innocente! Je suis innocente. (233)

[Please let me go. Let me be Madame Rolland again forever. Let me be rid of this game of death between you and Antoine. Innocent! Innocent! I'm innocent, you hear! (231)]

The multiplicity of narrative voices constructs Elisabeth's multiple personalities and conflictual aspirations: desire to be oneself and autonomous, but at the same time, rejection of any responsibility. To escape the madness of passion that had led her to internal conflicts, Elisabeth chooses conformity and social respectability. In relegating Nelson and her memory she rejects that authentic part of herself, only to settle into the dignified identity of Mme Rolland: a perfect, faithful, and caring wife, acknowledged as such by those who surround her:

> l'épouse modèle tient la main de son mari, posée sur le drap... *Voyez* donc comme Madame aime Monsieur! *Voyez* comme elle pleure... (250, emphasis mine)

> [The model wife, clasping her husband's hand in hers, poised on the sheet.... "Just look how Madame loves Monsieur! You see, she's crying... (249–50)]

Juletane is involved in a process of *dédoublement* similar to Elisabeth's. In the very act of writing a diary, the narrating subject of *Juletane* is acting simultaneously as the referent and as the referee. Writing as a "je" thus takes on the significance of a "je suis une autre." As for Elisabeth, the enclosed space from which Juletane tells her story and from which she writes creates for her a place of retreat, a space of her own in which the diary comes into existence. Juletane's *dédoublement* is also translated in the typographical arrangement of the text: the italics of Hélène's story in contrast to the roman print of Juletane's. This typographical juxtaposition highlights the crossing of Hélène's and Juletane's stories, creating a narrative "structure en abyme."

Hélène's story mirrors Juletane's in many ways, seeming to project Juletane's alter ego and her secret aspirations and shattered dreams, as illustrated by the following:

Juletane	Hélène
— from the French West Indies	— from the French West Indies
— writes a diary	— reads the diary
— *is married* to an African	— *marries* an African
— economically dependent	— economically independent
— an orphan	— happy childhood
— passive, controlled, submissive	— aggressive, in control
— first-person narrative	— third-person narrative
— intradiegetic narrator	— extradiegetic narrator
— abnegation	— "me first" philosophy
— total giving of the self	— marriage to satisfy her own needs
— ingenue	— cynical
— likes Beethoven's Ninth Symphony, especially the "Ode to Joy"	— likes the same

Juletane	Hélène
— includes a female character with a nervous condition	— a female character with a nervous goiter
— dies at the end of the novel	— finds new life and energy after reading the diary

Hélène's story thus reveals itself to be similar and very different at the same time. The extradiegetic narrator of Hélène's story summarizes her personality and philosophy of life: she is "her own woman," giving priority to "me first," and her life is ordered "watch in hand" (18).[5] She had definite opinions regarding marriage and the couple:

> Elle avait décidé depuis peu de se marier, dans l'unique but d'avoir un enfant tout à elle. Son futur mari: elle l'aimait bien. Il l'aimait bien. Il était plus jeune qu'elle de dix ans, un bel athlète d'un mètre quatre-vingt et de quatre-vingt kilos, doux, doux comme un agneau. Elle le dominait financièrement et intellectuellement trop indépendante, elle n'aurait pas pu supporter un mari qui commande, décide, dirige. (12)

> [She had recently decided to get married for the simple reason that she wanted a child of her own. She was fond of her husband-to-be. He was ten years her junior, a handsome athletic man, six feet tall, eighty kilos, gentle as a lamb. She was his superior financially and intellectually. Too independent by nature, she could not have tolerated a husband who would dominate her, make her decisions, take the lead. (1)]

This *dédoublement* can also be seen in the interaction of the narrator and the narratee, important to the articulation of the narrative.[6] After her husband's death, Juletane concludes her diary, aware that her husband, Mamadou, will never read it, implying thus that he was the narratee. Actually, the narratee turns out to be Hélène: through her act of reading, she conveys Juletane's ordeals to the reader, and at the same time recalls her own story. Hélène's and Juletane's stories seem to evolve in a parallel way. They actually merge in the very opposition between the intradiegetic narrator of Juletane and the extradiegetic one of Hélène, as well as in their shared reader. The use of a "structure en abyme" and the third-person narrator serve as narrative strategies that allow Juletane's *dédoublement* and distantiation from a projected personality to which she aspires, but which she is probably too weak to endorse or become. In other words, the whole process of writing the diary and the entire narrative of *Juletane* embody Juletane's failed attempt to come to terms with herself by becoming her own person. In the process of writing, she reaches at least the awareness of the therapeutic virtues of writing a diary and its capacity for empowerment, for she realizes that "coucher ma peine sur une feuille blanche pouvait m'aider à l'analyser, la dominer et enfin, peut-être, la supporter ou définitivement la refuser" (60) ("putting down my anguish on a blank page could help me to analyse it, to control it and finally, perhaps to bear it or reject it once for all" [30]).

Writing in the first person is for Juletane a means of self-assertion, a way of coming into existence. Like Elisabeth, but in a different manner, she has been stripped of her identity and name. Being a West Indian, descendant of slaves, her true identity and name have been "gommée sur le registre du temps" (13) ("erased from the register of time" [2]). The name she has now was, at any rate, a "borrowed name." In France, she was "une jolie négresse" or "la petite noire." Once in Africa, she is also nameless, and without identity. Marginalized and almost outcast, she is endowed with a new racial identity "the toubabesse," meaning white woman, and a new name and social identity are bestowed upon her: "the madwoman."

The stories of Elisabeth, Juletane, and Hélène are, in fact, the same story: a woman struggling with herself and with society in order to find her identity and self-worth. In shifting regularly from Juletane's to Hélène's story, the author of *Juletane* replicates Elisabeth d'Aulnières's predicament, the instability of her identity: Elisabeth d'Aulnières, Madame Antoine Tassy, Madame Jérôme Rolland. Juletane too is variously seen as West Indian, French, African.[7] The question mark in their quest is thus "Who am I?" Powerless, unable to take responsibilities and confront their present reality, both Elisabeth and Juletane become dependent on their dreams: the dream of a romantic love, and for Juletane, the dream of a mythical Africa. Both Juletane and Elisabeth live in ambiguities. After the murder of her husband Antoine Tassy, Elisabeth is unable to accept the realization of her dream, the freedom to love George Nelson. Juletane goes to Africa with the hope of reconnecting with the land of her ancestors, yet she is without any knowledge of the local language or customs. When her husband settles for polygamy, Juletane, disillusioned, withdraws herself into a "vegetable life" (41), thus capitulating in front of her co-wives. She does not engage in any action that could perhaps have changed her miserable life or put an end to it. Although writing a diary constitutes a tool for autoanalysis and self-exploration, she does not try to sort out her motivation for coming to Africa nor to come to terms with her mythical construction of Africa and of Mamadou.

Orphaned at an early age, Juletane was raised in the limited and enclosed world of her godmother, Marraine: she was a lonely young girl, cut off from the rest of the world. Mamadou appears in her life as an epiphany. He becomes not only her Prince Charming but also her whole world:

> Croyant trouver en Mamadou toute la famille qui me manquait, je ne l'aimais pas seulement comme un amant, un mari. C'était aussi toute cette affection filiale débordant en moi que je reportais sur lui. (35)

> [I thought I had found in Mamadou the family I missed, so I did not love him only as a lover, a husband. I *transferred* to him all the filial affection which was overflowing in me as well. (15, emphasis mine)]

Elisabeth also went through an emotional orphanhood. After her father's death, her mother withdrew in her mourning, leaving the responsibility for the young Elisabeth to her unmarried aunts, who henceforth took her whole upbringing in their own hands. Physically and emotionally motherless and fatherless, Elisabeth and Juletane have been dispossessed of their childhood. Raised in dependence and hyperprotectiveness, neither Elisabeth nor Juletane had learned to exercise responsibility or autonomy. All major decisions had been made for them. R. D. Laing, although not involved in the study of women's conditions, shows in *The Politics of the Family* how such patriarchal attitudes as oppression and possessiveness are reproduced in the family structure, and how such a family context prevents the young girl from reaching a self-definition or a sense of self-worth.[8] On the other hand, Juletane's and Elisabeth's orphanhood could be read as a rejection by the mother. In *The Reproduction of Mothering*, Nancy Chodorow emphasizes the mother's role in the constitution of her female child's mental well-being. A lack of maternal nurturance and emotional bonding can lead the female child to a reaction of emotional disturbance or hysteria,[9] a thematic present in many other francophone women writers, such as Marie Cardinal, Calixte Beyala, and Jeanne Hyvrard.[10]

Elisabeth and Juletane find surrogate mothers in the three aunts and in Marraine, while Doctor Nelson and Mamadou clearly become father figures. The two heroines' dreams and lives are inscribed within the limits of a room. The enclosed space, the source of their creativity, functions as a maternal metaphor: it is, in its enclosure, a womblike space providing security, calm, and intimacy. A subtext of Elisabeth's and Juletane's quest for identity is their search for love and intimacy. In the frequent retreat to the enclosed room, there is an unexpressed or repressed desire to go back to the mother, to the origins. Juletane goes to Africa and Elisabeth lives with her aunts, longing for the house of her birth and childhood:

... la rue Georges et ma maison natale. Echapper à l'emprise de cette redoutable demeure de la rue Augusta.... Ne puis-je fuir cette époque de ma vie? Retrouver le *lieu de ma naissance*? Le doux état tranquille d'*avant ma naissance*? Ma mère en grand deuil me porte dans son ventre, *comme un fruit son noyau.* (51, emphasis mine)

[Rue Georges and the house where I was born. Escape from the clutches of this frightful place on Rue Augusta.... Can't I run away from that part of my life? Back to where I was born? Back to the gentle, peaceful time before I was born? My mother deep in mourning, carrying me in her womb. Like the stone inside a fruit. (47)]

In using the present tense in conjunction with the closeness of "fruit" and "noyau," Elisabeth is reenacting the uterine state of well-being and bonding with the mother. The desire to go back to the mother's womb embodies the refusal to grow and assume responsibility. Hysteria, split personalities, and unstable identities map Elisabeth's and Juletane's psychological states. The desire reflects their asymmetric relationship to society's demands and their difficulty internalizing well-defined and predetermined social roles, when, at the same time, they cannot really cope with their aspirations for autonomy. Asocial behavior, madness, illness, and murder reflect the incapacity of the characters to reconcile both sides: their aspirations and the social norms. In her intense love and desire for George Nelson, Elisabeth instigates her husband's murder. During a period of hallucinations, Juletane has visions in which she kills one of her co-wives. In reality, she disfigures her forever, killing her socially, by throwing hot oil on her pretty face.

There is in Elisabeth and Juletane an ambivalent madness: a sign of their maladjustment but also a manifestation of their repressed desire to challenge a social order in which they feel inadequate. Juletane "the madwoman" actually ends up in a psychiatric hospital. Francophone women novelists have frequently represented female illness and the topos of madness. In *Juletane,* there is a reference to two other deserted or betrayed wives who undergo psychiatric treatment. So does Jacqueline in Mariama Bâ's *Une si longue lettre.* In Calixte Beyala's *C'est le soleil qui m'a brûlée,* Ateba is mad. Mireille, also a betrayed wife, in Mariama Bâ's *Un Chant écarlate* kills her husband in a moment of madness. In Simone Schwarz-Bart's *Pluie et vent sur Télumée Miracle,* another deserted wife goes into madness and withdraws from the community until her recovery. Women's literary works from other cultural areas as well have frequently represented female characters engulfed in illness, madness, or hysteria.[11]

In view of these numerous ill and/or mad female characters, one can only repeat in wonder Phyllis Chesler's statement in *Women and Madness*: "Perhaps the angry and weeping women in mental asylums are Amazons returned to earth these many centuries later, each conducting a private and half remembered search for her Motherland — a search we call madness."[12] Almost with joy, Elisabeth acknowledges her adulterous passion as a form of insanity:

> Oui, oui je suis folle. C'est cela la folie, se laisser emporter par un rêve, le laisser croître en toute liberté, exubérant, envahissant. (23)

> [Yes, no doubt I am mad. That's what it means to be out of your mind. To let yourself be carried away by a dream. To give it room, let it grow wild and thick, until it overruns you. (17)]

Her acknowledgement of "folie," thus a dissymmetry with the norm, conveys an affirmation of her right to romance and sexual pleasure, as opposed to the marital relationship and marital sex, performed only as a "conjugal duty." Juletane, on the other hand, refuses to accept that she is mad and questions what madness really means if not just a social construct:

> Ici, on m'appelle "la folle," cela n'a rien d'original. Que savent-ils de la folie? Et si les fous n'étaient pas fous! Si un certain comportement que les gens simples et vulgaires nomment folie, n'étaient que sagesse, reflet de l'hypersensibilité lucide d'une âme pure, droite, précipitée dans un vide affectif réel ou imaginaire? Pour moi, je suis la personne la plus clairvoyante de la maison. (13–14)

> [Here they call me "the madwoman," not very original. What do they know about madness? What if mad people weren't mad? What if certain types of behavior which simple, ordinary people call madness, were just wisdom, a reflection of the clear-sighted hypersensitivity of a pure, upright soul plunged into a real or imaginary *affective void*? To me, I am the most lucid person in the house. (2, emphasis mine)]

Juletane, probably without realizing it, is also questioning the Freudian assumptions in the biologization of women's illness and hysteria, seeking a more psychosomatic interpretation.[13] In *Le Discours antillais* Edouard Glissant, referring to the psychoanalyst Frantz Fanon, reminds us that somatic manifestations reflect other problems, for instance, a lack of possibility for expression. As Ernest Pépin quotes him:

> Le corps souffrant, Fanon l'a bien montré, n'est pas à proprement parler le corps malade. C'est le lieu d'un discours malheureux qui s'énonce sous forme de malaise et de mal d'être. (187)[14]

[The suffering body, as Fanon has shown, is not strictly speaking the diseased body. It is the site of an unhappy discourse that presents itself in the form of malaise and ill-being.]

Madness functions rather as a metaphor of the female social condition and alienation. For the Antillaise woman, Pépin, echoing Fanon, diagnoses the problem as a muffled discourse:

Mal à l'aise dans le discours dominant, lequel est masculin, c'est avec son corps qu'elle parle. Sa colère, sa joie, ses désirs, ses déceptions et surtout le non-dit (le non dicible) s'expriment par les mouvements du corps. Elle grossit, elle maigrit, elle se déforme.[15]

[Ill at ease in the dominant discourse, which is masculine, she speaks with her body. Her anger, her joy, her desires, her disappointments, and especially the unspoken (the unspeakable) are expressed by the movements of the body. She grows fat or thin, she is deformed.]

As she recounts her ordeal of a failed marriage and betrayed love, Juletane mentions her physical deterioration, the manifestation of her psychological state of mind: "Je maigrissais, mes jupes devenues trop larges me donnaient l'allure d'un épouvantail" (50) ("I was losing weight, my skirts, which now were too big, made me look like a scarecrow" [24]).

As he alludes to women's social condition, Pépin is also pointing out the procedures that control or prevent a female discourse ("le non-dit, le non dicible" [the unsaid, the unsayable]), which then attempts to find an outlet by disguising itself in illness or in madness.

Elisabeth and Juletane embody the story of millions of women throughout time and space. Their oscillation between a "je" and a third-person narrator also points to some of the limitations in feminism. The "je" narrator makes possible the identification of any woman reader with the characters, suggesting a universality of women's condition within patriarchal structures. On the other hand, the use of a third person establishes a narrative distance between characters and narrator, and allows a certain distantiation from that Other who is a "je" in terms of gender but who is not "je," in terms of class, race, and culture. Yet the textual dialogue between *Juletane* and *Kamouraska* implicitly calls for greater solidarity, understanding, and exchange among women of the world, greater respect for that Other who is different from "je."

In the *dédoublement* of Juletane's diary writing, and in the insertion "en abyme" of Hélène's story, the author of *Juletane* has created a narratee who in discovering the diary and reading it, in sharing the narrative with the readers, contributes to making Juletane's voice heard. If Juletane and Elisabeth have not succeeded in their quest for a true Self, they have at least succeeded in transforming the meaning of women's enclosure and in sublimating madness or illness. The enclosed space has become the space that makes possible the constitution of their text. Madness or illness is the place from which their discourse emerges. In fact, without "démence" or "folie" Elisabeth would not have lived her story of passion with George Nelson, and a "normal" Juletane could not have challenged, even silently, the polygamic system by withdrawing from the household. Through literary creation, Elisabeth's and Juletane's discourse, muffled in madness and in the *dédoublement* of a narrative "je(ux)," has become a public discourse that makes possible their survival as female characters.

Notes

1. Anne Hébert, *Kamouraska* (Paris: Seuil, 1970); *Kamouraska,* trans. Norman Shapiro (New York: Crown, 1974). Page numbers are indicated in parentheses. For other studies of *Kamouraska,* see Agnès Whitfield, *Le Je(u) illocutoire: forme et contestation dans le nouveau roman québécois* (Quebec: Presses de l'Université Laval, 1987); Janet M. Paterson, *Anne Hébert: architexture romanesque* (Ottawa: Editions de l'Université d'Ottawa, 1985).

2. Emile Benveniste, *Problems in General Linguistics,* trans. Mary Elizabeth Meek (Coral Gables: University of Miami Press, 1971), 218.

3. Ibid., 220.

4. Ibid., 199.

5. Myriam Warner-Vieyra, *Juletane* (Paris: Présence Africaine, 1982); *Juletane,* trans. Betty Wilson (London: Heinemann, 1987). Page numbers are in parentheses. See Jonathan Ngate, "Reading Warner-Vieyra's *Juletane,*" *Callaloo,* 9, no. 4, (fall 1986): 553–64.

6. *Narratee* here translates the "narrataire," "c'est-à-dire quelqu'un à qui le narrateur s'adresse" (someone whom the narrator addresses). See Gerald Prince, "Introduction à l'étude du narrataire," *Poétique* 14 (1973): 178–96.

7. Juletane to some extent is more dispossessed and more alienated than Elisabeth. The new history, the official one, has erased her past and confused her identity. Her name is a foreign name: that of a former slave's master. One can play here with the polysemy of the word "person," indicating both the grammatical person and an individual. Without a name, talked about as a third person (une jolie négresse, la folle, la toubabesse), Juletane actually is a "nonperson," as Benveniste states it when he writes in *Problems in General Linguistics:* "The form that is called the third person really does contain an indication of a statement about someone or something, but not related to a specific 'person.' The variable and properly 'personal' element of these denominations is here lacking.... The consequences must be formulated clearly: the 'third person' is not a 'person'" (197–98).

8. For an evaluation of Laing, see Elizabeth Janeway, *Man's World, Woman's Place: A Study in Social Mythology* (New York: Morrow, 1971).

9. Hysteria as manifestation of mental disorder is reflected in its etymology, translating the social importance given to a woman's womb, and as a consequence, it becomes also important to her. Elisabeth and Juletane are longing for their mothers, from which they have been literally and metaphorically expelled. Juletane's mental state deteriorates after she has an accident that kills (expels from her womb) her stillborn baby and makes her unable to

have any more babies. Her womb, according to her husband's and society's expectations, has become useless and Juletane herself worthless.

10. Marie Cardinal is French from Algeria, Ken Bugul is from Senegal, Calixte Beyala is from Cameroun, and Jeanne Hyvrard is French and lived for some time in Martinique. See Françoise Lionnet, *Autobiographical Voices: Race, Gender, Self-portraiture* (Ithaca: Cornell University Press, 1989); Marguerite Le Clézio, "Mother and Motherland: The Daughter's Quest for Origins," *Stanford French Review* 19: 381–89; Elisabeth Mudimbe-Boyi, "Ken Bugul," in Anne Adams, ed., *Fifty African and Caribbean Women Writers* (Westport, Conn.: Greenwood Press, forthcoming).

11. See Sandra Gilbert and Susan Gubar, *The Madwoman in the Attic: The Woman Writer and Nineteenth-Century Literary Imagination* (New Haven: Yale University Press, 1979); Phyllis Chesler, *Women and Madness* (Garden City, N.Y.: Doubleday, 1972); Marilyn Yalom, *Maternity, Morality and the Literature of Madness* (University Park: Pennsylvania State University Press, 1985).

12. Chesler, *Women and Madness*, 4.

13. See Kate Millet, *Sexual Politics* (Garden City, N.Y.: Doubleday, 1970); and Betty Friedan, *The Feminine Mystique* (New York: Norton, 1963).

14. Ernest Pépin, "La femme antillaise et son corps," *Présence Africaine* 141 (1987): 181–93. I thank Kenric Tsethlikai for providing a translation of both Pépin's quotations.

15. Ibid., 192.

CHAPTER NINE

Mothers, Rebels, and Textual Exchanges

Women Writing in French and Arabic

MIRIAM COOKE

Seven years after their democratic revolution, the French invaded Egypt, the heart of the Arab world. They had come to share — and, en passant, to enhance — the glories of their civilization. Riding high on a self-congratulatory wave, they quickly moved on out of Egypt to the west and to the north. They seized as strongholds for their *mission civilisatrice* the Islamic Berber majoritarian Algeria and the multiconfessional and multicommunal Syria and Lebanon. Armed with high-sounding slogans, they proceeded to crush the Arabs' liberty, fraternity, and equality.

Unlike their British counterparts, who replaced them in Egypt and who later established hegemony in Palestine and Iraq, the French *colons* had a personal stake in the system they put in place in the Arab world. The *colons,* derived primarily from the lower, particularly rural, classes, sought their fortunes in this foreign adventure. Confident of their cultural and ethnic superiority over the "natives" they had come to rule and possess, they imposed their religion, systems of governance and education, and above all their language. By the end of the nineteenth century, French had become the language of instruction in Syria, Lebanon, and Algeria. It was also the preferred language of the elite in Egypt.

The impact of the French colonial venture in the Arab Mediterranean was not uniform, however. In Algeria, the French violently imposed a colonial

superstructure that alienated the indigenous population. The Algerians reacted by eschewing Western values and behavior. In reaction to attempts
by the French to educate and liberate Algerian women, the men cloistered
the women, lest the offending eye of the foreigner intrude upon the sanc-
tity of the home, their only arena of control. Although many of the women
acceded, not all did. A few Algerian women in the colonial period received
the benefits of the French system, particularly education. Yet, unlike the
men, they found that education was little or no guarantee of dignity or
status in society at large. Some strongly criticized the biculturalism inherent in a system that promoted women's self-confidence and self-assertion
outside the home but crushed any sign of autonomy within. Indeed, it was
those Algerian women who perceived the double standards of their education who were pioneers of francophone fiction in the Arab world. Unlike the
men who wrote just before and after the revolution of 1954–61, the
women did not write to distance themselves from the French but rather to
understand their own situation in a bicultural society. Discourse allowed
them to question values of a society that needed to marginalize women to
symbolize a control at the family level that could not be achieved at the
political level. Their writings at times attack Algerian men and praise the
colonial system for giving women advantages, despite the fact that they realized that these attentions might alienate them from their own society. Although the women were not blind to such a ploy, some recognized that
hope for autonomy, however limited, lay in the hands of those who could
control the men who would control them.

Neither Algerian women nor men generally had access to Arabic except
as a purely religious idiom, and Berber was not considered a literary language; hence it was not repressed but rather ignored. The mother tongue,
whichever it might be, was degraded and outlawed. Thus, their post-revo-
lutionary dilemma was at once political and existential: they rejected the
language of the colonizer in favor of their own. But what was their own language? Arabic or Berber? Once writers, usually male, had made their choice,
they were confronted with another dilemma: audience. They were no longer
merely writing for and against the Parisians, although they could if they
chose. Their potential readership had multiplied. They could write for the
entire Arab world if they wrote in classical Arabic, or for the Algerian Arabs
if they picked a local dialect, or for Berbers should they master the Berber
language. In general, this search for an appropriate language was debilitating, and writers could find themselves confronted with what Eric Sellin has
referred to as the "page blanche."[1]

In the eastern Mediterranean countries exposed to French culture and language, there was considerably more linguistic freedom in the postcolonial period. Despite the weight of the French presence and influence in Syria, Lebanon, and even to some extent in Egypt, Arabic continued to be taught and used. Arabic was the medium of religious instruction; it was also indispensable for the education of the complete intellectual. Private tutors taught the sons but also the daughters of the upper and middle classes the belles lettres for which French was considered insufficient. And so, contrary to current wisdom, it appears that a few Syrian, Lebanese, and Egyptian women were already writing Arabic poetry and literary prose in the 1860s.[2]

Unlike the Algerians, most educated Syrians, Lebanese, and Egyptians who wrote in the postcolonial era had the linguistic tools that allowed them to choose between French and another language. The French had left Egypt early in the nineteenth century; hence, the use of their language had long been a matter of choice, of snobbism even. When the French left Lebanon in 1943, their departure did not radically change the educational and linguistic situation. Because a majority of Lebanese were Christian and therefore pro-French as a result of centuries-long contact, there were few in power who called for radical reform that would threaten and possibly undermine the dominance of French. Although some writers, like the Muslim Layla Baalbaki, deplored the preference for French and even English, their protest was as much directed at their own bourgeoisie as it was at the departed mandatory power. In Syria, on the other hand, French influence was much weaker, and therefore the end of the mandate in 1946 did not confront the Syrians with a great dilemma.[3]

Hence, of the Arab countries colonized by the French in the nineteenth century, Lebanon and Egypt are the only two that had a relatively easy relationship with the language of the French after their departure. In each case, those who spoke and wrote in French did so as a result of a choice. These choices could be "passive" or "active." I define a passive choice as one that is made by another; for example, parents who send their sons and daughters to lycées, assuming that such an education is a surer provider of status, deprive them of their ability to choose. An active choice is made by the subject. By the time Egyptians and Lebanese graduated from high school, most found themselves more at home in one of the two languages or cultures. They then proceeded to hone that language, but without necessarily sacrificing the other. The second language provided the richness, the otherness that allowed the writer to appropriate the first. This appropriation was most commonly achieved in French by arabizing, by making French strange to the French. In some cases, when both languages were equally perfected, writers confronted the linguistic choice each time they put pen to paper.

This essay will examine a selection of Lebanese and Egyptian women's novels written in French and in Arabic. My concern here is not with the why of the linguistic choice but rather with its effect. What difference, if any, does the choice of language make in representing a political or social condition? A comparative reading of some francophone and Arabic novels by women during two periods, the 1950s, when postcolonial Arab patriarchies were in formation, and the mid-1970s to early 1980s, when the patriarchies were in deformation, should serve to illustrate the difference language choice makes in the epistemology of an Arab woman's literary text.

The 1950s novels are the Egyptian Andrée Chedid's *Le Sommeil délivré* (1954) (*From Sleep Unbound*) and the Lebanese Layla Baalbaki's *I'm Alive* (Ana ahya, 1958). The significance of this period is that it is soon after independence and acquisition of self-rule, when "the Arab world was swept with nationalist, socialist and communist ideals."[4] This period saw the rise of male power determined to marginalize any and all who might stand in its way.[5] Both novels describe a woman's struggle to assert herself against a society that is as yet unsure of itself and unready to accept such female self-assertion. The later novels are all by Lebanese: the francophone works are Etel Adnan's *Sitt Marie Rose* (1978) and Evelyne Accad's *L'Excisée* (1982); the Arabic novels are Hanan al-Shaykh's *The Story of Zahra* (Hikayat Zahra, 1980) and Emily Nasrallah's *Those Memories* (Tilka al-dhikrayat, 1978). These later novels deal with the first half of the Lebanese Civil War, 1975–82. This war provided a turning point for women writers. Social and political fragmentation allowed for the decentering of dominant male voices and the emergence of those of women whose writings with time and multiple translations have acquired a wide audience at home and abroad.

Le Sommeil délivré[6] is an anti-bildungsroman. It tells the story of a young girl who is snatched out of school in the middle of a class to be wed to an older, unattractive man whom she has never before seen. Her remonstrances are not heard; her recalcitrance is chastised. Education was supposed to qualify her for a good marriage, not for independence and personal fulfilment. Samya's story scripts the systematic destruction of a woman's life and imagination. Like the protagonist of Charlotte Perkins Gilman's *The Yellow Wallpaper*, she ends up sick, psychosomatically paralyzed, and alone in her coffinlike, velvet-curtained room, where she is daily visited by her repulsive husband and his sadistic sister. Any attempts to leave the prison/ room, or even only to make it more congenial, are immediately punished, and status quo is quickly restored. Her only distraction is a village girl whose passion is the fashioning of clay figurines. Ammal, whose name means Hope, symbolizes the creativity Samya cannot realize. The stifling tedium and prohibition on imagination and self-expression are briefly interrupted by the birth of Mia. But the little girl is soon dead, too fragile to survive the weight of the room. Samya turns her attention and hopes to Ammal. Finally, the unchanging prospect becomes unbearable. The future, shrouded in the dark, heavy velvet curtains that her husband keeps closed, stretches out bleakly before her. She summons up what little strength is left her; as Boutros bends over his immobile wife to plant his blubbery lips on her cool forehead, he feels the dagger enter his heart. Samya has virtually committed suicide.[7] But it is not a complete suicide, for Ammal is there, watching: "She knows she must go away from this place. When your fingers can give birth to creatures who are closer to life than the living will ever be, you are not alone. She must go away, far from the suffocation and decay that came from fear" (141).

Layla Baalbaki's *I'm Alive* is a less desperate, though equally angry novel. Lina Fayyad, the daughter of a wealthy entrepreneur, contravenes all the rules of her social station even as she claims that she wishes to conform (296–97). Without consulting her parents, let alone asking their permission, she answers an advertisement for employment. The employer, a friend of her father, is surprised but hires her on the spot. She gets no "job satisfaction" and soon matriculates in the university. She is disappointed in the students and faculty and withdraws. Aware of the social opprobrium attached to interaction with young men, she becomes involved with an Iraqi, Baha. Far from withdrawing into her shell, as did Samya, Lina lashes out at all who would try to block her search for freedom from social convention and the apparently inescapable fact of possession by men. She clearly articulates her goal and tells Baha: "You're a slave to the Party, I am free. I shall never submit to the ideas of any living being, even if that being were a god" (192). When she realizes that she has come to need Baha, she imagines his fragmentation into furniture and café objects so that she may leave them/ him (265–67). In the end, she wills him out of her life. She watches him dissolve only to be replaced by "a large idol called pride: my pride" (335). She must not rely on another to construct her future. The novel closes with her walking down the street, weeping for the loss of Baha. She runs into a woman in mourning who lost her son thirteen years ago. Weeping, she tells Lina, will not bring back the departed. Lina then makes a half-hearted attempt to get run over, but again she fails . . . or, again she succeeds to live.

Whereas Samya is afraid of everyone, Lina is filled with contempt for those with whom she comes into contact: her father for his ruthless exploitation and collusion with the French when they held mandatory power; her mother, as representative of all submissive women in this society, for her cowardice and acceptance of her husband's dalliance as well as his iron fist; her sisters for their empty-headedness; her boss for his puffed up arrogance as well as for his associations with her father; her colleague for his inability to see her beyond his own desires; the university students for their indifference to learning and their hollow ideological positions; men for their inability to relate to women except as sex objects;[8] Baha the good Communist when he announces that he is off to Saudi Arabia "to get a bit of money" (206). But above all, she despises herself when she finds herself doing what others expect, and when she is forced to participate in a corrupt system because, for example, of her father's successful international business deals, the profits of which are shared among the family members (e.g., 77, 97), or when she discovers that the company for which she works is in fact putting out anti-Communist propaganda.

Although *Sommeil* and *I'm Alive* are written in the first-person feminine, the perspective of the first is that of the wife and becoming-mother, whereas the perspective of the second is that of the daughter. Samya's mother died when she was very young, and she scarcely figures in the narrative. It is almost as though Samya must eliminate her own mother so as to exculpate her for what happens. Samya acquiesces to her situation until she finds and adopts someone better able than she to fulfill her dreams and aspirations for herself but also for other women. Whereas Samya has given up on her own sexuality and subjectivity and therefore needs to see beyond herself to a different future for women, Lina is the opposite. She may invoke her mother whenever she is in need, but when the reality of her mother becomes manifest, she remembers how inadequate her mother is as a role model.[9] For her part, her mother is horrified at her daughter's insistence on being different and uncontrollable. She urges marriage, but the only models that Lina has are those of her parents, of the Syrian colleague whose husband raped her every night (113–14), and of Baha's uncle who thought that beating his wife was a necessary part of matrimony (254–55)! Lina declares that she will never accept a man that her parents "buy" for her. When her mother slaps her for insolence, Lina has to rush to her room lest she return the slap (325). With considerable satisfaction, Lina remembers her mother's outcry: "Since when has a woman in our family walked the streets like a prostitute? Since when has one sat with men and stuck her nose into their affairs? Since when has one smoked and within her mother's sight? Tell me, when? Tell me, what's driven you to this rebellion, this non-conformity? What do you need: a dress? a car? money? a house?" (181–82). So these are the values that her mother advocates and that Lina repudiates.[10] In despair, thinking that she has lost everything by giving up work and university, Lina decides she would like to have a baby. At the first hint of what she is about to propose, Baha is outraged. Without protest, Lina accepts that there shall be no baby (319–22). She will never turn to anyone other than herself to weave her future, even if in the process she must commit millions of murders (334). Lina fights to fulfill her own dreams: if she cannot succeed for herself then all is lost. Lina is not struggling for other women except, perhaps, prescriptively.

Samya and Lina establish very distinct relationships with their environment. Samya's entire story transpires within the confines of oppressing rooms, the climax coming in her married home where as a paraplegic she cannot move out of the mausoleum of her room. Her imagination, so fertile when she was a child, becomes barren. Lina, on the other hand, moves around freely between home, work, street, and university. She has her own room; more, she has a key to this room, and she knows that it is here that her future must be made (340). She finds ways of having the space and luxury to exercise her imagination, even in the face of prosaic reality. Every encounter is accompanied by an internal commentary that allows her to hold on to her own perspective: while talking to her boss she keeps imagining the death she has planned for him (183–86, 222). Lina imagines people as things so that they should not have dominion over her (200). Alienation from her surroundings allows her to escape into the world of her imagination whenever necessary and thus to keep control.

Another major difference between these two novels can be read in these women's abilities to control their bodies. Samya is surrounded by people who tell her how she must move and dress. In fact, she ultimately discovers that the only control she has over her body is to paralyze it. This kind of repressive control leads to a rage that drives her to murder her husband, and through his murder, which assures her own physical destruction, she is making room for her vicarious survival. Marianne Hirsch's analysis of Euro-American literature, which explores mothers' anger, is helpful in understanding Samya's anger: "To be angry is to claim a place, to assert a right to expression and to discourse, a right to intelligibility... If we see anger as a particularly pointed assertion and articulation of subjectivity, we can use it as an 'instrument of cartography' to map the subjectivity of those who are denied it by culture and discourse."[11]

Sommeil begins and ends with an enactment of the murder, the only act that Samya can initiate and complete. The whole plot revolves around this moment of catharsis. *I'm Alive,* on the other hand, revolves around the daily activities of the heroine. Family, friends, colleagues, and acquaintances try to do to Lina as had been done to Samya, but she tirelessly and defiantly rejects others' attempts to curb and commodify her. In what has become a typical move among protagonists of women's Arabic fiction, she cuts her hair. She feels that her mother had tried to instill pride in her hair as a way to control her (31). Her mother's wistfulness at the loss of the beautiful hair is greatly exceeded by the father's anger: "Go away! Get out of my sight! Don't let me see you before your hair has grown back!" (32). To which outburst she responds: "My father's a fool." Lina's mother gives up trying to control her and instead hopes to deceive herself and the world that she has not in fact lost this control, and even if she has why then surely the father has not (167)! But they have lost control, because rebelliousness is as necessary to Lina's existence as food to her body. Even her body rebels: "I looked down to examine my body. It was enveloped in thick cloth that could not, however, hide the rebellion of my breasts" (140).[12] Again and again, she talks explicitly about pleasure (*lidhdha*). Her mother accuses her body of generating *lidhdha* (e.g., 141), and Lina keeps coming back to this accusation to enjoy its licentiousness. It empowers her so that she can describe the body of Baha with desire.[13] Desire makes her feel alive and centered: "I live life fully whereas they live on its margin" (153). Awareness of desire makes her reject motherhood because mothers cannot be sexual beings.

Each of these novels emerges out of a similar social and political context in which newly independent Arab states in the process of establishing infrastructures and of developing political systems are seeking to establish control. Their management of resources and people is reflected in the family, where control of women connotes not only social but also political power. In *Sommeil,* Samya does not know how to deal with the men who need to possess and dispose of her. Her only answer is to drain the life out of her legs. Her final and only act of volition is violent, and it will invite a violent response. The violence of Samya's end—a figuration of a woman's impotence against male domination—haunts the novel. Lina, on the other hand, never submits. She fights in any way possible to hold on to her destiny, but unlike Samya and all the people she knows (274–77), she cares less about the future than she does about the present. The struggle may appear reckless, but it is never suicidal.

The first half of the civil war in Lebanon, which stretched from 1975 until 1982, witnessed the formation of the first school of Arab women writers, the Beirut Decentrists. Decentered from the fighting and also from the putative heart of Lebanese culture, they found that the war temporarily suspended rigid social norms. With no helmsman at the wheel of Lebanese literature, rules of admission broke down. In unprecedented numbers women began to write and publish, and their versions of the war, a war of senseless violence become routine, began to be read. Their novels provide a counterpoint to those of the 1950s. Whereas the latter document women's lives during a period of national self-definition, the former are written about women who are living through a crisis of political but also of personal identity. Women's writings of the 1950s express a rebellion against the emergence of what Hisham Sharabi has called neopatriarchy; women's writings on the Lebanese war announce women's growing self-confidence and political effectiveness.

Etel Adnan's *Sitt Marie Rose*[14] is a prose elegy to a Christian teacher who was killed by four Maronite men upon their learning of her affair with a Palestinian man. The murderers are filled with dread at the enormity of her crime but also at Sitt Marie's strength and consequently her threat to them. The narrator assures the militiamen and the reader that destroying Sitt Marie will avail them little for she is but one tree in a forest. But the men know only how to kill, so they seek a solution in this killing. Assigning to themselves the role of judges, they condemn her to death. Sitt Marie does nothing to stop them. She does not try to justify herself to them, to argue, to fight. There is a sense of inevitability that pervades the novel. Savagely ripping her body apart under the stricken gaze of the deaf and dumb pupils who are Sitt Marie's students but also her adopted children, the men are consciously creating a new generation. It could be that this generation will re-create the violence they have just witnessed. We are allowed to hope that they will take on their teacher/mother's mission and forge links of love.

L'Excisée[15] hovers on the edge of the war. E cannot stand the restrictions of her life in Lebanon. She feels her father at every turn, even in the privacy of her own room. P, her lover in Beirut, provides hope of release, and so they marry. She follows him to his native village in some distant Arab land. E soon learns the vanity of expecting release through the agency of a man. He wraps her in a veil, relegates her to a harem, and expects her to act in the same way as the village women. He forgets their liberated meeting and respectful courtship. Stunned, E accepts until she is threatened with clitoridectomy. In fear for her own body and for the child now growing in her womb, she escapes. Only when she has reached the sea, the symbol of liberty, can she do away with herself and with her child. But she leaves an heir. The little village girl Nour, whose name means Light, accompanies her to the sea. As though sensing the destiny E has determined for her so that she may die without guilt, Nour allows herself to be handed over to an Egyptian woman, who whisks her away to freedom where she might fulfill E's ambitions. Nour closes the novel:

> Je veux qu'elle puisse être fière de moi, car elle m'a sauvée. Sa venue m'a sauvée. Grâce à elle, j'ai vu le soleil et la lumière. Grâce à elle, je ne porterai jamais de masque étouffant sur ma figure. Grâce à elle, on ne me coupera jamais le ventre comme on l'a fait à ma soeur, qui est sûrement en train de crier de douleur aujourd'hui. On m'a appelé Nour à ma naissance, mais sans elle je ne connaîtrais jamais le jour. Il faut que je vive pour aider mes autres soeurs. (170)

> [I want her to be able to be proud of me, because she has saved me. Her arrival saved me. Because of her I have seen the sun and the light. Because of her I shall never wear a stifling mask. Because of her, my stomach will not be cut like that of my sister, who is surely still screaming with pain. When I was born, they called me Nour (light), but without her I would never have known daylight. I have to live to help my other sisters. (translation mine)]

E combats the violence of her husband's society by doing violence to herself. Neither Sitt Marie nor E entertains the idea of killing the men who oppress them. To eliminate individual men is as useless as eliminating individual women. What matters is that there should be other women to carry on the mission.

Protagonists in the Arabic novels focus on themselves with little or no reference to another as an expression of hope beyond the self. They seek autonomy. Although Maha in Nasrallah's *Those Memories*[16] is a mother, her children enter the narrative indirectly only as details that flesh out her life. Maha had decided long ago that she had to leave her village and her mother and go to Beirut so as to hope to make a life for herself. The absent village and mother haunt the novel. The novel tells the story of her conversation with her best friend, Hanan, who had early in the events run away from her mother and the war. Although these two women, who had both run away from their mothers, had been very close friends, their relationship upon Hanan's return is adversarial. Maha feels that their different experiences during the period of the war have made it impossible for them to communicate. At the end, Maha realizes that living through the war has thrown her upon her own resources and that she can rely on no one other than herself. Elsewhere I have interpreted their relationship as embodying the two aspects of a single woman's struggle to come to terms with her environment. Should she stay or leave war-torn Lebanon? Maha recognizes that staying is existentially important for her. She has found a role for herself, one that will allow her to live fully in the present, and fully in the war.

Hanan al-Shaykh's Zahra is an unmarried woman obsessed by her mother and especially by her mother's contempt. At the beginning of *The Story of Zahra*,[17] Zahra describes herself as being as close to her mother as the navel is to its orange, a simile that evokes prebirth union. But the action contradicts this assertion or, perhaps, hope of symbiosis. Zahra's mother uses her daughter to conceal an affair, and later she openly mocks her. Like Maha when she left her village and her mother, Zahra begins to come into her own when she leaves Beirut and her mother. It is only then that she begins to achieve a level of autonomy free from the need to escape into an idealized community with another. Hirsch has written of such mother-daughter relationships that the daughter's

> imagination is fueled either by a longing to re-experience symbiotic union with the mother (by identification with her) or by a struggle against an identification which still reveals a profound and continued closeness. The content of plot is not a process of successive distancing but, rather, is a struggle with a bond that is powerful and painful, that threatens engulfment and self-loss even while it offers the very basis for self-consciousness. In these writings the pre-oedipal realm figures as a powerful mythic space, not irrevocably lost but continually present because it is recoverable in ideal(ized) female relationships. Pre-symbolic and pre-cultural, it points to an alternative to patriarchy and the logos — a world of shared female knowledge and experience in which subject/object dualism and power relations might be challenged and redefined.[18]

The war liberates Zahra from her need for her cruel mother so that, like Lina, she can relish the thought of hurting her, of publicly shaming her.

Continual sexual abuse makes Zahra act in a way that is labeled mad. She accepts the label and the accompanying electroshocks as long as she can escape to a bathroom when the outside world becomes too much to bear. Zahra can thus lock others out of her own precious space. The war reverses norms, and where others are disoriented by the chaos, Zahra finds new orientation. The woman who had always escaped interaction with others initiates a sexual liaison with a sniper. She daily returns to his lookout post to resume the previous day's adventures. When she finds herself too pregnant to abort safely, she, like Lina before her, decides that she would like to have a family. But the logic of the novel militates against such an outcome. Zahra has decided to live, but not in the war and not through herself but through another. The woman who wants to reproduce herself in another who will continue her struggle cannot survive. The man she has chosen to realize her newfound drive and orientation kills both her and the fetus. If she alone cannot forge an appropriate future for herself in this strangely congenial context, then there can be no future either for herself or for others. However, unlike the violent deaths of the protagonists of the francophone novels on the war, Zahra's is gentle, oneiric. It is an abstract dying dealt by the abstracted symbol of the war, the sniper.

All of the novels, whether they were written in the 1950s or over twenty years later, have strong women protagonists who resist society and the pressure to conform and obey, despite the knowledge that when they do, the community will try to destroy the rebel. As Dale Bauer tells us, society "responds with a counterstroke to overturn, negate, or appropriate the resistance. In this way, resistance is homogenized and made part of the community, made tame and domesticated . . . The individual's struggle against the social conventions which define and inscribe subjectivity into sociality reveal the structure by which the body (and especially women's bodies) is controlled, seduced and manipulated."[19]

It would seem that the structures by which Arab women's bodies are controlled, seduced, and manipulated and their ability to respond appropriately are perceived differently by women who write in French from those who write in Arabic. In the francophone novels, women are depicted as victims of destructive men and/or their surrogates. They express no desire for men, because men are the source of their woes. It is men, rather than society, who are responsible for women's oppression. Heroines of the Arabic novels are open in their articulation of their desires. They can approach men, make them listen to their point of view. It seems that it is not so much men as society that is to blame for everyone's oppression. The men may not listen, but they are presented in such a way that the reader feels that there is hope for change; men are educable; moreover, there seems to be a mandate to educate men.[20] None of the francophone heroines has a room of her own, a space that is free of men's physical or psychological invasions or even presence. All of Samya's attempts, however feeble, to rearrange and thus make her own the room to which she has been relegated are immediately undone. This is not a room in a home but a solitary confinement cell. Sitt Marie Rose had thought herself to be in charge of the schoolroom and the pupils until the butchers arrived and proved their mastery of the space.[21] E had escaped her room in Beirut, thinking that her father's crushing presence could be escaped. But she soon learned that there was no space she could possess that was not already possessed by a man. Almost as though taking this Western Woolfian construct and turning it on its head, these protagonists deny the possibility of escape within the culture. Rooms of one's own connote separation. And this separation is depressingly familiar to those who have been brought up in a segregated society. This is no escape but a prison guarded over by a male who has total, socially sanctioned power. Prison-consciousness pervades these works, as the women struggle to find some outlet for their pent-up emotions and desires. In each case, the struggle is too much, and the woman dies violently.

Protagonists of Arabic novels do not share this anguished relationship to their space. They may wish to escape the prison of the home, but home is more a mental construct than a concrete structure. The women struggle to assert themselves within their context, which they hope thereby to change. Each demands that others acknowledge the value of her independent existence in the hope that such an acknowledgment will change the one who made it. The women work within their context so as to achieve a measure of control that will allow for transformation. They are not restricted to special spaces but roam around freely, able to find refuge in a locked room, a bathroom, or the home.

The death of the francophone protagonists finds reprieve through the "birth" of another, through an adopted daughter who will carry the baton. Adoption is key, for none is survived by a biological daughter. Because the mother's body is implicated in the system, to be survived it must be transcended. Hirsch's description of the ways in which Euro-American women write mothers out of their texts is instructive: "Women writers' attempts to imagine lives for their heroines which will be different from their mothers' make it imperative that mothers be silent or absent in their texts, that they remain in the prehistory of the plot, fixed as both objects of desire and as examples not to be emulated."[22] Each protagonist constructs herself as a mother beyond the biological possibility of her body so that she may continue to function and to dream through the adoption of one or more children who will not be tainted by genetic association. The mother's body must be erased because it reifies the persistence of tradition and of a patriarchal system. The mother's body blocks the possibility of autonomy for women. Even before her own daughter dies, Samya in *Sommeil* has elected Ammal whose clay figurines symbolize the future she is expected to construct; Sitt Marie Rose is survived by her deaf and dumb schoolchildren who did not hear her screams and could not speak but who did witness her dismemberment and who will re-member her; E in *L'Excisée* adopts Nour before she kills herself and her fetus and then sends her into the world to do what she and her natural daughter could not have done. These adopted heirs are always innocent vessels for the needs and aspirations of foster mothers. For the future to be different, it must follow a break.

The Arabic protagonists are rarely mothers, and if they are, that is the least significant aspect of their lives. They present themselves as daughters of at best inadequate mothers. Their criticisms of their mothers facilitate their separation from them and particularly from their collusion in their own oppression. They cut the umbilical cord so as to take the first step toward subjectivity. They live intensely in the present and do not contemplate escapist options that would exonerate them and put the burden of responsibility and solution-finding on another in an impossibly distant future. It is they who must construct the future, and when they turn to others, their failure immediately announces itself.

Despite the difference in strategy, these Arabic and francophone women's writings all reject biological motherhood. By eliminating the physical fact of motherhood from a mother's perspective, as in the francophone novels, or from a daughter's perspective, as in the Arabic novels, the protagonists escape what Hirsch has called the "debilitating dichotomies of the maternal and the sexual, the maternal and the creative. By not being a mother, she can avoid being eliminated in the service of her son's or daughter's plot."[23] It is noteworthy that the francophone protagonists do not become foster mothers until the end of the novel. Thus, throughout the novel the woman remains in tension between her sexual self and her idealized self. Each sacrifices the sexual at the end of her story, having lived its potential in the text. Although mothers' bodies are excluded from all the texts, their metaphorical presence is felt throughout. In the francophone novels, mothers of the protagonists are absent. These women have no positive models; hence, they cannot themselves provide good examples. To become good mothers they must sever heredity and look for someone who does not need a model, who has an inherent power to create, to influence, and to change. Protagonists of Arabic novels have set themselves the task of making the break. Again and again, they remind themselves of their mothers' complicity in the system. They must cut the umbilical cord so as to be reborn without mothers and to fashion themselves anew for themselves.

Can we generalize beyond the texts under consideration? Generalizations are fraught with dangers, but they seem plausible and justified in considering the language-specific nature of Arab women's writings. A test case is Nawal Saadawi's Arabic *Woman at Point Zero*[24] (Al-mar'a 'ind nuqtat al-sifr, 1973). At first glance, it seems to subvert my thesis. The novel revolves around the execution of a prostitute for the murder of her pimp. Is this murder not a suicide very much in the vein of Samya's murder? I would argue that it is not. We meet Firdaws after the event, and we hear her tell the story defiantly and without despair. Firdaws tells her story to a psychiatrist on the night before her execution. It is a story of rebellion against all who tried to exploit her vulnerability. None could tame her. Every escape from someone who was trying to abuse her body ironically placed Firdaws in a situation better than the one she had just left. Each change put her a little more in control of the body others so coveted. Although she did finally commit murder and knew that her fate was sealed, she remains unrepentant and strong. This strength is demonstrated in her interview. Not a detail is slurred. She had not once given in but had lashed her way out of every corner into which they had tried to push her. The murder was not suicide but rather an affirmation of a woman's determination never to say yes. She lives in a society that makes women's lives impossible. To say no to such a society is to say yes to oneself. Her final act is the culmination of her nay-saying. She is completely in control, for she will not allow the interviewer to interpose even one word. Her physical death recedes in importance as the narrative of her successful rebellions takes center stage. A latter-day Scheherazade, she preserves her life in its telling.

Arab women's francophone writings seek hope from *outside*; their Arabic counterparts seek it from *inside*. Each sees clearly the problems in Arab society that prevent women from realizing their potential and their rights. These problems are both internal and external, requiring for their resolution a synthesis of both strategic approaches. The francophone Algerian woman Assia Djebar wrote an introduction to the French translation of Saadawi's *Woman at Point Zero*. It is a landmark event in this synthesizing project. Djebar's text constitutes a francophone Arab woman writer's recognition of the significance of the feminism of an Arabic text written by another Arab woman. It is an acknowledgment that a single woman who has the courage to sacrifice herself in the path of self-fulfilment is not crazy, weak, and overwhelmed by forces beyond her control. She is a strong woman who refuses to live in a society that will not respect her. Her anger for herself is a model and guide for others who must learn how to say no so that they may live beyond their narrative.

Notes

1. Eric Sellin, "Obsession with the White Page, the Inability to Communicate, and Surface Aesthetics in the Development of Contemporary Maghrebian Fiction: The *Mal de la page blanche* in Khatibi, Fares, and Meddeb," *International Journal of Middle Eastern Studies,* 20/2 (May 1988), 165–73.

2. A few examples of this early women's literary production may be found in Margot Badran and Miriam Cooke, eds., *Opening the Gates: A Century of Arab Feminist Writing,* (Bloomington: Virago/Indiana University Press, 1990).

3. Layla Baalbaki is disturbed by her own preference for things French, including food, and insists three times in a single paragraph: "I'm not French!" (77). When a stranger in *I'm Alive* says hello, Lina responds inwardly: "Hello . . . Hello . . . I hate the English language" (95); *I'm Alive* (*Ana ahya* [Beirut, 1958]). English became the preferred second language, as is the case in other Arab countries that rid themselves of French colonial rule.

4. Bouthaina Shaaban, *The Prism and the Promise,* forthcoming (Indiana University Press).

5. In *Both Right and Left Handed* (Bloomington: Indiana University Press, 1991), Bouthaina Shaaban writes of men's fear of women that overrides all other fears.

6. Andrée Chedid, *Le Sommeil délivré.* I have not had access to the original French, hence the quotations are taken from Sharon Spencer's English translation, *From Sleep Unbound* (Athens, Ohio: Swallow Press, 1983).

7. This Egyptian Clytemnestra, to quote Marianne Hirsch, must "be killed because she is not the virgin mother who had become a cultural ideal: she is guilty of having murdered her husband, and, worst of all, she is politically active and aware." *The Mother/Daughter Plot: Narratives, Psychoanalysis, Feminism* (Bloomington: Indiana University Press, 1989), 30.

8. When she went to the cinema alone, men sniffed around her unable to believe that she was not a prostitute (60–67). The same was true when she sat alone in the café (263–64). Even the philosophy professor whom she had admired when she first went to university was really only interested in young women (130).

9. This is a good example of what Elaine Showalter has called "matrophobia," which she defines as self-hatred that is experienced as a "fear of becoming one's mother." "Toward a Feminist Poetics," in *The New Feminist Criticism,* ed. Elaine Showalter (New York: Pantheon Books, 1985), 135.

10. "I don't care about my mother. I don't love her. I don't respect her. I'm just used to having her in the house" (259).

11. Hirsch, 169–70.

12. But this body does not rebel against her; she is so much in control that she considers herself to be responsible for whatever her body does, even when it is conforming: "I create my body to live a trivial life like that of other bodies, so that it will be praised" (118).

13. "I had a crazy wish to touch his hands" (152). After Baha tells her of his wish to beat her, he imagines how she would defend herself by pressing her body close to his (257).

14. Etel Adnan, *Sitt Marie Rose,* trans. Georgina Kleege (Sausalito, Calif.: Post-Apollo Press, 1982).

15. Evelyne Accad, *L'Excisée* (Paris: L'Harmattan, 1982).

16. Emily Nasrallah, *Those Memories* (Tilka al-dhikrayat) (Beirut: Muassasat Naufal, 1980).

17. Hanan al-Shaykh, *The Story of Zahra* (Hikayat Zahra) (Beirut: Dar al-Nahar li al-Nashr, 1980).

18. Hirsch, 133.

19. Dale M. Bauer, *Feminist Dialogics: A Theory of Failed Community* (Albany: SUNY Press, 1988), 167.

20. Baha reveals to Lina how society has forced him to act in certain ways. His appetite for the female body is not his but one that is imposed, and to rid himself of the need to see nudity, he keeps going to the cinema (179). He tells Lina defiantly that for him she is just another woman. Lina predictably is infuriated (180). He tells her that he had wanted to beat her to a pulp the previous day "just like Uncle used to pulverize his wife's body." Lina realizes that even though he could not possess her in real life, he would try to do so in his dreams (254–55). This was the way he was educated; he knew no other model.

21. "In the classroom, held in their bewildering simplicity, is the group of justices, Mounir, Tony, Fouad, and Bouna Lias. Before them, Marie-Rose, beneath the extinguished electric light bulb hung by a cord, and the deaf-mutes. On the wall there is a crucifix. But, in this room, Christ is a tribal prince. He leads to nothing but ruin" (104).

22. Hirsch, 34.

23. Hirsch, 64.

24. Nawal Saadawi, *Woman at Point Zero* (Al-mar'a 'ind nuqtat al-sifr) (London: Zed, 1984).

CHAPTER TEN

"Nouvelle écriture" from the Ivory Coast

A Reading of Véronique Tadjo's
A vol d'oiseau

MICHELINE RICE-MAXIMIN

Véronique Tadjo is a relatively new and radically different voice in African literature written in French. This literature was dominated by male writers until Mariama Bâ from Senegal, author of *Une si longue lettre* (*So Long a Letter*) (1979) gave African women writers in French international recognition. Tadjo differs from the best-known first generation of African women writers and from most of her contemporaries, such as Mariama Bâ, Aoua Kéita, Aminata Sow Fall, Aminata Maïga Ka, Catherine N'Diaye, Nafissatou Diallo, Werewere Liking, and Ken Bugul. What sets her prose and poetry apart is the way in which her work signals a new sensibility that marks the advent of a new moment in postcolonial African literature.

Although the book jacket of *A vol d'oiseau* describes it as a "novel," this text is a nontraditional narrative in which Tadjo makes unusual use of typeface, typography, fragmentation, irony, parody, and transgression. Moreover, her use of the ancestral art of storytelling helps undermine the tale's only apparent fragmentation, as she mimics and defies the conventions of the traditional novel. The author does not tell us explicitly what she wants us to see or understand, because she does not herself know the answers to the questions she poses and the situations she presents. The changes in style, genres, scenes, moods, emotions, or voices actually establish, at times, both a distance and a connivance between the narrator and the reader.

Véronique Tadjo was born in Paris in 1955 and raised in the Ivory Coast. Beginning in 1984, she traveled and lived in Washington, D.C., Great Britain, Mexico, Nigeria, and France. As she says, she discovered her country away from home. And she quickly began to write about her experiences and observations. In 1983 Hatier published her first poetry book, *Latérite*, which received the prize of the Agence de Coopération Culturelle et Technique. Hatier also published *La Chanson de la vie et autres histoires,* and J. B. Lippincott published *Lord of the Dance: An African Retelling* (1989), which tells the story of the Senufo people of the Ivory Coast. Tadjo herself did the art work and illustration for these two works. Her second novel, *Le Royaume aveugle,* was published in 1991 by L'Harmattan. *A vol d'oiseau,* her first "novel," was published by Nathan in 1986.

The title *A vol d'oiseau* suggests not only something "easy" to read but also the modes of perception of a flying bird. Tadjo invites the reader to enter, see, read, and hear her text from such a vantage point. The size of the book is unconventionally small.[1] Ninety-six pages contain ninety-two chapters divided into twenty-one larger units. All ninety-two chapters are given plain Roman numerals, whereas the twenty-one units all start on the right-hand page and have bold Arabic numerals. There are also eight blank pages. The editing and publishing information[2] follows the text at the bottom of pages 2 and 96, showing that "il n'y a pas de frontière" (10) (There are no borders to cross) between the various environments or situations in which we can find ourselves, in the same way that there exists none for the bird in space.

Tadjo underlines the interconnectedness of things, a sense of borderless distance and vision, with an accurate eye for details. Like birds that tend to have a cyclical existence, her book seems to turn on itself in telling about destruction and reconstruction, and in beginning and ending with images of decay and rebirth. The narrator-bird finds herself in the middle of various cities (with characteristic urban problems), various world events (mainly painful ones), or everyday life happenings. Above all is a love affair turned sour. Like some birds flying in long stretches, the narrator-bird literally flies from one site to another, from one mood to another, from one story, tale, or report to another, an overall design as fragmented as the landscape seen during a flight.

A vol d'oiseau is indeed a different "novel." An unidentified italicized voice speaks of "une histoire sereine avec un début et une fin" (a simple story with a beginning and an ending) only to add that this is not reality. And only at the very beginning do we find a traditional, conventional, chronologically constructed story, that of a love affair that ends as "une sale affaire" (6) (a sordid affair).

An anonymous voice speaking through the epigraph invites the reader, in an intimate tone, to some form of total love:

Si tu veux aimer
Fais-le
Jusqu'au bout du monde
Sans faux détours
A vol d'oiseau.

[If you want to love
Do it
To the ends of the earth
Without deviation
Straight as the bird flies.]

Should we not also take this as a subtle clue to read the text in a global manner, from a bird's-eye view, that is, seen from above or at a distance, hence in an overall and cursory manner, hastily, superficially, and rapidly with little attention to detail?

At the same time, however, *A vol d'oiseau* betrays a conscious love for small details, for careful observations and descriptions. The narrator thus entices the reader to enter her mind, her intimacy, in a very calculated way. In fact, nothing is superficial, random, or rapid. Such a contradiction between the title and what seems to be the reality of the book almost leads us astray and certainly tests our vigilance.

Following the opening and inviting voice of the epigraph is another voice, in italics. This time the reader gets a distinct feeling of entering in the middle of an ongoing conversation or argument. The new voice is confessional, almost defensive, as if under attack by some almighty authority on style and form:

Bien sûr, j'aurai moi aussi aimé écrire une histoire sereine avec un début et une fin. Mais tu sais bien qu'il n'en est pas ainsi. Les vies s'entremêlent, les gens s'apprivoisent puis se quittent, les destins se perdent. (2)

[Naturally I, too, would have liked to write a simple story with a beginning and an ending. But you know very well that this is not possible. Lives intermingle, people become close and then move apart, destinies fade away.]

The narrator's desire for an unconventional structure reflects her constant questioning, not only of what happened to her but also of the complex relationship between reality and imagination, between reality and art, between reality and literature. Although puzzling, these three paragraphs provide a concise summary of and a guide to the fascinating stories that follow.

At one level *A vol d'oiseau* tells of the consequences of a love affair between a young African woman and the husband of her American host family in Washington, D.C. Tadjo writes this story, the traditional, conventional, chronologically constructed one of chapter I, in the third person as a condensed novel in itself. She starts with a physical description of "l'homme" with an emphasis on his voice and continues with the events that lead to his divorce:

> En le regardant allumer le feu, elle sut qu'elle allait l'aimer. . . .
>
> Un matin, elle écrivit ces quelques mots sur un bout de papier et le lui tendit: "Je suis désespérément amoureuse de vous."
>
> . . . Ils commencèrent par se voir seuls en ville, puis ils passèrent des après-midi ensemble. Tous les soirs, ils rentraient séparément.
>
> . . . Il lui arrivait aussi de partir en promenade avec sa femme . . . elles sympathisèrent. . . . Elles avaient l'impression d'être amies.
>
> Un jour, elle tomba malade de cette situation.
>
> . . . Elle décida que ce serait leur dernier rendez-vous. Dans la chambre d'hôtel, ils se dirent des mots d'adieu.
>
> Pourquoi a-t-il fallu que ce fût justement ce jour-là ? Pourquoi a-t-il fallu que sa femme les vît sortir de là?
>
> Il paraît que la maison est à vendre. Elle a gagné son divorce et les enfants sont à sa charge. (4–6)

> [Watching him light the fire, she knew that she was going to love him. . . .
>
> One morning, she wrote the words, "I am desperately in love with you," on a piece of paper and handed it to him.
>
> . . . They started by meeting alone in town, then they spent their afternoons together. But every night, they came home separately.
>
> . . . Sometimes she would also take a walk with his wife.
>
> . . . They came to know each other. . . . It seemed as if they were friends. But one day, she grew sick of the situation.
>
> . . . She decided that this would be their last time together. In the hotel room, they said their goodbyes.
>
> Why did it have to be that same day? Why did his wife have to see them leaving there?
>
> It seems the house is for sale. She won the divorce and the children are in her custody.]

This detached and rapid account ends the conventionally told version of the love affair and contrasts with the rest of the text written in a radically different style. This stylistic shift reveals how, at another level, *A vol d'oiseau* is an impressionistic and cubist rendering of the narrator's state of heart, mind, and body following the broken love affair. She tells of her almost uncontrollable desire for "l'homme," of her trying desperately to rid herself of that desire, and the beginning of her relationship with a new lover. She portrays this against a harsh background of the contemporary miseries afflicting the African, American, and European continents. The contradictions she feels in her desire for "l'homme" and a desire to free herself of him parallel the many paradoxes of modern life in big cities such as Washington, D.C., or Abidjan.

After writing this traditionally recounted story of the love affair, the first unit of the book begins to change totally, dispersing and falling apart to such a point that its last chapter (VII) is but one single sentence: "Il n'y a pas de frontière" (10). Here we embark on a different journey where we have to abandon our tendency to compartmentalize our general vision of life. We have to do this to understand and solve the issues raised by the novel as well as the narrator's private, public, or collective problems. Still another sentence (from the voice in italics) tells us what the narrator intends by telling and retelling tales and myths, all addressing personal and public survival, whether it is the survival of the young woman in the initial love story (chapter I), the survival of a beggar (chapter XIII), the survival of a young dancer, or the more global survival of the African continent: "Ta force surgira de tes faiblesses éparses et, de ton humanité commune, tu combattras les tares érigées en édifices royaux sur les dunes du silence" (2) (Your strength will spring from your scattered weaknesses, and with your shared humanity, you will be able to fight the defects erected as royal edifices on the silent dunes).

The narrator expresses herself in a polyvocal way, using first-, second-, and third-person singular as well as the passive voice. However, the voices all represent a single narrator-bird-storyteller. The blank pages provide a rest, a pause in the telling of the stories, similar to an appropriate stop in flight and a closing down of vision or the shutting of the eyes in landing for a bird. Indeed, as privileged readers we are this bird in flight, far above the earth and every so often, zooming down from a global, panoramic, puzzlelike view to a more myopic, detailed one. In this text, Tadjo's strategy is multifaceted. Various devices play different roles in the portrayal of the characters, as can be seen in chapter XIII with the subtle, progressive, and somewhat generic portrayal of a young deaf teenager stabbed by a jealous older beggar:

> Pourtant, le matin *il* était là. Toujours à la même place, comme hier et comme demain sans doute. *Il* était là avec son boubou sale et son turban aux couleurs fanées, assis contre un arbre, la canne à ses côtés. *Il* avait le

visage fatigué et les mains osseuses. *Il paraissait rêver, mais à quoi ressemblent les rêves d'un homme usé?* (25–26, emphasis added)

[And still, in the morning *he* was there. Always in the same place, like yesterday and again tomorrow without a doubt. *He* was there with his dirty boubou and his turban of faded colors, sitting against a tree with a cane at his side. *He* had a tired face and bony hands. *He* seemed to dream, but of what does an exhausted man dream?]

Then follows the description of the arrival of the teenager: "Seulement, voilà, un jour *l'enfant* arriva. On ne sait d'où, mais un jour, il fut là, planté comme un jeune manguier" (26, emphasis added). (Only, then, one day *a child* arrived. No one knew from where but, one day, he was planted there like a young mango tree.)

We are left with a feeling of anonymity and distance but at the same time with a definite and precise vision of the characters. Another form of anonymity in *A vol d'oiseau* is the fact that all the characters have only generic names such as "l'enfant sourd," "l'autre," "le vieux," "le garçon." The narrator herself remains nameless just as her lovers do. The exception is Akissi, the only character called by her name: "Il fait chaud, il fait noir, et je pense à Akissi" (12) (It is hot, it is dark, and I think of Akissi). We should note that in Tadjo's work Akissi is a rather mysterious intertextual character, first mentioned in *Latérite*.[3] In *Le Royaume aveugle*, she is the daughter of King Ato IV and only then becomes a fully developed character. In fact, Tadjo's first two works—*Latérite* and *A vol d'oiseau*—seem to be a sort of introduction to Akissi's life story as fully recounted in *Le Royaume aveugle*. Generally, only various epithets identify people or places, such as "la grande ville de pierre qui maintenant a froid" (the big town of stone that now feels the cold) or "cette ville qui n'a pas d'odeur" (the town with no smells). The narrator names explicitly only Washington, D.C., Abidjan, and other African or European cities that are the sites of crucial events in her life or world disasters. The other unnamed sites, describing general misery, could be almost anywhere on the various continents—thus their generic character.

The impression of vagueness and anonymity produced by this effect introduces not only ambiguity but also a certain universality. In this anonymity, the polyvocal narrator can find the power to avoid narrow definitions, enjoy a greater freedom as well as a sense of liberation that gives her more strength. She can act like and assume the different voices composing her personality. This particularity also underlines cultural differences, and at times, for instance, the narrator calls upon our sense of vision and smell to become part of our reading experience, a practice uncommon to the traditional way of relating to a written text. Furthermore, this anonymity reinforces the allegory and potentially makes everything allegorical.

At still another level *A vol d'oiseau* is concerned with the "humanité commune" as reflected in those various tales, mythical, real, or surreal, told in the only nonfragmented units (2, 3, 5, 9, 10, 16, and 17), giving them more strength and fullness on the page — as we see them — as well as to our ears — as we hear them. These tales represent the collective consciousness, the popular wisdom and memory of the people. They have, each in its own way, a cathartic function for the narrator. They sustain her and eventually help in her healing process. They also participate in the creation of her new conscious self, capable of speaking in different voices, each recalled by the triggering of specific memories.

Indeed, interspersed allegorical tales are crucial to the development of the narrative. For instance, one tale (chapter XXXI) symbolizes the narrator's relationship with "l'homme" as it reaches an apocalyptical high, ending with her own symbolic death. A blank page follows, allowing the narrator and the reader a long needed respite as after a traumatic experience. In the next tale (chapter XXXII) the narrator clearly identifies with a young invalid boy: "Pour la jeune fille, le garçon est devenu une écharde dans sa chair, une vision de sa propre blessure, comme cette maladie qu'elle porte en elle et qui lui ronge l'âme" (43) (For the young girl, the little boy is like a thorn in her flesh, a reminder of her own wound, like the illness she carries within herself and torments her soul). Caring for him and giving him some money alleviates her own anguish, and later she befriends him. After the young boy is robbed, she gives him a large amount of money to restock his stolen cigarettes and candies. Afterwards, however, he avoids her: "ils ont pris l'habitude de se considérer comme deux étrangers dans la ville" (46) (they now behave like any two strangers in the city). At this, the narrator of *A vol d'oiseau* then realizes how she, too, has become estranged from "l'homme," avoiding him, because of a sense of betrayal.

Another tale (chapter LXIII) tells of a couple madly in love who have a child. They teach him to be generous. They teach him love and also to believe in himself. They want him to rebuild the cities destroyed by violence and oppression. The narrator strongly identifies with that child, who like her

> ne voyait que désespoir. Bien sûr, la ville était brillante de lumières et
> d'envies mais il suffisait de faire un pas pour rencontrer la boue et la saleté.
> Les gens étaient parés d'or mais il suffisait de tourner la tête pour voir des
> infirmes en haillons et des enfants sauvages. (70)

[saw nothing but despair. Of course, the city shimmered with lights and desires but it took him only one more step to see the mud and the filth. The people were decorated with gold but only a turn of the head brought into view the disabled in rags and wild children.]

Just like the narrator, this child feels exiled, and "ses yeux filmaient chaque chose" (his eyes recorded everything). Like her, he feels that he is changing a great deal and losing faith. Like her, he is assaulted by anguish, and it is at this very moment that he falls in love with a woman who considers herself asexual, for whom time is no obstacle and love not a primary concern. She is innocent. He burns with desire for her. Like the narrator of *A vol d'oiseau*, he is obsessed with the smell and the scent of his loved one who is not yet ready for a serious love relationship. And because the young boy is not ready to take no for an answer, one evening he gives her something to drink and then rapes her. In the morning, she wakes up pregnant: "Je me meurs.... Cet enfant n'est pas de moi. Il amènera le malheur" (72). (I am dying.... This child is not mine. He will bring unhappiness.) The young man realizes the horror of his act and wants to undo it. But it is too late. Everything has been destroyed:

> Un souffle d'air violent brûla les êtres et renversa les buildings. La peau se détacha en plaques. Les yeux s'asséchèrent. Les cheveux tombèrent par touffes. Tous moururent violemment. Le fer se mit à fondre et coula le long du sol. Un énorme nuage-champignon sculpta l'horizon incendié. (72)

> [A violent breath of air burned the people and upturned the buildings. Skin pulled away in layers. Eyes dried up. Big tufts of hair fell out. Everyone died violently. Iron melted and swept down to the soil. The inflamed horizon sculpted itself into a huge mushroom cloud.]

In this apocalypse, all physical signs of beauty as well as organs of visual sensation are violently obstructed, so as to prevent anyone from ever seeing and reporting. For the narrator this event recalls her own affair with "l'homme," and she realizes that she, too, has lost all feelings of sensation and now experiences a sort of illness: "Je la connais cette maladie qui me ronge les veines et me fait un sang d'encre. Je la sens cette maladie qui me fait tourner la tête en plein soleil" (79). (I recognize this illness that gnaws at my veins and turns my blood to ink. I can feel this illness that makes me turn my head in the face of the sun.)

The next and last tale (unit 17) follows this apocalyptic tale of death, but without a pause this time although it will be followed by a blank page of rest. This tale is about a magician visited by a young woman who wishes access to the formula of eternal happiness. She tells the old magician that she does not know why she has come to see him, then continues:

> Je ne connais pas la nature de ma joie. Elle apparaît et disparaît. Rien ne semble statique. Tout est mouvant et je suis prise dans un tourbillon. Je ne vois plus la différence entre le rêve et la réalité. (75)

> [I do not know the nature of my joy. It appears and disappears. Nothing seems static. All is mobile and I am drawn into a whirlwind. I can no longer see the difference between dream and reality.]

The narrator shares this young woman's state of confusion, constantly oscillating among several worlds, countries, cities, lovers, and emotional states in which reality and dream are blurred. Then, after the protagonists of this tale have made love, while the magician sleeps, the young woman decides to open his brain, after having gone with him through a glass labyrinth, symbolic of the transparency and openness of her vision. She will finally find herself in his brain, and what she sees frightens her:

> C'était un désert de tristesse et de solitude. On aurait dit un champ de bataille....
>
> Elle allait s'enfuir, quitter cet endroit de désolation quand, au loin, elle remarqua un lac et, au-delà, une plaine dont l'herbe semblait verte et souriante. La terre y était riche. (75)

> [It was a desert of sadness and solitude. It looked like a battlefield....
>
> She was going to run away and leave that place of desolation when, in the distance, she noticed a lake and, beyond that, a plain on which the grass seemed green and smiling. The soil there was rich.]

She desperately tries to reach this haven, a synonym not only of freedom but also of hope, just like the narrator's freedom from "l'homme" and her hope for a new self. Through this tale of love and excessive curiosity, the narrator reveals herself more intimately. Just like the the young woman of the tale, she, too, seeks the key to happiness. She, too, first loses her own identity in order to find herself after her traumatic love affair.

While showing the evolution of the narrator's feelings through the ordeal of her recovery, these four tales (units 9, 10, 16, and 17) also tell of events in society on both a collective and an individual level. At the same time they provide emotional support for the hardships encountered in her everyday life. These four different tales are autonomous intertexts that can easily be detached from the general personal text. The narrator emphasizes their oral, traditional, and thus independent nature by constantly pointing out that these are transmitted stories:

On m'a raconté cette histoire et c'est ainsi que je vous la livre. (23)

[I am telling you this story exactly as it was told to me.]

Ce n'est pas moi qui le dis. Je l'ai lu quelque part. (38)

[These are not my words. I read them somewhere.]

These passages recall the traditional formulas that African griots and storytellers in the Caribbean use at the conclusion of storytelling gatherings called to entertain and educate. As in the oral tales, the narrator gives up her voice to a protagonist who in turn tells her or his own story. The result is an unbroken chain of stories told in a succession of voices. However, these independent intertexts, far from being digressions, establish a relation of analogy between the narrator's story and the other ones serving as background. They link the past to the present. They are the narrative thread contributing to the evolution of the global story and of the narrator. As she says, the stories have to be told and heard whatever their nature is, for

Il y a une histoire en chaque être. (15)

[There is a story within each human being.]

L'histoire de la misère se raconte. (23)

[The story of misery can be told.]

L'amour est une histoire qu'on n'arrête pas de conter. (53)

[Love is a story that keeps on being told.]

The narrator realizes more and more that the ancestral art of storytelling is the connection that can help her hold together the various events of her life, past, present, and future. The repetitive structure of the text fuses both the personal and the public spheres in her desire to give a voice to those who cannot speak or be heard well enough. In fact, she is just like the young actress of the tale in unit 3, who says that in the play, "je *représente* le peuple. Symboliquement" (20, emphasis added). (I *represent* the people. Symbolically.)

These tales also play another important role. Throughout the novel they are the elements cementing the sufferings and dilemmas as well as the joys assailing the narrator. They give her new hope and lead her to an understanding and reconciliation. Furthermore, their very pattern adds to the circular structure of the text, reflecting the narrator's way of thinking. There are important differences between the chronological and traditional story of chapter 1 and the other ninety-one chapters, which move in a different rhythm, involving a pattern of call and response, as in the African and Caribbean oral tradition. Although much remains implicit, it is the reader's task to decipher the somewhat complex reality of this polyvocal text.

For the narrator, the stories of both her country and her personal life are thus closely tied. The African continent becomes a metaphor for her own burning unsatisfied desire, a feeling linked to hunger and famine: "je découvrais la famine de mon désir" (80) (I was discovering the famine of my desire). She therefore can see starving Ethiopian children with their "ventres ronds comme des ballons de carnaval" (stomachs as round as carnival balloons) or the "petite fille qui refuse la nourriture parce que son corps a oublié" (83) (the little girl who refuses food because her body too has forgotten it). In Tadjo's text, "desire" is a key "character" through whom the narrator can actually win access to her very past and present. Desire is also like a second skin on her body, an integral part of herself, a force capable of burning her. In a lyrical passage desire appears as a phoenix, a symbol of her new life, and goes through the test of fire in order to be reborn and purified, with a new consciousness. Desire reconciles her with her past. In this oscillation between public and personal recollections, the narrator's own misery becomes part of the global one, because as she said earlier, "Il n'y a pas de frontière." Whether she deals with time, space, or human experiences, everything is in a state of fusion. In the text, images of war and cataclysms evoke that fusion, or the terror felt, while images of calm waters and green pastures signify promises of tranquillity and hope. In playing with these different elements, the narrator recognizes that there are no borders in the unfolding of our lives. Her refusal to isolate events, to inscribe them in her text in a controlled frame, or always to find a beginning and an end reflects what Carol Gilligan calls a "feminine consciousness," which, we think, is not solely confined to women:

> The psychology of women that has consistently been described in its greater orientation toward relationships and interdependence implies a more contextual mode of judgment and a different moral understanding. Given the differences in women's conceptions of self and morality, women bring to the life cycle a different point of view and order human experiences in terms of different priorities.[4]

This passage describes Tadjo's textual strategy well. Her apparently fragmented text is actually a very unified story that conveys a stream of consciousness–like style that adds an oral dimension to her text. The ninety-two chapters are carefully streamed into a cyclical "puzzle" with a dynamic, circular, evolving pattern. The very writing of that puzzle helps the narrator to "fleurir en hibiscus épanouis" (96) (bloom as a full-blown hibiscus) and also satisfies the reader willing to follow the narrator's words:

> Je réarrange le puzzle, déplace les moments, récupère les souvenirs. Tu vis ta vie, je vis la mienne. Il y a mille histoires, mille saisons du cœur. . . .
> Je juxtapose les destins, enregistre les sensations. . . .
> Je dépasse les années, opère des flash-back et analyse les gestes. (91)

> [I am rearranging the puzzle, displacing moments, and recovering memories. You live your life, I live mine. There are a thousand stories, a thousand seasons of the heart. . . .
> I juxtapose destinies, record sensations. . . .
> I move beyond the years, enact flashbacks, and analyze the gestures.]

Indeed when the narrator refers to a particular element, fact, character, or story, it is up to us to make the appropriate or multiple connections. Tadjo makes us consider reality globally in order to survive in our chaotic world. There is no distinction between personal and collective suffering. As for the representation of time, there is no distinction between past, present, and future. Jeanne Hyvrard calls this "fusional" time, allowing us to "dire le futur et le passé"[5] (evoke both past and present at the same time). At other times, it does seem as if narrator and reader play a game of hopscotch, jumping in and out of both space and time. The reader experiences a sort of horizontal cross-reading, transported back and forth by the movements created by the transgression from one genre, story, and country to another. At the end of her text, the narrator better appreciates the creative process that was at work in the writing of her text and in her life. She has a clearer sense of what happened to her in that "sale affaire." She realizes that she has created something bigger than the reality that has isolated her, and which now leaves her with a feeling of being in exile and of solitude:

> Ici, il n'y a plus de griots mais des poètes. . . . Tu t'ornes de ton écriture. Elle devient ton identité, ton gagne-pain, ta raison de vivre. . . . Tu t'enfermes dans ta création et les mots t'ensevelissent et les phrases te suffoquent. . . . (64)

> [Here there are no more griots but only poets. . . . You decorate yourself with your writing. It becomes your identity, your livelihood, your reason to live. . . . You shut yourself up in your creation and the words enshroud you and the sentences suffocate you. . . .]

At the end the narrator has come full circle and experiences a cathartic rebirth: "Il fallait être folle pour penser que les corps bombarderaient la solitude. Que le plaisir enfanterait un langage fertile" (86). (One had to be crazy to think that solitude would be assaulted by the body. That pleasure would give birth to a fertile language.) She resolves her contradictions and conflicts and gains a strong sense of freedom and empowerment, and nothing but her writing will remain (90). It is her anguish and hope that engender her creative writing. Writing personally and intimately helps her find that open space that will liberate her. Her strong desire for Memory, for the Past, for the Rituals provides the catharsis for her pain:

> Je veux verser du gin et appeler les dieux. . . . Dire les mots sacrés pour apaiser le feu, réduire en cendres les promesses données. (30)
>
> [I want a libation of gin and I want to hail the gods. . . . To utter the sacred words that will quiet the flames and turn the promises to ashes.]

> Retrouver le présent. . . .
>   J'ai besoin du fétiche qui efface les mémoires. (31)
>
> [To recapture the present. . . .
>   I need the fetish who erases the memories.]

> Croire aux contes et aux légendes. . . .
> La parole complète. Celle qui est à la fois silence et verbe, action et inertie. . . .
> Ces mots sur du papier blanc. Ce sont eux qui me disent à l'oreille les souvenirs. Qui chuchotent à mon âme les paroles momifiées. (90)
>
> To believe in the tales and legends. . . .
> The complete word. The one that is simultaneously silence and word, action and inertia. . . .
> These words on the white page. They are the ones who utter the memories into my ears. Who whisper the mummified words to my soul.]

The narrator is anxiously calling for the transformative power of the Word. The "mummified words" she refers to are these legends and tales of the oral tradition always kept alive, transmitted through the art of storytelling and therefore inscribed in her text. The various tellings and retellings are also always different, thus constantly changing, just like her own self. She finds writing a liberating refuge from her intense moments of exile and confinement. In fact, her personal crisis was the very catalyst that triggered her desire to tell/write her story, in her own voice. Her apparent fragmented writing is an interrogation, almost an archaeology of herself, of her country, and of the various places where she has lived. She stresses the importance of connectedness that is the source of empowerment in her life. Hence, on a trip to Washington, D.C., where she experiences extreme ennui and anxiety, she can no longer feel or "smell" the city. She feels like a caged animal. Suddenly her native country flashes to mind and becomes a new lover: "La nuit, il s'allonge à mes côtés et me fait l'amour" (64) (At night, it lies beside me and makes love to me). The narrator at times focuses on specific places— in Abidjan, Adjamé, Treichville, Yopougon, Cocody. By recalling these key places on the African continent, she enters a meaningful and deep communication with her culture and ancestors. Recalling all the social and political ills of many African countries and all their misery and poverty is also deeply disturbing. She needs to pause and meditate. After such rejuvenation and purgation, however, she can better appreciate her new direction, her new friend:

> Je sais bien que je n'ai rien à te reprocher....
> C'est seule, devant ma machine à écrire les journées qui passent, c'est toi, le soir, le dos courbé en mangeant....
> Mais quand la nuit commence à peine, blottie contre ton corps aussi chaud qu'un croissant, j'ai des visions de bonheur. (95)

> [I know very well that I can't blame you for anything....
> I am left alone in front of my typewriter, writing about the days that pass by. You, in the evening, your back bent over while you eat....
> But, when the night has barely fallen, and I am curled up against your body as warm as a croissant, and I have visions of happiness.]

She has reached a certain state of peace. She has come to a new understanding of herself, trying to rid herself of negative and destructive feelings such as jealousy or excessive possession. She remembers "l'homme's" wife, once her friend: "Pourquoi ne pas partager? Appartenir. Ce ne sont pourtant pas les luttes qui manquent" (88). (Why not share? To belong to someone. It is not as if there is ever a shortage of personal struggles.) Here, she fancies a new type of relationship, a more collective way of living and connecting and sharing with others, be they lovers or friends, and close to a form of polygamy. She realizes that two people can better help one another: "le chemin est long mais à deux ce sera plus facile" (40) (The path is long but it will be easier for two). This proverblike sentence also plays a crucial role in the allegory of love and death. In a key tale (chapter XXXI), a man is devastated by the long suffering of the woman he loves, and wishes to share in her suffering, ready to remain with her until death. And she reciprocates, asking him not to be mad at her although she is still in love with her former lover as well as with him. The context of this tale is the occasion for the narrator to realize how much she, too, has idealized "l'homme":

> "J'en ai fait un poète-génie, un esprit fantastique....
> Des mots simples, j'ai voulu faire un drame. Des gestes anonymes, j'ai inventé la suite" (90–91).

[I made him a poetic genius, a fantastic spirit. . . .
From simple words, I wanted to create a drama. With secret gestures, I
continued the story.]

Here the narrator expresses her desire to write, to create in order to survive
and to live.

We can now better appreciate Tadjo's overall design: the constant coming and going from one genre of stories to another, the numerous movements between the different continents and places, the different persons
afflicted with all sorts of misery as well as the differences between the narrator's two lovers, her varied moods, and her various reactions to her desires and her pain. Tadjo's stylistic innovations lie more in the form and
the rhythm of the narrative than in the language itself. She does not hesi-
tate to use typography as a stylistic device to convey her message together
with a poetic prose, reflecting yet again oral tradition. She expresses leaps
in time, space, and emotions with a lyrical poetry often full of anguish that
re-creates the irrationality of the world. The blank pages and the divisions
of her text are perfect examples of the semantic, artistic, and psychological
role played by space in her text, as if she were staging the indescribable
feelings of the characters. As readers of Tadjo's text, we are left, at times, a
little ill at ease, uncomfortable, or unable to "speak/read," as if we, too, were
experiencing the same traumas. She thus creates for the readers another
connection beyond the actual text. She also uses cinematographic techniques
that call upon our sight and hearing as if we were in front of a television
screen, viewing images of dreams or nightmares, such as in the narrator's
description of Marcory-pot-poto, with the rhythmical repetition of "je vois"
(11–13) (I see). Elsewhere, snapshots and fragments of films pass in front
of our eyes, as in the scene of a mother dying of cancer whose estranged
son returns to see her. In this story, the omniscient narrator's telling of his
mother's thoughts and reactions to his unexpected visit parallels the narrator of *A vol d'oiseau*'s painful and irremediable experience, and it helps
her rid herself of her own cancer, of "l'homme," and of her uncontrollable
desire for him. Once again she transforms death and destruction, learned
from a tale, into hope, survival, and life. All her suffering is but a pause,
with its cathartic value, in the cycle of life.

To read *A vol d'oiseau* is somewhat like flying over or working on a mosaic, reconstructing a — only apparently — dispersed story; as readers, we too
may have to "rearrange the puzzle" and resort to flashbacks. Tadjo's text introduces a new "third-world" narrative fragmentation, different from the "Western" postmodernist one. Her use or description of allegories, initiation

stories, traditional order, and popular life also reflects the search for empowerment of the narrator. At the end, however, we can still enjoy the global mosaic at a certain distance at the same time that we can also appreciate each of its small components. Véronique Tadjo's *A vol d'oiseau* has already changed the landscape of African literature. Her global preoccupations are closely linked with her style to emphasize the social and political comments found in her fiction. There is a parallel between her modernist representation and reading of the cultures of our contemporary world with its social and political events, particularly on the African continent. Her strategy does recall Hyvrard's concept of "identité de rassemblement de la planète" (connectedness through global gathering).[6]

Notes

1. The second edition of *A vol d'oiseau* was published by L'Harmattan (Paris) in 1992. For this essay, I am using the original text published by Nathan in 1986. This first edition's cover and size are different from the second edition's and more relevant to the text than those of the second edition. All translations are mine. I would like to thank Sarah Glass for sharing with me her working manuscript of her translation of *A vol d'oiseau*.

2. The reader is surprised at the outset by the unusual placement of the first epigraph. In this way, the fictional text overflows into the technical publication information, showing that no borders exist.

3. Akissi appears in the following poem: "Dans la nuit noire déserte, / sorciers occultes / et sacrifices rituels / les dieux sont là / à guetter l'inconnu. / Que fais-tu sous la lune / à déchiffrer le sable? / Ne sais-tu pas / qu'Akissi est morte / En portant son enfant?" in *Latérite*, (Paris: Hatier, 1984), 82.

4. Carol Gilligan, *In a Different Voice* (Cambridge: Harvard University Press, 1982), 22.

5. Jeanne Hyvrard, *Mère la mort* (Paris: Editions de Minuit, 1976), 53.

6. Hyvrard also talks of "identité collective" in the same interview by Euridice Figueiredo in *Conjonction* 169 (April–June 1986): 121.

CHAPTER ELEVEN

After Negation

Africa in Two Novels by Maryse Condé

CHRISTOPHER L. MILLER

I would like to begin with a paradox. In Maryse Condé's first novel, *Hérémakhonon*, Africa appears as a metaphysical trap, the object of a quest that turns out to be "vain."[1] The search for meaning, genealogy, and cultural identity that brought Véronica, the Guadeloupean narrator, to Africa proves futile, and an unbridgeable gap seems to open between her and the land of her ancestors: "Mes aïeux, je ne les ai pas trouvés. Trois siècles et demi m'en avaient séparée" (242–43). ("I didn't find my ancestors; three and a half centuries have separated me from them" [136].) By the end of the novel, Véronica knows that she has "cherché mon salut là où il ne le fallait pas" (312) ("looked for her salvation in the wrong place" [176, AT]), and she seems to have renounced cultural affiliation with the continent once and for all.

According to Françoise Lionnet's insightful analysis of *Hérémakhonon*, Véronica's experience is symptomatic of how the colonized subject can fall victim to internalized stereotypes, in this case the myth of Return to Africa. Véronica, according to Lionnet, is incapable of acting, of participating in the reality around her, which she is content to observe with detached irony. Véronica lacks a language of her own: she does not speak, she "is spoken" by the powerful discourses that surround her.[2] Lionnet borrows her terms from Edouard Glissant and his *Le Discours antillais,* and applying Glissant's vocabulary to Condé's work, Lionnet interprets *Hérémakhonon* as a cautionary tale about "the obsession of Oneness" ("cette obsession de l'Un"), the "non-Relation," known as Return.[3] *Détour,* the term by which Glissant describes deviation from totalities and hegemonies, is a "permanent exercise of turning away from transcendence" (32): *détour* is camouflage, ruse, and systematic "stammering." Return, on the other hand, reflects an unquestioning investment in Being, in a world of discrete cultural essences. Among the historical examples Glissant uses are Israel and Liberia. His description of African-Americans "returning" to Liberia has close resonances in Condé's work; he writes: "What are we to think about the fate of these people who come back to Africa, aided and prodded by the calculating philanthropy of their masters, *and who are no longer Africans?*" (30). The false assumption of "still being African" is the myth of Return that Condé addresses in *Hérémakhonon.*

Organized around the myth of Return, *Hérémakhonon* is taken by many as a fable of "failure" — and the word occurs often in critiques of this book.[4] Lionnet, however, does see in the end of the novel a new "wisdom" taking hold of the narrator, who begins to be more aware of the corner into which she has painted herself. At this point Lionnet seems to anticipate the reorientation in Condé's work that occurs after *Hérémakhonon,* namely the recourse to forms of literary expression more "committed" to Caribbean reality. Condé's physical and intellectual return to the Caribbean fits neatly into the scheme proposed by Glissant: the myth of Return to Africa having been repudiated, new cultural agendas must be set closer to home; an *antillanité* must emerge from *la prise en compte de la terre nouvelle* (a coming to terms with the new land).[5] From this point of view, Condé's *Hérémakhonon* becomes rereadable as groundwork, as the negation of Return that is necessary before new *détours* can be pursued. This interpretation is further supported by a recent interview in which Condé describes how she has "made peace with [her] island . . . and peace with [her] self."[6] This is not the paradox.

The problem with this very logical interpretation is that it ignores the ten years of literary production that separate *Hérémakhonon* from Condé's more recent treatment of Caribbean themes. Three more volumes of her fiction deal with Africa before she turns her attention back to the New World: *Une Saison à Rihata* and the two-volume opus *Ségou* precede *Pays mêlé* and *Traversée de la mangrove.*[7] The supposed "negation" of Africa in *Hérémakhonon* somehow does not erase a continuing interest in the continent, an ongoing Africanist discourse created by Condé. Here, then, is the paradox with which I would like to begin: if Africa is revealed to be a mere trap for the narrator of *Hérémakhonon,* why does it remain a preoccupation, an obsession, and a source of cultural identification within Condé's work?[8] In other words, how can one explain the existence of *Une Saison à Rihata* and *Ségou*? On the conceptual level, how are we to understand the logic by which the object of an apparent negation remains a foundation stone within an author's work? We can be sure of only one thing at this point: that this is the logic of Maryse Condé.

There is a hypothesis that would account for this apparent discrepency. If Condé and her work are nihilistic, then there is no real paradox in her continuing interest in a negated object. The fascination with a "black hole" (as Africa is described in *Hérémakhonon*[9]) and the destruction of identity— "je viens ici commis voyageur de l'Europe pour détruire d'autres identités . . . je viens ici oeuvrer à d'autres aliénations" (237) ("I come here as a traveling salesman from Europe to spoil other identities . . . and I come to work on other alienations" [133]) — could be explained, too easily in my opinion, as a form of nihilism. According to this interpretation, Véronica would represent the totally colonized mind, completely dominated by European Africanist discourse; formulas like "The Dark Continent" would be the signs of an internalized oppression that the narrator is unable to combat. We know that Condé is not afraid of appearing nihilistic from time to time. In an interview, she remarks, scandalously: "The only Caribbean author that I really like is V. S. Naipaul, who has a mind that is very contentious, very negative, very nihilistic. . . ."[10] I do not think, however, that this statement should be taken literally, even in the process of recognizing the important role that negation and negativity play within Condé's oeuvre. Her negativity must be analyzed, its limits explored. The symbolic use of Africa — this "difficult continent," as Condé calls it in her novels[11] — is perfect for this. In her critical study of the francophone Caribbean novel, Condé offered the following appraisal of her own work (referring to herself in the third person): "Maryse Condé [concluded that there was] a *difficulty if not an impossibility* in tying back together the broken threads" between Africa and the West Indies.[12] In the ambiguity between a "difficulty" and an "impossibility," there is all the difference between, on the one hand, a negative but committed form of thought and, on the other, a nihilism that must dead-end. Tempted by nihilism, which she does not wholly reject, Condé nonetheless opts for "difficulty," for the labor of reconstruction. In spite of the criticism that she directs against any Africanistic nostalgia in *Hérémakhonon*, there was no intention to reject Africa as a whole in the novel,[13] and Condé spends ten more years studying and explaining Africa in *Une Saison à Rihata* and *Ségou*, to which I will return presently.

I would like to suggest, therefore, that Condé's negativism requires closer scrutiny. The supposed "impasse"[14] of exile and of the internalized stereotype is in reality the object of *critical irony* on Condé's part, as she explains in an interview:

> When Véronica says "The Dark Continent," it's in a mocking, ironic tone. Africa has always been talked about as the Dark Continent. So she takes up the cliché with irony. *It is essential to know how to read and to not take everything at face value* [*il faut savoir lire et ne pas tout prendre au premier degré*].[15]

Such explicit instructions from an author should not be ignored. And yet, it is not always easy in a book such as *Hérémakhonon* to "know how to read." This novel is among the most narratologically complex works ever to come from the francophone African or Caribbean world; the author herself has described it as "a bit hermetic."[16]

One peculiarity of *Hérémakhonon* that has not escaped the attention of critics is the fact that the narrator, unlike all the other characters in the novel, is never directly quoted. On the level of explicitly represented actions, everyone speaks but her; meanwhile she alone *thinks,* and her internal reflections constitute the dominant point of view. The dialogues are asymmetrical, in that other characters speak within quotation marks but Véronica's "replies" are exclusively given in free-direct or free-indirect discourse. Can this lack of direct intervention and engagement be thought of as an impotent "silence" on Véronica's part, as a refusal of dialogism?

This is a case where things must not be taken at face value. If Véronica is silent on the level of written discourse, she is not silent at all on the level of represented reality: she speaks, and the reader can often infer what she has said by looking at the responses of her interlocutors. The apparent silence is in fact the sign of a deeper privilege, the privilege of *irony.* The first dialogue of the novel, in which Véronica is addressed by the customs agent of the African country in which she is arriving, is a good example of this:

> "Raison du voyage?"
> Vraiment ce policier met dans le mille.... Raison du voyage? Ni commerçante. Ni missionnaire. Ni touriste. Touriste peut-être. Mais d'une espèce nouvelle, à la découverte de soi-même. Les paysages, on s'en fout....
> "Bienvenue en terre africaine!"
> D'où sort-il celui-là?...
> "Vous êtes ici chez vous."
> Bon, il efface d'un coup trois siècles et demi. (12–13)

["Purpose of visit?"
The police officer is really hitting the nail on the head. . . . Purpose of visit? No, I'm not a trader. Not a missionary. Not even a tourist. Well, perhaps a tourist, but one of a different breed, searching for herself, landscapes be damned. . . .
"Welcome to Africa!"
Where did *he* spring from? . . .
"Consider yourself home."
With one word, he has wiped out three centuries and a half. . . . (12)]

Véronica's voice does not speak in this passage, yet her interior monologue clearly encompasses and undercuts the discourse of actual speech as represented by the *douanier*.

Furthermore, in other passages of *Hérémakhonon*, it becomes obvious that Véronica has spoken without being quoted directly. Free discourse, both direct and indirect, presents a part of what the narrator says and a part of what she thinks. In the following passage, for example, the lack of quotation marks surrounding Véronica's interventions does not prevent an actual dialogue from being represented:

"J'ai passé tout le Conseil des ministres à penser à vous."
L'aveu est de taille: je pourrais être flattée.
"Je me demandais si Abdoulaye arriverait à vous retenir. Et si demain matin, je n'apprendrais pas que vous avez encore été mêlée à une sale histoire."
N'exagérons rien! Des sales histoires, il n'y en a pas tellement!
"*Vous trouvez!* Dès votre arrivée, vous n'avez rien fait d'autre que vous lier au militant d'un parti interdit . . ."
Qui? Saliou? . . . Ce n'est pas ce qu'il est à mes yeux. Et de son parti, je ne sais rien. Il ne m'en parle jamais.
"*De quoi parlez-vous alors?*" . . . (220–21, emphasis mine)

["I spent the entire ministerial meeting thinking of you."
This is an enormous confession: I ought to be flattered.
"I was wondering whether Abdoulaye would manage to retain you. Or whether tomorrow morning I wouldn't hear that you have been mixed up yet again in some sordid affair."
Don't exaggerate. There haven't been that many.
"*Oh no?* As soon as you arrived you had nothing better to do than get involved with a militant of a banned party . . ."
Who? Saliou? That's not what he is in my eyes. And I don't know anything about his party. He never mentions it to me.
"*What do you talk about then?*" . . . (123, emphasis mine)]

In the italicized phrases here, Véronica's interlocutor responds to things that Véronica has actually said, not just thought. There is therefore a dialogue on the level of diegesis, even if, for reasons that remain open to interpretation, her speech is never given directly in the text between quotation marks. What she says is rendered only through the medium of free-direct or free-indirect speech. But in my opinion Véronica's discursive situation has nothing to do with either silence or failure. Her position is one of power, a means of critique that allows the narrator to present Africa in a certain light. Thus Véronica's point of view dominates the entire novel (as at the end of the passage quoted, Véronica adds this conclusion: "Cet homme est odieux. Lucidement, je m'en rends compte" (221). ("This man is obnoxious. I am now fully aware of it" [123].)

Véronica's consciousness and point of view are of course highly problematic. The "identity crisis" that brought her to Africa is profound and continues unabated; her political and cultural situation in Africa is completely ambiguous. She describes herself as "dans tout cela, un cheval avec des oeillères" (110) ("a horse with blinders in all this" [59]). Véronica's response to the complexities around her is "derision" and "sarcasm" (qualities that, incidentally, Condé professes to admire in other authors[17]); she insulates herself within a cocoon of irony.

What is happening in *Hérémakhonon* may thus be less a "failure of enunciation" (as Lionnet describes it) than a different type of enunciation that deserves closer scrutiny. There is indeed a barrier between the inside (Véronica's consciousness) and the outside (Africa and its politics); it is true that Véronica never breaks out of her ironic shell to commit herself to the outside world. But *Hérémakhonon* is hardly the "book on nothing" of which Flaubert dreamed: just as Véronica "speaks" without being quoted, the novel sends positive signals between its lines. *Hérémakhonon* does not attempt to resolve the identity problems associated with the African diaspora, but it stakes out a firm position on the question of Return. Enunciation does not fail in this novel; it is ideology that fails. The peculiar way in which Véronica's direct speech is excluded from the text is not the cause or consequence of her "failure." The myth of Return is to blame, and *Hérémakhonon* reads like a novelized indictment of false identification with Africa. The figure of Africa is demystified with some brutality, and *Hérémakhonon* becomes the antidote to negritude and its vision of Africa as One.[18] The narrator's consciousness, meanwhile — confused, blind, and sarcastic — nonetheless gropes for other solutions.

What those other solutions might be is not evident from a reading of *Hérémakhonon* alone; the problems raised here must be seen in the perspective of Condé's wider oeuvre. Condé's Africa, which is at first a myth to be exploded, becomes a *continent* to study, to criticize, and to explain. From *Hérémakhonon* to *Une Saison à Rihata* and from *Une Saison à Rihata* to *Ségou,* there is a progression, a gradual process of opening. This can be seen on the level of style: Condé begins to move away from the hermeticism that characterized *Hérémakhonon.* She marks the transitions between past and present and between Africa and the West Indies, she joins the majority of African and African-Caribbean writers who include explanatory footnotes in their novels, and in *Ségou* and *Moi, Tituba, sorcière noire de Salem,* she borrows devices from the popular historical novel. What is striking in this body of work, when looked at as a whole, is Condé's concerted effort to *reweave* the broken threads of the diaspora through the exploration of history. To analyze this process of reweaving, I turn now to the novel that followed *Hérémakhonon.*

The work of demystification, which one might have thought completed in *Hérémakhonon,* nonetheless continues in *Une Saison à Rihata* (which has not been translated into English), but the discourse and style of this novel are significantly different. Africa remains enigmatic, and the West Indian female narrator, Marie-Hélène, is still an isolated, slightly cynical figure, lost in an African country "that she had never made her own."[19] Like Véronica, Marie-Hélène is almost blind to African culture:

> A ses *yeux,* toutes les manifestations de la vie communautaire africaine étaient privées de sens [cf. *Hérémakhonon,* 111: "Plus rien n'a de sens"], vestiges mécaniques d'un passé dont rien ne subsistait. Elle s'y ennuyait à périr. (192)

> [To her *eyes,* all manifestations of African communal life were meaningless (cf. *Hérémakhonon,* 60: "Nothing has meaning anymore"), the hollow vestiges of a past of which nothing remained. She was dying of boredom.]

But this negativism concerning the sense of African culture is given a different spin in *Une Saison à Rihata,* a different discursive character. Now the narrator's isolation — which was accentuated in *Hérémakhonon* by her confinement to the outwardly "silent" but inwardly dominating free-direct and -indirect speech — is modified. Now the privilege of free-indirect discourse — and therefore of critical thinking — is parceled out to nearly all the characters in the novel. The power of thoughtful irony, which was monopolized by the narrator in *Hérémakhonon,* here belongs to everyone. Consciousness within *Une Saison* is thereby disseminated, fragmented, and shared within a community, and the narrator's point of view therefore becomes *relative* and open to critique. Whereas in *Hérémakhonon* Véronica alone controls the interpretation of events, in *Une Saison* a multiplicity of points of view—even that of a relatively minor character—can have access to free-indirect speech. Thus the ideology of the state itself is represented ("A sarcler, biner sous le soleil...la raison revenait vite!...L'étranger était le lieu dangereux où s'apprenait la détestable idéologie du marxisme-léninisme..." (117) (After enough weeding and hoeing in the hot sun, they'll come back to their senses!...Abroad was where they could pick up the repugnant ideology of Marxism and Leninism...), as is the point of view of a newly introduced character named Alvarez-Souza, the head of a delegation sent by a neighboring president:

> Alvarez-Souza, dévisageant Madou, éprouvait la plus profonde antipathie pour ce play-boy en tunique à la Sanjay Gandhi (Toumany avait ramené cette mode d'un voyage en Inde), dont l'air arrogant l'offusquait. *Etait-ce pour créer une pareille classe qu'on avait lutté si dur contre les Blancs?* (58, emphasis mine)

> [Alvarez-Souza, staring Madou down, felt the strongest antipathy for this playboy in a Sanjay Gandhi tunic (Toumany had brought this fashion back from a trip to India); Madou's arrogant manner offended him. *Did we struggle so hard against the Whites only to create a class of people like this?*]

Yet in the very next paragraph, free-indirect style returns to Madou:

> Madou, s'asseyant dans le fauteuil qui lui revenait, se demanda s'il avait conscience d'écrire une page importante de l'histoire de son pays. *Pas vraiment!* Tout au plus, à présent, il se sentait alerte comme un lévrier. *On allait discuter dur!* (58, emphasis mine)

> [Madou, sitting down in the armchair at his place, wondered if he was aware of writing an important page in the history of his country. *Not really!* At most, for the moment, he felt as alert as a greyhound. *Let's get on with the tough talking!*]

From one paragraph to the next, free style passes subtly from one character to another. (This egalitarian parceling out of the style is continued in *Ségou,* and in a fascinating and original way in the more recent *Traversée de la mangrove*).

Une Saison à Rihata thus marks an opening, a break with the narrative restrictiveness of *Hérémakhonon.* Not the least consequence of this opening is that Marie-Hélène's blindness to Africa is offset by the voices and thoughts of African characters, who seem to speak for their cultures. Condé therefore involves herself in a kind of fictional *ethnographic* writing; she adopts a form of narrative "ethnographic authority."[20] The customs of one African civilization and of one clan within it in particular are described in passages like the following, in which elders of the clan react to the adulterous affair between Marie-Hélène and her brother-in-law Madou:

> La société ngurka est habile à prévoir les réparations de toutes les fautes, de toutes les offenses. . . . Il n'était question que de Madou, car Marie-Hélène ne comptait pas. Elle n'était que "celle qui vient d'ailleurs," capable par conséquent de tout et qui le prouvait. . . .
>
> Les anciens en avaient décidés tout autrement. *Les deux frères devaient rester unis, du moins en apparence. La bouche ne sait pas ce que le coeur tait.* Quant aux enfants, quel qu'en soit le père, ils appartenaient au clan. *Chez les Ngurkas, il n'y a pas de différence entre fils et neveu, fille et nièce. . . .* N'étaient exigés que la répudiation de la femme, son départ avec le bâtard métis qu'elle avait imposé au foyer. *Ah, qu'ils s'éloignent tous les deux! Qu'ils rejoignent les rives marécageuses où ils avaient vu le jour!* (71, emphasis mine)

> [Ngurka society has clever ways of providing for the redressing of any fault or any offense. . . . Madou was everything, she didn't count at all. She was a mere "outsider," capable of anything, and she proved it. . . .
>
> The elders had decided quite differently. *The two brothers had to remain united, at least in appearance. What the heart holds silent, the mouth does not know.* As for the children, no matter who their father was, they belonged to the clan. *Among the Ngurka, there is no difference between son and nephew, daughter and niece. . . .* All that was demanded (by the elders) was the repudiation of the woman (Marie-Hélène), her departure with the mulatto bastard she had imposed on the household (her nephew and foster son Christophe). *Oh, let them go away, both of them! Let them go back to the swampy shores where they were born!*]

In this passage and elsewhere,[21] Maryse Condé takes a leaf from anthropological and ethnographic discourse, the method of attributing a *collective* voice to a group; this collective voice is often written in free-indirect discourse.[22]

Within the construction of *Une Saison à Rihata*, this polyphony means that Marie-Hélène's ethnocentrism and "missionary" spirit[23] are offset by a number of other perspectives. The principal characters — Marie-Hélène; her husband, Zek, who is marginal in his relation to state power; and Zek's brother, Madou, the Minister of Rural Development — are each in a different way in complicity with the nation's dictator, Toumany. Their dilemma is to be involved with a power that they know to be illegitimate, and all three see direct action as a very problematic possibility. Marie-Hélène is especially critical of the political culture in this (unnamed) country, while at the same time remaining perfectly aware of her position as an alien:

> Elle haïssait l'arbitraire et la corruption. Elle haïssait et méprisait la bourgeoisie ostentatoire et parasitaire, les arrivistes en tous genres que le pouvoir sécrétait. *Bien qu'elle ne fût jamais parvenue à le considérer comme sien,* elle éprouvait une profonde compassion pour ce peuple qui n'en finissait pas de souffrir et devenait ombre de son ombre, fantôme de son fantôme. (115–16, emphasis mine)

> [She detested everything arbitrary and corrupt. She hated and detested the middle-class show-offs and parasites, the *arrivistes* of all kinds that state power seemed to produce. *Although she never got to the point where she could consider herself one of them,* she had a profound compassion for these people, who never seemed to stop suffering, who wasted away like shadows of their shadows, ghosts of their ghosts.]

Thus it is Marie-Hélène who analyzes and critiques the contradictions of this society; it is she who sees the "fossé qui séparait les classes sociales dans le pays" (103) (gap that separates the social classes in the country); whereas the "nouveaux puissants entendaient prouver contre toute évidence que la société de Toumany ignorait les divisions en classes" (133) (newly empowered intended to prove against all evidence that Toumany's society knew no class distinctions).

Marie-Hélène would thus appear to be something other than a simple neocolonialist, blind to African culture. She critiques Toumany's regime, and she fails to understand traditional local culture, yet

> malgré les incohérences et le désordre de sa vie privée, elle avait gardé intactes les convictions de sa jeunesse, quand . . . elle rêvait d'une Afrique libre et fière qui montrerait la voie aux Antilles, entraînerait l'Amérique dans son sillage. Presque à son insu, elle avait communiqué un vocabulaire contestataire aux enfants, ce qui n'était pas sans dangers. (54)

> [in spite of the incoherences and the disorder of her private life, she had kept the convictions of her youth intact, her dream of a free and proud Africa that would show the West Indies the way and bring America along in its wake. Almost without knowing it, she had taught her children a vocabulary of protest, which was not without dangers.]

Within Marie-Hélène's mind, Africa can become a place to love, but only under two conditions: that the relation to the West Indies of her childhood and the problem of personal love both be resolved. As in *Hérémakhonon*, the personal and the political are intertwined. At one point in *Une Saison*, all of these factors come into a temporary equilibrium:

Oui, à Prahima, elle avait retrouvé la saveur de son enfance. Quand
Madou la prenait par la main, elle était capable d'aimer cette terre, de s'y
enraciner. (188)

[Yes, in Prahima, she had rediscovered the flavor of her childhood. When
Madou held her hand, she was capable of loving this land and putting down
roots in it.]

But this moment cannot last, because it depends on a forbidden love affair
with her brother-in-law (and we have seen how this is viewed by local society). At the end of the novel, the political and personal contradictions remain
unresolved, and the power of the dictatorship remains implacable. Condé
provides no easy formulas for popular revolution here or elsewhere.

And yet a decisive step is taken in comparison to Hérémakhonon. Certain characters in Une Saison à Rihata come to be aware of the power of
thought and of song in combating political oppression. In a group of political prisoners who have been rounded up in an effort to suppress resistance
to Toumany's regime, a griot named Sory begins to sing the epic of Bouraïna
(which bears a strong resemblance to the Sunjata epic of the Mande). From
this performance a clear implication emerges: when seen in light of the
grandeur of the past, the current situation makes one wonder, "Alors pourquoi à présent acceptait-il la domination?" (198) (Why should we now accept domination?). Singing the ancient epic proves to be "an action," an act
of "anger" and "revolt."[24] If the novel ends with arrests and executions ("public, of course!"), Condé has nonetheless sent a clear signal concerning the
value of critical thinking in situations of political oppression: thinking,
singing, and perhaps even writing, although they may not be the ultimate
solution, are at least the right place to start.

Thus if one reads Condé carefully, if one does not take everything "at
face value," it becomes possible to see that her Africa is not Joseph Conrad's
or even V. S. Naipaul's. She does not project, in the words of one of her
characters, a "somber fatalism" (154) onto the essence of Africa; she does
not, as has been alleged, substitute for "the ancient arsenal of clichés" a new
"Africa that is damned."[25] Her Africa is a continent that has been demystified, politicized, historicized, and examined from a point of view that is
admittedly very skeptical.

The foundations of Condé's Ségou are thus visible in Une Saison à Rihata; one sees the beginning of her immersion in African epics, anthropology, and history. If the recourse to history coincides with a greater degree
of popularization in her writing, this does not change the cultural function
or the power of Africa in her work. Following a model of identity that is

indeed "conflictual,"[26] Condé pursues an "irritating dialogue with [herself]"[27] and with the discourses of the postcolonial world.

Notes

1. "Laissons là mon identité. Est-ce que toute cette quête n'est pas vaine? *Vaine.*" *Hérémakhonon* (Paris: UGE, 1976), 167. "Let's forget about my identity. Isn't all this searching in vain? In vain." *Heremakhonon,* trans. Richard Philcox (Washington, D.C.: Three Continents Press, 1982), 91. Further references to the text and its translation will be placed in parentheses. In cases where I have found it necessary to alter the translation, I will use the symbol "AT."

2. Françoise Lionnet, *Autobiographical Voices: Race, Gender, Self-Portraiture* (Ithaca, N.Y.: Cornell University Press, 1989), 179.

3. Edouard Glissant, *Le Discours antillais* (Paris: Seuil, 1981), 30. Translations are my own.

4. See Lionnet, *Autobiographical Voices*; also Jonathan Ngate, "Maryse Condé and Africa: The Making of a Recalcitrant Daughter?" *A Current Bibliography on African Affairs* 19, no. 1 (1986–87), 5–20. Arlette M. Smith, however, argues against seeing *Hérémakhonon* as a story of failure and emphasizes the narrator's increased "perception of cultural realities" ("Maryse Condé's *Hérémakhonon*: A Triangular Structure of Alienation," *CLA Journal* 32, no. 1 [September 1988]: 52).

5. Glissant, *Le Discours antillais,* 31. Glissant's version of *antillanité* is described in his glossary to *Le Discours antillais*: under "Antilles," he says, "Je crois que la mer des Antilles ne resserre pas, qu'elle diffracte. Elle n'impose pas l'Un, elle rayonne du Divers"; and under "Antillanité, "Plus qu'une théorie, une vision" (495). ("I think that the Caribbean Sea does not enclose; it is an open sea. It does not impose one culture, it radiates diversity" [261].)

6. "Je me suis réconciliée avec mon île: une interview de Vèvè A. Clark," *Callaloo* 12, no. 1 (winter 1989): 133; an English translation appears on facing pages.

7. The blurb on the cover of *Pays mêlé* (Paris: Hatier, 1985) states: "*Pays mêlé* paraît annoncer un retour vers les Antilles natales, retour au demeurant déjà amorcé dans *Dieu nous l'a donné...*" (*Pays-Mêlé* seems to announce a return to the Caribbean birthplace, a return whose beginning is already indicated in *Dieu nous l'a donné...* [translation mine]). See *Ségou,* vol. 1, *Les Murailles de terre*; vol. 2, *La Terre en miettes* (Paris: Robert Laffont, 1984–85); and *Traversée de la mangrove* (Paris: Mercure de France, 1989).

8. As Ngate has pointed out, "while it would be foolish to deny that Maryse Condé is indeed a Caribbean woman, she is also one for whom Africa has been and remains an essential point of reference" ("Maryse Condé and Africa," 18). In a study that appeared after my essay was first drafted, Leah Hewitt makes an argument similar to mine about the implied logic that ties together *Hérémakhonon, Une Saison à Rihata,* and *Ségou*; see Hewitt, *Autobiographical Tightropes* (Lincoln: University of Nebraska Press, 1990), 165, 188.

9. "En fin de compte, je n'imaginais rien. Un grand trou noir. The Dark Continent" (*Hérémakhonon,* 106). ("Actually, I never imagined anything. A great black hole. The Dark Continent" [56].)

10. E. Shungu, "Maryse Condé: Guadelouyséenne, professeur et productrice," interview, *Jeune Afrique* 1216 (April 1984), 66–67.

11. "Condé, Afrique, un continent difficile," *Notre Librairie* 74 (April–June 1984), 23, translation mine.

12. Condé, *Le Roman antillais* (Paris: Fernand Nathan, 1977), vol. 1, 18, emphasis mine.

13. "Je me suis réconciliée," 121–23: "There was no question of rejecting Africa as a whole."

14. Lionnet, *Autobiographical Voices,* 175: "The narrator's failure to act upon the insights she gleans points to a passivity and a lack of will symptomatic of her colonial background

and ambiguous situation. She represents the impass of exile for the colonized self and the difficulty of finding a viable position within the cultural constellation of the 'other'..."

15. Condé, "Afrique, un continent difficile," 22, emphasis mine.

16. "Je me suis réconciliée," 120.

17. Shungu interview, 67.

18. This refers to negritude as elaborated by Léopold Sédar Senghor. Cf. Condé in Shungu (66–67): "Je ne lis Senghor que pour me persuader que je déteste tout ce qu'il a écrit. Il projette une image de l'Afrique que je n'aime pas du tout; une image de mémoire qui est un contre-modèle." (I read Senghor only in order to persuade myself that I detest everything he has written. He projects an image of Africa that I don't like at all, an image of memory that is a counter-model.) Cf. "Afrique, un continent difficile," 22: "Pendant un temps, les Antillais ont cru que leur quête d'identité passait par l'Afrique. C'est ce que nous avaient dit des écrivains comme Césaire et d'autres de sa génération; l'Afrique était pour eux la grande matrice de la race noire et tout enfant issu de cette matrice devait pour se connaître, fatalement, se rattacher à elle. En fin de compte, je pense que c'est un piège... La quête d'identité d'un Antillais peut très bien se résoudre sans passer, surtout physiquement, par l'Afrique." (For a certain period, the Antilleans believed their search for identity led through Africa. This is what writers like Césaire and others of his generation had told us; Africa was for them the great womb of the black race, and every child born of the womb, in order to know himself, had inevitably to identify himself with it. In the end, I think this was a dead end. The identity of an Antillean can very easily establish itself without going through Africa, especially in a physical sense.)

19. *Une Saison à Rihata* (Paris: Robert Laffont, 1981), 170; translations are my own.

20. See James Clifford, *The Predicament of Culture* (Cambridge: Harvard University Press, 1988), "On Ethnographic Authority," 21–54.

21. See also the example of the misunderstanding between Marie-Hélène's and Zek's children and their paternal grandmother, who has "des traditions et une conception du monde qu'elles ignoraient" (traditions and a concept of the world they didn't understand).

22. See Clifford, *The Predicament of Culture*, 47; and Dan Sperber, "L'Interprétation en anthropologie," *L'Homme* 21, no. 1 (January–March 1981): 76–78.

23. This is Pius Ngandu Nkashama's interpretation in "L'Afrique en pointillé dans *Une Saison à Rihata* de Maryse Condé," *Notre Librairie* 74 (April–June 1974).

24. It is Victor, the assassin of the minister Madou, who begins to understand this idea.

25. Alain Baudot, "Les Ecrivains antillais et l'Afrique," *Notre Librairie* 73 (January–March 1984): 45.

26. Edmond Marc-Lipiansky, "Des images et des hommes: la quête d'identité dans *Hérémakhonon* de Maryse Condé," *Revue d'ethnopsychologie* 2–3 (1980): 136.

27. *Une Saison à Rihata*, "irritant dialogue avec lui-même," (149).

CHAPTER TWELVE

Rewriting "America"

Violence, Postmodernity, and Parody in the Fiction of Madeleine Monette, Nicole Brossard, and Monique LaRue

KAREN GOULD

The image of "America" has been given increasing prominence in Quebec fiction since 1960. Whether viewed with interest, apprehension, or outright contempt, the influence of American culture and ideology on the imaginative terrain of contemporary Quebec letters has been substantial, engendering a seemingly endless variety of images, themes, and narrative forms that idealize, disparage, and sometimes parody the power and cultural hegemony of the United States in North America.[1]

Historically speaking, American characters, cities, and modes of thinking have often been negatively portrayed in the Quebec novel. For many nineteenth- and early twentieth-century authors of Quebec's popular *romans du terroir* (novels of the land), the "American presence" and U.S. industrialization in the Northeast, which lured young francophone farmers south, represented a serious threat to accepted Québécois values—especially rural life, the traditional family unit, the French language, and Catholicism. Because of its expansionist history and relative economic strength, the neighboring United States was therefore viewed as hazardous to the socioeconomic future and cultural survival of Quebec's francophone population. Literary representations of the United States have frequently emphasized this threat.

American influences have left their adverse and occasionally positive marks on the Quebec novel in numerous and profound ways, precipitating identity crises in francophone protagonists, aggravating tensions among cultural, political, and economic forces in the novel, and at times contributing to the erosion of social cohesiveness within the francophone communities depicted in tradition-bound Quebec novels. By foregrounding issues of collective minority identity and cultural survival, the intrusion of American socioeconomic interests and cultural values into the unfolding plots of both traditional and modern Quebec fiction has usually functioned and been read by Quebec critics as textual proof of the damaging effects of "American cultural imperialism." Indeed, since the 1960s, politically engaged novelists and essayists such as Hubert Aquin, Victor Lévy-Beaulieu, Jacques Godbout, and Pierre Vadeboncoeur have portrayed the ever-expanding, controlling nature of American materialist culture as a serious threat to nationalist solidarity and political autonomy in Quebec.

In the case of the postwar Montreal novel (1945–70), however, Jean-François Chassay offers a more nuanced reading, arguing that "[t]he proximity of the United States is both a worry and a delight, a distressing situation or an invaluable opportunity, depending on the point of view. The Montreal novel has never effaced the tensions created by what might be considered American control."[2] Insisting on a more ambivalent, modernist view of the Quebec–U.S. connection, Chassay's comments would appear to apply equally well to the continuing pleasure and anxiety that the U.S. presence and "Americanness" provoke in recent fiction from Quebec.

A number of critics have already noted the centrality of American values and mythologies as well as the importance of American history and popular culture in contemporary Quebec writing.[3] Novels by Jacques Godbout, Jacques Poulin, Jacques Marchand, and Pierre Turgeon are an indication that American influences, the current fascination with l'américanité, and Quebec–U.S. border crossings — whether geographical or imaginary — are injecting new themes and fresh perspectives into Quebec letters. At the same time, the increasing frequency of journeys southward in the contemporary novel also means that Quebec writers are commenting on America's cultural landscape and its myths with greater insight and in considerably more detail. Although some readers in Quebec and in the rest of Canada as well will doubtless view this current literary preoccupation with border crossings as further proof of American cultural intervention and the general weakening of Quebec's nationalist project, it can also be read as a sign of assertiveness on the part of Quebec writers and intellectuals who have begun to confront and critique America close-up by positioning their works inside U.S. borders. Moreover, Quebec novelists often express their keen desire to reflect upon life and culture in the United States directly in their narrative dialogue, as Madeleine Monette does through the exhortation of one of her characters: " 'Allez. Avale encore un peu, et dis-moi ce que tu penses de l'Amérique.' "[4] ("Come on. Drink a little bit more and tell me what you think of America.")

With this growing interest — both positive and negative — in life, letters, and culture south of the border, it is not surprising that France and the prestige of French cultural authority are less present today in Quebec fiction than in the past. Rather than define themselves primarily in response to and against the "Hexagon," a number of Québécois writers are exploring questions of identity and difference in terms of their most proximate neighbor. Not unlike their male counterparts, women writers in Quebec have been similarly inspired by the appeal and the peril of *l'américanité*—a word much in vogue in Quebec since the early 1980s that translates as "americanness" or "North Americanicity." As they look south, however, writers such as Marie-Claire Blais, Madeleine Monette, Nicole Brossard, Madeleine Ouellette-Michalska, Monique LaRue, and others represent America's cultural and political landscapes in somewhat starker and more discernibly gendered terms.[5] Jovette Marchessault's *Lettre de Californie* (1982),[6] for example, evokes the historical brutality of "New World" colonization and reminds us that America remains, for some, the land of conquerors and witch-hunts. And in Marie-Claire Blais's *Visions d'Anna* (1982),[7] transcultural problems such as poverty, urban alienation, racism, environmental pollution, drugs, sexism, homophobia, and the disintegration of families plague the North American continent with little respect for national borders or for notions of distinct cultural identity and nationhood.

Along with insisting on the North American character of contemporary Quebec society, Madeleine Monette's *Petites Violences* (1982), Nicole Brossard's *Le Désert mauve* (1987),[8] and Monique LaRue's *Copies conformes* (1989)[9] evoke the inescapable magnetism of American culture, the alienation produced by American urban life, and the invasive character of American ideology — themes that have been explored by a number of male authors as well, as I have already noted. However, their novels also underscore issues of gender politics, cultural violence, and female self-discovery in contemporary American settings. Not surprisingly, these gender-inflected themes affect both the perception and the descriptions of "America" in significant and sometimes paradoxical ways.

Situating their novels in New York City, the southwestern United States, and California, respectively, Monette, Brossard, and LaRue use geographi-

cal and cultural displacements to underscore issues of flight and exploration, alterity and extraterritoriality, themes that, as Simon Harel points
out in works by Jacques Poulin and Jacques Godbout, signal a break with
the closed space of Quebec and a new form of "continentalism" in Quebec
letters.[10] By virtue of this extraterritorial shift in perspective, Monette, Brossard, and LaRue have, like their male counterparts, challenged the boundaries of Quebec writing by locating francophone cultural intervention beyond provincial borders. In so doing, they have also extended their feminist
critique of contemporary gender relations to encompass the North American continent, thereby encouraging readers to reflect on the status of women
and men in a broadened cultural context. At the same time, their combined
efforts to reenvision "America" through francophone eyes underscore the
importance of creatively interrogating the dominant culture from the margins. Refiguring "America" thus means rewriting the American story ("une
histoire américaine")[11] from the point of view of gender, francophone minority culture, and transculturalism — perspectives that repeatedly overlap and resist one another in the works of these three female novelists.

Madeleine Monette: *Petites Violences* (1982)

A resident of New York City since 1979, Madeleine Monette writes both from
within and outside the cultural landscape of the United States. Her 1982
novel, *Petites Violences* (*Little Acts of Violence*), reveals a double vision of
urban America, which is both intriguing and disturbing, and which, when
viewed through "foreign eyes," reflects some degree of cultural ambivalence on the part of the author. New York, the American city best known
for its dazzling wealth and cultural sophistication, becomes in this work a
site of cultural estrangement, tough-minded economic activity, violence,
and death. It is also portrayed as a complex geocultural space of proliferating social codes and competing identities. Elements of seduction and danger, which further underscore New York's contemporary mystique, are in
constant conflict throughout the narrative. Indeed, Monette's account of
the crossing of borders from Montreal to Manhattan leads to a crucial re-
assessment of the contradictory appeal of urban America.

Highlighting Quebec as a point of narrative and cultural origins, Monette articulates a vision of "Americanness" in *Petites Violences* that raises issues of gender, minority cultural status, and postmodernity in distinct and
powerful ways. At the same time, the act of viewing the francophone female
subject through the lenses of a neighboring but different culture provides

an intriguing context for reenvisioning the self. The textual and autobiographical links here are complex, given that Monette's decision to move to New York predates the writing of this novel. More importantly, the necessary trajectory of geographical displacement, cultural critique, and enhanced self-knowledge, which maps both the novel's narrative course and the parameters of the female narrator's psychological development, clearly preoccupies the author as well. Monette "travels" to America in this novel in order to explore and reenvision it, while her narrator-protagonist journeys to New York to escape her past and to reinvent her life.

In theme and form, *Petites Violences* draws attention to the sexism, violence, and gender stereotypes that figure in and are reproduced by American mass culture. As several critics have argued, the novel can fruitfully be read as a feminist critique of a "stifling and abusive relationship" and, concomitantly, as a narrative of female self-affirmation.[12] Postmodern in outlook, the novel also highlights the paradoxical play of extraterritorial identification and cultural estrangement, as well as the conflicting impulses to problematize and affirm female subjecthood. This double narrative gesture becomes an important mode of political contestation in Monette's text.

Violence is explicitly foregrounded in *Petites Violences,* as its title suggests. Even though the narrative intrigue focuses primarily on the problem of destructive personal relationships and lingering emotional ties, various forms of cultural violence in urban America are also emphasized. Thus, the text's New York setting both confirms and reinforces Monette's principal themes. Montreal emerges through a series of flashbacks and irrepressible emotions as the site of a past life and an abusive love affair that the narrator attempts to flee.

During a train ride from Montreal to New York, which serves as the novel's menacing prologue and strategically marks Monette's unfolding narrative, a scene of domestic violence is made public. Having decided to return home after abandoning her spouse and children, an anonymous American wife is slain during a violent struggle with her husband as impassive travelers look on while others become agitated over the train's delay. Martine, the narrator-protagonist, describes the couple's final agonizing battle in grim detail, emphasizing the sense of desperation and incomprehension that overtake them:

> Animés de poussées violentes, les deux corps s'étaient mis à rouler le long du wagon. Les bras et les jambes empêtrés jusqu'à se fondre dans une étreinte lourde et maladroite, ils basculaient l'un sur l'autre et gesticulaient dans le vide, sans plus savoir s'ils cherchaient à s'agripper ou à se repousser.

Surgissant au creux d'un coude, sous la raideur d'une épaule ou à travers
une masse de cheveux ébouriffés, la lame du couteau apparaissait et
disparaissait comme une source de lumière vive et intermittente entre leurs
deux visages apeurés. (29)

[Animated by violent shoves, the two bodies had begun to roll alongside the
car. Their arms and legs entangled to the point of merging in a heavy,
awkward embrace, they toppled over one another and gestured in the
surrounding emptiness, without knowing whether they were still trying to
grab on to one another or to push away. Shooting up out of the hollow of
an elbow, under the stiffness of a shoulder or through a mass of disheveled
hair, the knife's blade appeared, then disappeared, like a source of
intermittent, intense light between their two frightened faces.]

In this contorted, grisly scene of intertwining, rivaling bodies, death appears to be the only way out of the entanglement. Herself a former victim of domestic abuse, Martine recognizes the destructive elements of the
"abused wife syndrome" and accurately predicts its *dénouement* even before the nameless woman gets off the train. Indeed, the kind of brutal resolution to a failed relationship that Martine witnesses in this prefatory
scene is precisely the ending she hopes to escape by traveling to New York.
As a result of her American journey and temporarily severed cultural ties,
Monette's protagonist intends to close the chapter on the humiliating relationship in which she had become entangled. But Martine's manipulative
and sometimes violent Québécois lover, Claude, will follow her nonetheless, and the brutality of New York will be unrelenting. Although the cultural border crossing in *Petites Violences* is significant, the potential for violence does not ebb; on the contrary, it intensifies on the mean streets of
Manhattan.

Even before arriving in New York City, which Lise Gauvin refers to as
America's "mythic and mystifying" megalopolis,[13] a black conductor tries
to prepare Martine for the harsh realities of what he calls "une ville de fous"
(16) (a city of crazy people). On this score, New York does not disappoint.
Amid the incessant noise and jostling crowds, Martine confronts the daily
peddling, scavenging, and stark poverty of the city's underclasses. With a
mixture of apprehension and interest, she observes the activities of police
squads and protesters, hustlers and dope dealers, prostitutes and pimps,
streetwise cabbies and bruised bag ladies. Criminality, conflict, provocation,
and contempt result in tough street scenes and forceful fashion statements.
As Martine's inventory of her friends' designer fashion collection indicates,
the rudeness of city life and the aggressiveness of New York clothing trends
seem inextricably linked:

Les couleurs et les styles sont agressifs, les tons heurtés, les épaules
rembourrées et pointues, les imprimés tranchants, le plus souvent
géométriques, les tissus élastiques, satinés ou transparents. On se croirait
dans le salon d'habillage d'une héroïne de bandes dessinées, dont les
costumes stylisés et sexuellement audacieux annonceraient une femme
hybride, mi-Barbarella, mi-Marilyn Monroe. (61)

[The colors and styles are aggressive, the tones clashing, the shoulders
padded and pointed, the prints forceful, usually geometric, the fabrics
elastic, satin, or transparent. You'd think you were in the fitting room of a
comic-strip heroine whose stylized and provocative clothing seems to
suggest a hybrid woman, half-Barbarella, half-Marilyn Monroe.]

Martine is both drawn to and repelled by the violent acts and cultural
images that characterize American urban life. But New York also captures
her imagination as a heterogeneous site of differences and excess that provides a necessary, if unlikely, refuge. Along with the conflict and human
suffering that she witnesses, Martine views New York as a turbulent, postmodern space of high and low culture, whose contrasting elements include
The Rocky Horror Picture Show and an academic conference on violence in
literature, chic fashion models and street people, gay and lesbian activists
and Joan Crawford fans, transvestites and straights, angry pornographers,
patronizing psychoanalysts, and feminist intellectuals, as well as a variety
of races and ethnic groups.

Martine's quick-paced, inventory-like style of sketching New York scenes
paints the diverse character and competing activities of the city's population in broad strokes. At the same time, her terse descriptions suggest a certain narrative distance that evokes the detached voyeurism and noninvolve-
ment of American urban dwellers when faced with the misfortunes of others.
Most importantly, the vibrant street movement and short, vivid descriptions
of New York's diverse population enable Monette's narrator-protagonist to
"collide" with differences, to experience her own status as francophone outsider, and to confront her most repressed fears without relief.

By virtue of her novel's New York setting, Monette's view of America is,
of course, limited. Moreover, despite Martine's attraction to the experience
of "foreignness," she attributes a seductive and specifically sexual magnetism
to this American city. Based in part upon earlier visits as a tourist, Monette's
narrator initially associates New York with an exciting lover who demands
complete submission to the dictates of desire. Like the city of Montreal,
which has often been personified as an alluring sexual partner or sensual
body in Quebec poetry,[14] New York both impassions and confuses Martine:
"électrisante comme une main sous une chemise de nuit, déconcertante

comme une averse sur une robe de soirée" (32) (electrifying like a hand under a nightgown, disconcerting like a shower on an evening dress). By personifying the city in such a manner, Monette shifts the focus of the discourse on otherness and foreignness from the public domain of the streets to the private realm of the body and the emotions. And because the effect of this personification produces a more general blurring of the personal and the social, it underscores the interconnectedness of private and public forms of aggression.

Elspeth Probyn argues that "in thinking of how locale is inscribed on our bodies, in our homes, and on the streets, we can begin to loosen its ideological affects."[15] Throughout *Petites Violences,* the sense of excitement and ever-present danger on local New York streets punctuates Martine's personal memories of sexual enticement and domestic violence in Montreal. Likewise, living in New York keeps the cruelty of her former Québécois companion at the forefront of the narrator's consciousness. In this way, New York functions as a spatial and cultural trope for the violence that must be faced. Eventually, Martine will begin to analyze the meaning behind the magnetism of New York.

To the chagrin of some feminist readers, Martine does not develop a rigorous theoretical discourse on male violence toward women during her narration, no doubt in part because Monette herself does not privilege theory in her writing. At the same time, the fact that Martine appears to be implicated in the perpetuation of her own subjugation makes a staunch feminist stance on male violence more difficult. Martine is in fact both drawn to and repelled by Claude's domineering attitudes and vicious acts. Ironically, Monette uses the figure of Claude and the New York conference on the effects of violence in literature to ridicule American academic theorizing on violence, censorship, and artistic expression. As Martine remarks, such theorizing is often detached from actual practice. Claude's position in defense of freedom of artistic expression is seemingly more American than Québécois in outlook, and certainly contests what some Quebec intellectuals have viewed as the "natural" alignments of feminism and Quebec nationalism. More ambivalent and perhaps more cynical than some America-watchers in Quebec, Monette refuses to trade in easy gender stereotypes and cultural clichés. She prefers instead to accentuate the contradictions at work in the gender/culture/violence paradigm.

Although *Petites Violences* does emphasize the prevalence of aggressive behavior in contemporary American life and culture, it insists as well on the many transcultural forms that violence takes. Monette's ironic stance with respect to theory is, moreover, abundantly clear. Such is the case, for instance, with her characterization of Claude, whose well-received research on what motivates violent sexual behavior, which he delivers in New York, contrasts sharply with his pleasure at humiliating Martine; Claude's theoretical assumptions and scholarly conclusions thus contradict the reality of his private life. This conflict further underscores the conceptual slipperiness of dividing human experience into public and private spheres, a point Monette initially raised by "staging" the prologue's intimate death scene in full public view.

As I have already suggested, Monette reverses a number of cultural stereotypes in this novel, primarily through her characterizations of Claude, the francophone ex-lover, and Lenny, a former American boyfriend with whom Martine reconnects. Gender and culture are not represented as fixed identities in *Petites Violences,* and indeed Claude, the francophone, uses language — both French and English — to overpower and belittle Lenny in an unusual gesture of minority (i.e., francophone) dominance. Monette's portrait of Lenny is not culturally predictable either. As an attentive lover who ghostwrites for a living, enjoys speaking French, and dreams of becoming a legitimate novelist, Lenny does not fit the stereotypical image of the macho American male and may to some extent deconstruct it. But Lenny exerts his masculinity over Martine elsewhere — through his physical advances and in the act of lovemaking.[16] His sexual aggressivity thus results in another kind of "battle" of the sexes:

> Lenny a cette façon de prendre sans demander qui réveille en moi des fantasmes mal enfouis, une envie mal réprimée d'être subjuguée par un corps plus entreprenant que le mien, une volonté plus tranchante que la mienne. (81)

> [Lenny has a way of taking without asking that stirs up barely buried fantasies, a not-so-repressed desire to be subjugated by a more assertive body than mine, a more compelling will than mine.]

As this passage suggests, the romantic love quest has all but disappeared in *Petites Violences.* Accordingly, the discourse of love that we might expect to find in the descriptions of the lovers' encounters has been replaced by a discourse of sexuality and possession. For Martine, the sustainable heterosexual relationship she longs for is one in which her sexual desire is responded to without detriment to her psychological or physical vulnerability. Hence, feelings of safety and trust are paramount. Although Martine prefers her sense of self in Lenny's company to the degraded object she had become with Claude, she is nonetheless uncomfortable with Lenny's liter- ary obsessions. His writing projects, which include a fictionalized account of an actual murder of a female violinist and a novel about an aging de- fender of pornography who served time for the murder of a prostitute, re- veal Lenny's own fascination with male dominance and sexual violence. Both Lenny and Claude are influenced by and implicated in an American cul- tural outlook—nurtured by the popular media—that promotes the eroti- cization of violence toward women and the sensationalization of abusive sexual conduct. By foregrounding the contradictions at work in the medi- ated male perspectives on violence and desire in *Petites Violences,* Monette exposes some of the embedded gendered fantasies of humanist (male) cul- ture. The successful interweaving of domestic and social themes in this novel encourages the reader to consider the ways in which the circulation and proliferation of violent images in North American culture fuel the every- day violence ("*petites violences*") that occurs in the private lives of contem- porary couples.

As Monette's novel draws to a close, Martine's fear of Claude remains greater than her fear of New York. The physical distance she has placed be- tween herself and an abusive ex-lover, between a past identity rooted in in- adequacy and submission and a more positive sense of self, has allowed Martine to confront her disappointments and her desires, and to acknowl- edge her own need to create. In fact, this need to live and write "elsewhere," outside Quebec and beyond the borders of her cultural homeland, has re- peatedly marked Monette's work. Thus, despite the hazards it represents, and despite the uneasy strangeness Martine experiences, living in New York has a therapeutic effect. Having confronted the city's aggressiveness and her own complicity in the subjugation she has endured, Monette's narrator- protagonist is able to sever ties to an injurious past and face the project of writing with a renewed sense of self-awareness and determination. In a typ- ically self-reflexive, postmodern gesture at the end of the narrative, Martine links her strategy for self-renewal to the anticipated writing of a novel that deals with the domestic and social implications of *les petites violences.* Monette's novel has come full circle.

Martine's ambivalence toward cultural difference, which Homi Bhabha characterizes as a postmodern, postcolonial stance,[17] makes her decision to stay in New York at the end of the story not only possible but credible as well. From the point of view of Quebec nationalism, of course, this choice can only be viewed as disappointing and problematic. For Martine, however, and for Monette as well it seems, issues of gender and power complicate the politics of cultural difference and also mitigate to some degree the shock of geocultural displacement.

Nicole Brossard: *Le Désert mauve* (1987)

Nicole Brossard's *Le Désert mauve* (*Mauve Desert*) is a postmodern triptych whose themes and form stretch the literary and cultural boundaries of women's writing in Quebec.[18] It is also the author's most accessible, most "American" novel to date. Brossard's choice of the American Southwest as the principal setting is hardly innocent since the interpretive changes that result from wearing different cultural lenses constitute one of the text's central interrogations. In this new and crucially "foreign" desertscape setting, Brossard presents a story of adolescent desire and unexplained murder. Drawing attention to the intimate processes of reading, reflection, and rewriting, Brossard's text also incorporates the story of a Québécoise reader (Maude Laures) who has become captivated and troubled by the seemingly inexplicable elements of the strange murder plot. Maude Laures's meditations on the female victim and the escalating violence of North American society are central to her translation project and to the author's own cultural rereading of contemporary America.

The heterogeneous character of Brossard's work pushes the formal and aesthetic limits of the contemporary Quebec novel on a number of fronts. Privileging interdiscursivity over conventional literary forms, *Le Désert mauve* blends disparate literary and paraliterary elements, including brief narrative sequences, frequent use of poetic imagery and alliteration, historical intertexts, journal entries, blurred photographs, imaginary dialogues, theoretical reflections on the process of translation, and a translated version of part 1 that repeats the initial story in French from the fictional reader's point of view. It is, among other things, a novel that undoes itself in order to imagine, if not reinvent, another kind of ending.

Traditional north-south boundaries are also problematized in this North American novel of love, murder, and translated hope. On the one hand, *Le Désert mauve* depicts a female reader's imagined movement back and forth over the U.S.–Quebec border, as she reflects on the southwestern story from her Montreal locale. But it also blurs geographic and cultural boundaries between the United States and Mexico through the selective use of Spanish and English words as competing cultural signifiers as well as through desert descriptions that seem to transcend national borders. Brossard gives additional emphasis to her transcultural outlook by assembling a cross-border community of women's voices in her narrative. Most importantly, the novel's major themes (love, violence, and creative rewriting) know no national borders. Brossard's use of these boundary-breaking strategies effectively undermines the hegemonic effect of the very concept of *américanité*.

The tripartite construction of Brossard's novel highlights three interrelated narrative moments: (1) the presentation in part 1 of a fictitious book, *Le Désert mauve*, written by a fictional and presumably American writer, Laure Angstelle; (2) Maude Laures's notes and assembled materials in part 2; and (3) her translation of Angstelle's *Désert mauve*, which she retitles *Mauve, l'horizon*, in the third and final section of the book. As I have remarked elsewhere, this triple narrative focus introduces questions of "interpretation and translation from one novel to another, from one 'language' to another, and of course, from one woman to another."[19] The trope of translation, which Brossard exploits here with remarkable originality, also engenders a series of reflections on subjectivity and alterity, unity and diversity, which place the work of creative reinscription at the center of a feminist reading aesthetic.[20] At the same time, the emphasis on translation in *Le Désert mauve* also marks an interpretive shift in vision from one culture, geography, and history to another. Brossard's novel moves us from the American cultural perspective of Laure Angstelle to the Québécoise cultural horizon of Maude Laures, from the arid topography of Arizona and New Mexico to the December snows of Montreal, from the advent of the atomic era in America to the transcultural present of proliferating firearms and misogynist crimes that circulate within and across national borders. Space, like subjectivity and sexuality, is not singular or rigidly controlled.

As we learn from her reader's notes, Maude Laures's has become enamored with Laure Angstelle's southwestern text, which she purchased in a used book store in Montreal. The passion she experiences for a story whose meaning remains elusive is what drives Maude Laures's preoccupation with her own project of translation: "Maude Laures s'était laissé séduire, *ravaler* par sa lecture. Il n'est pas toujours possible de rêver sans avoir à donner suite aux images" (59). ("Maude Laures had let herself be seduced, *sucked in* by her reading. It is not always possible to dream without having to follow through on the images" [55].) But before she can rewrite the original American story that has heightened her emotions and sparked her creativity, Maude Laures must reflect on the meaning behind Angela Parkins's enigmatic murder and expand upon Angstelle's narrative elements (places, objects, characters, scenes, key concepts) in order to make sense out of the senselessness of the narrated crime that concludes Angstelle's story.

Brossard's reader-translator resists easy translations and a simple concurrence of views. She will, for example, develop background sketches for each of Angstelle's characters, place her own self-portrait alongside those of the characters she contemplates, put extra revolvers into circulation — including one in the hands of "l'homme long" (the long man) — and quiz Laure Angstelle about the murder of Angela Parkins in an imaginary dialogue. In this way, Brossard acknowledges the feminisms within feminism through the different "angles" of vision in *Le Désert mauve*. At the same time, she underscores what Teresa de Lauretis has termed the "feminist deaesthetic," a nontraditional, noncanonical, participatory aesthetic that valorizes the reader — in this case a woman — rather than the author of the text.

The American desert initially serves as a haven in this text because of its seductive beauty, exhilarating expansiveness, and the anonymity it affords the lesbian couple who have made it their home. For the impatient adolescent daughter and narrator, Mélanie, it is a space of unlimited possibilities: "s'enfoncer dans la nuit avec des cernes autour des yeux, des espaces absolument délirants à proximité du regard" (12) ("driving into the night with circles under my eyes, absolutely delirious spaces edging my gaze" [11]). In the end, however, the American Southwest is a failed oasis inasmuch as the violence Brossard's female protagonists and fictional reader hoped to avoid cannot be escaped. Retreat into the desert does not prevent the murder of Angela Parkins while she is dancing in Mélanie's arms, nor does it diminish the proliferation of weapons and cultural intolerance that foreshadow it.

Even when rewritten by a more sanguine Québécoise reader, who would like to erase Angela Parkins's murder scene and, with it, the history of America's nuclear arms race and frontier "conquest" mentality, Laure Angstelle's inaugural story of lesbian awakening and unanticipated violence in the Arizona desert will result in the same scenes of calculated death — the unexplained death of one woman in the arms of another and the fantasized (and historically real) atomic deaths of millions. As Maude Laures explains in her imaginary dialogue with the author, the realities of the landscape will make their way into the translated text despite differences of interpretation and intent: "les paysages vrais assouplissent en nous la langue, débordent le cadre de nos pensées. Se déposent en nous" (143) ("true landscapes loosen the tongue in us, flow over the edge of our thought-frame. They settle into us" [133]).

Through the eyes of her fictional author, narrator, and reader-translator, Brossard maps the American desert as a vast space of ardent fascination and troubling contrasts, painting it in mauve, white, red, and gold colors that will be associated with passion, vulnerability, violence, and hope. Due to the disparate, abandoned objects of former lives, her postmodern desertscape retains traces of "la présence soupçonnée de l'humain" (73, 74) ("the suspected presence of the human element" [69]). But this same arid geography of striking beauty and disguarded junk, of white light, deserted pools, and desolation also suggests a decomposing world that evokes a feeling of "hyperreality" (DM 71; MD 67). Through analogy, the desert as wasteland is thus linked to the progressive barrenness of American cultural values.

Brossard insists on the "Americanness" of her novel by privileging Laure Angstelle's southwestern setting, plot, and site of publication. The desert's American topography is emphasized through characteristic descriptions of motels, swimming pools, fast cars, television violence, bars, and revolvers. Female responses to the aggressive nature of American culture are traced in the simple gestures of daily life:

> Je renversai mon verre de lait et la nappe se transforma en Amérique avec une Floride qui se prolongeait sous la salière. Ma mère épongea l'Amérique. Ma mère faisait toujours semblant de rien quand les choses étaient salies. (12)

> [I spilled my glass of milk and the tablecloth changed into America with Florida seeping under the salt-shaker. My mother mopped up America. My mother always pretended not to notice when things were dirtied. (12)]

Brossard appropriates several American cultural icons for her own deconstructive purposes. Parodying the "on-the-road" identity and American wanderlust of Jack Kerouac, who has become an influential literary icon in Quebec as well as in the United States, Maude Laures names Mélanie's anonymous lesbian mother "Kathy Kerouac"; Maude Laures wants to believe that Kathy Kerouac's voice and love for another woman can subdue the culture of violence that is transmitted daily on television. The most imposing American cultural icon, however, is the atomic physicist Robert Oppenheimer, whose veiled identity is revealed in the destructive, tormented visions of "l'homme long," and whose final deadly act is foreshadowed and historicized in the numerous references to the desert test sites for the atomic bomb and to the recorded comments of Oppenheimer and others after the first atomic explosion near Los Alamos. Brossard's portrait of "l'homme long" incorporates many of the well-documented habits, trademarks, and intellectual interests of Robert Oppenheimer, director of the original atomic bomb project at Los Alamos, New Mexico (1942–45) — in particular, the cigarettes, felt hat, awkward thinness, interest in Sanskrit and Hindu philosophy, East Coast education, mathematical genius, and his fascination and acknowledged concern with atomic experimentation and weapons production. Brossard also includes Oppenheimer's frequently cited reference to the *Bhagavad-Gita,* "I/am/become/Death" (17), which he reportedly uttered at the moment of the first atomic bomb explosion in the American desert, along with Kenneth Bainbridge's reply: "Maintenant nous sommes tous des fils de chienne" (23) ("Now we are all sons of bitches" [21]),[21] which Maude Laures subsequently mistranslates as "Maintenant nous sommes tous des chiens" (193) ("Now we are all dogs" [177]), although her motivation may in fact be to rid the phrase of its sexism.

Through the depersonalized portrait and blurred photographic images of "l'homme long" (who becomes "l'homme ob'long" in Maude Laures's translation), Brossard undermines the discourses of democracy, science, and military might that the United States has constructed for itself in order to legitimize its pursuit of nuclear superiority. Questioning the reasons behind the murder of Angela Parkins thus "triggers" further questions about the role of superpower militarism and televised violence in the shaping of a nation's cultural psyche. Like Monette, Brossard views contemporary American culture through the prism of gendered aggression, but in Brossard's novel the forces of aggression have explicit historical roots. Moreover, unlike Monette's *Petites Violences,* reflections on male violence in *Le Désert mauve* occur exclusively among women and among lesbians who are located on the margins of mainstream culture.

In sum, it matters that Brossard's postmodern setting and story of lesbian transgression and death are American in origin. Far from the social constraints and urban violence of New York, Montreal, and other North American cities, the female characters, fictionalized writer, and reader-translator of *Le Désert mauve* are confronted nevertheless with both the history of America's destructive power and the violent sexism promoted in contemporary popular culture, especially as portrayed on commercial television. Brossard's experimental text is a cross-border tale of creative resistance that speaks allegorically of the culturally sanctioned violence and intolerance that women and men must face. Maude Laures's act of translation in the concluding section of this work is an effort to reinvent the American desert and transform a menacing cultural horizon so that life, not death, is painted there. As Brossard herself has written more recently, "[l]e pays qui entre en nous comme le rêve dans la vie est un pays qui s'invente" (the country entering us as a dream might in real life is a country in creation).[22]

Monique LaRue: *Copies conformes* (1989)

Feminist parody of classic male texts has emerged in recent years as a popular subgenre of women's writing.[23] Some examples of its success in Quebec are Louky Bersianik's burlesque parodies of the Bible and Plato's *Symposium* respectively in *L'Euguélionne* and *Le Pique-nique sur l'Acropole*[24] as well as Lise Gauvin's pointed rewriting of Montesquieu's *Lettres persanes* and the European male essay tradition in her widely read *Lettres d'une autre*. The intent of this imitative subgenre in the hands of feminist writers such as Bersianik and Gauvin is both subversive and complicitous because of the value placed on the original appropriated text. As Linda Hutcheon notes, feminist parody is primarily a political gesture that both acknowledges and resists the vision and power of a particular book, icon, or cultural tradition.[25]

Monique LaRue's third novel, *Copies conformes* (Exact copies), both parodies and enacts an extraterritorial rereading of Dashiell Hammett's American classic *The Maltese Falcon*, published in 1930. More than simply a parodied intertext, however, Hammett's well-known detective novel frames the narrative structure, story line, and cultural landscape of LaRue's work; it also furnishes the pivotal themes of deception, disguise, and ethical emptiness that LaRue will give another, markedly different slant. The parallels with Hammett's plot are numerous and easy to recognize. In *The Maltese Falcon*, detective Sam Spade tries to determine who killed his partner by helping the beguiling Brigid O'Shaughnessy, an enigmatic woman who has become involved in the theft of a maltese falcon statuette. Before returning home to Montreal with her son, LaRue's narrator-protagonist, Claire Dubé, must recover her husband's missing computer disk that contains information on multilingual translations. Thievery in LaRue's version of Hammett's story has gone high-tech.[26] During her search for the truth behind the disk's disappearance, the Québécoise mother-turned-sleuth encounters characters of excess who, due to their deceit, jealousy, and greed, evoke Brigid O'Shaughnessy, Joel Cairo, and the inscrutable Gutman in the original *Maltese Falcon*.

The "Americanness" of *Copies conformes* is doubly accented because of the importance placed on Hammett's infratext and because of the mythic California setting that is foregrounded both in the original American

detective mystery and in LaRue's rewritten story. Likewise, and in keeping
with the self-reflexive gaze of postmodern fiction, LaRue's protagonist has
reread *The Maltese Falcon* and recounts the story line to other characters.
LaRue thus acknowledges her fascination with American popular culture
and mirrors her own retelling of the detective plot. As in Brossard's *Le Désert
mauve*, the act of rereading leads to the translation (rewriting) of American
cultural signs. In *Copies conformes*, however, the differences of gender, motherhood, and francophone minority identity are more explicitly framed and
more ironic.

Making humorous use of the conventions and redundant format of
American male detective writing, LaRue — like Hammett — highlights the
question of identity and the slipperiness of truth. Sam Spade's efforts to
get to the bottom of a tangled intrigue of theft and murder define the parameters of Hammett's classic detective plot, which LaRue repeats in a different voice. In fitting postmodern fashion, her female protagonist adopts
a de-centered position of narrative uncertainty when speculating about
the motives of individual characters and the veracity of their statements.
Confusion over individual identities and the blurring of subjectivity are
linked to other postmodern preoccupations as well, such as issues of geographic and cultural displacement, transculturalism, multilingualism, and
the work of translation.[27] *Copies conformes* also contains a distinctly "nationalist" discourse that underscores the fragility of the francophone collectiv-
ity when confronted with the material, cultural, and linguistic imperialisms
of the neighboring United States.[28] The image of a voracious, assimilating
America is reinforced by the vast scale of California's high-tech economic
interests and by the fierce arrogance of its entrepreneurial elite, as exem-
plified in the remarks of Ron O'Doorsey, who is LaRue's version of Hammett's conniving Gutman:

> Il peut bien avoir étudié à Harvard, au MIT, travaillé pour Hewlett Packart
> [sic], I.B.M. On s'en fout. Les grands prêtres des ordinateurs aboutissent
> tous chez nous. (22)

> [Whether he's studied at Harvard, M.I.T., or worked for Hewlett Packard, IBM.
> We don't give a damn. The high priests of computers all end up with us.]

LaRue reveals her feminist concerns in this text through the attention
accorded her female narrator, the problematizing of male modes of representation, and the valorizing of maternal thinking. Interweaving a parody
of the American detective plot with a story of francophone marginaliza-

tion and maternal conflict and care, LaRue presents an intriguing blend of feminist, nationalist, and postmodernist stances and textual moves.

In LaRue's tongue-in-cheek version of Hammett's story, the setting is once again San Francisco, but the geocultural map now extends beyond the famous city streets of *The Maltese Falcon* to include the intellectual community of Berkeley, Silicon Valley, and, through nostalgic moments of comparison and contrast, the city of Montreal and francophone culture in North America. For Claire Dubé, who has accompanied her husband to Berkeley on his research leave, this transcultural stretch proves problematic. As in Jacques Godbout's *Une Histoire américaine*, the act of leaving Quebec for California engenders a narrative of extraterritorial estrangement that plays on tensions of alterity and identity.[29]

Along with its geocultural shift, *Copies conformes* relocates the site of the crime in the body of a woman. In so doing, LaRue's text enacts what Annette Kuhn views as the double mystery paradigm of Hollywood's film noir genre, which is "typically structured around crime and its investigation by a [male] detective figure."[30] Kuhn argues that in the film noir of the 1940s, "it is very common for a woman character to be set up as an additional mystery demanding solution, a mystery independent of the crime enigma. . . . [T]he focus of the story may [in fact] shift between the solution of crimes and the solution of the woman-question."[31] In Hammett's novel and in John Huston's 1941 film version of *The Maltese Falcon*, Brigid O'Shaughnessy (alias Miss Wonderly, alias Miss Leblanc) is the female riddle Sam Spade (and the reader/spectator) needs to solve. The confusion surrounding Brigid's identity explains much of her charm and potentially subversive power because conformity to traditional notions of femininity remains ambiguous.

In the figure of Brigid O'Doorsey, LaRue gives us a grim caricature of Hammett's representation of woman as mysterious schemer and dangerous seductrice. LaRue's Brigid dons elaborate disguises and consciously imitates "the look" of Hammett's Brigid O'Shaughnessy, even though she is too old for the part and strangely out of sync with the times. This postmodern Brigid lives a simulated life based on cliché-ridden Hollywood images that reify femininity (and masculinity) to keep women in their place as objects of beauty, mystery, and desire. LaRue's parodic stance with regard to this character is unequivocal: Brigid will self-destruct. Her obsession with aging has made Brigid the easy prey of cosmetic surgeons and a believing accomplice in her own destruction:

Peu à peu l'obsession de l'épiderme s'insinuait dans sa vie. Des dizaines et
des dizaines d'interventions avaient été pratiquées, semblent-il, sur son
visage livré aux aiguilles à coudre de richissimes doctoresses qui effaçaient
les traces du temps, dans de louches cliniques de beauté . . . Une droguée du
scalpel. (73–74)

[Little by little the obsession with skin crept into her life. Dozens and
dozens of operations had apparently been performed on a face given over
to the wealthy female doctors' needles, which erased all traces of age, in
shady beauty clinics . . . A knife addict.]

LaRue, like Kuhn, defines the place of woman in the American detective
novel and film noir tradition as one of confinement to an image that has
proved ruinous, even deadly for real women. By emphasizing Brigid's fascination with the engineered beauty of a Hollywood image and her increasingly self-destructive behavior, LaRue reframes the question of who is being murdered in the male detective plot. As a result, her narrative becomes
a site of political undoing from which to challenge the construction of
woman as objectified "other" in American popular culture. Through Brigid
O'Doorsey's displaced narcissism and pitiful efforts to "mirror" an image
she desires as her own, LaRue also critiques Jean Baudrillard's essentialist
notion that seduction and artifice are the inherent realm of the feminine.[32]

In *Copies conformes,* Brigid's brother, Ron O'Doorsey, who helped found
the "Maltese Falcon" software company, is also a great admirer of Dashiell
Hammett — the "Maltese Falcon" computer game he designed is their hottest
product. In the high-pressure computer world in which he operates, legit-
imized thievery through copying and the chronic raiding of other people's
ideas mean that originality is no longer possible or even ethically necessary. The third member of Hammett's revived trio, who most resembles
Joel Cairo, is Brigid's estranged husband, Diran Zarian, an Armenian computer copyright expert who has abandoned his own cultural roots and
family ties in order to succeed in Silicon Valley. Unfamiliar with Hammett's
famous story, Diran nevertheless rivals the novel's original characters for
his egoism and his keen interest in retrieving the "original." The only significant additions to Hammett's cast of original characters in LaRue's rewritten script are two children: Phil, Claire's five-year-old son, who does not
want to leave California, and Joe Zarian, the obese, lonely child from Diran
Zarian's first marriage. Their presence signals the importance of maternal
concerns in LaRue's text.

Along with the ironic transformation of *The Maltese Falcon* plot, LaRue
fills *Copies conformes* with autoreferential elements that remind us of the

popularity of Hammett's book, his life in California as a private investigator, writer, and Hollywood celebrity, and the 1941 film version that made both Hammett and Humphrey Bogart famous. But Claire also casts a shadow over Hammett's ethical conduct in "real life" when referring to the 1921 rape/murder trial in which then detective Hammett defended an accused male actor (61). References to the Dashiell Hammett fan club and the "Maltese Falcon Tours," which exist beyond the life of LaRue's novel, further confuse the fictional and the real; they also remind us of Hammett's preeminent status as an American cultural icon. These autoreferential moments underscore the self-reflexivity of LaRue's work and the way in which the author borrows from existing cultural images and earlier texts.

Despite the important role parody plays in LaRue's text, *Copies conformes* is more than a clever Québécois critique of an American detective story because the search for meaning occurs outside the revised detective plot, in the other, more mundane narrative of mothering and maternal work. Mother of three, professor, and writer, Monique LaRue does not approach the topic of mothers from a distance, as her public discourse and other writings indicate.[33] In *Copies conformes*, she questions the paradoxical space of the mother in contemporary culture, a mother who has often been the disparaged "other" of white, middle-class feminism since Simone de Beauvoir and Shulamith Firestone.[34]

Far away from Montreal, her "langue maternelle," and the values of her own minority culture, Claire Dubé maintains a sense of connectedness and commitment through her child. Paradoxically, the range of Claire's activity during their six-month stay in Berkeley has been "reduced" to the task of mothering in large measure because of insecurities regarding the English language and the fast-paced, foreign culture in which she finds herself. In California, the lowly status of married housewife contrasts sharply with the hustling, success-at-any-price careerism of Silicon Valley elites. Among the high-tech computer crowd, and even to herself, she appears embarrassingly traditional: "Moi, Claire Dubé. Trente-cinq ans, mariée, un enfant. Profession perdue en cours de route" (10) (Claire Dubé. Thirty-six, married, one child. Career lost along the way). Yet for a brief time Claire will be drawn into the suspenseful romance of the California mystique. Efforts to retrieve the missing disk cause her to take to the highways and neglect her child. Once she has fallen for the charm of Diran Zarian, who is also keen on solving the computer disk theft, Claire begins to doubt her emotional commitment to her husband, eventually succumbing to a one-night fling with Zarian.

In the novel's concluding pages, LaRue's protagonist finally perceives her situation clearly: her child, maternal tongue, and place of origin, as well as her spouse, represent values to which she ultimately clings. Refusing to idealize them, she knows they are nevertheless part of her identity and sense of stability in the world. In an era of microsecond communication, proliferating computer copies, confusing identities, and ethical emptiness, the value Claire attaches to human connectedness and preservative love is similar to the feminist ethics articulated by sociologist Sara Ruddick in her work on "maternal thinking."[35] Both Ruddick and LaRue link the kinds of activities mothers perform to serious thinking about caring for others and for the larger collectivities in which they live. In the process of unraveling the basic elements of the computer caper in which she has become entangled, Claire retrieves the values that lead her "home" to Montreal.

Unlike Zarian, who has forgotten his Eastern European roots and marginalized Armenian culture, except when he speaks French, Claire remains connected to her Québécois past. Is the maternal that which reminds us of our origins — in this case, French-speaking Quebec? Claire's reaffirmation of maternal values contrasts sharply with the disintegrating, dysfunctional California families of Zarian and Brigid. Having stayed in closer touch with the day-to-day needs of children, Claire worries about the future of a culture steeped in greed and falsehood in which, increasingly, children and loved ones are neglected. Although LaRue's "mother-woman" seems almost to belong to another era, the estrangement and nagging guilt that Claire experiences during her offbeat California odyssey are very much in keeping with contemporary times. Motherhood in *Copies conformes* is presented as both a cultural handicap and a source of creative power. Unlike Hammett's detached, self-absorbed male hero, LaRue's protagonist forges an identity — not without difficulty — in relation to intimacy and care.

By subverting key elements of the American male detective genre, including the dominance of the male point of view, LaRue's maternal subplot reclaims the realm of women's daily experiences, reestablishes interaction between private and public space, and emphasizes the importance, rather than the material game, of social relations. Through the changes brought to Hammet's original plot, *Copies conformes* thus suggests a number of ways in which the act of rewriting can link American and Québécois literary traditions, even as it contrasts the gendered visions and cultural perspectives of Hammett and LaRue.

"How," Jean-François Chassay wonders, "when faced with such a stifling and aggressive neighbor, can the contemporary Quebec novel invent its own version of America?"[36] Although Madeleine Monette, Nicole Brossard, and Monique LaRue have responded to the inescapable lure of the United States and to the very meaning of *américanité* from various artistic stances, their novels nevertheless suggest that francophone cultural reinvention can be compelling. Despite important differences in philosophical outlook, Monette, Brossard, and LaRue have articulated a vision of "Americanness" that raises issues of gender, minority cultural status, and postmodernity in distinct and powerful ways.

Petites Violences, Le Désert mauve, and *Copies conformes* are examples of how Quebec women writers can successfully cross national borders without abandoning uniquely francophone perspectives on "America." Monette, Brossard, and LaRue borrow from, critique, and rewrite the American cultural scene not to capitalize on some new form of postmodern literary exoticism nor to succumb to the lure of Americanization itself. Rather, they seek to expand the geocultural sphere in which women's lives are refigured and the idea of culture is itself reshaped.

Notes

1. See Benoit Melançon, *La Littérature québécoise de l'Amérique: guide bibliographique,* Rapports de recherche 6 (Montreal Centre de Documentation des études québécoises, 1989).

2. Jean-François Chassay, "L'autre ville américaine: La présence américaine dans le roman montréalais (1945–70)," in *Montréal imaginaire: Ville et littérature,* ed. Pierre Nepveu and Gilles Marcotte (Montreal: Fides, 1992), 280. My translation. All subsequent translations are my own unless otherwise indicated.

3. See *Urgences* 34 (1991), a special issue on "Mythes et romans de l'Amérique." See also Laurent Mailhot, "*Volkswagon Blues,* de Jacques Poulin, et autres Histoires américaines' du Québec," in *Le Roman québécois contemporain (1960–1986) devant la critique. Oeuvres et critiques* 14, 1 (1989): 19–28; Jonathan Weiss, "*Le Premier Mouvement* de Jacques Marchand: un roman américain?" *Etudes françaises* 26, 2 (1990): 21–29; and Simon Harel, *Le Voleur de parcours: Identité et cosmopolitisme dans la littérature québécoise contemporaine* (Montreal: Le Préambule, 1989), 159–60.

4. Madeleine Monette, *Petites Violences* (Montreal: Quinze, 1982), 96.

5. See Lucie Guillemette's study of gendered discourse on "America" in "L'Amérique déconstruite et les voix/voies féminines dans *La Maison Trestler* de Madeleine Ouellette-Michalska," *Dalhousie French Studies* 23 (fall–winter 1992): 61–67.

6. Jovette Marchessault, *Lettre de Californie* (Montreal: Nouvelle Optique, 1982), 17.

7. Marie-Claire Blais, *Visions d'Anna* (Montreal: Stanké, 1982).

8. Nicole Brossard, *Le Désert mauve* (Montreal: Hexagone, 1987); *Mauve Desert,* trans. Susanne de Lotbinière-Harwood (Toronto: Coach House Press, 1990).

9. Monique LaRue, *Copies conformes* (Montreal: Lacombe, 1989).

10. Harel, *Le Voleur de parcours,* 159–60.

11. *Une Histoire américaine* is the title of Jacques Godbout's parodic novel about consumerism, conservatism, and West Coast political resistance (Paris: Seuil, 1986).

12. Janine Ricouart, "Entre le miroir et le porte-clés: *Petits Violences* de Madeleine Monette," *Dalhousie French Studies* 23 (fall/winter 1992): 16–17.

13. Lise Gauvin, *Lettres d'une autre* (Montreal: Hexagone, 1984), 36.

14. Pierre Nepveu, "Une ville en poésie québécoise contemporaine," in *Montréal imaginaire: Ville et littérature*, ed. Pierre Nepveu and Gilles Marcotte (Montreal: Fides, 1992), 323–71.

15. Elspeth Probyn, "Travels in the Postmodern: Making Sense of the Local," in *Feminism/Postmodernism*, ed. Linda J. Nicholson (New York and London: Routledge, 1990), 187.

16. Frédérique Chevillot, "Les Hommes de Madeleine Monette," *Québec Studies* 15 (fall /winter 1993): 17.

17. Homi Bhabha, *The Location of Culture* (London and New York: Routledge, 1994).

18. See Karen Gould, "Féminisme, postmodernité, esthétique de lecture: *Le Désert mauve* de Nicole Brossard," in *Le Roman québécois depuis 1960: méthodes et analyses*, ed. Louise Milot and Jaap Lintvelt (Saint-Foy: Les Presses de l'Université Laval, 1992), 195–213, reprinted in *L'Autre Lecture: La critique au féminin et les textes québécois*, ed. Lori Saint-Martin (Montreal: XYZ, 1994); and Janet Paterson, *Moments postmodernes dans le roman québécois*, expanded edition (Ottawa: Presses de l'Université d'Ottawa, 1993).

19. Karen Gould, *Writing in the Feminine: Feminism and Experimental Writing in Quebec* (Carbondale and Edwardsville: Southern Illinois University Press, 1990), 98.

20. See Sherry Simon, "La traduction inachevée," in *L'Etranger dans tous ses états: enjeux culturels et littéraires*, ed. Simon Harel (Montreal: XYZ, 1992), 37.

21. See Richard Rhodes's recounting of the first atomic explosion in *The Making of the Atomic Bomb* (New York: Simon and Schuster, 1986), 675–76.

22. Nicole Brossard, *La Nuit verte du parc labyrinthe* (Laval: Editions Trois, 1992), 14.

23. A slightly different version of this analysis of *Copies conformes* has appeared as an article, "*Copies conformes*: la réécriture québécoise d'un polar américain," *Etudes françaises* 29, 1 (1993): 25–35.

24. Louky Bersianik, *L'Euguélionne* (Montreal: La Presse, 1976; reprint, Montreal: Stanké, 1986) and *Le Pique-nique sur l'Acropole* (Montreal: VLB Editeur, 1979; reprint, Montreal: L'Hexagone, Collection Typo, 1992). For a discussion of Bersianik's parodic writing, see my chapter on Bersianik in *Writing in the Feminine*, 150–99; and Evelyne Voldeng's essay, "La Parodie carnavalesque dans *L'Euguélionne*," in *Féminité, subversion et écriture* (Montreal: Remue-ménage, 1983), 119–26.

25. Linda Hutcheon, *The Politics of Postmodernism* (London and New York: Routledge, 1989), 102.

26. Susan Ireland makes an interesting analogy between the stolen disk and LaRue's own acknowledged "thievery" of Hammett's story in "Monique LaRue's *Copies conformes*: An Original Copy," *Québec Studies* 15 (fall 1992/winter 1993): 23–24.

27. Sherry Simon has noted the recurrence of the theme of translation in contemporary Quebec novels where travel to the United States occurs. See her essay, "La culture en question," in *L'Age de la prose: romans et récits québécois des années 80*, ed. Lise Gauvin and Franca Marcato-Falzoni (Montreal: VLB Editeur; Rome: Bulzoni, 1992), 58–59. See also Sherry Simon, *Le Trafic des langues: Tradition et culture dans la littérature québécoise* (Montreal: Boréal, 1994).

28. In Quebec, *nationalist writing* has been overtly associated with the project of an independent Quebec. Nationalist-leaning discourse in *Copies conformes*, however, is more postcolonialist in sentiment than *indépendantiste*.

29. Harel, *Le Voleur de parcours*, 190.

30. Annette Kuhn, *Women's Pictures: Feminism and Cinema* (London and Boston: Routledge and Kegan Paul, 1982), 35.

31. Ibid.

32. Jean Baudrillard, *De la séduction* (Paris: Denoël, 1988).

33. LaRue has lamented the trivialization of motherhood in contemporary writing in "La mère aujourd'hui," *La Nouvelle Barre du jour* 116 (September 1982): 53.

34. On maternal discourse in Quebec women's writings, see Karen Gould, "Refiguring the Mother: Quebec Women Writers in the 80s," *International Journal of Canadian Studies/ Revue internationale d'études canadiennes* 6 (fall 1992): 113–25; and "Vers une maternité qui se crée: l'oeuvre de Louky Bersianik," *Voix et Images* 17, 1 (fall 1991): 35–47; Mary Jean Green, "Redefining the Maternal: Women's Relationships in the Fiction of Marie-Claire Blais's *Visions d'Anna,*" *Québec Studies* 2 (1984): 94–104; Lori Saint-Martin, "Gabrielle Roy: The Mother's Voice, The Daughter's Text," *American Review of Canadian Studies* 20, 3 (fall 1990): 303–25; Patricia Smart, *Ecrire dans la maison du père: L'émergence du féminin dans la tradition littéraire du Québec* (Montreal: Québec/Amérique, 1988).

35. Sara Ruddick, *Maternal Thinking: Toward a Politics of Peace* (New York: Ballantine, 1989).

36. Jean-François Chassay, "Reflet des Etats-Unis dans le roman québécois: une version de l'Amérique," *Urgences* 34 (1991): 15.

CHAPTER THIRTEEN

Blurring the Lines in
Vietnamese Fiction in French

Kim Lefèvre's *Métisse blanche*

JACK A. YEAGER

Although by their numbers men have dominated Vietnamese francophone literature since its beginnings in the early 1920s, women writers have made important contributions to this corpus and have been producing texts since the appearance of collaborations by Trinh Thuc Oanh and Marguerite Triaire in the late 1930s and early 1940s.[1] Moreover, from the outset women characters have played important roles in narratives written by men.[2] In the late 1960s, however, both women's and men's voices fell silent, an event I noted with some pessimism in the mid-1980s.[3] But in recent years a new group of Vietnamese francophone writers has emerged, signaling at once a reawakening of this narrative voice that fell silent in the 1960s and new directions in novels in French by Vietnamese writers. Ly Thu Ho's 1986 novel *Le Mirage de la paix* (The mirage of peace) bridges the silence of the 1970s and early 1980s, linking the old and the new. Many facets of the Vietnamese francophone experience explored in her earlier novels reappear in this text, the completion of her trilogy.[4] The works of Kim Lefèvre, Bach Mai, Nguyen Huu Khoa, and Linda Lê, however, all writers who have published since 1985, show important new fields of examination and present new situations in original ways that in some cases bear only distant connections to previous texts or to each other. Nguyen Huu Khoa and Linda Lê seem to break radically with the work of their predecessors,[5] whereas both Bach Mai and Kim

210

Lefèvre reorient the debate toward current issues such as the refugee problem, Amerasian and Eurasian children, and the drug trade.[6] With the exception of Nguyen Huu Khoa, all these new writers are women.

Kim Lefèvre[7] develops the marginalized body as the crux of her text
Métisse blanche (White métisse).[8] The publication of this narrative in 1989
caused quite a sensation in France as witnessed by numerous favorable
reviews[9] and an appearance by Lefèvre on Bernard Pivot's *Apostrophes*.[10]
Lefèvre's autobiographical narrative,[11] which she herself has called a novel,
traces the childhood and adolescence of a Eurasian girl in colonial Viet Nam.[12]
The narrator effectively sets the tone in the opening lines of the text: "Je suis
née, paraît-il, à Hanoi un jour de printemps, peu avant la Seconde Guerre
mondiale, de l'union éphémère entre une jeune Annamite et un Français"
(17). (It seems I was born in Hanoi on a spring day, not long before the
Second World War, [the child] of the ephemeral union of a young Annamese
woman and a French man.) On the one hand, like her literary predecessor
Ly Thu Ho, Lefèvre fixes the historical backdrop, the final years of official
French colonialism and its aftermath, and the implications of the wars to
come. This short phrase, then, determines an entire historical, political, and
cultural context: French Indochina, colonialism, and the overlay of French
cultural influence on Vietnamese traditions.

But this first sentence also struggles against any kind of specificity because it also indicates the narrator's place in Viet Nam, a place that will always be imprecise and temporary, "paraît-il" (it seems) and "éphémère"
being the operative words in this opening phrase. It is not a "place" at all,
because it can never be fixed or defined. As a young girl, the narrator lives
with various relatives, sometimes with her mother, who at one point gives
up her daughter to an orphanage only to rescue her later. This changing,
unstable, and unreliable family situation is reflected in a constant shifting
and relocation, moving from one house to another, in and out of the orphanage, from one town to the next, from North to South Viet Nam and
back, and finally from Saigon to France. The physical displacements have
various causes: the family's financial hardship, the war, the narrator's own
changing attitudes about the culture into which she was born, and of course
her status as *métisse* (biracial). The voyage motif runs throughout the text;
the narrator is always on the way somewhere, on the move physically or psychologically: "Ma vie était comme une fuite en avant mais pour aller où?"
(144) (My life was a forward flight, but to go where?).[13]

The narrator's own situation seems to tell us about the plight of the
Vietnamese people as well. Their culture, shaken to its foundations by colo-

nialism and wars for independence, is in turmoil, destabilized, changing. Because of the war, the Vietnamese are forced to leave their homes and see their villages destroyed and their identity questioned in a culture tied as it is to the land. Lefèvre evokes this sense of loss and change in a moving scene in which villagers attempt to deal with leaving home, with the Viet Minh burning their village in the face of advancing French troops: "Comment! la maison bâtie par leur grand-père, où avait vécu leur père, anéantie à jamais? C'était inacceptable" (115) (What? The houses built by their grandfathers, the houses where their fathers had lived, destroyed forever? It was unacceptable); and later: "Les vieilles recueillaient un peu de terre qu'elles enveloppaient dans un mouchoir, pour qu'on la jetât plus tard dans leur tombe. Leur grand regret était de devoir mourir loin du sol où elles étaient nées" (115). (The old women gathered a bit of earth that they wrapped up in a handkerchief so that it could be thrown into their own graves later. What they regretted most was to have to die far from the land where they were born.)

Everything in this text, however, leads back to the narrator's métissage, that undefinable site. She feels herself to be a part of the Vietnamese community and culture only to be rejected and humiliated by those to whom she wants to belong. This rejection is somehow incomprehensible to the young girl who feels Vietnamese. Lefèvre, reliving her childhood on *Apostrophes,* slipping into the present tense, recalled: "Dans ma tête il y a des paysages vietnamiennes, il y a des airs de chansons vietnamiennes, donc je ne comprends pas pourquoi je ne pouvais pas l'être, je ne comprenais pas et c'était pour moi une très grande injustice." (In my head there are Vietnamese landscapes, there are melodies of Vietnamese songs, so I don't understand why I couldn't be Vietnamese, I didn't understand and it was for me a very great injustice.) As a child, the narrator is not really aware of her physical difference, having only rarely looked at herself in a mirror.[14] When finally she sees her reflection for the first time, she too is shocked at her unexpected facial features, at seeing what others see. Up to then, she had always thought of herself as looking like her mother and sisters (133).

The mode of being out of place, "étrangère," is a common thread running throughout *Métisse blanche* (18, 28, 50, 51, 63, 78, passim). The narrator's first photograph shows the image of an "étrangère" (133), the face, "étranger" (134). Buying herself a mirror, she finds the reflection that of an unknown person: "Etrangère, à moi-même, je l'étais également aux yeux des autres" (137) (A stranger to myself, I was equally strange in the eyes of others). Mme N, described as an "étrangère" (256, 259), serves as the narrator's benefactor, paying for her schooling at the exclusive Couvent des Oiseaux. Having to learn French literature not as "étrangère" but as if it were the narrator's own strikes her as odd (290).

The narrator's realization of her "strangeness" both explains and sharpens the unexpected title, the devaluing of what usually has value in a colonial context (or elsewhere), the denial of "la part blanche" (the white part).[15] She dreams of a kingdom, "peuplé de métisses" (37) (populated with métisses), a place where she will be normal, where she will fit in: "J'aurais un père métis, une mère métisse, un oncle métis, et même mon institutrice serait métisse. Personne ne me remarquerait car je serais comme tout le monde" (37). (I would have a mixed-race father, a mixed-race mother, a mixed-race uncle and even my schoolteacher would be biracial. No one would notice me because I would be like everyone else.) Ironically, that place turns out to be the orphanage: "je constatai avec stupeur qu'il n'y avait parmi [les jeunes fille de l'orphelinat] aucune Vietnamienne, qu'elles étaient toutes métisses, comme moi" (49). (I noticed with amazement that none [of the young girls in the orphanage] was Vietnamese but that they were all biracial like me.) Fitting in can only occur outside the family, the basic social unit in Viet Nam where Confucian social relations regulate all social interaction and where replication of the idealized past is paramount. At one point in her text, the narrator invents a history for herself, a past, where she has Vietnamese parents.[16] Legitimate history is associated with having a father (72), and yet at other times she wants to purge herself of her French blood. The ephemeral is thus reinforced in the narrator's ambivalence about her heritage. The invented history foreshadows *Métisse blanche* and Lefèvre's coming to writing.

To the narrator's Vietnamese relatives in a society that prizes its sons, she is also the useless daughter ("inutile" [122]) to her stepfather in addition to being untrustworthy because of the French blood within her. This view of her makes her the scapegoat of colonialism as well as the constant reminder of it. At a local village school she becomes bored and loses interest; the teacher punishes her often, as the narrator writes, "avec une ardeur quasi patriotique, comme si en s'acharnant sur moi elle sauvait le pays entier du venin colonial" (36) (with an almost patriotic fervor as if in going after me so relentlessly she was saving the whole country from the colonial venom). She is finally expelled in humiliation. In another instance the Viet Minh who come to her village test her loyalty to the cause of independence and berate her when she fails, but she is only a child, learning to respond to shifting power and authority by trial and error. Even her mother wonders aloud to her daughter what her own life would have been like if she had never met the Frenchman: "Qui sait ce que je serais devenue si je n'avais pas été enceinte de toi" (232) (Who knows what I would have become had I not been pregnant with you); or if her child had been a boy: " 'Que n'es-tu un garçon?' " (171) ("Why weren't you a boy?"), reminding her daughter once again that women and girls are powerless in a society regulated by Confucian filial piety.

The narrator's appearance then sets her apart and reminds the observer not only of Viet Nam's own humiliation at the hands of the French but also that the narrator's mother transgressed Vietnamese traditional morality, having a child outside of marriage and having had sexual relations with the enemy (86). The narrator represents the mother's shameful relationship with a Frenchman, cause for her own rejection: "Mon existence signait sa faute et son exclusion" (92) (My existence was a sign of her mistake and her exclusion), a situation the man her mother eventually marries always holds against her. The daughter's movement over the landscape recalls the original sin of her mother and the daughter's métissage, the "porteur d'immoralité" (320) (carrier of immorality), on her face for all to see (198). The daughter is the potentially guilty witness of her mother's ruined life (298). As a site of shame and humiliation, at the same time she reacts and becomes obsessed with guarding her own virtue because as her mother tells her and as her life illustrates, a woman who loses her virginity loses everything in traditional Viet Nam. Referred to as her "trésor" (treasure), the narrator's virginity creates her worth and constructs her femininity in a world controlled by men: " 'Une femme n'a qu'un trésor, c'est celui de sa virginité' " ("A woman has only one treasure and that's her virginity"), the narrator's mother tells her at the moment of her first period—and she speaks from experience. "Làdessus, elle me racontait les lamentables histoires de ces filles répudiées par leurs époux parce qu'elles n'étaient plus vierges. Il ne leur restait que le recours à la prostitution ou une vie misérable. Car les hommes savent toujours reconnaître une fille qui a perdu sa virginité" (110). (Upon that, she told me the pitiful stories of girls rejected by their husbands, because they were no longer virgins. The only recourse left for them was prostitution and a life of misery. For men can always recognize a girl who has lost her virginity.) The mother frames her assessment, knowingly: " 'Crois-moi, ma fille, je sais de quoi je parle. Ne commets pas les mêmes erreurs que ta mère' " (110). ("Believe me, my daughter, I know what I'm talking about. Don't make the same mistakes as your mother.")

Throughout *Métisse blanche* the narrator associates Viet Nam with her mother, France with her father. At the outset the absent father is deemed arrogant and detestable (17); the narrator dreams of accidents that would empty her of the French blood within her (18). At the end of the text, the association still holds: "La France, c'est l'image du père qui m'avait abandonnée" (340) (France is the image of the father who abandoned me): the narrator is the impure fruit of her mother's betrayal (342). By contrast, "Viêtnam, c'est la douceur du visage de ma mère" (340) (Viet Nam is the sweetness of my mother's face). When her mother retrieves the narrator from the orphanage, an environment where French is spoken, she in essence "returns to Viet Nam" and must relearn Vietnamese (64–65, 71). "J'avais une mère" (71) (I had a mother), the narrator writes, who had thought herself abandoned. Recovering her mother signifies recovering a country, a culture, a language. "Comme j'aimais ce pays, le Viêt-nam, mon pays…" (32) (How I loved this country, Viet Nam, my country…); "C'est un pays cher à mon coeur" (340) (The country is dear to my heart). Not surprisingly, the narrator learns about the role of women in traditional Vietnamese society from her mother: the expectations of domestic work (83, 84), how a Vietnamese woman should behave (109–11), her position of powerlessness relative to men, and the dangers of succumbing to their desires: "Prends garde à ne pas te faire engrosser, ta vie serait ruinée pour toujours" (210) (Be careful not to get pregnant or your life will be ruined forever), her mother says. Successfully resisting sexual desire to safeguard her virginity makes the narrator worth the same as "Vietnamienne de pure race" (304) (pure Vietnamese [woman]).

According to Vietnamese tradition, then, men determine the value of women; women are defined by men, exchanged by them. In this context, the narrator can be sold like her literary ancestor, Kieu, in the most famous of Vietnamese verse romances, *Kim-Van-Kieu*.[17] She can consider herself like merchandise, to be bought and sold. Other women characters in the book, portrayed as prostitutes, give weight to the mother's warning. But the narrator's development of a sense of self-worth and self-respect contrasts with the traditional view of women and counteracts it, showing a new level of consciousness.

The narrator's false start in the Vietnamese village school suggests the need to pursue other forms of knowledge, for indeed, according to *Métisse blanche*, it is education and more specifically a Western education in French that will free the narrator from her degraded state and gain her some measure of self-respect and esteem, in a sense revalorizing what had been devalued, while at the same time she struggles against the hatred she feels for her father. The desire on the part of the narrator to prove her self-worth motivates her to succeed at school. Even her stepfather shows some respect for the young girl when she passes her examinations and earns her degrees. Confucianism, too, held education in high esteem.

Learning French provides the key to "other knowledge." The narrator's first contacts with this language take place at the orphanage. Later on her mother finds her cousin Odile, again also a Eurasian, "celle qui avait désespéré de faire de [la narratrice] une Française" (150) (the one who had tried desperately to make a French woman [of the narrator]). Odile decides it would be unworthy of the girl's French blood to leave her uneducated and takes her in to "[l'] initier à un style de vie plus conforme à [sa] nature" (150) (initiate [her] to a lifestyle more in line with [her] nature). Eventually, the narrator finds her way to the prestigious Couvent des Oiseaux near Dalat, the Catholic school where the better part of her education takes place. Presented as an enclave in the mountains, the convent school is separated from its surroundings, cut off from the momentous events happening around it: the war against the French, governmental repression, Dien Bien Phu, the Geneva Accords, and the division of the country at the seventeenth parallel. The inroads that Vietnamese culture have made at the school appear on closer examination superficial to the narrator and her friend Do. Both feel out of place there, surrounded by their Vietnamese classmates who seem very French (273) in what they see as another world (285–86).[18] The narrator feels as disoriented in this isolated location as she did anywhere else, "étrangère." Likewise Do, the more traditional of the two young women, becomes the reference point for her French-influenced, Catholic peers who act as though France were their native land and the Gauls their ancestors. Do finds that the community at the convent school seems oblivious to the impact of colonialism on Viet Nam, as if it had not even existed. Do's enthusiasm about the defeat of the French at Dien Bien Phu can, it seems, only be shared by the narrator.

On the other hand, the narrator's French Catholic education at the convent school makes her feel superior to her own family to the extent that while she is home she misses school.[19] Her arrogance alienates her from her family. These attitudes then seem to measure her conversion to French culture. And the narrator tells her story to an imagined French reader who is non-Vietnamese, like other texts in the Vietnamese francophone corpus. Consequently, she explains Tet, the social role of Chinese in Viet Nam, the story of the Trung sisters, proper behavior, and the like.[20]

Identifying traditional Viet Nam with the mother and France with the father would seem to reinforce the conventional dichotomy of the feminine East and masculine West. This binarity is continually challenged and clouded, however, by the narrator's ambivalence. Formal education in *Métisse blanche* takes place in French settings, and the narrator finds pleasure in learning: "Je connus enfin la joie d'avoir accès à la connaissance. Mon francais s'améliorait de jour en jour" (54) (I finally knew the joy of having access to knowledge. My French improved day by day). The mother, realizing the importance of a French education to her daughter, tells her that she is not suited for domestic work and "pushes" her from the kitchen: "Une fille de ta race n'est pas une paysanne!" (86) (A girl of your race is not a peasant); "Si tu étais élevée en France, tu recevrais une éducation au lieu de vivre comme les gens d'ici!" (86) (If you were being raised in France, you would receive an education instead of living like the people here). Moreover, the mother sees education as an arm against adversity for her daughter (143). As a result, the narrator progressively leaves behind her Vietnamese education for French schools (244). Significantly, following her mother home along the narrow dikes of labyrinthine rice fields, they get lost, stuck in the mud (72).

At the same time the narrator is drawn irresistibly by the knowledge of France, rejecting the culture that considers her a monstrosity (18). She hates her straight hair and dreams of being French (29); after the coolness of the convent school, located in the mountains, she claims she will never adapt to the heat and humidity of her country (259). While on vacation at her family's house, she thinks nostalgically of the convent school, where everything is beautiful (286). Contrary to the Vietnamese communal way of life, the narrator demands privacy in her family's house (286–87). Likewise, she disdains her mother, considering her a peasant, a "Nha-quê" (287). Using this Vietnamese word, appropriated by the French to refer pejoratively to the Vietnamese, is the ultimate insult and rejection. Finally, the mother accuses her daughter of losing all notion of filial piety (263). The transformation seems complete when the narrator writes that as a teacher in Saigon, she expresses herself naturally in French "comme tout professeur qui se respecte" (334) (like any self-respecting teacher). And yet, even these feelings are always tempered, never categorical, always clouded. The narrator would do anything to make her mother happy and yet wants to erase the memory of her mother's failed life (242). As for teaching, the narrator considers herself as a pioneer, one of the first generation of teachers in an independent Viet Nam: "Je me considérais pleinement comme une enfant du Viêt-nam, comme une citoyenne du Viêt-nam. Ce pays était le mien, c'était mon sol et ma patrie. Je désirais y vivre jusqu'à la fin" (324) (I considered myself to be fully a child of Viet Nam, a citizen of Viet Nam. This country was mine, it was my land, my fatherland. I wanted to stay there for the rest of my life). A few pages later, given the opportunity to pursue her studies in France, the narrator writes: "L'idée de pouvoir quitter le Viêt-nam me suffisait. Elle constituait ma protection contre une société qui m'avait de tout temps sourdement refusée. C'était ma cuirasse, ma porte de sortie. Je me contentais de ce rêve de revanche" (337) (The idea of being able to leave Viet Nam was enough for me. It constituted my protection against a society that had forever rejected me in silence. Leaving was my armor, my escape. I contented myself with this dream of revenge). And yet, as with the nostalgic ending of the text, the narrator, in hindsight, measures her attachment to Viet Nam, assesses its deep imprint on her personality, admitting that the land of her birth formed the core of her being (339). Right up until the actual departure, she debates whether to go or stay (330), likening her leaving to a child "qu'on aurait brutalement arraché du sein maternel" (340) (brutally snatched from its mother's breast).

This ambivalence is compounded by the way that métissage provides the basis not only for rejection and humiliation but also for value and beauty, another duality lying at the heart of the narrative. The narrator's grandmother tells her: "'Tu es un alliage, ni or ni argent, ta vie sera difficile. Mais celui qui recherche la rareté sera heureux de te trouver'" (35) (You are an alloy, neither gold nor silver; your life will be difficult. But the man who is looking for rarity will be happy to find you), a conversation recalled later (49). Years later, the narrator is considered in France as an "objet rare" (77) (rare object). Often, she is beautiful (241) and desirable precisely because she is métisse (104–5, 150, 151). Duc, the music teacher in Nha Trang with whom the narrator has a platonic affair, tells her so: "Mais tu me plais justement parce que tu n'est [sic] pas vietnamienne tout à fait. Vois-tu, tu es vietnamienne sans l'être, c'est là ton attrait. Quand je te regarde, tu m'es à la fois familière et étrangère. Et j'aime ça" (217–18) (But you please me precisely because you aren't completely Vietnamese. You are Vietnamese without being it, see, that's your attraction. When I look at you, you are at once familiar and strange. I like that). Once discovered, their cross-generational affair is easily explained because of the narrator's métissage; she is, in effect, "métisse, immorale, folle" (225) (biracial, immoral, crazy). The narrator is constantly torn by her desire to purge herself of her French blood and yet seeks to develop that part of her nature. In the end she cuts herself off from the site of her humiliation, rejection, and shame and heads for France. But her birthplace, too, will always be within her: "les haies de bambou, l'étang de mon enfance, les visages aimés et le dos satiné de la vieille nourrice qui m'emportait dans les rues silencieuses d'Hanoi, par une nuit de crachin" (343) (the bamboo hedges, the pond of my childhood, the beloved faces and the satin-smooth back of the old nurse who carried me through the hushed streets of Hanoi on a drizzly night).

Throughout the text the narrator's marginalization plays itself out in unresolved duality, in ongoing ambivalence. She sets this up in the first line of the text and in presenting the text itself both as an autobiographical "récit" (account) and as a novel. What then is this text? Where is this text? Somewhere between genres, blurred between autobiography and novel, the convergence typical, in fact, in this literature, here the story of the author herself growing up as métisse in colonial Viet Nam, but presented too as a work of the imagination, supported by extensive detailed dialogues cited verbatim, submerged in the depths of memory. Reality and invention blur, seem deliberately confused. The editor integrates Lefèvre's mother's identification card photograph into the cover design of the book in a way similar to Marguerite Duras's American editor's incorporating a photograph of the writer as a young girl between the titles on the cover of the American edition of L'Amant.

In Métisse blanche Lefèvre creates a narrator that by her presence alone upends the cultural, social, political, and racial worlds of tradition and colonialism. She is the constant reminder of and challenge to all these categories and expectations, out of place and yet present, there.

In its originality, this text suggests, then, a continually evolving trajectory of Vietnamese francophone literature. This literature was born within and nurtured on the dilemma of cultural métissage with such salient examples as Hai in Nguyen Phan Long's 1921 novel Le Roman de Mlle Lys (The novel of Mademoiselle Lys),[21] Sao in the 1930 text Bà-Đầm (the rendering of Madame in Vietnamese) by Truong Dinh Tri and Albert de Teneuille,[22] the narrator in Pham Van Ky's 1947 novel Frères de sang (Blood brothers),[23] and so many others. The reawakened voice of the mid-1980s remembers this problematic cultural blending, but both Bach Mai and Kim Lefèvre present racial métissage for the first time in their texts. Those whose lives were determined by cultural métissage could hide this blending resulting from education, could "pass" if need be while coping with the desire to assimilate and the eventual realization that becoming the other is impossible. The racial métisse, by contrast, demonstrates her blending by the presence of her body, there for all to see.

I would suggest, however, that Lefèvre plays with sexual roles and performances in conscious ways that are rare in this literature. In *Métisse blanche* she broaches questions of gender and sexuality, of androgyny. Almost offhandedly, comments appear unexpectedly in the text, creating a pattern in their repetition. Mme Moreau, the narrator's French teacher at a religious school in Saigon, has a masculine air about her that her students admire:

> C'était une grande femme rousse à la chevelure flamboyante coupée très court, dont la peau incroyablement blanche était couverte de taches de rousseur. Toujours vêtue d'une saharienne et d'une jupe blanche, elle ressemblait à ces officiers de marine que j'avais vus dans les films américains. . . . Nous admirions son allure masculine, son assurance. (230)

> [She was a tall, red-headed woman with flaming hair cut very short and whose incredibly white skin was covered with freckles. Always dressed in a safari jacket and white skirt, she looked like one of those naval officers I had seen in American movies. . . . We admired her masculine air, her assurance.]

And teaching is viewed as a "profession pas assez 'virile'" (profession not virile enough) by the narrator, who would prefer to be a doctor or an engineer (231). Later she decides to become a teacher, encouraged by Mme Moreau, who tells her she is not good enough in mathematics to be in science, and disappointing her mother, who saw her daughter working as a midwife. After Moreau leaves (following her husband, who has been transferred to Africa), one of the sisters at the school, a soeur Aimée, protects the narrator, taking care of her when she is ill, "alliant le dévouement d'une mère au zèle d'une amante" (238) (combining the devotion of a mother with the zeal of a lover). In this same section of the book, the narrator mentions that the sisters try to prevent the schoolgirls being "au dortoir en tête à tête afin de les soustraire à la tentation des amours coupables. Mais certains couples se formaient quand même, quelques filles s'aimaient entre elles" (237) (in the dormitory in intimate conversation in order to shield them from the temptation of forbidden love. But some couples developed in spite of it; some girls loved each other among themselves). The narrator explains, however: "Nous avions de quatorze à seize ans, une sensualité naissante, des élans d'amour sans objet, sur qui d'autre déverser ce trop-plein? Les religieuses elles-mêmes avaient leurs préférées auxquelles elles vouaient une passion interdite et non exclue de sensualité" (237). (We were fourteen to sixteen years old and had an emerging sensuality, passionate transports without object; on whom else could we unload our overflowing emotions? The nuns themselves also had their favorites to whom they declared a forbidden passion that did not exclude sensuality.) The sister that greets the narrator upon her arrival at the airport to take her to the Couvent des Oiseaux in Dalat has bushy eyebrows like those of an old "mandarin" and a "voix presque masculine" (267–68) (almost masculine voice), setting the precedent for the register of sexual ambiguity at the school. Before the narrator's departure for France, she sees two young women caressing each other at a student residence in Saigon. The girls are described by another as "le couple du second étage" (312) (the couple from the second floor).

Similar blurrings in *Métisse blanche* reinforce the challenge to gender boundaries and prescribed roles. At the orphanage, the girls are taught that France is "notre mère nourricière, notre patrie" (62) (our nurturing mother, our fatherland). To avoid the fate of women, powerless in traditional Viet Nam, the narrator considers disguising herself as a man like the heroines in her books (120). Attracted by the photographs of languid women (247), she later expresses a desire to read *La Religieuse* (289). The narrator's role as teacher in a newly independent Viet Nam (324) extends to a wish to remain single and autonomous (299), a trait she will pass on to her students for whom education will be a liberating force just as it was for the narrator (324). She describes one of her own friendships with another woman as "presque virile" (342).

Although experimenting, searching, and confusion would fit the portrayal of adolescence, androgyny and challenging gender roles in Lefèvre's text seem more long lasting. The perceived ambiguity of these situations recalls the undefinable quality of the narrator herself, her "ephemeral" beginnings. The incidences of transvestism and same-sex coupling in *Métisse blanche* would reinforce the narrator's own life on the margins. Moreover, as Marjorie Garber has pointed out: "one of the most important aspects of cross-dressing is the way in which it offers a challenge to easy notions of binarity, putting into question the categories of "female" and "male," whether they are considered essential or constructed, biological or cultural."[24]

A seemingly undefinable "third," like the Eurasian child in Lefèvre's narrative, is thus introduced that disturbs binarity and creates crisis, but as Garber indicates, this third is not a term nor is it a sex; rather "the 'third' is a mode of articulation, a way of describing a space of possibility. Three puts in question the idea of one: of identity, self-sufficiency, self-knowledge" (11). In francophone literature from colonial and postcolonial contexts, the third would challenge any dominant power.[25] The presence of a third "puts in question identities previously conceived as stable, unchallengeable, grounded, and 'known'" (13), as well as questioning "the very notion of the 'original' and of stable identity" (16). The category crisis Garber articulates means that borders become "permeable," and for her that permits "border crossings from one (apparently distinct) category to another" (16). Transvestite figures, then, necessarily blur and erase seemingly stable and immutable boundaries.

Although transvestism and gender boundary crossing are infrequent in *Métisse blanche,* these moments disrupt the narrative often enough to call attention to themselves, concentrated as they are in the last third of the text. For Garber even rare moments such as these are meaningful and point to a "category crisis elsewhere."[26] Furthermore, these most noticeable disruptions occur most tellingly in educational settings: a pension in Saigon, the convent school, a dormitory for school girls. The cultural ambiguity that defined generations of Vietnamese francophone texts, of course, originated here. For the narrator of *Métisse blanche,* the convent school, at first like another planet (269), protected from the outside, comes to capture life between two worlds, a liminal space. On a visit to nearby Dalat, the narrator remarks: "Deux mois vécus en ce lieu protégé, dans une sorte de flou culturel où nous étudiions la langue de Racine mais communiquions en vietnamien entre nous, m'avaient fait oublier ces images familières [de la vie dans une ville vietnamienne]. J'étais en train de perdre progressivement mes racines" (283) (Two months spent in that protected place, in a kind of cultural flux in which we studied the language of Racine but communicated among ourselves in Vietnamese had made me forget these familiar images [of life in a Vietnamese city]. I was in the process of gradually losing my roots [a play on words with Racine]). And, as we have seen, the narrator's mother reproaches her daughter for having lost the notion of filial piety, so influenced as she is by her French education.

The blurred border zone exposed by the cross-dresser is revealed equally by the métisse, for it is precisely this space that the narrator inhabits in *Métisse blanche.* At the same time, it is the site of the text itself, somewhere between the worlds of fiction and autobiography, the territory so well mapped by Françoise Lionnet and other critics.[27] Constriction and limitation, from tradition or colonialism, necessitate the experimentation and crossover we see in Lefèvre's narrative, a search for new possibilities, challenges to tradition. Here, as in previous texts, these potentials came in the form of, say, French education. In *Métisse blanche* the act of imagining a different future takes place also in communities of women, recalling Trinh Thuc Oanh and

Marguerite Triaire as well as Ly Thu Ho.[28] Kim Lefèvre's presentation of crossover, of challenging the expectation of gender roles, however, upends these
worlds as well, suggesting a new métissage of sexual identity and gender
performance. This and all other aspects of *Métisse blanche* conspire to blur
and cloud notions of race, gender, and genre, effectively capturing a life
caught between worlds, undefinable, standing in sharp contrast to post-
industrial assertions for linguistic purity and against cultural ambiguity.
"[L]e monde à l'envers" (275) (The upside down world) of *Métisse blanche*
challenges those who insist on the drawing of lines in the struggles against
diversity, multiculturalism, and ambiguity, in an effort to define and cate-
gorize. In this way, Kim Lefèvre's text is timely and controversial. More importantly, her narrative also traces a new path in the drama of colonial and
postcolonial Viet Nam.

Notes

1. These collaborations include two novels, *En s'écartant des ancêtres* (Distancing from
the ancestors) (Hanoi: Imprimerie d'Extrême-Orient, 1939) and *La Réponse de l'Occident* (The
answer of the West) (Hanoi: Imprimerie d'Extrême-Orient, 1941), and a collection of short
narratives, "contes du pays d'Annam," *La Tortue d'or* (The golden turtle) (Hanoi: Imprimerie
d'Extrême-Orient, 1940). I discuss the two novels in *The Vietnamese Novel in French: A Literary Response to Colonialism* (Hanover and London: University Press of New England, 1987),
chapter 6.

2. In one of the first novels published, *Le Roman de Mlle Lys*, Nguyen Phan Long casts a
woman character as protagonist. For further discussion, see *The Vietnamese Novel in French*,
chapter 6, "Women as Character and Symbol."

3. My conclusions, written in 1985, in *The Vietnamese Novel in French* were anything if
not pessimistic.

4. Ly Thu Ho, *Le Mirage de la paix* (Paris: Promédart/Les Muses de Parnasse, 1986),
winner of the Prix de l'Asie from AUPELF in 1987. See my analysis, "La Politique 'intimiste':
La Production romanesque des écrivaines vietnamiennes d'expression française," *Présence francophone* 43 (1993): 131–47. Ly Thu Ho, *Printemps inachevé* (Unfinished spring) (Paris: J. Pey-
ronnet, 1962), and Ly Thu Ho, *Au milieu du carrefour* (At the crossroads) (Paris: J. Peyron-
net, 1969) are the first two novels in the trilogy. See analyses of these texts in *The Vietnamese
Novel in French*, chapter 5.

5. Nguyen Huu Khoa has published three novels: *Le Temple de la félicité éternelle* (The
temple of eternal happiness) (Paris: La Différence, 1985), *La Montagne endormie* (The sleep-
ing mountain) (Paris: La Différence, 1987), and *La Métamorphose de la tortue* (The metamorphosis of the turtle) (Paris: La Différence, 1995); Linda Lê has published four novels: *Un
si tendre vampire* (Such a tender vampire) (Paris: La Table Ronde, 1987), *Fuir* (Flight) (Paris:
La Table Ronde, 1988), *Calomnies* (Calumnies) (Paris: Christian Bourgois, 1993), and *Les
Dits d'un idiot* (The tales of an idiot) (Paris: Christian Bourgois, 1995); four interlocking
novellas that could be considered a novel, *Les Evangiles du crime* (The gospel of crime) (Paris:
Julliard, 1992); and finally a collection of short stories, *Solo* (Paris: La Table Ronde, 1989).
See my discussion of new narrative voices in *Vietnamese Literature in French* (New Orleans:
CELFAN Review Monographs [Tulane University], 1996).

6. Bach Mai has published one novel, *D'Ivoire et d'opium* (Of ivory and opium) (Sherbrooke: Editions Naaman, 1985). This novel figures in the discussion of new narrative voices

in the aforementioned monograph, note 5, as well as in my article, "Bach Mai's Francophone Asian Voice: Remapping Margin and Center," *Québec Studies* 14 (spring/summer 1992): 49–64.

7. Kim Lefèvre has lived in Paris since her departure from Saigon, recounted at the end of *Métisse blanche*. She returned to Viet Nam during the summer of 1990, her first trip back since leaving in 1960, and published a second text titled *Retour à la saison des pluies* (Return to the rainy season) (Paris: Editions Barrault, 1990) about that experience. According to her editor, she also plans to continue the story begun in her first narrative. I discuss the second narrative in: "*Retour à la saison des pluies*: Rediscovering the Landscapes of Childhood," *L'Esprit Créateur* 32, 2 (summer 1993): 47–57.

8. *Métisse blanche* (Paris: Editions Barrault, 1989). The word *métisse* means a blending of different strands and commonly refers to women of mixed race. There is no equivalent in English that carries the same connotations as the French word; witness the translation of Mathieu Kassovitz's recent film, *Métisse*, as *Café au lait* in the United States. Editions Barrault has gone out of business; all their records and contracts were transferred to Flammarion. *Métisse blanche* has since been republished in a "J'ai lu" paperback edition. Page numbers will appear in parentheses. Translations are mine.

9. These articles were in the press dossier at Editions Barrault, Paris. All records are now housed at Flammarion. See note 8.

10. Broadcast on Antenne 2, April 7, 1989.

11. See also Michèle Sarde's excellent introduction to the text.

12. Kim Lefèvre presented her work and responded to questions at the Nhà Viêt-Nam (Viet Nam House) in Paris, May 28, 1989.

13. The voyage motif captures life between cultures and runs strongly through most Vietnamese francophone narratives. Biculturals during the colonial period often found themselves in what Vietnamese nationalists termed the halfway house of culture.

14. On *Apostrophes* she explained why she hated the French blood within her body: "je me sentais vietnamienne en tout, dans mon âme, dans la culture, je me suis . . . je n'ai jamais vécu qu'au Viêt-Nam, jusqu'à cet âge et je n'ai vu que des Vietnamiens." (In every way I felt Vietnamese, in my soul, in the culture, I was . . . I had only lived in Viet Nam [and] up until that time I had only seen Vietnamese people.) In *Métisse blanche*, the narrator writes: "Les souvenirs de mon enfance sont imprégnés de son climat, de ses paysages, de ses odeurs, de la musique de sa langue. Je me surprends parfois à fredonner des airs anciens que je croyais ensevelis dans l'oubli" (340) (The memories of my childhood are imbued with its [Viet Nam's] climate, its landscapes, its odors, the music of its language. I sometimes find myself humming old tunes that I thought were buried in oblivion).

15. On *Apostrophes* Bernard Pivot asked her why the title was not *métisse jaune* and the following dialogue ensued: Lefèvre: "Eh bien justement parce qu'en général quand on dit métisse, on pense couleur. Et là justement ce qui est rejeté dans cette société où vit cette petite fille c'est sa part blanche qu'on ne veut pas. On ne veut pas de cette part-là. Et c'est pour ça qu'on la renvoie sans arrêt comme on dit aux gens de sa race, c'est-à-dire aux Français." Pivot: "Mais au fond en France quand vous êtes venue à ce moment-là vous étiez une métisse jaune." Lefèvre: "Oui, mais en France, vous savez, quand je suis arrivée en France et que je dis que je suis vietnamienne, les gens me croient tout à fait tout de suite. Alors qu'au Viêt-Nam si je dis que je suis vietnamienne, on me regarde et on dit non, tu n'es pas vietnamienne, tu es métisse. Et maintenant avec une certaine accoutumance à avoir énormément d'Asiatiques ici en France, maintenant quand je dis à un Français que je suis vietnamienne, eh bien le Français me regarde et il me demande, sans aucun mélange?" (KL: Well, because in general when one says *métisse*, one thinks color. And there, of course, what is rejected in that society in which the little girl lives, it's her whiteness that no one wants. They don't want anything to do with that part of her. And that's why they are always sending her back, as they say, to people of her own race,

that is to say, to the French. BP: But in the end, in France when you came, at that time you were a yellow *métisse*. KL: Yes, but in France, you know, when I arrived in France and I say I'm Vietnamese, people believe me right away without question while in Viet Nam if I say I'm Vietnamese, they look at me and say non, you're not Vietnamese, you're a métisse. And now with people getting more accustomed to having a large number of Asians in France, now when I say to a Frenchman that I'm Vietnamese, well, he looks at me and asks, with no [racial] mixing?) In *Métisse blanche* the narrator writes: "ce que le Viêt-nam m'avait refusé, la France me l'a accordé: elle m'a reçue et acceptée. Tout compte fait, je n'en suis pas déçue. Ici [en France], les choses me paraissent simples. Si je dis que je suis vietnamienne, on me prend comme telle, si je dis que je suis française, on me demande de quelle origine je suis: sans plus" (340) (France granted me what Viet Nam refused; France received and accepted me. All things considered, I am not disappointed. Here [in France], things seem simple to me. If I say I'm Vietnamese, people believe me; if I say I'm French, they ask about my origins, nothing more).

16. "J'inventais une histoire où j'étais l'enfant de deux Vietnamiens de souche" (104). Later, during her hours of playing hooky in a nearby cemetery, she imagines herself a "[p]rincess sans royaume" and invents "un arbre généalogique, des sujets, une histoire" (36).

17. See, for example, Nguyen Du, *The Tale of Kieu*, Huynh Sanh Thong, trans. (New Haven: Yale University Press, 1983). This unique edition presents the *quôc-ngũ* rendering of the original Vietnamese text in *chũ-nôm* with the English translation on facing pages.

18. Of the other students at the convent school, Do says: "elles n'ont rien de commun avec nous. Elle ne connaissent rien de notre histoire, de notre littérature. Elles sont incapables de te citer le nom d'un seul poète. C'est à peine si elles savent qui est Nguên [sic] Du" (273) (They have nothing in common with us. They don't know about our history or our literature. They are incapable of naming a single poet for you. They scarcely know who Nguyen Du is). Nguyen Du wrote the most famous of Vietnamese verse romances, *Kim-Van-Kieu*. See note 17.

19. "J'avais la nostalgie du couvent des Oiseaux de Dalat. Là-haut, tout était beau" (286) (I was nostalgic for the Couvent des Oiseaux in Dalat. Up there, everything was beautiful).

20. These explanations are typical in this literature. See *The Vietnamese Novel in French*, 54–60.

21. Hanoi: Imprimerie Tonkinoise, 1921. See the discussions in *The Vietnamese Novel in French*, chapters 4 and 6.

22. Paris: Fasquelle, 1930. See the discussion of this text in *The Vietnamese Novel*, chapter 4.

23. Paris: Editions du Seuil, 1947. See *The Vietnamese Novel*, 82–83, as well as Thuong Vuong-Riddick, "Le Drame de l'Occidentalisation dans quelques romans de Pham Van Ky" (The drama of Westernization in some of Pham Van Ky's novels), *Présence francophone* 16 (spring 1978): 141–52; Angela Shipman, "*Frères de sang*: le drame d'un prodigue" (*Blood Brothers*: the drama of a prodigal son), *Vietnam Forum* 11 (winter/spring 1988): 204–13; and Nguyen Hong Nhiem, "L'Echiquier et l'antinomie je/moi comme signe et substance du conflit Occident/ Extrême-Orient dans les oeuvres de Pham Van Ky" (The chessboard and the I/Me antinomy as sign and substance of the West/Far East conflict in the works of Pham Van Ky), (Ph.D. diss., Univ. of Massachusetts-Amherst, 1982). To date *Frères de sang* is the only Vietnamese francophone novel translated into English: *Blood Brothers* (New Haven: Yale Southeast Asia Studies Center, 1987). Sadly, it is now out of print, but a second edition is promised.

24. Marjorie Garber, *Vested Interests: Cross-Dressing and Cultural Anxiety* (New York and London: Routledge, 1992), 10. Further references are in parentheses in the text.

25. Garber illustrates her idea with three examples, including the "third" world: "The Third World is only a 'third' in that it does not belong to one or another of two constructed regions, the developed West and what used to be described as the Communist bloc. What the

so-called Third World nations have in common is their post-colonial status, their relative poverty, their largely tropical locations, their largely non-Caucasian population, and the fact that they were once subjected to Western rule. Very little else made the Third World an aggregation; the new nations that came into being as a result of decolonization have in other respects little similarity to one another. 'Third World' is a political term, which simultaneously reifies and dismisses a complex collection of entities" (11). This example "involve[s] moving from a structure of complementarity or symmetry to a contextualization, in which what once stood as an exclusive dual relation becomes an element in a larger chain. Thus the United States and the Soviet Union once saw one another, in effect, as rivals dividing up the world, each invested in the fantasy that only the other was in the way. The so-called 'Third World,' which was always 'there,' but was invisible to Cold War myopia except as a potential sphere of influence against the encroachment of the 'other' superpower, paradoxically contributed to the lessening of Cold War tensions by becoming more politically and economically visible — by (to use a once popular term) 'emerging.' The Cold war focus on one 'other' was thus rendered both impractical and impossible" (12).

26. Garber writes, "The apparently spontaneous or unexpected or supplementary presence of a transvestite figure in a text (whether fiction or history, verbal or visual, imagistic or 'real') that does not seem, thematically, to be primarily concerned with gender difference or blurred gender indicates a *category crisis elsewhere*, an irresolvable conflict or epistemological crux that destabilizes comfortable binarity, and displaces the resulting discomfort onto a figure that already inhabits, indeed incarnates, the margin" (17, emphasis in the original).

27. See Françoise Lionnet, *Autobiographical Voices: Race, Gender, Self-Portraiture* (Ithaca: Cornell University Press, 1989) as well as the work of Liz Smith, Estelle Jelinek, Sidonie Smith, Julia Watson, Bella Brodzki, and Celeste Schenk. See also Lionnet's essay in this volume. Mary-Kay Miller's and Ronnie Scharfman's essays, also in this volume, indicate the importance of métissage in creating ambiguity and challenging binarity. See particularly Scharfman's discussion of oxymoron in light of Lefèvre's title, *Métisse blanche*, and Miller's references to Lionnet and the artificial division between fiction and autobiography as well as the coexistence of the multiple strands of métissage.

28. Lefèvre's are not the first references to cross-dressing in narrative literature in French from Viet Nam. For example, Chau Long, the protagonist in Mai Khanh's novel *Châu Long ou l'âme d'une jeune fille orientale* (Paris: La Pensée Universelle, 1987), disguises herself as a man to protect herself and to gain access to an educational world reserved for males in traditional Viet Nam.

PART III

Engendering the Postcolonial Subject

CHAPTER FOURTEEN

Theorizing Terror

The Discourse of Violence in Marie Chauvet's *Amour Colère Folie*

RONNIE SCHARFMAN

Between the acting of a dreadful thing and the first motion, all the interim
is like a phantasma or a hideous dream.
Julius Caesar

The lunatic, the lover and the poet are of imagination all compact.
A Midsummer Night's Dream

Comment agir, o coeur volé?
Rimbaud, "Le coeur volé"

Under the regime of the Duvaliers and their Tontons Macoutes, what does it mean to speak of violence, as Marie Chauvet does in her 1968 trilogy, *Amour Colère Folie?* In a universe where all are susceptible to arrest, rape, torture, disappearance, even murder at any moment and for any reason, where Kafka has become concrete and real, down to the last detail of daily life, is it possible to explore a violence that would be specifically discursive, and if so, what sense would such an exercise have, confronted by the horrors of the lived? As the beginning of a response to this question, I would like to propose the hypothesis that this work functions as an act of resistance to the violence from which it springs, but that it can only resist by repeating, by violating the reader as it proceeds, dragging us in as accomplices and voyeurs to the very heart of darkness, of which it is both the semblance and the conscience.

The story of the trilogy's reception, or rather of its violent suppression, is worthy of note. Published in Paris in 1968, *Amour Colère Folie* is the fourth novel written by Marie Chauvet, who was born in Port-au-Prince in 1919. Her first book, *Fille d'Haiti*, was crowned by the Prix de l'Alliance Française. The third novel, *Fonds des nègres*, won the Grand Prix France-Antilles in 1960. She would seem, then, to be a respected, recognized, established writer. In Haiti, she presided over a salon where she welcomed young poets.[1] But when Gallimard published the text in question, Chauvet's husband bought all the copies, confiscated them, and locked them up, where they stayed for twelve years! In the meantime, Marie Chauvet fled her husband and exiled herself in New York, where she died in 1973, poor and unknown, exiled again outside of the immediate community of the Haitian intelligentsia in the United States.

Does her novel explode in the reader's hands to have been thus suppressed? It would certainly have scandalized the Haiti of Papa Doc and his Duvalieristes on the one hand, because of the scathing portraits of those in power, and the *bien pensante* mulatto bourgeoisie on the other. This was Marie Chauvet's own milieu, as daughter of one bourgeois highly placed both in society and government, and wife of another. The terror of scandal and the hypocrisy and cowardice it engenders constitute one of the most important themes that link these three novels.

Since 1980, when it was rediscovered, the trilogy has become almost a cult object for Haitians of Marie Chauvet's class in exile in the United States. It is thanks to such a network that I myself finally procured this text, which, like all her others, is out of print and nearly impossible to obtain.[2] Written in a pure French, "le français de France," by a bourgeoise who denounces the conventional cowardice of the bourgeoisie, by a mulatto who deconstructs the racism of the mulattoes, by a Haitian who seeks to expose and subvert the oppressive regime under which she lives, by a woman who, as one of the rare female writers in her country, explores female eroticism on the one hand and its violent oppression on the other, the trilogy demonstrates unusual psychological probity and political courage.

The text does not scandalize the foreign reader. It does worse: it traumatizes. It shocks us, not in our morality, but rather in the depths of our being. It wounds, confuses, haunts. Each time that I reread it, I approach it with feelings of intense fear, rage, impotence, claustrophobia, and disgust but also with fascination, pity, and admiration. It also happens that I avoid this text, forget what I have read even as I reread it, or I no longer assimilate what I am in the process of reading because it is too terrifying. In short, I recognize behavioral variants of denial, which characterize what psychiatrists define as post-traumatic stress disorder and which link me with many of the characters portrayed in the novels.[3] Like a nightmare that undermines rest by haunting it, Chauvet's discourse does violence to our reading habits by transgressing the pleasure of the text. Because she is as merciless toward her reader as the world that she depicts is toward its victims, Chauvet provokes both resistance and fascination. But she does not leave the reader indifferent.

Two important and admirable essays on this text that paved the way for my own work, one by Madeleine Cottenet-Hage and the other by Joan Dayan, have treated *Amour,* the first part of the trilogy, and *Amour Colère,* the first and second parts, respectively.[4] Is trying to deal with the entire trilogy going to the end of the night? One of the terrifying problems of this text is that one advances while regressing, in the strongest sense of the latter term. To work one's way through the trilogy is to touch the heart of darkness. Not only do we advance-regress, as the title indicates, from Love to Madness, by passing through Rage; not only do these three states reveal themselves to be coextensive and thus contaminated each by the others; but also, and perhaps this is the worst part when one looks at them closely, they are, in fact, nothing but their own opposites.

In the case of *Amour,* we are dealing with two loves, in fact, imagined by a very dark-skinned mulatto called, ironically, Claire. Two loves fantasized in her head, confessed to her diary. The first is for her brother-in-law Jean Luze — white and French, married to her sister Felicia. This impossible love, which Claire never admits to openly, becomes an obsession, a perversion, an aggression, and, finally, a destructive force. Her second love, lived out also only on the level of fantasy and dream, equally unacceptable, is in fact a warped hatred for the local commandant, a black sadist, Caledu (whose name, in Creole, means somebody who beats hard).[5] Caledu represents Duvalier's regime, one that imprisons mulatto women from the bourgeoisie in order to torture them, whipping their genitalia, while screaming furiously: "Aristos, bande d'aristos, mulatres-aristos, je vous estropierai tous, aristos, aristos..." (163)[6] (Aristos, bunch of aristos, I'll cripple all of you, aristos, aristos). Caledu's obsessive-compulsive behavior fuses race, class, and gender in one single horrific gesture of punishment. This man whom Claire detests, who terrifies her, obsesses her sexually, too, and it is with him that she will celebrate the only hymen permitted to her, and to which I shall return shortly.

As for the novel *Colère,* the rage that the entire Normil family experiences over the unwonted, unexplained, unjustified, and violent invasion of their lands will be experienced in a different way by each of the story's characters. But no matter how furious the rage, each time it explodes it leads only to impotence or to some form of sacrifice that cannot resolve or save anything. This suffocated anger will end in the death of the young girl of the family, Rose, who allows herself to be violated every day for a month in the most abject conditions describable, hoping by her Faustian pact to save the family's property and future.

And in the third novel, *Folie,* four starving, drunken, terrified poets are holed up together in the single room of a stinking hut, hallucinating what they call the devils, and thereby articulating the profound truth of the situation surrounding them without, however, being able to name the enemy directly. Paralyzed by ancient, unresolved cultural and psychoanalytic terrors as well as by the undecidability of the characteristics of the evil that is suffocating them, they cannot make a single gesture that would break through their immobility. Trapped together between those four walls, they make each other both crazier and more lucid, so that the boundaries distinguishing between these two states become more and more fluid. They are finally arrested by Duvalier's "devils," judged sane, ironically, by a corrupt doctor, and shot as subversive traitors by the very devils they cannot name. Pathetic, delirious creatures who dream of saving their country and winning love and respect! In such a story, on which side can we place the appellation "mad"?

If I have briefly sketched this summary of the three novels starting from their titles, each of which undermines itself, it is to demonstrate that one of the versions of violence that is at work in this text, and that threatens the reader, is situated on the discursive level in the form of the oxymoron, or its rhetorical relative, the paradox. The oxymoron both contains and expresses ambivalence; it produces ambiguity. This text does violence to us by subverting our habitual concepts of notions such as love, anger, madness, but also of terms such as black and white, power and submission. The oxymoron is the textualization of a profound truth in the Haitian context, which is that of the contamination of terms, and which hides, in turn, that of the contamination of races. I would even suggest that the violence of Chauvet's text is governed on the level of the unconscious by that unnameable oxymoron that is repressed by the appellation "mulâtre," and that would be "white nigger." In other words, this trilogy violates us because certain of its textual apparatuses, including the oxymoron, destabilize our perception of the world. We do not know how to read it, if we have "gotten" it, on which side to take a position, because nothing is quite what it seems. Chauvet's text seizes us, transgresses us in our comfort by deconstructing our illusion of exteriority and innocence. Jean Luze speaks early on in *Amour* of an "infernal paradise." Its power is getting us to participate in the psychodramas that are taking place, which threaten us in our integrity. By weaving us as witnesses into its powers of horror, the text warps us. And our terror comes in part from the effect of feeling possessed by it, contaminated by it, dispossessed of ourselves. Vodoun comes to mind here, and each time that vodoun erupts in these three novels, it is always with the violence of the return of the repressed. Religion of the black peasantry, reminder of an Africa that many gallicized Haitian mulattoes would prefer to forget, vodoun in this text represents both a mystifying, mysterious primitivism that the French institutions — school, church, and racial lactification — would have wished to erase, and a return to the authenticity of its people. We are at the heart of the kind of contradiction Chauvet is exposing in all its tension.

These remarks focusing on the function of the oxymoron to effect a certain kind of discursive violence can be expanded to an allegorical reading of the Haiti of Duvalier. This republic, independent since its revolution in 1804 and where, according to Aimé Césaire's expression, "négritude stood up for the first time," has known only regimes of violence, and racial, economic, political, and natural disasters since its inception. Chauvet speaks of the results of such a history in the opening pages of *Amour*:

> Nous nous exerçons à nous entr'égorger depuis l'Indépendance. Les griffes du peuple se sont mises à pousser et se sont acérées. La haine entre nous est née. D'elle sont sortis nos tortionnaires. Ils torturent avant d'égorger. C'est un héritage auquel nous nous cramponnons, comme au français. Nous excellons dans le premier et sommes encore médiocres dans le second. (14)

> [We have been practicing cutting each others' throats since Independence. The peoples' claws began to grow and became sharpened. Hatred among us was born. From it came our torturers. They torture before they slaughter. It's a heritage we hold fast to, like the French language. But we excel in the former, and we are still mediocre in the latter.]

The irony of this observation does not exclude the author's sensitivity to the tragic dimension of Haiti's national history. But it is not this direction that I propose to explore in this essay. I only mention the allegorical and politico-historical interpretation in passing to emphasize my argument that a certain textual violence emanates from the internal contradictions within this society as they are articulated at the level of the discourse itself. They would function as a reflection of and on, as well as a resistance to, the immense contradiction that was Duvalier's Haiti, where all of the usual equivalencies between class, race, and power were overturned, deconstructed, and perverted with the violence and terror that we all associate with that regime.

But what I am concerned with here is rather the textual functioning of this violence and its cumulative effect on the reader. "Lasciate ogni speranza, voi ch'entrate," as the gates of Dante's Inferno read, for once inside Chauvet's text, one feels imprisoned. For if, on the one hand, there is the coexistence of opposites, on the other, there is the erasure of certain defining distinctions, and the effect is claustrophobic. Not only the physical and vital space but also the mental space within which the characters act and reflect shrinks from one novel to the next. In the third novel of the trilogy, one suffocates as if one would go mad. The closed space is echoed by all the gazes that hide or look away, that accuse or covet, but that do not disclose. In the small provincial town where all of the episodes of the trilogy take place, the streets are always deserted, but everybody sees and knows everything. The whole town watches, posted behind windows, curtains, shutters. The other is there, s/he is watching me, but never to share anything. S/he is there, threatening to denounce me without me knowing. In terror, paranoia reigns: all solidarity is forbidden. "We have become mean by contagion," says the narrator of *Amour*. The victims do not unite, do not consecrate the community by diverting violence from it, as in the analyses of René Girard.[7] On the contrary, in Chauvet's world gone mad, power afflicts, inflicts violence arbitrarily, instead of protecting society from it, all the while forbidding the relief of any purifying catharsis. The progressive degradation of any possibility for action, the constant humiliation of human beings, leads to the truth of the total abjection of the four poets/drunkards/beggars/madmen/visionaries of *Folie*. This truth seems to reside in the relationship that all the characters entertain with the anonymous but omnipresent enemy who prowls just on the other side of the shutters, or the closed door, or the posts. This is a relationship that repeats and parodies, in a grotesque and terrifying way, that of the black slave to the white master during the period of colonization. What characterizes this relationship, as we well know, is the total power of the master over the slave, his arbitrary brutality, including all forms of sexual sadism, rape, and violence, and the negation of the being of the other. On the slave's side of the equation — silence, submission, acceptance, and interiorization of the declared inferiority, or, but more rarely, resistance, revolt, suicide. The two actors in this drama are inextricably, dialectically bound.

In *Amour* it is this negative transmission, across the generations and social hierarchies, of a white superego at once colonialist, paternalistic, and internalized, that Claire's father attempts to inculcate in his daughter as he raises her. To liberate herself, Claire will have to revolt against this paternal figure. Her triumph, at the end of *Amour*, is that after having denied herself so much, she does not sacrifice herself but, rather, externalizes her aggression. Claire's father violates her in her sexual identity, brutalizes her, and, by his own admission, treats her like a slave. Following are some flashbacks from her journal:

> J'étais réprimandée pour rien, épiée odieusement... Pour m'endurcir et me faire payer sans doute ses espérances paternelles déçues, il décida brusquement de m'élever comme un garçon.... (104–5)

> [I was reprimanded for nothing, spied on odiously. To harden me, and no doubt to make me pay for his disillusioned paternal hopes, he decided abruptly to raise me like a boy.]

> A la maison, il revenait à mon père de me faire travailler. Chaque jour, à cause des pâtés que je faisais sur ma page d'écriture, j'étais punie. La punition consistait à rester à genoux, à quelques pas de mon père, les bras croisés et la tête droite. Tremblotante de fatigue, j'attendais, les yeux fermés, le "lève-toi" qui devait arrêter le supplice. Quelquefois, je pleurais et la punition durait bien plus longtemps. (105)

> [At home, it was my father's role to make me do homework. Every day, because of the ink blots I made on my page, I was punished. The punishment consisted of my remaining on my knees, a few steps from my father, my arms crossed and head straight. Trembling from exhaustion, I awaited, eyes closed, the "get up" that would stop the torture. Sometimes I cried, and the punishment lasted much longer.]

Because precisely what he fears for his daughter is a kind of pollution by contagion, the violence of his repression takes the form of a kind of incestuous voyeurism. He interrogates her about her relations with others and beats her, sometimes so terribly that the doctor must come to treat her.

> Que voulez-vous, mon cher ami, j'inculque des principes et j'entends être obéi... C'est une race indisciplinée que la nôtre, et notre sang d'anciens esclaves réclame le fouet, comme disait feu mon père... Mon sang à moi est en voie de régression et... j'ai hérité certaines qualités qui vont lui faire défaut à elle, si je ne la corrige pas. (110–11)

[What can I say, my dear friend, I am inculcating principles and I mean to
be obeyed . . . Ours is an undisciplined race, and our former slaves' blood
calls out for the whip, as my late father used to say . . . My (black) blood is
in a state of regression, and I've inherited certain qualities that she will lack
if I don't correct her.]

Claire's father looks upon métissage as a kind of impurity, or pollution,
if not an oxymoron, that must be exorcised, like the black blotches of ink on
her notebook. Claire is punished in part because she is very black, a living
reminder of the excess of black blood. The return to blackness, the return of
blackness, represent the father's most primitive fears. As a constant reminder to him of what he is repressing, Claire must be victimized, violated,
by the paternal whip, which would effect both a symbolic genocide and
gynocide. The father's racial self-hatred reveals itself even more violently
when Claire discovers that he secretly practices vodoun each time he visits
the peasants who work his coffee plantations. When Claire first sees this
unknown face of her father, "the black Parisian" with his neck "paré de col-
liers multicolores et sa tête . . . ceinte d'un foulard rouge" (115) (adorned
with multicolored necklaces and his head bound with a red scarf), she is
shocked and conflicted. She sees him, in a painful and ironic reversal, as the
nigger. What symbolic register must she now obey — her biological father,
whom she fears but feels betrayed by, or her spiritual father, the priest Paul
and the church he represents? Claire's father has mixed feelings toward her,
because she is black and a woman, and yet, at the same time, she reincarnates
his own mother, a Negress from whom he has inherited the command to serve
the loas. For her part, Claire will also experience deep ambivalence toward
her father once she discovers this practice.

In *Amour*, the complex relationships among class, race, sexuality, and
violence form a knot around the father-daughter dyad. What the father
will end up inculcating in his daughter in the final analysis is the importance
of a secret life, because the integrity of her racial and sexual identities has
been violated. Self-conscious and suffering from a complex about her color,
Claire confesses to her journal that she had begun to detest the ancestor
whose black blood had somehow slipped into her veins after so many generations.

Forever wounded in her primary narcissism, Claire renounces love, believing herself monstrous. Her upbringing will have made of Claire a repressed creature, if not a perverted one, who comforts herself for the lack
of tenderness in her life by practicing onanism in her room, motivated by
pornographic postcards and *Lady Chatterly's Lover*. This somewhat masculin-

ized eroticism is tempered by Claire's playing with a doll/child whom she showers with frustrated maternal affection. The disquieting effect of Claire's short-circuited eroticism stems from the subversive aspect of its self-suffi-ciency. And yet Claire's body becomes the locus where all of the conflicts of the novel—psychic, social, racial, erotic, even, eventually, political— wage their wars. The parental messages that should constitute the language with which Claire can construct herself are scrambled. She speaks only silently, secretly, through her journal, which we read like voyeurs. In public, she is quiet. Similarly, avid for her brother-in-law, she sublimates her desire through a warped plot to encourage a liaison between him and the third sister.

This confusion reaches its paroxysm in the strange relationship that de-velops between Claire and the commandant, Caledu. We have seen that sexuality and sexual identity are bound up with mechanisms of power and with both the desire for and terror of submission. The black Caledu, who both dehumanizes and desexualizes women, serves to crystallize all of Claire's impotent rage against her father. But being both very black and phallic, Caledu is endowed at the same time with an identificatory attraction for Claire to the repressed. What both terrifies Claire and makes her feel guilty is her own unquenched, unquenchable sexuality, which she displaces, and replaces, little by little over the course of the narrative from her obsession with her brother-in-law to one with Caledu. A critical moment in the text in terms of Claire's *prise de conscience* about herself comes in the guise of a nightmare, which I will quote at length because it is crucial to my discus-sion. In the dream, Claire is no longer caught up in one of her erotic fantasies where she makes love to herself by playing the role of Jean Luze.

The violent eroticism of this nightmare is punitive, humiliating, and, in the final analysis, fatal, as she orchestrates her subjugation to the desired and detested Caledu. Her conscious sense of being degraded by the political situation is condensed into the sexual imagery of her debasement in the dream:

> Mon rêve d'hier soir me bouleverse encore: j'étais seule, debout en pleine lumière, au milieu d'une arène immense surmontée de gradins où gesticulait une foule terrifiante. Elle hurlait et m'interpellait en me montrant du doigt. De quoi m'accusait-elle? Je courais, honteuse de ma nudité, cherchant en vain un coin obscur pour m'y cacher, quand, tout à coup, je vis se dresser devant moi une statue de pierre. A cet instant, les clameurs de la foule devinrent assourdissantes. La statue pourvue d'un phallus énorme tendu dans un spasme de voluptueuse souffrance était celle de Caledu. La statue s'anima et le phallus s'agita, fiévreusement. Je me jetais à ses pieds, à la fois soumise et révoltée, osant à peine lever les yeux, les

cuisses serrées. J'entendis crier "à mort, à mort." C'était la foule qui poussait Caledu à m'assassiner. Le froid d'un métal me caressa la peau du cou en même temps qu'un éclat de rire féroce succédait seul aux cris de l'assistance, tout à coup silencieuse. L'arme s'enfonça doucement, profondément dans ma chair. Je restai un long moment immobile, figée d'horreur. Puis, me relevant, je marchai dans une brume épaisse, les mains en avant, décapitée, avec ma tête qui se balançait sur ma poitrine. Morte et vivant ma mort.... (145)

[Last night's dream still stuns me: I was alone, standing in full light, in the middle of an immense arena surmounted by steps where a terrifying crowd was gesticulating. They were screaming and questioning me while pointing at me. What were they accusing me of? I was running, ashamed of my nudity, looking in vain for some obscure corner to hide in when, suddenly, I saw a stone statue standing before me. At that instant, the clamoring of the crowd became deafening. The statue, supplied with an enormous phallus tensed in a spasm of voluptuous suffering, was Caledu's. The statue moved and the phallus waved about feverishly. I threw myself at his feet, at once subdued and indignant, hardly daring to raise my eyes, my thighs tightly closed. I heard them cry "death, death." It was the crowd pushing Caledu to assassinate me. A cold metal caressed the skin of my neck at the same time that a ferocious burst of laughter followed the cries of the audience, all at once silent. The weapon drove softly, deeply into my flesh. I remained immobile for a long moment, frozen with horror. Then, getting up, I walked through a thick fog, hands ahead, decapitated, with my head rocking on my chest. Dead, and living my death.]

This passage is one of the most cruel, one of the most violent in the entire trilogy, and merits elaboration. Where does the violence originate in this text? The dream articulates both Claire's terror and her desire, but such an inadmissible desire that she must turn it around as violence against herself. The aspect of self made spectacle here is terrifying: Claire is naked, exposed, vulnerable, before an anonymous crowd demanding her death for a crime of which she is ignorant. What, in fact, is she guilty of? Desiring? But what, or whom? Once again, it seems that one can identify a discursive violence in the tension of the oxymorons "un spasme de voluptueuse souffrance" and "morte et vivant ma mort." This then extends to the confusion between rape and murder. She submits to the phallus, her thighs tightened, as if to protect herself from violation, but the phallus transforms itself into a weapon, which "penetrates deeply, gently into my flesh." Paradoxically, it is the arm that penetrates her, not the phallus, but in fact this weapon symbolically kills her. This horrible scene leaves the reader frozen, like Claire herself. But it violates us further by identifying us, putting us in the role of the anonymous crowd. There is a certain contagion in the spectacle of violence.

The epilogue to the scene situates the dream in a long line of repeated night-mares that all have as their theme Claire's victimization, her terror of the brutality and bestiality to which she is reduced at the hands of her father, her feelings of being trapped and the resulting claustrophobia, the fusion and confusion of rape and violence. The nightmare functions as a memory of real and imagined scenes as well as a prefiguration. For Claire understands, without being able to articulate it yet, that the only way to escape from her nightmare will be to reverse the terms of her submission and to turn the violence on her paternal aggressors, oppressors.

Having once received a dagger as a gift from Jean Luze, Claire fantasizes turning her aggression against several people. She thinks she is furious with her sister Felicia, of whom she is jealous because of Jean Luze, but her rage is displaced each time she imagines giving vent to it. For her sister is not really the person at whom her hatred and violence are aimed. Once, at night, she hears someone being led away by Caledu and crying out for help. Frustrated and furious, she hallucinates a dagger shining before her and just as quickly tries to erase the dangerous thought by burying herself in memories.

This vision that Claire glimpses is that of her future, of the violent act that she will have to commit to free herself. More used to passivity and masochism and what she herself calls her cowardice, the image of the vio-lent gesture that she must accomplish terrifies Claire so that it provokes a regression into the past. But it is precisely that past where she was so violently abused by her sadistic father. Where, then, can she flee, and how can she act? The past is painful, the present, nightmarish, the future, terrifying. The reader is caught up in this claustrophobic atmosphere precisely because s/he is present at the moment that thought is actually constituted, because Chauvet has so mastered the internal monologue that what we read seems to be precisely what is being formulated in Claire's consciousness.

Two decisive events help Claire to externalize her aggressive impulse and to transform the genocide and gynocide she has symbolically suffered into homicide, rather than the contemplated suicide. The first is the profound disillusionment she experiences after realizing once and for all that she can never replace her sister as Jean Luze's wife and mother of their child. But having burned her substitute sex objects, Claire finds herself completely deprived of the "ersatz consolations," as she calls them, behind which she had managed to hide. She has reached a point of no return. The moment is critical, pivotal, for Claire can no longer breathe behind the masks she has created for herself. The idea of crime is slowly being transformed into one of revolt. The second momentous event is the arrest of her friend Jane and Jane's son, and their torture by Caledu. The narrative economy will now drive Claire inexorably toward the one act of authentic liberation possible. The phallic dagger, originally aimed at the sister whom Claire dreams of doing away with, is now desperately turned on Claire herself. But the ineluctable climax of the drama will displace the dagger one last time, to aim it at the real enemy, Caledu. A riot in front of her house draws Claire out of the delirium in which she is preparing to kill herself as if it were a tryst with a lover. To stab herself in her bed with the dagger, metonymy for Jean Luze and symbol of Caledu's murderous nightmare phallus, would condense suicide, rape, orgasm, and hymen. But by killing Caledu, Claire frees herself from all of these self-destructive convergences. She enacts a symbolic hymen with herself. This is figured in the blood from the dagger that she allows to flow freely, recalling the black blotches on her schoolwork, and thus restoring her right to express herself. This violent phallic gesture allows Claire to become the aggressor, both father and Caledu, thereby destroying the whip, the rape, negritude as an inferiority complex, the cruelty to which she had been subjected. Claire opens a space for herself where the constitution of an autonomous identity is inscribed in blood, at the same time that she liberates the city. Individual liberation will take on a communal sense, and violence, a sacred one. The doors of the houses that open at the end of the story also free the reader. We leave the claustrophobic space of Claire's obsessions. The end of *Amour* is like a deep breath, and the novel ends on a positive, if somewhat ambiguous note.[8] Claire is alone, but free. And the violence that destroys Caledu is satisfying, both psychologically and aesthetically, because the arm/phallus that had so terrified Claire in her nightmare is transformed by her into an instrument of liberation.

The next two novels of the trilogy are progressively more implacable and abject. When I first undertook this research on Chauvet, I thought it was to explore the textual functioning of a specifically feminine discourse of violence and terror. If such a discourse existed, I told myself it would be situated at the level of the experience of rape. Although rape of women figures as a fundamental obsession in *Amour* and occupies center stage in *Colère*, Chauvet deepens and expands the meaning of rape, exceeding its literal sense without minimizing that sense. She gives us intolerable graphic descriptions of female rape and terror to expose an even more abject sense of shame that defies all sexual or generic categorization. I would like to argue here that we are touching on the psychology at work in the concentration camps, one that subjects the victim to degradation at the same time that it makes the victim an active, complicit collaborator in this degradation, forcing him/her to bear silent witness. Making the victim believe that s/he is responsible for the humiliation endured leads to self-doubt and paralysis.

By staging a relationship where one being has absolute power over another, Chauvet uses rape as a synecdoche, as a manifestation of a kind of violence that is far more universal, one that threatens the physical and psychic integrity of all beings at all moments and is that of total oppression on the side of the powerful one and total impotence on the side of the victim. If in *Colère* there is an eroticization of abjection, we should note at the same time what I shall call a desexualization of rape as its corollary or, rather, a bestialization of it on the one hand and a ritualization on the other. The passages where Rose undergoes and describes her repeated rape by the man in the black uniform with the gorilla's hands who has neither a face nor a name for her are among the most terrifying in literature. Rose has made her pact with the devil: she will allow herself to be violated for thirty days, at the end of which her family's lands will be restituted to them. The invasion of the Normil family property, which constitutes the opening of the novel, is punctuated by the hammering of the stakes that demarcate a kind of transformation of the beloved, hard-earned land into a prison. The Normils are henceforth at the mercy of the Tontons Macoutes who stand guard at the edge of their property. The opening scene is a metaphorical rape of the property, a rape that Rose will try to redeem by substituting that of her body proper. The sound of the stakes driving into the earth prefigures not only her violation but also her martyrdom and death, as if the entire family were being buried alive. The house-become-prison is implicitly compared to a casket. They are all barricaded inside, untouchable, petrified, immobile, nailed down. The impotence of each one of the family members is symbolized by the youngest, the disabled Claude, who fantasizes himself as the savior of them all, but who is, in fact, condemned to crawl on the ground because of his physical paralysis. He is the ironic incarnation of the end of a line. Gifted with a heightened, almost visionary sensibility, it is he who first realizes Rose's secret compromises, and who pronounces the critical oxymoron of the text: "Rose stinks," he declares, after one of her outings to the gorilla. The paradox signals the end of all innocence, the point of no return.

Yet the tragedy of the novel is that Rose, alone, acts, and she must do so with her body — the only weapon of her youth and her femininity. We witness her degradation first through the eyes of her brother, incestuously attached to her, who, in a long interior monologue, moves from a kind of jealous rage to disgust to pity when he confronts the torment that his sister experiences. The reader participates from the outside, so to speak. It is not until the next chapter that we have Rose's own terrible narrative in the first person. We are present at her reification, her humiliation, her violation, and the mental as well as physical torture to which she subjects herself:

> Commencez donc à vous déshabiller, m'a-t-il ordonné comme s'il réclamait de moi un simple travail de bureau ... Tu ne te débattras pas, tu ne crieras pas, me recommanda-il, parce que si tu le fais, tu t'en repentiras ... Couche-toi, dit-il, couche-toi, les jambes ouvertes, les bras en croix ... Tu vas tout gâcher, me souffla-t-il, si tu me résistes, je ne pourrai rien faire. Il faut obéir, obéir sans hésiter, autrement, tout est fichu, tu comprends? Je ne peux être un homme qu'avec les belles têtes de saintes de ton espèce, les belles têtes de martyre vaincu ... Tu es vierge, n'est-ce pas? Tu ne m'as pas menti? Je vais te faire mal, très mal, mais tu ne diras pas un mot, tu m'as compris? Pas un mot ... Il s'enfonça en moi d'un seul coup terrible, brutal et, aussitôt, il râla de plaisir. Je mordis mon poing, de souffrance et de dégoût ... Lorsque je fus nue, il se jeta sur moi si brutalement que je criai. ... Je t'ouvrirai jusqu'à ce que mon poing entier y passe, me cria-t-il. (283–84)

> [Begin to undress, he ordered, as if he were asking me for some simple office task. You won't struggle, you won't scream, he recommended, because if you do, you'll regret it. Lie down, he said, lie down, legs spread, arms crossed. You'll ruin everything, he whispered to me, if you resist me, I won't be able to do anything. You must obey, without hesitation, otherwise, all is lost, understand? I can only be a man with your kind of beautiful saints' heads, beautiful faces of vanquished martyrs. You're a virgin, right? You didn't lie to me? I'm going to hurt you, very badly, but you won't say a word, understand? Not a word. He thrust into me with one brutal, terrible push and right away groaned with pleasure. I bit my fist, out of suffering and disgust. ... When I was naked, he threw himself on me so brutally that I screamed. I'm going to open you up until my whole fist gets in, he screamed at me.]

The conditions imposed by the "gorilla" represent a kind of ritualization of total submission upon which his sense of power and virility depend. But that it is a question of absolute, sadistic power that goes beyond sexual violation in the strict sense is borne out by the terrifying substitution of the clenched fist for the penis as the instrument of penetration and punishment.

Rose's horror at what she is forced to undergo and observe is redeemed to some extent by her lucid consciousness. Her unrelenting self-scrutinization and interrogation belie her apparent passivity and resist the gorilla's efforts to dehumanize her. As in all of Chauvet's universe, and, indeed, in that of the concentration camps to which I have alluded, the subject's worst fear is that of contamination, collusion, complicity, pollution. Rose's ongoing internal monologue throughout her ordeal is her guarantee of her humanity and her morality. By splitting off from herself, she remains, intellectually, intact and can recognize the other in all his monstrosity, reduced to the bestiality of pure aggression, of which rape is here the chosen manifestation. Rose's hope is to be oxymoronically purified through her defilement, as she projects herself into the future, beyond torture, as more modest and innocent than before her ordeal. But her terror is that, in acquiescing to the gorilla's inhuman demands, she will be forever, irreversibly, tainted. Her scrupulous soul-searching even as she is being tortured is all the more disturbing as she questions the possibility of her own complicity, and even pleasure.

Rose's specifically gendered tragedy is characterized by the way she is rejected at home. Having sacrificed herself for her family, she finds herself debased by them as well. Paralyzed by their own cowardice and inability to act, they accuse her of prostituting herself. To the gorilla who has "bought" her and abuses her sexually, she is a saintly martyr; to the family she has acted to save, she is a whore. We find the same kind of impossible tension of the oxymoron when we identify Rose as the virginal whore, and it is a contradiction that she herself cannot sustain. The progressive annihilation of her feminine body traces Rose's passage from life to death. Once sensuous and the very image of youthful joie de vivre, Rose's violated body takes on the aspect of the living cadavers of concentration camps. When her brother discovers her dying, he pronounces, "exténuée, ils l'ont exténuée" (330) (They have debilitated her).

Perhaps what is most effective in this discourse of terror as Chauvet articulates it is the shrinking range of possible gestures of resistance and the devalorization of those that remain. Not only are the family's fantasies of heroism impossible dreams that they entertain to defend against their impotence, but the one individual who seeks to act is made to suffer unbearably, and, in the final analysis, her suffering is unredeemed. Chauvet does not allow the reader the comfort of a catharsis, and this is perhaps the most violent effect of all. As an allegory for Duvalier's Haiti, *Colère* is both a scathing indictment of all those who refuse to act as well as a merciless portrayal of the double bind of the meaningless suffering entailed by those who would try to act in a totalitarian universe.

Degradation, claustrophobia, paranoia, and derangement reach their paroxysm in the third novel, *Folie*. Although I cannot analyze this text fully here for reasons of space, I would like to enumerate some of the characteristics that would define madness in a world gone mad. The suffocation of the word, because this is the story of four poets, and the resulting misunderstandings punctuate this text, figuring the most abject impotence.[9] Messages are lost en route, literally and figuratively. We witness bits and pieces of conversations, deaf/dumb dialogues, delirious discussions where language, having been so muffled, distorted, and perverted, communicates only lack, fear, or confusion. This is the grotesque, violent version of the absurd dialogues and quid pro quos of Beckett's hoboes in *Waiting for Godot*. But here reality is worse than any hallucination, or, rather, we find it impossible to distinguish between the two. The figure for this undecidable contamination is the cadaver that rots in front of René's door as the story advances and that none of the four can identify for sure: is it that of a man, or of a dog? Is there, then, so little difference? The reality of madness and the madness of the reality in this novel are such that a man and a dog are equivalent.

For his part, René is immoblized by his fidelity to the maternal body in the guise of the vodoun practices his mother has bequeathed to him. All that remains to him in his hovel are the objects of worship that serve her loas, including some rum that he considers it a sacrilege to drink. Paralyzed by conflicts, including a grandiose love for his lighter-skinned, upper-class neighbor for whom he writes poetry, René yearns to break out of his cage and lead a community to victory over the devils. Instead, he and his friends will be executed.

Marie Chauvet revolted against a regime of absolute evil and gratuitous violence by writing this trilogy profoundly rooted in the psychosocial reality of Haiti under Duvalier. When violence is seated in the very hands of those in power, we experience unmitigated terror, for nothing protects us any longer. By arrogating author-ity to herself in such a context, she challenges the regime, subverts its assumptions of total control, and therefore resists its definitions of female vulnerability, even as she excruciatingly details the representation of that vulnerability.

The immense return of all of Haiti's repressions — racial, social, sexual, religious — that constitutes Marie Chauvet's discourse deconstructs oppressive power by exceeding it through the violence of the text. To speak the horror in order to violate those who would prohibit freedom of expression — this is the essence of Marie Chauvet's violent resistance.

Notes

A French version of this essay appeared in *Violence, Théorie, Surréalisme*, J. Chenieux-Gendron and T. Mathews, eds. (Paris: Collection Pleine Marge, Lachenal & Ritter, 1994). I would like to thank the editors for permission to publish this English translation.

1. I am grateful to Professor Raymond Mitton of the Hackley School in Tarrytown, N.Y., for sharing his personal reminiscences about Chauvet's "salon" in Haiti, as well as her life in exile in New York.

2. Professor Joan Dayan of the University of Arizona has shared her Chauvet research with me with infinite generosity. It is to her that I owe thanks for locating a copy of the trilogy through the New York Haitian network.

3. See, for example, "Diagnostic Criteria for Post-traumatic Stress Disorder," in *Diagnostic and Statistical Manual of Mental Disorders* (Washington, D.C.: American Psychiatric Association, 1987), 247–51.

4. Madeleine Cottenet-Hage, "Violence Libératoire, Violence Mutilatoire dans *Amour* de Marie Chauvet," *Francofonia* 6 (spring 1984): 17–28; Joan Dayan, "Reading Women in the Caribbean: Marie Chauvet's *Love, Anger and Madness*," in *Displacements: Women, Tradition, Literatures in French*, ed. Joan de Jean and Nancy K. Miller (Baltimore: Johns Hopkins University Press, 1991), 228–53.

5. Dayan, 234.

6. Marie Chauvet, *Amour Colère Folie* (Paris: Gallimard, 1968). Page numbers will appear in parentheses. Translations are mine.

7. See, for example, René Girard, *La Violence et le sacré* (Paris: Grasset, 1972).

8. See Cottenet-Hage's discussion of the end of this novel in *"Violence Libératoire."*

9. I use Julia Kristeva's notion of the abject here as delineated in her *Pouvoirs de l'horreur* (Paris: Seuil, 1982). An interesting critique of Kristeva's concept, and of interest for my discussion here because it argues that she has voided it of any political effectiveness, is Paul Smith, "Julia Kristeva et al.; or, Take Three or More," in *Feminism and Psychoanalysis*, ed. Richard Feldstein and Judith Roof (Ithaca: Cornell University Press, 1989), 84–104.

CHAPTER FIFTEEN

Postscripts

Mariama Bâ, Epistolarity, Menopause, and Postcoloniality

KEITH L. WALKER

L'Histoire marchait, inexorable. Le débat à la recherche de la voie juste
secouait l'Afrique occidentale. Des hommes courageux connurent la prison;
sur leurs traces d'autres poursuivirent l'oeuvre ébauchée. Privilège de
notre génération, charnière entre deux périodes historiques, l'une
de domination, l'autre d'indépendance. Nous étions restés
jeunes et efficaces car nous étions porteurs de projets.
L'Indépendance acquise, nous assistions à l'éclosion
d'une République, à la naissance d'un hymne
et à l'implantation d'un drapeau.

[History marched on, inexorably. The debate over the right path to take
shook West Africa. Brave men went to prison: others following in their
footsteps, continued the work begun. It was the privilege of our
generation to be the link between two periods in our history,
one of domination, the other of independence. We remained
young and efficient, for we were the messengers of a new
design. With independence acheived, we witnessed the birth
of a republic, the birth of an anthem and the
implantation of a flag.]
Mariama Bâ, *Une si longue lettre* (*So Long a Letter*)

The early phases of francophone literary culture are characterized by assertion of identity, the reinvention of language, the quest for selfhood, the

unification of Blacks in the commonwealth of the French colonial experience, and the struggle for decolonization and nationhood. The emphasis on language is crucial, for the expropriation of the French language by the early francophone writers was a first step in the decolonization of the mind. The transformation of language is inseparable from social transformation and the reinvention of concepts of the European and the emancipated self. Decolonization, independence, and postcoloniality are redefinitions of nation, self, and what it means to be a man or a women in the formerly colonized spaces of the globe.

During the French colonial phase, African and Antillean men and women demonstrated a fierce solidarity, and their combined voices were a univocal expression of the aspirations of a people to end colonial domination. As Frantz Fanon points out, "Decolonization unifies the people by the radical decision to remove from it its heterogeneity, and by unifying it on a national, sometimes a racial, basis."[1]

A consequence of decolonization and nationhood has been that African women have become accustomed to speaking out, alongside their men, have come in revelatory contact with the world, notably with women on a worldwide scale, and have become aware of the improved status of women in other societies. African women now have the perspective, privilege, political space, and right to attend to their own agenda distinct from that of the African male. The social transformation in Africa involves not only the couple Europe and Africa but also the African man and the African woman vis-à-vis traditional African society and mores. The agenda has shifted from the raising of the consciousness of the masses to the expression of intracultural difference and consciousness, or perhaps, as Julia Kristeva would say, to "the demassification of cultural difference."[2] The perplexing new space is that of the African woman in post-independence society.

In broad terms, francophone literary culture is concerned with transitional social realities and the ever-shifting construction of the francophone identity as it responds to the pressures of the political, the economic, the social, and the legal. In this sense the letter should not be a surprising form of literary expression for a francophone woman writer. As an artifact the letter is *in transit*, crisscrossing borders and barriers, negotiating the national and international *in-between* places where, in francophone literature, difference, displacement, differ*ance*, change, and conflict are signified.

Menopause and decolonization have in common, among other shared traits, that certain traditions have treated them both as disabilities. Medicine and the colonial powers that were opposed to decolonization have a shared vocabulary of doom and curse that is potentially disabling to those who internalize it. A cultural analysis of reproduction and an ethnopsychoanalytical analysis of colonialism make the point. First, speaking of menopause, Emily Martin notes the following in *The Woman in the Body*:

> This period during which the cycles cease and the female sex hormones diminish rapidly to almost none at all is called the *menopause*. The cause of the menopause is the "burning out" of the ovaries . . . Estrogens are produced in subcritical quantities for a short time after the menopause, but over a few years, as the final remaining primordial follicles become atretic, the production of estrogens by the ovaries falls almost to zero. Loss of ability to produce estrogen is seen central to a woman's life: "At the time of the menopause a woman must readjust her life from one that has been physiologically stimulated by estrogen and progesterone production to one devoid of those hormones."[3]

Moving beyond the physiological bases of menopause, Martin is very direct concerning the descriptive language of menopause:

> What is the language in which menopause is described? In menopause, according to a college text, the ovaries become "unresponsive" to stimulation from the gonadotropins, to which they used to respond. As a result the ovaries "regress." . . . Diminished, atrophied relics of their former vigorous, functioning selves, the "senile ovaries" are an example of the vivid imagery brought to this process.[4]

> After the MENOPAUSE a woman is usually unable to bear children. . . . Everywhere else there is regression, decline, atrophy, shrinkage, and disturbance.[5]

> Eliminating the hierarchical organization and the idea of a single purpose to the menstrual cycle also greatly enlarges the ways we could think of menopause.[6]

At this point, it is important to consider Fanon's discussion of the politics of the descriptive language of decolonization:

> During the period of decolonization, the native's reason is appealed to. He is offered definite values, he is told frequently that *decolonization need not mean regression* [my emphasis], and that he must put his trust in the qualities that are well tried, solid and highly esteemed.[7]

> The well being and the progress of Europe have been built up with the sweat and the blood of Negroes, Arabs, Indians, and the yellow races. We have decided not to overlook this any longer. When a colonialist country, embarrassed by the claims for independence made by a colony, proclaims to the nationalist leaders; "*If you wish for independence, take it, and go back to the Middle Ages,*" the newly independent people tend to acquiesce and to

accept the challenge; in fact you may see colonialism withdrawing its capital and its technicians and setting up all around the young State the apparatus of economic pressure. The apotheosis of independence is transformed into *the curse* of independence, and the colonial power through its immense resources of coercion condemns the young nation to *regression*. In plain words, the colonial power says "*Since you want Independence, take it and starve.*"[8]

Both menopause and colonial independence involve the transition from one state to another. Menopause, as a state, is viewed as regression, decline, atrophy, shrinkage, disturbance, the negation of reproduction, and as such entails a dramatic change in the identity of the female subject. The move to colonial independence also involves a shift in the identity of the colonized subject in which the social, political, and economic transitions are viewed by segments of the society as "regression, decline, atrophy, shrinkage, disturbance (folly, madness), and the negation of reproduction."[9] The tension is between the loss of the capacity to bear and the birth of the nation. Ramatoulaye, the letter-writer of *Une si longue lettre,* dispatches a hymn to the new nation after independence, a hymn to marriage, to the couple and the family, drawing our attention to the tie between personal narrative and the narrative of nation. Mariama Bâ reveals what Edward Saïd would call the "sensuous particularity as well as historical contingency"[10] of a woman living on the borderline of historical transition. Bâ's statement cited as an epigraph to this chapter insists on this point: "*It was the privilege of our generation to be the link between two periods in our history, one of domination, the other of independence. We... were the messengers of a new design*" (25, my emphasis).

Here, Bâ's text presents the correspondences and ironies of the coincidence of a woman's change of life and national emancipation. To qualify the postcolonial condition as menopausal is to admit a consciousness of the ambiguities in the experiences of struggle for decolonization and independence: it is to view emergent nationhood as a prolongation of trauma and pain, as temporary loss and disablement and deferral of full blossoming. This is the sense of the words of Ben M'Hidi, Leader of the FLN, speaking to the young revolutionary Ali Lapointe in the film *The Battle of Algiers*: "It is difficult to start a revolution... More difficult to sustain it... and still more difficult to win it. But it's later when we've won that the real difficulties begin. There is still a great deal to do. I hope you are not tired."

The association of the change of life with birth leads to Bâ's refusal of the menopausal state as a psychically, socially, and physically disabling state. The identity and the discourse of the menopausal woman and the post-

I subject are experienced as altered and enabled: both are experi-
ıere, ultimately as emancipation from subjugation. Despite the surface simplicity of expression, *Une si longue lettre* (*So Long a Letter*) is dense
with emotional, political, and ironic complexity springing from watershed
experiences, and from the aftermaths of national trauma, the birth of a nation, abandonment, death of a loved one, and the loss of youth and illusions.
Bâ experiences the limits of race and gender and translates the differences
as well as her woman's pain into a kind of solidarity with women of her
class and condition as well as with African men.

Bâ's novel, as its title suggests, is in fact one long letter with embedded
shorter letters, examples of which we have seen within its texture. The letter as a form is silence broken, solitude broken. The epistolary form allows
for the dictation of the discourse of the other; it is a privileged format for
inscribing silent awarenesses and speechlessness into reality, into being, like
the experimental poetry of the surrealists, the negritude poets, and African-
American novelist Alice Walker's text *The Color Purple.*[11]

The epistolary form is potentially a particularly feminist form. It permits
the notation of the social history of a people, that is, the details of domestic life, the perhaps peculiarly female perspective on politics, the inclusion
of trivia (by male standards), tangential realities, and digressions; psycho-
analytically, it permits the transcription of the free association of stream of
consciousness; and ultimately, it permits the liberation of the subscon-
scious and the unconscious self — the other. In particularly feminist terms,
it promotes bonding between the correspondents who share their secrets,
intimate fears, aspirations, and political agenda. The letter allows Ramatoulaye a space in which to articulate a grassroots feminist pride that includes a praise song to domesticity and cleanliness:

> Nous sommmes vendredi ... L'odeur du savon m'enveloppe ... Les femmes
> qu'on appelle "femmes au foyer" ont du mérite. Le travail domestique
> qu'elles assument et qui n'est pas rétribue en monnaies sonnantes, est
> essentiel dans le foyer. Leur récompense reste la pile de linge odorant et
> bien repassé, le carrelage luisant où le pied glisse, la cuisine gaie où la sauce
> embaume. Leur action muette est ressentie dans les moindres détails qui
> ont leur utilité: là, c'est une fleur épanouie dans un vase, ailleurs un tableau
> aux coloris appropriés, accroché au bon endroit ... L'ordonnancement du
> foyer requiert de l'art. (93)

> [Today is Friday ... The smell of soap surrounds me. The cleanliness of my
> body pleases me ... Those women we call house-wives deserve praise. The
> domestic work they carry out, and which is not paid in hard cash, is
> essential to the home. Their compensation remains the pile of well-ironed,

sweet-smelling washing, the shining tiled floor on which the foot glides, the gay kitchen filled with the smell of stews. Their silent action is felt in the least useful detail: over there, a flower in bloom placed in a vase, elsewhere a painting with appropriate colours, hung up in the right place. The management of the home is an art. (63)]

Francophone literature is replete with insurrectionism, anger, suffering, and frustration, but it is also sensuous, sexual, about love, loving, embracing, and particularly, there is prayer for deliverance from hatred. Bâ ends her letter with a litany of one-line observations, versets, in which she expresses the desire to transcend her pain, to articulate courageously the love she cannot suppress or transform into hatred, and finally to underscore the importance of the couple and the family. The tone is not strident. It is the considered reflection of a middle-aged widow too old for first love, wise enough to face the future, strong enough to keep her eyes and heart open to happiness:

Les irréversibles courants de libération de la femme qui fouettent le monde, ne me laissent pas indifférente . . . Mon coeur est en fête chaque fois qu'une femme émerge de l'ombre. Je sais mouvant le terrain des acquis, difficile la survie des conquêtes: les contraintes sociales bousculent toujours et l'égoisme mâle résiste . . . Instruments des uns, appâts pour d'autres, respectées ou méprisés, souvent muselées toutes les femmes ont presque le même destin que des religions ou des législatures abusives ont cimenté . . . Je suis persuadée de l'inévitable et nécessaire complémentarité de l'homme et de la femme. . . . L'amour si imparfait soit-il dans son contenu et son expression, demeure le joint naturel entre ces deux êtres . . . C'est de l'harmonie du couple que naît la réussite familiale . . . Ce sont toutes les familles, riches ou pauvres, unies ou déchirées, conscientes ou irréfléchies qui constituent la Nation. La réussite d'une nation passe donc irrémédiablement par la famille. (129)

[I am not indifferent to the irreversible currents of women's liberation that are lashing the world. . . . My heart rejoices each time a woman emerges from the shadows. I know that the field of our gains is unstable, the retention of conquests difficult: social constraints are ever-present, and male egoism resists. . . . Instruments for some, baits for others, respected or despised, often muzzled, all woman have almost the same fate, which religions or unjust legislation have sealed . . . I remain persuaded of the inevitable and necessary complementarity of man and woman . . . Love, imperfect as it may be in its content and expression, remains the natural link between these two beings . . . The success of the family is born of a couple's harmony. . . . The nation is made up of all the families, rich or poor, united or separated, aware or unaware. The success of a nation therefore depends inevitably on the family. (89)]

Une si longue lettre is addressed from Ramatoulaye to her girlhood friend, Aissatou, across the ocean. *Une si longue lettre* is also a letter in a bottle tossed into the sea of humanity. *Une si longue lettre* is dedicated "To all women, *and to men of good will*" (1, my emphasis). It is addressed to all who would see the condition of women improved.

Une si longue lettre is punctuated within and especially at the end by incomplete significance: "Tant pis pour moi si j'ai encore à t'écrire une si longue lettre..." (131) ("Too bad for me if once again I have to write you so long a letter... [89]). It does not end, but rather stops, in a suspended and elliptical space, perhaps at a threshold of understanding and self-affirmation. The gallant and amorous Dr. Daouda Deng functions to underscore the fact that in African societies, divorce, widowhood, middle age, and menopause are not synonymous with death for a woman and need not foreclose the possibilities of sexuality or marriage. Ramatoulaye has gotten "man off her eyeball," as Sug would say in *The Color Purple,* at least for a while, and consequently there is no resolution of the economic, social, and affective dimensions of the marital mourning or menopausal conflicts through a happy remarriage ending. *Une si longue lettre* resists closure by simply stopping inconclusively because of a sense of exhaustion, because it is the end of the day, or because Ramatoulaye is running out of words. The addressee-reader is offered a brief valedictory tinged with a note of delay, deferment, and disarticulation. Although remarriage is forestalled, the letter ends at a point in the process of personal exploration and experimentation heretofore denied Ramatoulaye.

In transitional social realities, the need to write often leads to the search for new forms of expression. Most often, existing art forms are recovered, reformulated, and revalued. The "threshold," "aftermath," or "watershed" literatures of francophone production express their blurred realities and borderline living in mixed genres or hybrid forms. Bâ recovers and exploits the letter maximally. *Une si longue lettre* is a chronicle of Ramatoulaye's mind, her body, her age, her time, and her nation as a woman thinks them. As judge and defendant, herself and her society on trial, Ramatoulaye has written an epistolary apostrophe that is, in the jurisprudential sense, a letter missive, a letter dimissory, or a letter of appeal. As a transmission of pain and knowledge to her African woman friend in America, the letter is an SOS to African women of her class and polygamous condition around the world[12] as well as to future generations of readers. When addressing the nation, the letter assumes the cadences of Koranic discourse and the biblical form of versets as in the apostolic Epistles. As she works her way through the "various sounds and juxtapositions of words," her letter becomes a "mystic writing pad" where Ramatoulaye lives in the full sensuous mystery of language, characters, script, and calligraphy, finding refuge and revelation in their interstices as she seeks a phonics of difference and affirmation.

Absence, silence, abandonment, solitude, and, one might hazard, a measure of preciousness and sentimentality are the nodal points of European female epistolary expression as typified in French by *Les Lettres portugaises* (perhaps written by a man) and to some extent in the writings of Isabelle de Charrière. *Une si longue lettre* seems to pressure these points differently and thereby wrench women's epistolarity from many of its commonplaces and traditions, moving it from the intimate to the community and from the community to the nation and beyond. Ramatoulaye, the correspondent, is not a passionate woman in love, alone and tormented, who through the *projective* epistolary gesture seeks to turn her lover's absence into an imagined presence and her soliloquy into an imagined and fulfilling dialogue. Ramatoulaye's letter is a *retrospective*, written, indeed, under the traditional epistolary sign of absence, but with the distinction that she has been abandoned *utterly* — through infidelity, remarriage, and her lover-husband's death. There is no hope or possibility of dialogue and presence ever again. Her letter writing as therapy and retrospective will seek "to penetrate the deepest abysses of being."[13]

African Muslim polygamous societies are, by definition, relationships of permanent Koran-sanctioned social inequality in which the power of the husband reinforces the domination, subordination, and submission of women. This power is rationalized by the elders and their Koranic explications of what "ought, should, better" be and of what is "right, good, and bad." Bâ's text is a *letter of appeal* in the legal sense for traditional patriarchal societies to rethink the economic, legal, and affective consequences of polygamy and culturally sanctioned gender inequality. Bâ, the Senegalese woman writer, manages with passion, compassion, and discernment to crystallize the sense of the situation of an educated, professional, intellectual black mother-wife called to an uncommon destiny by a white woman, her high school teacher, in a polygamous Muslim West African urban center. In *Une si longue lettre* Ramatoulaye, a fifty-year-old teacher and mother of twelve, is abandoned after twenty-five years of marriage by her first and only love, her husband, Modou Fall, in order to marry their oldest daughter Daba's best friend, Binetou. The letter begins with the correspondent in a state of total divorce and wordlessness. Ramatoulaye spins in madness, inertia, and devastation, accepting with difficulty what is not there: no husband

and no words in language that can express her spiritual disarray after having been abandoned by her husband. The family, especially Ramatoulaye and the daughter Daba, reel in pain and disbelief. Ramatoulaye laments:

> Et dire que j'ai aimé passionnément cet homme, dire que je lui ai consacré trente ans de ma vie, dire que j'ai porté douze fois son enfant. L'adjonction d'une rivale à ma vie ne lui a pas suffi. En aimant une autre, il a brulé son passé moralement et matériellement. Il a osé pareil reniement. Et pourtant, que n'a-t-il fait pour que je devienne sa femme! (23)

> [And to think that I loved this man passionately, to think that I gave him thirty years of my life, to think twelve times over I carried his child. The addition of a rival to my life was not enough for him. In loving someone else, he burned his past, both morally and materially. He dared to commit such an act of disavowal. And yet, what didn't he do to make me his wife! (12)]

Une si longue lettre systematically analyzes a middle-aged mother-wife's perspective and modes of thinking *in contrast* to those of a man. Ramatoulaye presents the woman's body as a text upon which the abjectness of her social condition is writ large. In contemplating her mirror image, Ramatoulaye regards herself as an abject object:

> L'éloquence du miroir s'adressait à mes yeux. Ma minceur avait disparu ainsi que l'aisance et la rapidité de mes mouvements. Mon ventre saillait sous le pagne qui dissimulait des mollets développés par l'impressionnant kilométrage des marches qu'ils avaient effectuées, depuis le temps que j'existe. L'allaitement avait ôté à mes seins leur rondeur et leur fermeté. La jeunesse désertait mon corps, aucune illusion possible. Alors que la femme puise, dans le cours des ans, la force de s'attacher, malgré le vieillissement de son compagnon, l'homme, lui, rétrécit de plus en plus son champ de tendresse. Son oeil égoïste regarde par-dessus l'épaule de sa conjointe. Il compare ce qu'il eut à ce qu'il n'a plus, ce qu'il a à ce qu'il pourrait avoir. (62)

> [I looked at myself in the mirror. My eyes took in the mirror's eloquence. I had lost my slim figure, as well as my quickness of movement. My stomach protuded from beneath the wrapper that hid the calves developed by the impressive number of kilometres walked since the beginning of my existence. Suckling had robbed my breasts of their round firmness. I could not delude myself: youth was deserting my body. Whereas a woman draws from the passing years the force of her devotion, despite the ageing of her companion, a man, on the other hand, restricts the field of tenderness. His egoistic eye looks over his partner's shoulder. He compares what he had with what he no longer has, what he has with what he could have. (41)]

The social context of this fiction is not contrived and as a construct is instructive on the universal condition of women — Black, White, Yellow, Red, Brown, European, American, Third-World. Traditional twentieth-century

Muslim[14] and black communal societies are hierarchical visions of human connection, and as such dramatize in the boldest terms the issues, frustrations, concerns, and visions of feminism today. Structured on gender inequality, these groups reveal that between men and women there are different ideologies (myths, images, concepts, and ideas) of justice, care, sexuality, and economics. These societies allow little recognition of the dual perspectives in these areas. The woman, especially, has little exercise of choice. On the one hand, the "network" or "web"[15] of interconnectedness in these religious, polygamous tribal contexts seems to protect the man from entrapment, betrayal, humiliation, rejection, and deceit by the woman. On the other hand, in exchange for protection from isolation, the society offers women roles of dependence, nurturance, self-sacrifice, submission, and susceptibility to abandonment at the very stage of her development when she is most vulnerable: middle age. The voice in *Une si longue lettre* is the voice of a middle-aged woman in mourning, struggling to overcome rejection and the image of herself as an "abject object."[16]

This epistolary confession presents the psychopathology of a middle-aged mother of twelve who, as an adolescent, had imagined a life of intimacy and activities through which family relationships would be woven and connections sustained in an interdependence of love and care rendered increasingly coherent and safe with the passage of time. Instead, after twenty-five years of marriage, she finds herself in a state of moral nihilism because the loss of affiliation with her husband and the disruption of her family cohesion are perceived and experienced as a veritable loss of self. Before its transcendent closing, *Une si longue lettre* is a statement of mourning in triplicate. The novel begins with the death of Ramatoulaye's husband and only love. This ostensible mourning of her husband's death allows her to mourn the greatest transition of her life, which had preceded his death by several years: his abandonment of her for an adolescent girl. Occasioned by the same man, this double mourning gives rise to melancholia, self-deprecation, and despair that exacerbate the third normal transition of midlife with its attendant crises of menopause. Ramatoulaye struggles to see herself as worthwhile. The contemplation of the mirror image of her body reveals to Ramatoulaye and perhaps to women universally the integration of the social being and the personal being. In this case, with its "inscriptions" that record the travail of twelve childbirths and years of walking, aging, and internalized pain, the body itself is the *first text*, the *pre-text* to the actual letter. Indeed, the body is the original secret text in which are encrypted and encoded the revelations of the subsequent letter. The letter must be read, then, as a secondary trace, as a *post-script* to the original body text. Here one intuits the potential of a woman's body to become a cult to which she alone is the initiate; it is a secret, a chamber, to which she alone holds the key and through which she thinks:

> *toutes les femmes ont presque le même destin que des religions ou des législations abusives ont cimenté.* (129)

> [*all women have almost the same fate, which religions or unjust legislation have sealed.* (88, my emphasis)]

Polygamy and abandonment can entail emotional as well as economic humiliation. The consequences of Modou's newfound passions are economically devastating for the family. Ramatoulaye and the twelve children are left almost destitute except for her teacher's salary. They no longer have the car that Modou drives, while the new mother-in-law drives a new car and Binetou, the new wife, changes her two new Alfa-Romeos according to fancy. And, then, there is the affective humiliation of the statutory conjugal visits from Modou on a tidy, routine rotational basis. Despite her abiding love, Ramatoulaye can no longer suffer his deceitful embrace. She confides:

> Je n'étais donc pas trompée. Je n'intéressais plus Modou et le savais. J'étais abandonnée: une feuille qui voltige mais qu'aucune main n'ose ramasser, aurait dit ma grand'mère. (77)

> [I was not deceived, therefore. I no longer interested Modou, and I knew it. I was abandoned: a fluttering leaf that no hand dares to pick up, as my grandmother would have said. (57)]

Ramatoulaye describes herself as a fluttering leaf that no one dared pick up. And yet, Ramatoulaye picks herself up and reaches out across the distance, across the sea to her best girlhood friend, Aissatou, who presently lives and works in Washington, D.C. One of the felicitous consequences of Ramatoulaye's abandonment is the bonding that occurs between the two modern women of the same ethnic, national class who share a mutually inclusive reality that neither had theretofore discussed. Aissatou's husband, Mowdo, had inflicted upon her what, despite tradition, was for her an irreparable, unpardonable hurt. Before Modou, Mowdo had also taken a younger wife at the insistence of his mother, who had always despised Aissatou. On the day of his marriage Aissatou gathered her four children and disappeared without a trace, leaving only a letter:

> Mawdo, Les Princes dominent leurs sentiments, pour honorer leurs devoirs. Les "autres" courbent leur nuque et acceptent en silence un sort qui les brime. Voilà schématiquement, le règlement intérieur de notre

société avec ses clivages insensés. Je ne m'y soumettrai point. Au bonheur
qui fut nôtre, je ne peux lui substituer celui que tu proposes aujourd'hui.
Tu veux dissocier l'Amour tout court et l'amour physique. Je ne rétorque
que la communion charnelle ne peut être sans l'acceptation du coeur, si
minime soit-elle. . . . tu peux procréer sans aimer . . . est inadmissible . . .
d'un côté, moi, "ta vie, ton amour, ton choix," de l'autre "la petite Nabou à
supporter par devoir" . . . Je me dépouille de ton amour, de ton nom. Vêtue
du seul habit valable de la dignité, je poursuis ma route. Adieu. (50)

[Mawdo, Princes master their feelings to fulfill their duties. "Others" bend
their heads and, in silence, accept a destiny that oppresses them. That,
briefly put, is the internal ordering of our society, with its absurd divisions.
I will not yield to it. I cannot accept what you are offering me today in place
of the happiness we once had. You want me to draw a line between heartfelt
love and physical love. I say that there can be no union of bodies without
the heart's acceptance, however little that may be. . . . you can procreate
without loving . . . is unacceptable to me: on one side, me, "your life, your
love, your choice," on the other, "young Nabou, to be tolerated for reasons
of duty" . . . Clothed in my dignity, the only worthy garment, I go my way.
Goodbye. Aissatou. (31–32)]

Aissatou's departure is an act of refusal in which she transcends victimization, asserts her dignity, withdraws from participation in a system that
humiliates her, and makes the move to self-reliance. Aissatou's example will
sustain Ramatoulaye.

There is a man willing to pick up Ramatoulaye "fluttering like a leaf" —
the handsome, wealthy, intellectual assemblyman, the medical doctor Daouda
Deng, who had asked her to marry him when they were teenagers. His love
for her has never wavered. He declares that still at age *fifty* her grace has
kindled his passion. Ramatoulaye is warmed by his expression of love, but
she sends him a letter of regret and explanation that although she holds
him in high esteem, esteem is not enough for marriage, whose snares she
knows from experience. Perhaps more important, Ramatoulaye's solidarity
with other married women and her refusal to be complicitous in the perpetuation of the abuses of polygamy lead her to point out that recently
abandoned herself because of a woman, she could not lightly bring herself
between Dr. Deng and his family.

Tu crois simple le problème polygamique. Ceux qui s'y meuvent
connaissent des contraintes, des mensonges, des injustices qui alourdissent
leur conscience pour la joie éphémère d'un changement. Je suis sûr que
l'amour est ton mobile, un amour qui exista bien avant ton mariage et que
le destin n'a pas comblé . . . C'est avec une tristesse infinie et des larmes aux
yeux que je t'offre mon amitié. (100)

[You think the problem of polygamy is a simple one. Those who are involved in it know the constraints, the lies, the injustices that weigh down their consciences in return for the ephemeral joys of change. I am sure you are motivated by love, a love that existed well before your marriage and that fate has not been able to satisfy. It is with infinite sadness and tear-filled eyes that I offer you my friendship. (68)]

Farmata, the messenger, returns to act out the pain apparently displayed by Daouda upon reading the letter. Farmata severely criticizes Ramatoulaye for having *rejected* Daouda. Farmata does not understand Ramtoulaye's empathy and solidarity with Daouda's wife and that women who question the justice of polygamy must not perpetuate its injustices even for, or perhaps especially for, personal comfort. Further, Farmata fails to comprehend Ramatoulaye's deferral, which is not foreclosure of any relationship with Dr. Deng. Ramatoulaye wishes to assert that sometimes a woman might, as she says, "want to be *something else* besides a mother" or a wife: "Je souhaitais 'autre chose' à vivre. Et cette 'autre chose' ne pouvait être sans l'accord de mon coeur" (102). ["I wanted *'something else'*. And this 'something else' was impossible without the full agreement of my heart" (70).]

Through the bonding between two women, both traumatized by abandonment and by the "rights" of men in a polygamous society, the reader observes the variable definition of family. It is the support of her friend in moral, spiritual, and financial terms that sustains Ramatoulaye and her family during their time of stress. Family, including the friend Aissatou, is the "smallest organized, durable network of Kin and non-Kin who interact daily, providing the domestic needs of children and assuring their survival."[17] Often, as in *Une si longue lettre* and in *The Color Purple*, family culminates in a network of women abandoned by men.

Bâ writes with deft simplicity. In a passage where Ramatoulaye is ostensibly talking about books, one discovers a Riffaterrian "paradoxical depth of the surface":[18]

> les livres te sauvèrent. Devenus ton refuge, ils te soutinrent... Puissance des livres, invention merveilleuse de l'astucieuse intelligence humaine. Signes divers, associés en sons; sons différents qui moulent le mot, agencement de mots d'où jaillit l'dée, la Pensée, l'Histoire, la Science, la Vie... Les livres soudent des générations au même labeur commun qui fait progresser. Ils te permirent de te hisser. Ce que la société te refusait, ils te l'accordèrent. (51)

> [books saved you. Having become your refuge, they sustained you... The power of books, this marvelous invention of astute human intelligence. Various signs associated with sound: different sounds that form the word.

Juxtaposition of words from which spring the idea, Thought, History, Science, Life... Books knit generations together in the same continuing effort that leads to progress... They enabled you to better yourself... What society refused you they granted. (32)]

The passage stands out because it seems to be a graft,[19] an intervention, that describes the text's own procedures. The passage repeats the structures it is analyzing. It seems an act of deconstruction in that it consists of moving from one concept to another by reversing and displacing a conceptual order. Bâ's meta-writing reveals the dynamics of Ramatoulaye's as well as her own writing processes and suggests what Bâ hopes will be the reception and interpretation of Ramatoulaye's letter, Bâ's book, by Aissatou, the first of generations of readers. Although the passage is very much about the power of reading for all Africans, in context it also suggests metonymically or through displacement the power of writing and the dire need of African women, as represented by Aissatou, to read books written by African women, as represented by Ramatoulaye. Further, the passage pressures differance in that it underscores and bridges the gap of significance between the letter as correspondance—postal missive and the letter as correspondance between sound and sense, as printed character, representation of sound. There is a desire to return to the African woman the power to live in language and not submit to it, to find herself in the letters, sounds, and juxtapositions. Writing is difficulty, effort, struggle, work, and resistance to predescription and prescription, but above all, it is refuge, freedom, and power "granted" when a woman writes the letters that correspond to the sounds emanating from within. *Une si longue lettre* must also be read as the transcription of a phonics of difference.

Ramatoulaye's letter is an epistolary cogito, a groping toward significance, self-determination, self-definition, and subjectivity in which she thinks in order to write in order to be. This groping for significance is evident in the passage of unusual density cited previously wherein Ramatoulaye is in search of a phonics distinctly her own. The missive is transmission of knowledge, a sharing of pain, a tracing of feminine affect, and a search for a language of her own. It is a letter of grief, transfiguration, and conversion in which Ramatoulaye wishes to shed her capacity for self-sacrifice. Like the journal, the dream, and the daydream, the letter allows intimacy with self and emergence of the unconscious self—the other that has almost lost its voice under the weight of inequality, subordination, submission, and self-abnegation. As a process of self-examination, the epistolary form allows Ramatoulaye to place herself on trial, dialoguing with herself, quarreling with herself as judge and defendant. As writer, Ramatoulaye is author of self and other. The letter of Ramatoulaye represents the unconscious or the discourse of the other. The other is therefore the place, the letter itself, in which is constituted the "I" who speaks with her/herself who hears her true voice for the first time. There is, of course, a change in register: epistolarity, normally associated with the privacy of the "I," is here socialized, politicized, nationalized, and even internationalized by Aissatou's location. The link between writing, textuality, and difference is enacted. Writing here in Bâ's text is performing the construction of an alternative personal consciousness within the nation — the demassification of difference. The postcolonial and the poststructural are conjoined in the correspondants, Ramatoulaye and Aissatou, who are mutually constructed disseminations of pain.

Ramatoulaye finds salvation and refuge through writing: she does not speak out, rather she writes herself out of her passivity of dependence, self-abnegation, and paralysis of initiative, action, choice, and thought. Finally, the mother of twelve gives birth to herself through the process of parthenogenesis that is in fact her act of letter writing for survival. Her life had been oriented toward others: virtue resided in self-sacrifice and a reluctance to judge or hurt others.[20]

The letter continues with some reflections on the nature of the mother-daughter relationship and particularly with observations on the distinction between love and friendship:

> L'Amitié a des grandeurs inconnues de l'amour. Elle se fortifie dans les difficultés, alors que les contraintes massacrent l'amour. Elle résiste au temps qui lasse et désunit les couples. Elle a des élévations inconnues de l'amour. (79)

> [Friendship has splendours that love knows not. It grows stronger when crossed, whereas obstacles kill love. Friendship resists time, which wearies and severs couples. It has heights unknown to love. (54)]

One particular friendship, brief but of profound importance, was with her high school teacher, another woman, a white woman. The middle years of a woman's life readily appear a time to return to the unfinished business of adolescence. For Ramatoulaye it is the remembrance of the utopian experience of the girls' school with its white headmistress who called her girls to an uncommon destiny, the recall of which helps Ramatoulaye to orient her desperate condition toward the future and visions of transformation, self-enhancement, self-development, and a new morality of love that includes obligations to self.

> Aissatou, je n'oublierai jamais la femme blanche qui, la première, a voulu pour nous un destin "hors du commun"... Des amitiés s'y nouaient, qui ont résisté au temps et à l'éloignement. Nous étions de véritables soeurs destinées à la même mission émancipatrice... Nous sortir de l'enlisement des traditions, superstitions et moeurs; nous faire apprécier de multiples civilisations sans reniement de la nôtre; élever notre vision du monde, cultiver notre personnalité, renforcer nos qualités, mater nos défauts; faire fructifier en nous les valeurs de la morale universelle; voilà la tâche que s'était assignée l'admirable directrice... Elle sut découvrir et apprécier nos qualités. Comme je pense à elle!... la voie choisie pour notre formation et notre épanouissement ne fait point hasard. Elle concorde avec les options profondes de l'Afrique nouvelle, pour promouvoir la femme noire. (27–28)

> [Aissatou, I will never forget the white woman who was the first to desire for us an "uncommon" destiny. Friendships were made that have endured the test of time and distance. We were true sisters, destined for the same mission of emancipation.... To lift us out of the bog of tradition, superstition and custom, to make us appreciate a multitude of civilizations without renouncing our own, to raise our vision of the world, cultivate our personalities, strengthen our qualities, to make up for our inadequacies, to develop universal moral values in us: these were the aims of our admirable headmistress. She knew how to discover and appreciate our qualities.... How I think of her!... it is because the path chosen for our training and our blossoming has not been fortuitous.... It has accorded with the profound choices made by New Africa for the promotion of the black woman. (15–16)]

Returning to the meta-writing passage cited earlier allows for closure as well as overture: Books / knit / generations / together. The syntagmatic development of this sentence progressively signifies and complicates the idea of text. The field of signification expands from the personal textual (books) to the social, economic, and aesthetic textile (knit) to the corporal and bio-psychological network of human connection (generations) and finally to the spirituality of cultural identity, solidarity, and community (together). Perhaps the operative word is "knit," which invites the contemplation of African literary, genealogical, intellectual, social, political, and textual arachnologies or Anance's web, which finds its correspondance in the telegraph and telephone wires that establish the networks of communication in Simone Schwarz-Bart's, novels, especially *Pluie et vent sur Télumée Miracle*. In Dogon mythology the relationship between text and knitting or speech and weaving is made explicit:

> "Speech Which Is Inside Cloth"
> By now, we expect that the origin of the relationship made in Dogon mythology between speech and weaving has been made sufficiently clear, a relationship of both a physiological order, since the mouth organs are parts of a loom that "weaves" the sound material emitted by the larynx and gives it color and form, and of a social order because all the individual "words" intertwine like threads weaving human relationships together and making, as it were, a wide band of cloth that continues uninterrupted from generation to generation.
> If speech is weaving, weaving inversely is "speech" in the broad sense because it is created by human activity. It is also "speech" in the restricted sense because the threads intertwine like elements of language, animated by the regular creaking of the pulley and the sound of the tensors and shuttle. This combination of sounds is "the voice of Nommo who speaks softly." The mysterious message registered in the cloth designs is enigmatic, and in the system of correpondence, this speech type is associated with the "speech of weaving." The thread receives this message and becomes a band of cloth. Before it can be altered, its substance requires speech.[21]

As secondary trace or as postscript to the original menopausal *body* text, *Une si longue lettre* weaves the connections between the middle-age woman's body and the postcolonial condition, between the personal and the social symbolic. The significances respectively of menopause and of the nation's coming into being are altered by their juxtaposition and friction in the text. Just as independence from colonial rule is experienced as birth as well as the prolongation of trauma and pain, menopause is presented as loss as well as redefinition and rebirth. Writing as a connotative system is progress as well as loss and incomplete significance. Writing is contribution to the progress of society that is itself "in transit," in transition, moving from state to state as in the situations of the menopausal woman, the birth of the nation, and the trajectory of the letter crisscrossing political, intellectual, psychological, and social boundaries. The letter-book knits a network of understanding between Ramatoulaye and Aissatou, and it dreams that there are possibilities for life other than those of the life lived. The letter is so effective because, in its effect, it is insinuative and noncoercive while it seeks to subvert the dominant ideology and mindset that have been lived and experienced as oppression. The closing of the letter points to the healing dimension of Bâ's epistolary as therapeutic storytelling, as "a writing cure," and an act of psychic self-preservation against subordination. "Decolonized" and "postcolonial," not unlike "menopausal," are imperfect markers of change. Neither decolonization nor postcoloniality is a completed act or state. Both decolonization and postcoloniality or post-independence are ongoing temporalities and processes of political, social, and psychological revaluation of nation, race, couple, family, and gender. Letter writing is an act of incomplete significance or severed communication and, as such, is appropriate to the transcription of the disjointed temporality and ongoing cultural questioning, revaluation, and healing that is the postcolonial: Bâ's valedictory suggests that the African woman will take up the pen again if she does not find silence without oppression.

Ramatoulaye lives in a culture with inherited laws that no longer work for her. Ramatoulaye's story is a statement of refusal in which she transcends victimization, asserts her dignity, and withdraws from participation in a system that humiliates her. Her love for Africa, her hopes for the nation, and her belief in the importance of the couple and the family are unshakable. The tension is between *to change* and *to evolve*. Fundamentally, what Ramatoulaye seems to long for is to see the laws that govern polygamy *evolve* so as not to be out of sync with, or even in opposition to, gender equality by taking into account the changing economic, political, and cultural forces of post-independence Africa and their impact on the reconstruction of the identity of the African woman.

Notes

1. Frantz Fanon, *The Wretched of the Earth* (New York: Grove Press, 1968), 46.

2. Julia Kristeva, "A New Type of Intellectual: The Dissident," in Toril Moi, ed., *The Kristeva Reader* (Oxford: Blackwell, 1986), 298.

3. Emily Martin, *The Woman in the Body: A Cultural Analysis of Reproduction* (Boston: Beacon Press, 1987). Although this is not the place for a clinical discussion of menopause, I feel it proper to present data that support my descriptions of the menopausal. From the many possible sources, I find this text to be the most direct and comprehensive.

4. Ibid., 42.

5. Ibid., 43.

6. Ibid., 51.

7. Fanon, *The Wretched of the Earth*, 43.

8. Ibid., 97.

9. Mariama Bâ, *Une si longue lettre*. (Dakar: Les Nouvelles Editions Africaines, 1980). *So Long a Letter*, trans. Modupe Bode-Thomas (Portsmouth, N.H.: Heinemann, 1989), 25. Page numbers will be given in parentheses in the text. The dangerous "follies" of independence are reinforced in the text through a secondary character, Jacqueline, an Ivorian who, against the wishes of her Protestant parents, marries a Senegalese and returns with him to Senegal, where she faces ostracism in a largely Catholic and Muslim society. The rejection pushes her into depression, psychosomatic disorders, fears of insanity, and thoughts of suicide (41–45). Her case also addresses the demassification of difference among Africans spoken of earlier. The text addresses it directly: "Coming to Senegal, she found herself in a new world, a world with different reactions, temperament, and mentality from that in which she had grown up. In addition, her husband's relatives — always the relatives — were cool toward her because

she refused to adopt the Muslim religion and went instead to the Protestant church every Sunday.

"A Black African, she would have been able to fit without difficulty into a black African society, Senegal and the Ivory Coast both having experienced the same colonial power. But Africa is diverse, divided. The same country can change its character and outlook several times over from north to south or from east to west" (42).

10. Edward Saïd, *The World, the Text, and the Critic* (Cambridge, Mass.: Harvard University Press, 1983), 39.

11. Alice Walker, *The Color Purple* (New York: Harcourt Brace Jovanovich, 1982).

12. The term is normally applied to traditional societies, but it is my view that the issue of polygamy is of great pertinence in urban and rural America.

13. Jacques Derrida, *La Carte postale* (Paris: Flammarion, 1980).

14. Tahar ben Jelloun, *La Plus haute des solitudes* (Paris: Seuil, 1977).

15. Carol Gilligan, *In a Different Voice* (Cambridge, Mass.: Harvard University Press, 1982).

16. See Julia Kristeva, *Powers of Horror: An Essay on Abjection* (New York: Columbia University Press, 1982).

17. In particular the chapter "Visions of Maturity" in Gilligan, *In a Different Voice*, addresses the issues of concern in Bâ's text.

18. Michael Riffaterre, *Text Production* (New York: Columbia University Press, 1983), 12.

19. Jonathan Culler, *On Deconstruction* (Ithaca: Cornell University Press, 1982), 141.

20. Gilligan, *In a Different Voice*.

21. Marcel Griaule, *Conversations with Ogotemmeli. An Introduction to Dogon Religious Ideas* (London: Published for the African Institute by the Oxford University Press, 1965), 642.

CHAPTER SIXTEEN

The Intertext

Werewere Liking's Tool for Transformation and Renewal

IRÈNE ASSIBA D'ALMEIDA

Tu dis un mot et tu engendres le monde.
Bernard Delvaille

Werewere Liking is a Cameroonian artiste in the full sense of the word: poet, playwright, singer, theater and movie actress, stage producer, novelist, essayist, painter, jeweler, and researcher. She stands out among African writers, male and female alike, not only for the profusion and diversity of her oeuvre but also because her mode of expression constitutes a *nouvelle écriture*, a new way of writing. She is well aware of the peculiarity of her style: "Je n'ai pas une écriture conventionnelle. Elle est difficile à faire accepter parce qu'elle travaille sur elle-même en tant que forme d'art." (I do not have a conventional writing style. It is difficult for my writing to find acceptance because of its work on itself as artistic form.)[1] It is precisely the reflexive nature of her writing that makes Liking unique,[2] and that leads to an abundant, imaginative use of intertextual material allowing her to rework previous signifying systems within the context of writing about Africa.

Of her three novels, I will examine the second here, *Elle sera de jaspe et de corail* (It will be of jasper and coral), her most technically innovative, a book whose imaginative originality resides in the happy mixture of narrative modes, in the multiplicity of voices, and in the richness of intertextual space. In fact, more than any of her works, this intriguing novel is replete with diverse intertextual indicators that rely above all on abundant explicit or implicit allusions, such as those to the mythologies of Cameroon (especially among the Bassa, Liking's ethnic group), Egypt, and Greece. Elsewhere she uses biblical, Buddhist, and Islamic references either in isolation or in a syncretic manner. In this book, allusions to literary texts abound. Moreover, like most African writers, Liking incorporates elements of orature in her writing, an incorporation that can also be seen as an intertext.[3]

Following in the steps of Mikhail Bakhtin, Julia Kristeva, who coined the term "intertext," has written that "every text builds itself as a mosaic of quotations, every text is absorption and transformation of another text."[4] Despite the divergence of opinion of critics such as Roland Barthes, Jacques Derrida, and Michael Riffaterre, a wider concept of intertextuality seen as incorporation into a new text of previous citations, references, quotations, fragments of quotations, and allusions has endured; after retracing the history of the concept, Jonathan Culler concludes that "the study of intertextuality is not the investigation of sources and influences as traditionally conceived; it casts its net wider to include anonymous discursive practices, codes whose origins are lost, that make possible the signifying practices of later texts."[5]

Liking's use of the intertext goes beyond the question of source and influence; her intertext is, as Séwanou Dabla rightly points out, all-pervasive:

> Le livre de W. Liking... ne dédaigne pas les moyens du récit moderne que l'on retrouve... dans l'intertextualité permanente qui distingue *Elle sera de jaspe et de corail* dans la littérature africaine.[6]

> [W. Liking's book... does not disdain the techniques of modern narrative that can be found in... the permanent intertextuality that makes It will be of jasper and coral a unique book in African literature.]

I would also argue that the vast intertextual space created by Liking is not incidental. For her, intertextuality serves as a tool in the process of making new meaning; from her complicated pattern of reference emerges both a critique and a metamorphosing of sources.

From among all the intertextual possibilities contained in this novel, and even though the Bible is a very common point of reference, I would like to concentrate on what I consider to be two of the most salient and developed intertextual markers in *Elle sera de jaspe et de corail*, the allusions to aspects of negritude philosophy and feminist discourse. These intertextual elements are important in themselves, but I will also use them to demonstrate how Liking uses intertextuality as a textual strategy to convey a specific message, in other words, how intertextuality operates in this text.

Elle sera de jaspe et de corail is set in Lunaï, a fictitious and sordid village intended to epitomize Africa. The novel describes the creative process that the *misovire*, its main protagonist, is going through. *Misovire*, a term coined by the novelist, should mean "a woman who does not like men" because of its etymological roots, but, in fact, it has a different meaning, as we will discover later on. The misovire is attempting to write a journal composed of nine "pages," each dedicated to specific themes ranging from the creation of a new language to the raising of children. Through writing, the misovire wants to create a new race that will be, as the title of the novel suggests, "de jaspe et de corail... de souffle et de feu" (10) (of jasper and coral... of breath and of fire). The symbolic value of the title is apparent when one knows that coral, a limestone formation in dramatic shapes, displays bright colors of tan, orange, yellow, purple, or green. Jasper, a red stone, is extremely hard; ancient Greeks and Romans believed it could heal illnesses and draw the poison from a snakebite. Fine grades of both jasper and coral can also be polished into gems. Like these beautiful stones, the new race, then, will be strong, precious, and capable of healing old wounds.[7] Above all, however, it will be a rainbow with "coral-rose" and "sapphire-blue-jade-green" children. This way of seeing the new race in terms of nonconventional colors subverts the usual black and white dichotomy, which only serves to polarize and divide people.

The misovire is a represented narrator who, in a first- and third-person narrative, describes the journal being written as a "texte-jeu," a text-game, and poses herself both as the "game leader" and as a sort of prophet heralding the forthcoming birth of the new race. She is the essential voice, the unifying principle of the story, seen through her eyes. Her thought processes constitute the kernel of the narrative, but its motor is the dialogue between the protagonists of the story, Grozi and Babou. These two intellectuals, whose names are replete with suggestive and connotative flavors, reflect on the African situation. Yet a fourth voice is that of "Nuit Noire" (Black Night), in Dabla's words, "a character 'in absentia' " (191), a mythical character whose very name constitutes yet another way of subverting conventional symbols. Indeed, Black Night connotes a double darkness with all the negativity commonly surrounding the word *black*. Nuit Noire embodies light, clarity of mind and vision, of knowledge and consciousness. Finally, a "Little Spirit" occasionally intervenes in the narrative. The novel, which Liking describes as a "chant-roman" (song novel) and which she subtitles "Journal d'une misovire," is constructed in such a way that the misovire's thoughts are constantly interrupted, or provoked, by her own reflexive voice, by her own interventions expressed in a poetic form, by Grozi and Babou's dialogue, and by Nuit Noire and the Little Spirit, who always intervene in a poetic "voice off."

In this "texte-jeu" the narrator will unveil some of Africa's shortcomings. But, of course, she is aware that others have written with the same intention, and thus she opens her novel with a cluster of intertextual signifiers, each making titular allusion to a book written by a prophet of doom speaking from outside the continent: *L'Afrique est mal partie* (*False Start in Africa*) by the French sociologist René Dumont, as well as "L'Afrique étranglée" (Strangulated Africa), "L'Afrique en danger" (Africa in danger), and "L'Afrique trahie" (Africa betrayed). The narrator recognizes that these titles reflect some of the painful realities of Africa that she herself denounces:

> La parole n'a plus de sens. Le regard, le plaisir, l'amitié sont figés dans le mitigé. Les désirs originels sont pervertis. Les intellectuels sont creux et vasouillards. Les hommes tremblent dans leur bourses et les femmes sont de la vraie merde. Les vieillards sont pourris les enfants contaminés. (7–8)

> [The word no longer has meaning. Looking, pleasure, friendship are stuck in the mitigated. Primordial desire is perverted. Intellectuals are hollow and muddleheaded. Men tremble in their balls and women are real shit. Old people are rotten and children contaminated.]

The misovire contends that, while all of this is true, it is not true *only* of Africa, *only* of Lunaï. For a change, the narrator wants to be a prophet in her own land, to unveil the sordid aspects of life in Lunaï, and to show another view of its cultural history. She insists on her alternative perspective by repeating twice that "il y a d'autres vérités" (7–8) (there are other truths) and that "un peuple ne tombe jamais en faillite totale" (8–9) (a people never goes totally bankrupt). She therefore constitutes herself as the simultaneous voice of despair and hope. Indeed, she eloquently demonstrates that in spite of all the death wishes that others have for Africa, Africans remain frightfully resilient, perpetual survivors who steadily ensure the continuation of the race: "Et le plus étonnant c'est qu'il persiste dans ce fouillis des éclats de lumière" (8) (and the most astonishing thing is that in all this chaos sparkles of light still linger). There is no doubt that from those sparkles the new race will be born.

However, after discarding as the sole representations of the African reality the ideas contained in the titles of these foreign books, the narrator almost immediately reappropriates them into a statement expressing her inability to write: "Et elle [la misovire] vogue de faille en faiblesse, de 'mauvais départ' en 'trahison' sans jamais réussir à démarrer son 'journal'" (9) (and she [the misovire] drifts from rift to weakness, from "false starts" to "betrayals" without ever being able to get her journal underway). The use of foreign titular allusions to describe a writer's block suggests, of course, the consequence of the paralyzing inhibition that outsiders have inflicted upon Africa through colonization, and that they continue to inflict upon the continent through new tactics of demoralization, the utterly negative, pessimistic looks cast on Africa, and the hopeless predictions made about its future.

This statement about the misovire's inability to write is very important in understanding the textual strategies and techniques contained in *Elle sera de jaspe et de corail*. Indeed, although the narrator announces that she intends to write a journal of nine "pages," the first "page" starts on the actual page 23 of the novel and ends on page 55; the misovire's "page" 2 runs from page 55 to 74, "page" 3 from page 74 to 96, and the same pattern continues until the end. In the printed text all of the fictional "pages" start in the middle of an actual page, with the exception of "page" 6, which, significantly, is devoted to the concept of choice. Further, on page 54, at the close of "page" one, the misovire is still looking for a person to whom to dedicate her journal, having found no one worthy of it because all the inhabitants of Lunaï are "tse-tse flies," even including Grozi and Babou. Finally she gives up on the idea of an orthodox dedication and opts for an unconventional one: the journal will be dedicated to the *ideas* of Grozi and Babou, "à leur idées capables de fécondation" (54) (to their ideas capable of bearing fruit). When the misovire has reached her ninth "page" (149), she still declares that she has not been able to write the journal and is still asking herself: "Dois-je vraiment écrire un journal de bord? Serai-je capable de l'écrire? Est-ce utile?" (149) (Must I really write a log? Will I be able to write it? Is it useful?). At the close of her novel of 155 pages, which she claims are not written, she plans to retire to a hermitage, where she hopes to find the inspiration and peace to begin writing.

What then is the meaning of this apparent intent to "deceive" the reader? Her inability to write is caused by several factors, including the negative influence of colonization and the related fact that Lunaï, a "village merdeux et merdique" (13) (village shitty to the core), is such a tormented and tormenting world that it cannot nurture any kind of inspiration. In such an environment, the misovire is "encore trop imbibée de merde et de pus" (151) (still too saturated with shit and pus). Another interpretive perspective emerges, however, the issue of women being silenced in their artistic expression. This silencing reveals why the misovire describes her text as a "texte-jeu," a concept that operates at many different levels. This symbolic "play" or make-believe divulges a sophisticated narrative trick in which the misovire continually announces that she is unable to write, while she is in fact writing profusely. In this context where the text is at once a text and not a text, where the text is being created "in spite of," the misovire (whose identity is clearly that of a woman) represents the woman who, in spite of the prohibitions imposed on her by patriarchal society, is in the process of creating for herself a subjectivity. By claiming not to be a subject, while, in fact, being a subject through the creation of a novel that is a kind of literary Trojan horse, she is able to manage what I call a "prise d'écriture" (the seizing of writing). Not to write would be compliance; to write is resistance. This is a very postmodern approach where the intertext becomes a way of denying and defying women's absence and silence. The intertext becomes necessary to mock the idea of women's muteness because through it the misovire exhibits her enormous literary knowledge and weaves into her own story all possible forms of literature.[8]

In this written book that is not written, one of the most striking networks of intertextual references is Liking's allusions to aspects of the negritude philosophy. Using key phrases, such as "humanisme africain" (African humanism), "Civilisation de l'Universel" (Civilization of the Universal), and "métissage" (crossbreeding), the misovire creates a very explicit intertextual framework and alerts the reader to some of the tenets put forth by Léopold Sédar Senghor, one of the "fathers" of negritude, in Liberté, his four volumes of essays.[9] The allusions are made more obvious as intertextual markers when Liking invents a character named Ségar, a name recalling Sédar, the middle name of Léopold Senghor. This onomastic allusion is further emphasized because the first time Ségar appears, he is speaking of métissage, a notion close to Senghor's heart.[10] Ségar is also said to be speaking of humanism, to be extolling African values. Here Liking exhibits the satirical humor that pervades her text: "Le soir à Lunaï on entend passer des mots comme amitié hospitalité, solidarité fraternité dignité, é, é, é, et l'on croit rêver debout" (4) (In the evening in Lunaï you hear the passage of words like friendship hospitality, solidarity fraternity, dignity, y, y, y, and you think you are dreaming awake).[11] This string of words represents "la longue histoire de notre humanisme, depuis que le sens a vidé les lieux du mot" (42) (the long history of our humanism, ever since the word has become devoid of meaning).

Liking's ironic play with negritude is also worked out in the identity of the two characters Babou and Grozi. Although their racial identities are not explicitly mentioned anywhere in the novel, several clues indicate that Babou — whose name is suggestive of "bagou" (glibness) — is a white man, whereas Grozi — whose name is suggestive of the adjective "gros" (big) and the slang word "zizi" (dick) — is a black man.[12] The suggestive nature of their names is stereotypical, seeming to fit certain tenets of Senghor's very Manichean negritude; however, Grozi and Babou act and react exactly contrary to what is expected of them. For instance, Grozi, wanting to have just one child, marries a white woman because she comes from a society where "le fils unique est chose courante et honorable" (136) (the only son is a common and honorable thing). Unfortunately, this woman's reproductive cycles are upset because she took birth control pills for so long that she is turned into a "guinea-pig," producing a multitude of babies, now in pairs, triplets, or quintuplets. The white Babou, on the other hand, wishing to have "une floppée d'enfants sauvages intuitifs" (137) (a multitude of intuitive savage children) marries a black woman who gives him an only child! Thus cleverly and amusingly Liking overturns stereotypes.

"L'émotion est nègre, comme la raison héllène" (Emotion is Black, as reason is Hellenic), the well-known statement made by Senghor in his essay "Ce que l'homme noir apporte" (*Liberté* vol. 1, 24), has provoked considerable criticism from many quarters, but Liking attacks it through the medium of satire. Senghor affirms in the same essay, "C'est dans le domaine du *rythme* que la contribution nègre a été la plus importante, la plus incontestée... le Nègre [est] un être rythmique. C'est le rythme incarné" (*Liberté*, vol. 1, 37) (It is in the area of rhythm that the Black man's contribution has been the most important and the most undeniable... the Black man is a rhythmical being. He is rhythm incarnate). To mock this statement, Liking establishes a role reversal in which Babou, the white man, is fascinated by rhythm, dreams of Black emotion, and is annoyed to be labeled a fake black man. On the other hand, Grozi, the black man, "se décrète cartésien commet des thèses sur la raison et en perd sa langue maternelle" (16) (decrees himself a Cartesian commits theses on reason and loses his mother tongue in the process).[13] Grozi's goal is to attain a White intellect, and he is annoyed to be labeled a fake white man. Liking thus satirizes not only Senghor's rigid racial stereotypes but also the intellectuals, black or white, who attempt to abide by them.

To put an end to all this nonsense, Nuit Noire advocates instead a "rythme mental" (mental rhythm) that will be "l'atout premier de la nouvelle race"

(21) (the first asset of the new race). Genuinely using the concept of "métissage," Grozi amalgamates the notions of rhythm, reason, and emotion to
arrive at a new form of thought:

> Elle (la pensée) doit être approfondie, par delà la raison. Elle doit tailler et
> ciseler l'émotion au point de la formuler, de la créer.... Je veux une rigueur
> intellectuelle plus vraie que la raison ... (25)
>
> [It (thought) must be deepened past reason. It must cut and chisel emotion
> in such a way that emotion will be formulated, created.... I want an
> intellectual rigor that is truer than reason ...]

The same idea is reiterated when Grozi speaks of how those who hide behind
traditional masks must be unmasked to allow for a real metamorphosis:

> A nouveau
> Le corps engendrera l'émotion
> L'émotion accédera à la pensée
> La pensée atteindra la volonté
> Et la volonté s'enracinera dans la conscience ... (105)
>
> [Once again
> The body shall generate emotion
> Emotion shall extend to thought
> Thought shall activate willpower
> And willpower shall take root in consciousness ...]

By using her characters to criticize the philosophy of negritude, Liking challenges its dominating philosophical code and destabilizes its authority.

A second key group of intertextual markers in *Elle sera de jaspe et de
corail* is one that echoes the language of feminism, using words such as
"phallus," "macho," and "male." Liking differentiates "male" from "man."
Indeed, it seems that throughout the novel the narrator distinguishes between "l'homme" (man), a valorized notion, and "le mâle" (male), regarded
as a perversion of manhood. Only because of Grozi's presence can the misovire stand living in Lunaï, because Grozi "possède des tas de possibilités a
des tas de vertus ... et il a du talent" (60) (has a lot of potential a lot of
qualities ... and he is talented). At the same time, she is repelled by him,
"parce qu'il a en lui les gènes je le crains de la pourriture de la civilisation
macho qui a régné depuis tant de siècles et qui voit tout en phallus!!! Je
parie qu'il visualise l'élan de l'âme comme un phallus dressé!" (67) (because
I am afraid he has in him the genes of the rottenness of the macho civilization that prevailed for so many centuries and that sees everything through
the phallus. I'll bet he visualizes the leap of the soul as an erect phallus!).

The misovire speaks here of the "page" that she would dedicate to "desire," and she carefully differentiates the type of desire she has in mind from what she calls the "phallic desire":

Ce désir phallique [est] caractérisé par son impossibilité d'accéder à l'éternité: un désir s'érigeant constamment en épées en fusils en missiles en monuments architecturaux un désir se vidant avec autant d'aisance en guerres en sang en pus... un désir raide la nuit et flasque le jour....(67)

[This phallic desire (is) characterized by the impossibility of reaching eternity; a desire constantly setting itself up as swords as missiles as architectural monuments a desire emptying itself so easily in wars in blood in pus... A desire stiff at night and limp by day....]

The misovire suggests that, faced with their finitude, males suffer an existential anguish and seek to compensate for it by a sexual desire that would like to be transcendental but instead remains pathetically earthbound. This phallic desire is associated with images of war, considered a manifestation of great deeds by men but only as destruction and putrefaction by the narrator. The description relies on the stiff/limp metaphorical opposition, an idea the narrator reinforces:

Et les hommes ont construit leur vie sur la philosophie d'un désir aux élans caractérisés par la raideur des débuts et la mollesse des fins et dont le symbole—la force—serait la clé de la vie. (67)

[And men have constructed their lives on the philosophy of desire whose elans are characterized by the stiffness of their beginnings and the limpness of their endings and whose symbol—force—would be the key to life.]

Here again stiffness followed by limpness symbolizes some kind of failure. Yet in their dealings with women, men exhibit an arrogance that the status of being a male in patriarchal society confers on them. This arrogance seems to have no limit:

A-t-on jamais vu un mâle se juger indigne d'un morceau de roi? Le plus laid le plus vulgaire et le plus démuni stupide ne s'inquiète pas de faire des avances à la meilleure des femmes à la déesse elle-même et ne se demande jamais ce qu'il peut proposer apporter dans ce dialogue. Sans doute parce que les hommes s'imaginent que leur phallus suffit à tout compenser. (150)

[Have you ever seen a male think himself unworthy of a prize fit for a king? The ugliest the most vulgar the most impoverished stupid has no qualms about making advances to the best of women to the Goddess herself and he never wonders what he can bring to the dialogue. Probably because men believe that their phallus alone is enough to compensate for everything.]

Liking uses feminist discursive markers to address important epistemological issues concerning women, their relationship to men, and their relationship to the very act of writing. She intimates that women cannot let
the present state of affairs continue. They need a strategy, one contained in
the idea of the misovire, which is, I believe, an alternative word for "feminist." Continuing in her work of transformation, Liking, then, offers a means
of reconceptualizing feminism in African terms. She invents the word *misovire* much in the way that Alice Walker invented "womanist," with the difference, however, that Walker's term has positive connotations; it is a celebration of womanhood.[14] Misovire, by contrast, is a word invented *against*
men, though, as we will see, it is not intended to convey an entirely negative meaning. The very act of its invention is in itself of primal importance
as Liking engenders a new language, fashioned by a woman to bring into
being that which is not. It is also intended to fill a void, because in the
French language no word exists to describe someone who does not like
men. Liking's invention is critical in that it shows how gender ideology
pervades all spheres of human endeavor, including linguistic constructions,
and it is precisely to counter these forms of dominant patriarchal ideologies that Liking, an expert at mixing categories, combines Greek and Latin
morphemes to invent *misovire*.[15]

Her invention is all the more important because the creation of the word
also creates the function, and the possibility of another reality. Yet, disre-
garding the literal etymological meaning of *misovire* as "man-hater," Liking
offers a very different definition for her neologism: "une femme qui n'arrive
pas à trouver un homme admirable" (a woman who cannot find an admirable
man).[16] Her definition clearly demonstrates that she does not advocate separatism. Her stance does not limit itself to anti-male rhetoric but stresses
instead a balance between demand and persuasion. She thus exerts force
by the act of inventing misovire, and yet moderates that force with a certain subtlety through the special definition she gives the word. This is the
balancing act that remains at the heart of how women negotiate their demands, indeed their positions, within African societies. With the redefinition of woman as misovire, Liking emphasizes men's shortcomings in contemporary society, reminding them of a lack of dignity and a lost sense of
values that cause women to move away from them:

> Elle (la femme) se sent entourée par des "larves" uniquement préoccupées
> par leurs panses et leurs bas-ventres et incapables d'une aspiration plus
> haute que leur tête, incapable de lui inspirer des grands sentiments qui
> agrandissent, alors, elle devient misovire.

[She (the woman) feels that she is surrounded by "larvae" solely preoccupied with their bellies and their loins and unable to aspire to something that reaches higher than their heads, unable to inspire her with feelings that can uplift her, therefore, she becomes a misovire.][17]

As Anne Adams points out, "our diarist does not really want to be a misovirist, she's forced into the posture, she says, by the men's misogynist behavior."[18] And the diarist insists that women also have their share of responsibility: "Il faut l'avouer: si Lunaï est aussi caduque c'est parce que les femmes sont devenues de la vraie poisse, des Tsé-tsés" (74) (One must admit this: if Lunaï has become so lame, it is because women have become tacky, real tsetse flies). Also, if men have turned into "des sexes sans couilles" (89) (sexes without balls), women have accepted that situation and do not pull their men toward greater things either. Thus, in an incident highly reminiscent of a scene in Ferdinand Oyono's *The Old Man and the Medal*, where a politician keeps a whole village waiting for him in the sun and then has the audacity to demand a young woman for his siesta, no man dares denounce him, but at the same time "aucun homme n'avait trouvé en sa femme le miroir qui aurait pu lui renvoyer une image de lui impossible à accepter une image qu'il aurait refusée . . ." (89) (no man could find in his wife the mirror that reflected an image of himself impossible to accept an image he had to reject . . .].

Women too have betrayed an ideal of transcendence, and using orature as an intertext, Liking explains the deterioration of relationships between men and women through a mythical tale of origins that goes back to the time when Lunaï was called "berceau en coeur," "the heart-shaped cradle." At that time the Gods wanted to keep knowledge for themselves and not share it with men. But Hilôlômbi, the Elder, decided to send to men "Masques en mission de civilisation" (Masks with a civilizing mission). The allusion to the French "Mission Civilisatrice" (Civilizing Mission) is obvious. Here, however, the term connotes a more positive value, for the Masks' first objective was to "initier l'homme à la sagesse c'est-à-dire à la connaissance et à son bon usage" (76) (initiate man into wisdom, that is to say into knowledge and its good use). It was a great period of initiation that yielded positive results. But soon, man started to wallow in the animal world, and so to punish him, he was deprived of wisdom. Um, one of the Masks sympathetic to man, stole knowledge for man and hid it in a hole. No man tried to seek for it. It was a woman, Soo, the twin sister of Njock, the elder of man's twins, who did so because *she* was inhabited by a strong desire for love. She heard the voice of the Mask who encouraged her and asked her to marry him:

Et c'est ici que Soo commit la première bêtise de femme: elle eut peur! Elle eut peur de sa trouvaille de la puissance de son désir elle eut peur d'elle-même... L'homme appelé à son secours s'empara d'Um et de ses secrets et les garda jalousement pour lui dépossédant totalement la femme. (80)

[And it is at that time that Soo made her first mistake as a woman! She got scared of what she found, scared of the force of her desire scared of her own self... She called man to her rescue and he took possession of Um and of his secrets and kept them jealously for himself thus completely dispossessing woman.]

However, the woman was left with something fundamental:

Soo put garder la sensation de la chaleur de ce premier contact des feux des dieux et des hommes ainsi que le souvenir de cette voix d'Amour et de Connaissance qu'elle avait été la seule à entendre et qu'elle n'oublierait jamais. (80)

[Soo was able to keep the sensation of the warmth generated by the contact of the fire of gods and men as well as the memory of the voice of Love and Knowledge that she alone had heard and that she would never forget.]

And that is why she became demanding, and why the "lâches les médiocres et les malhonnêtes perdirent toute chance de survie" (80) (cowardly mediocre and dishonest men lost all chance of survival). Reintroducing initiation, she put men on the right path again, and as a reward, Hilôlômbi said to her, "Désormais tes désirs seront les miens ta volonté mienne" (81) (From now on, your desires will be mine and your will mine). Soon, however, Hilôlômbi became disappointed because woman's will became synonymous with material desires. Losing her sense of exigency, becoming increasingly materialistic, woman thus lowered herself to the level of men. Liking has set this myth of origins from the African tradition of orature in a sense against the terms of Western feminism, not to negate those terms but to complicate them and to appropriate them to an African context. The pattern of intertextual references produces a new synthesis.

Now faced with this abdication of responsibility displayed by most women in Lunaï, the misovire wonders if she can still sing the praises of women and be proud of being a woman:

Oserais-je parler de la fécondité de la femme alors qu'elle n'en veut plus? Pendant qu'elle parle d'une émancipation difficile à définir au moment même où elle perd la conscience de sa valeur et ne désire plus que de devenir l' "homme", pire que le mâle... à l'heure où elle se laisse entretenir tout en se gargarisant de mots creux: égalité émancipation féminisme vais-je pouvoir chanter l'Etre? Me lever et dire je suis femme? (93)

[Would I dare to speak of the fecundity of woman when she no longer wants it? At a time when she is speaking of an emancipation that is difficult to define at the very moment when she is losing awareness of her worth and desires nothing more than to become a "man," even worse than a male... at a time when she accepts to be a kept woman while she revels in empty words: equality emancipation feminism will I be able to sing the Being? To stand up and say: I am a woman?]

This passage reveals the confusion women experience in the process of self-definition, as well as the gap that exists between their words and their deeds. Yet unrelentingly, the misovire will continue her song about women, hoping that an orphan who lost her mother might hear her and "redresserait le corps et la tête reprendrait confiance et fierté d'être femme éternelle mère de la Mer grande noble généreuse" (94) (would straighten her body and her head would regain confidence and pride in being a woman eternal mother of the Sea great noble and generous).

Liking's invention of the word *misovire* and the special significance she attributes to the word are not intended to alienate men from women but to make men think about gender relationships. It is also intended to put pressure on men to make them active agents in achieving the goal of social transformation heralded by the emergence of the "new race." The invention of misovire, therefore, does not constitute a gratuitous act; it is done for a redressive purpose, for besides filling in a linguistic void, the word aims to destabilize the status quo, and at a revitalization of society. And because, like men, women too must learn the process of self-renewal, Liking's position reveals an interest not so much in feminism but in a new form of humanism capable of transforming society as a whole.[19] It is in that sense that she dreams of a new race that will be "of jasper and coral" and can only be born:

Quand l'homme ne jouera plus au porc
Quand la femme ne sera plus chienne en chaleur
Quand je ne serai plus misovire et qu'il n'y aura
plus de misogynes... (153)

[When man will no longer be a pig
When woman will no longer be a bitch in heat
When I will no longer be a misovire and when men will no
longer be misogynists...]

In the conclusion to one of his essays on intertextuality, Marc Angenot declaires that "la question n'est pas de savoir ce que 'veut dire' *intertextualité*, mais 'à quoi ça sert' et cette utilité est elle-même relative au moment historique" (the question is not what *intertextuality* "means" but "what its use is" and this use is itself relative to the historical moment).[20] What, then, are the uses of the intertextual referents utilized by Liking in this historical moment of African literature? Through the voice of the misovire, Liking seems to use Senghor's works to critique the negritude movement, but she does so for the purpose of transformation and thus to invent a new discursive order.[21] Her critique represents the culmination of a long reflection on negritude, its meaning, and its function. Indeed, Liking's ideas on the question have evolved from a belief and acceptance of negritude in *A la rencontre de*... (1980),[22] to a questioning of its main tenets and its relevance in *Orphée-Dafric* (1981), to the search for a new formulation in *Elle sera de jaspe* (1983). Or perhaps the attempt at reformulation is already present in *Orphée-Dafric* when Orphée comes to the realization that

> Il serait temps d'élargir notre humanisme et de l'appliquer concrètement; qu'il cesse d'être une notion abstraite dont nous cernons difficilement le contenu et dont nous ne voyons pas l'efficacité. (56)
>
> [It is high time for us to broaden our humanism and to apply it to concrete things; it must cease to be an abstraction whose contents escape us and whose effectiveness we cannot see.]

In *Elle sera de jaspe,* we have seen that Liking advocates a "mental rhythm"; she then proceeds to champion not a rejection of emotion but a transformation of it, to make it more effective, just as the whole negritude concept should be transformed to achieve a revitalization of Africa. As Babou points out:

> Maintenant que je me suis converti à "l'Emotion-Nègre" je la voudrais plus puissante que jamais mais aussi plus subtile... Il faudrait provoquer de l'enthousiasme pour des activités ayant des buts autres que des fins personnelles réallumer le feu sacré en somme pour une idée qui exalte et va chercher au fond de tout la vraie Emotion enfouie depuis des siècles par l'habitude de perdre en ayant raison. (25)
>
> [Now that I am converted to "Black-Emotion" I would like it to be more powerful than ever and also more subtle... One should be able to generate enthusiasm for activities whose goals do not necessarily lead to personal gains in sum rekindle the sacred fire for an idea that exalts and goes back to the core to find the genuine Emotion buried for centuries because of the habit of losing while being in the right.]

The end of this quote touches another literary intertext, as Babou alludes to Cheikh Hamidou Kane whose *L'Aventure ambiguë* (*Ambiguous Adventure*) explains how colonizers came to Africa and overwhelmed the African people, who realized only belatedly that they too had to go to the white man's school to "apprendre chez eux l'art de vaincre sans avoir raison" (47) (learn from them the art of conquering without being in the right) (37).[23] In this intertextual transformation the loss of genuine emotion is traced to the habit of losing while being in the right. This, in turn, is an invitation to break away from such debilitating habits, to seek the sacred fire that will ignite people, exalt them, transform the tsetse flies that they have become into real human beings.

Liking's agenda is one of radical change. We began with Kristeva's definition of the intertext as "absorption and transformation of another text."[24] Here, Liking absorbs and transforms several texts, not as mere artistic device, for beyond the textual transformation, Liking aims at a transformation of society. This is expressed in a multitude of ways, starting with the very title of the book, It will be of jasper and coral, referring to the advent of a new race. Social transformation also involves a new moral order that will be brought about by the reintroduction of initiation rites into contemporary African life. Babou, Grozi, and the misovire herself all dream of a "rencontre initiatique" and are of the opinion that all leaders should go through initiation seen as a key factor in social reconstruction: "Ce qu'il nous faudrait à nous / C'est une Initiation / Rigoureuse comme un couperet" (151) (What we need / Is an Initiation / As precise as a scalpel].

The new society will be sustained by a new philosophy that will go beyond the surface of things, a new way of life that would take into account the lessons of colonization, a new language that will speak to all senses and recover primordial meaning, a new art that will move away from the facile reproductions of ancestral African art because it is not possible to say that "l'Artiste est le témoin de son temps" (62) (the artist is the witness of his/her times) and demand, at the same time, that this very artist remain in the museum of the Africa of bygone days. Babou and Grozi advocate a new theater, a theater of Masks to unmask all kinds of false masks whether civilizing or colonizing, mediating or tyrannical. A new understanding and practice of sexuality, away from Grozi's masturbation, will be essential to reinstate the art of loving. Also, a new sensuality is advocated by the "Little Spirit," using poetry to enlighten Grozi as to the richness of the senses:

La beauté d'une perle d'eau
D'un reflet d'or sur une peau noire
L'éclat moiré d'un velours de soie
L'ondulation frisée de poils sur une peau lisse
La brise du soir dans les cheveux

La fraîcheur d'une goutte de rosée sur la joue
La vraie valeur d'un contact de peau
D'une caresse... (121)

[The beauty of a water pearl
Of a golden ray's glow on a black skin
The shimmering sheen of silky velvet
The wavy undulation of hairs on a smooth skin
The evening breeze in the hair
The coolness of the drop of dew on the cheek
The true value of touching skin
Of a caress...]

This poetic passage is, like many others, inscribed in the mixture of genres that characterizes *Elle sera de jaspe et de corail,* a work described by Liking as a novel, a song, a journal. The text also presents many characters who function as voices in dialogue, as if in a call and response mode, much as in theater. Although corresponding to a postmodernist strategy, this approach also finds its roots in orature:

Je ne veux pas me préoccuper des scissions de genres. Je n'adhère pas à la scission systématique des genres. L'esthétique textuelle négro-africaine est d'ailleurs caractérisée, entre autres par le mélange des genres. Et ce n'est qu'en mélangeant différents genres qu'il semble possible d'atteindre différents niveaux de langues, différentes qualités d'émotion et d'approcher différents plans de conscience d'où l'on peut tout exprimer.

[I do not subscribe to the systematic separation of genres. Black African textual esthetics is characterized, among other things, by the mixture of genres. It is only by mixing different genres that it seems possible to reach different levels of language, different kinds of emotions and to reach different levels of consciousness from which everything can be expressed.][25]

The incorporation of feminist intertextual markers makes it possible for Liking to give feminism an African face, as it were. She recasts feminism in an African mold to fit the contours of issues faced by women in contemporary society. By inventing the term *misovire,* Liking frees herself from referential bounds to make new meanings, form new paradigms, build new codes. This position is one of self-affirmation. It is important to remember that Liking's journal is a text-game where the novelist, through the misovire, is indisputably the game leader using the act of writing to set the rules, to seize the right to speak up, to expose, to define, to assess, to predict. She thus positions herself in discourse with great confidence and becomes a powerful voice that must be contended with. The voice makes ample use of orature, not only in its salient characteristics such as the retelling or reworking of myths and legends, not only in the abundant use of repetitions, interjections, and insults, but also in the corrosive nature of the language, so vividly reminiscent of the satirical songs that were the forte of women in oral traditions, in fact one of their only means of defense.

The mocking mode is enhanced by parody so skillfully executed that the reader can only react to it with laughter. If we do not want to interpret intertextuality in such a narrow way as to see it only from an intraliterary perspective, we may agree with John Hannay and with Yuri Lotman before him that the intertext also derives from cultural norms. From this standpoint, it is possible to say that Liking restores to literature the cultural norms of laughter. With only a few exceptions such as Ferdinand Oyono and Mongo Béti, most African writers adopt a very serious, austere tone.[26] This is understandable because the literature deals with some of the dismal problems Africa is confronted with. In so doing, however, the writers rob their readers of an important cultural trait, the joie de vivre that, in spite of everything, is always present in African societies and often expresses itself with heartfelt laughter and an extraordinary sense of humor.

Even though Liking is vividly alive to the numerous problems that plague and seem to paralyze Lunaï, laughter and humor are strongly foregrounded in Elle sera de jaspe, not only in the description of comical situations but also in semantic configurations. In doing so, Liking dislocates signifiers and dislodges stereotypes. This linguistic innovation, also a critique of reprehensible social behavior, is characteristic of Liking's language, which is totally liberated, uninhibited, clearly provocative, even scandalous. This linguistic liberation can be seen as yet another resistance and defiance of the patriarchal order which imposes silence on women, especially in matters concerning sexuality.

Thus, Liking's project becomes evident. She uses intertextuality as a tool for transformation and renewal, supporting the belief that for Lunaï to survive: "Il nous faudra tout repenser, tout reformuler, tout reconstruire" (33) (We will have to rethink everything, reformulate everything, rebuild everything). Her novel-song perfectly matches Laurent Jenny's definition of intertextuality as "le travail de transformation et d'assimilation de plusieurs textes opéré par un texte centreur qui garde le leadership du sens" (the work of transformation and assimilation of several texts operated by a centering text that maintains the leadership of meaning).[27] Liking uses this technique brilliantly. She is a modern woman who, refusing to be confined to the Africa of yesteryears, brings in all kinds of intertextual markers from all literatures and cultures. Yet, she does maintain the leadership of meaning by controlling, containing, and making all this knowledge work for her design of transformation. Thus, she situates the intertextual elements in such a way as to use them without dislodging either the central text or the core culture. Through the mediation of the intertext, her beautifully written book becomes a powerful collage, with all kinds of intersections and interconnections aiming at turning attention to the necessity for change. In Liking's hands, intertextuality is both deconstruction and revision for the purpose of a twofold transformation of art and society. This approach reveals a measure of the sociopolitical commitment that this lucid, impassioned, and highly original writer brings to bear to make a plea for a return to social wholeness on the African continent.

Notes

1. Werewere Liking, "La femme par qui le scandale arrive" (The Woman who causes scandal), interview by Sennen Andriamirado, *Jeune Afrique* 1172 (June 22, 1983): 68–70. This translation and all subsequent ones are mine.

2. Werewere Liking is one of the most prolific female writers in French-speaking West Africa. Some of her works include *On ne raisonne pas le venin* (One does not reason venom), poems (Paris: Saint Germain-des-Prés, 1977); *Orphée-Dafric*, novel, followed by *Orphée d'Afrique*, ritual theater by Manuna Ma Njock (Paris: L'Harmattan, 1981); *Elle sera de jaspe et de corail* (*Journal d'une misovire*), chant-roman (It will be of jasper and coral [Journal of a "*misovire*"]), a song-novel (Paris: L'Harmattan, 1983); *L'amour-cent-vies* (One hundred lives of love) (Paris: Publisud, 1989). As a playwright, she has published *La puissance de Um* (Um's power) (Abidjan: CEDA, 1979); *La queue du diable* (The devil's tail) in *Du rituel à la scène chez les Bassa du Cameroun* (From ritual to the stage among the Bassa of Cameroun) (Paris: Nizet, 1979); *Une nouvelle terre* (A new land) followed by *Du sommeil d'injuste* (Unjust sleep) (Dakar: Les Nouvelles Editions Africaines, 1980). Many other plays, not yet published, have been produced on stage.

3. This is not to disregard *Orphée-Dafric*, Liking's first novel, where the intertext begins with the title and is embedded in the very structure of the narrative. In an article titled "Echoes of Orpheus in Werewere Liking's *Orphée-Dafric* and Wole Soyinka's *Season of Anomy*" (*Comparative Literature Studies*, 31, 1, [1994]: 51–70), I show how Liking, taking the classical myth of Orpheus as a metaphorical and archetypal foundation, revises and transforms it to weave an African narrative. Also, in *L'Amour-cent-vies* (One hundred lives of love), it is obvious that Liking rewrites intertextually the story/history/epic of Soundjata Keita.

4. Julia Kristeva, *Sêmiôtikê* (Paris: Seuil, 1969), 52.

5. Jonathan Culler, *The Pursuit of Signs: Semiotics, Literature, Deconstruction* (Ithaca, N.Y.: Cornell University Press, 1981), 103.

6. Séwanou Dabla, *Nouvelles ecritures africaines: Romanciers de la seconde génération* (Paris: L'Harmattan, 1986), 192.

7. For an elaboration on the symbolism of what Anne Adams calls the "rock motif," see her essay, "To w/rite a New Language: Werewere Liking's Adaptation of Ritual to the Novel," *Callaloo* 16, 1 (1993): 165.

8. In *Elle sera de jaspe et de corail*, there are numerous literary allusions to other writers' works: Cheikh Hamidou Kane's *L'Aventure ambiguë* and Ferdinand Oyono's *Le Vieux Nègre et la médaille*, Ayi Kwei Armah's *The Beautyful Ones Are Not Yet Born* and *Two Thousand Seasons*; Yambo Ouologuem's *Le Devoir de violence* (*Bound to Violence*), some of Jean de la

Fontaine's *Fables*, André Gides's *Les Nourritures Terrestres*, Pascal's *Pensées*, Birago Diop's poem "Souffles," Wole Soyinka's criticism of negritude. The intertext also incorporates elements of popular culture, especially when Liking imitates "Zombie," a song (banned by the military government when it came out) by the Nigerian singer Fela.

9. See in particular *Liberté*, vol. 2 (Paris: Seuil 1971), "La Négritude est un humanisme du XXe siècle" (69–79); "Négritude et modernité ou la Négritude est un humanisme du XXe siècle" (215–42). For an interesting commentary on the "Civilization of the Universal," see Sylvia Bâ Washington, *The Concept of Negritude in the Poetry of Léopold Sédar Senghor* (Princeton: Princeton University Press, 1973), 179–80.

10. Senghor expatiated on the notion of crossbreeding in "De la liberté de l'âme ou l'éloge du métissage," *Liberté*, vol. 1, *Négritude et Humanisme* (Paris: Seuil, 1964), 98–103; in "L'Afrique et l'Europe: deux mondes complémentaires," *Liberté* vol. 2, *Nation et voie Africaine du socialisme* (Paris: Seuil, 1971), 148–157; and in "Asturias le métisse," *Liberté* vol. 3, *Négritude et Civilisation de l'Universel* (Paris: Seuil, 1977), 506–14.

11. Needless to say, the translation loses part of the comic effect of the textual and euphonic correlation of the ironic é, é, é and "et."

12. Anne Adams offers another interpretation of the names, which seems to me less convincing: "The Lunaïans, dubbed by the diarist 'tsetse' flies, are represented by Grozi (whose name is plausibly a corruption of *grogui*, 'vendor of cheap goods') and his partner-foil Babou (plausibly from *babouche*, 'cheap goods' itself)" ("To w/rite a New Language," 159). That interpretations can be so widely different points to the fact that Liking's use of language is very rich and opens her novel to a multiplicity of readings.

13. Here again, the ambiguity and pun contained in "[il] en perd sa langue maternelle" is lost in the translation. This expression is a calque on the expression "en perdre son Latin," which literally means "to loose one's Latin," that is, one's language, but which also means figuratively "to have no sense of direction," "to be lost."

14. See Alice Walker, *In Search of Our Mothers' Gardens* (San Diego, New York, London: Harcourt Brace Jovanovich, 1984).

15. In the French context, Monique Wittig has invented the word *misandre*, which, etymologically, has the same meaning as *misovire*.

16. Werewere Liking, "A la recontre de ... Werewere Liking," Interview by Bernard Magnier, *Notre Librairie* 79 (1975): 18; my translation. The key to this ambiguity resides in what linguists call the lexical aspect of the verb *arriver* "to succeed" in the syntagma *ne pas arriver à*, "to fail," "to be unsuccessful"; the expression thus negatively modalizes the *attempt* to find a man worthy of admiration.

17. Ibid.

18. Adams, "To w/rite a New Language," 164.

19. Filomena Chioma Steady makes a similar point when she speaks of a "humanistic feminism" in "African Feminism: A Worldview Perspective," in *Women in Africa and the Diaspora*, ed. Rosalyn Terborg-Penn, Sharon Harley, and Andrea Benton Rushing, (Washington, D.C.: Howard University Press, 1987), 3–24. I am aware that the term "humanism" has historically been overused and misused, and served as a concept meant to exclude "others." Here, however, the word "humanism" is used in a most positive sense. The new form of humanism advocated by Liking vigorously rejects all forms of exclusion.

20. Marc Angenot, " 'l'intertextualité': enquête sur l'émergence et la diffusion d'un champ notionnel," *Revue des Sciences Humaines* LX 189 (Jan.–Mar. 1983): 132.

21. Two of the most mordant criticisms of Senghorian negritude were made by Marcien Towa in *Léopold Sédar Senghor: Négritude or servitude?* (Yaoundé: CLE, 1971) and by Stanislas Adotévi in *Négritude et négrologues* (Paris: UGE, 1972). Liking is, to my knowledge, the only female novelist to offer a critique of this movement.

22. Werewere Liking and Manuna Ma-Njock, *A la recontre de*... (Dakar: Nouvelle Editions Africaines, 1980).

23. Cheikh Hamidou Kane, *L'Aventure ambiguë (Paris: Julliard, 1961); The Ambiguous Adventure*, trans. Katherine Woods (London: Heinemann, 1972).

24. Kristeva, *Sêmiôtikê*, 52.

25. Liking, "A la recontre de... Werewere Liking," 18.

26. It must be noted that Nicolas Martin-Granel found enough material to edit a book titled *Anthologie romancée de l'humour et du grotesque dans le roman africain* (Fictionalized anthology of the humorous and the grotesque in the African novel) (Paris: Sepia, 1991). However, even that "humor" is more of the nature of a biting, grating satire than the joyously funny popular humor I am referring to.

27. Laurent Jenny, "La stratégie de la forme," *Poétique: Revue de théorie et d'analyse littéraires* 27 (1976): 262.

CHAPTER SEVENTEEN

Writing (Jumping) Off the Edge of the World

Metafeminism and New Women Writers of Quebec

LORI SAINT-MARTIN

In Quebec, a few women writers, of whom the best known are Gabrielle Roy and Anne Hébert, have been critically acclaimed and widely studied by both men and women. Such experimental feminist writers as Nicole Brossard, France Théoret, Louky Bersianik, and Madeleine Gagnon have also been the subject of much critical work by women.[1] In fact, these powerful and well-established feminist writers, now in their forties and fifties, have been the focus of so much work by feminist critics that younger or less prolific women writers have not received all the attention they deserve. My aim is to read selected works of some of these newer writers from a double perspective: their problematic relationship to feminism — what I call their metafeminism — and the narrative strategies they use to underline and/or question the feminine.

Unlike the feminist writers just mentioned, who see writing as a form of political struggle whose ultimate end is the destruction of patriarchy and who believe, like many feminists elsewhere, that changing language will change the world,[2] the younger generation in Quebec has not generally come out in public as feminist and shows little interest in the idea of a female language. In fact, some newer writers have formulated a kind of declaration of independence from feminism. Carole Massé says, "I am first and foremost she-who-writes. And she-who-writes has no thesis, feminist or other, to illustrate in her texts."³ But in general, the relationship of these writers to feminism and to older feminists is not one of matricide. As I will try to show, their work incorporates certain feminist ideals and questionings in a new, problematic way. Far from being postfeminist (with all that word implies of dancing on a dead movement's grave), these works are, in their various ways, what I would call metafeminist.⁴ This term, which to the best of my knowledge has never been used to describe women's writing in Quebec, will help define the works I will discuss here and their common theoretical and formal background.

To illustrate both the concept of metafeminism and current trends in Quebec women's writing, I will be focusing on three representative novels: *La Maison du remous* by Nicole Houde, *Les Images* by Louise Bouchard, and *Maryse* by Francine Noël. Different as they are, these works have a great deal in common. All three incorporate the types of questions raised by radical feminist writing—women's place in culture and history, women and language, relationships between mothers and daughters—but abandon theory-fiction and avant-garde writing practices in favor of the traditional novel and a more accessible, neutral style.⁵ All three rework and refigure the past through literary or biblical references, linking that past to an examination of women's present status. But unlike experimental feminist texts, they contain few theoretical elements or political statements on women. Instead, they tell individual, highly introspective stories that focus on the personal as a means of dealing with the political, rather than the reverse. I will be studying various formal strategies used by these authors and pointing to the metafeminist ways in which individual and political concerns are intertwined in their works.

Metafeminism: The Example of Carole Massé

Perhaps by analogy with postmodernism, a notion much in vogue, there has been much talk in recent years about postfeminism, often from conservatives delighted by feminism's alleged demise (which the term postfeminism of course contributes to). However, as Toril Moi points out, "true postfeminism is impossible without post-patriarchy,"⁶ and that happy day is still far off. In the meantime, we need a term to describe works that do not formally resemble experimental feminist writing and yet clearly stem from or continue this writing in other directions. This is where the term *metafeminism* is useful.

Like its rival *post*, *meta* means "beyond," "after," or "behind"; in the United States in terms such as metacritism and metahistory, it stands for "higher, transcending." My use of the term does not in any way mean that feminism is outdated, nor that metafeminism transcends it; rather it relies on what the *Oxford English Dictionary* calls the chief senses of the word: "sharing, action in common; pursuit or quest; and esp. change (of place, order, condition, or nature)," as in metamorphosis. These meanings seem especially appropriate in the context of feminism, which prides itself on its ability to initiate collective action and to evolve and welcome new voices. *Random House Dictionary of the English Language* (1981 edition) also gives "along with" and "among," which suggest a companionable rather than an adversarial or transcendent relationship. As I will be using it here, the term *metafeminism* both includes and calls into question; it accompanies feminism, espouses its causes, incorporates it into new forms. It does not imply abandonment of what has come before but a new form of integration, a way of building on past accomplishments. Returning to Carole Massé, we see metafeminism at work in the contrast between her independent stand and her actual writing. She repeatedly lays claim to a personal voice, refusing political obligations:

> La femme à l'écritoire ne parle pas au nom de Dieu, de l'Histoire, des Femmes, du Réel ou d'un nom propre qui ne serait pas le sien, elle parle en son nom personnel... [7]

> [The woman with the writing case does not speak in the name of God, of History, of Women, of the Real, or of a proper name other than her own, she speaks in her own personal name...]

Massé's statements can be read as a declaration of independence from political commitment, and more particularly from feminism, with which many new women writers would no doubt agree. But despite such disclaimers, their works are not always apolitical or self-absorbed. In *Dieu* (God),[8] published in 1979, Massé examines the place of woman in the Western symbolic order through a long meditation on history and mythology, mothers and daughters, and patriarchal language and a possible woman's speech, concerns she shares with experimental feminist writers. Her formal strategies — free association, wide-ranging and extremely dense word play, and circuitous phrasing — also bring her closer to experimental feminist writers than to other new writers. Paradoxically, despite Massé's repeated claims to be speaking entirely in her own name, she is the young writer who shows the most affinities with experimental feminist writing. Her work illustrates the double nature of metafeminism, as it both challenges the strategies and focuses of "older" feminist writers and incorporates many of their concerns. This double movement, as I will try to show, is also characteristic of Nicole Houde, Louise Bouchard, and Francine Noël.

La Maison du remous: The Novel of the Land in the Feminine

The nineteenth century saw the rise in Quebec literature of the "roman de la terre" ("novel of the land"), chronicles of rural life that generally idealize that life and villify cities and their inhabitants. Remaining on the land is seen as a form of fidelity to Quebec's past, its traditional culture, religion, language, and way of life. As several feminist readers have shown, these novels consistently neglect female experience, killing off female characters early or portraying them as objects of male will and desire, not as subjects in their own right.[9] Even novels by women, such as Germaine Guèvremont's *Le Survenant* (1945) and *Marie-Didace* (1947), tend to eliminate the mother before the story begins.

La Maison du remous (The house by the whirlpool) by Nicole Houde, published in 1986, returns to this critical period for the early Quebec novel and for women's history, rewriting the past from a female point of view. A comparison of Houde's novel to the first novel of the land, *La Terre paternelle* by Patrice Lacombe (1846), will show the distance between a male- and female-centered vision of the same world.

Lacombe's novel focuses on the members of a small rural family. Through various wrongheaded decisions, they are ruined and forced to abandon their ancestral land to work as water carriers in the city. Finally, the younger son returns from work with the North West Company and buys back the old family farm, recreating the blissful state that marked the beginning of the novel. What is striking—and typical—about this novel, besides its heavy-handed moralism, is the small role female characters play in it. Their actions are never decisive; both ruin and prosperity are the result of action taken by the male characters, with the mother and daughter bravely or joyously accepting all. In one curious scene, however, Marguerite, the daughter, disrupts the novel's action without uttering a single word. Because the parents have decided to deed the farm to their oldest son in return for a yearly income, the whole family visits the notary, who teases Marguerite by pretending to think they have come for her marriage contract. Marguerite simply blushes and bows her head; everyone begins to laugh.[10] So far, Marguerite is correctly playing the modest womanly role expected of her, and the text moves smoothly on. A long squabble on the division of property follows, and Marguerite suddenly bursts out laughing, shocking the others:

> En même temps un éclat de rire, mais étouffé presque aussitôt, fit tourner tous les yeux du coté de Marguerite qui, depuis longtemps, faisait tous ses efforts pour se contenir.
> Le notaire la regarda, en fronçant légèrement les sourcils.
> "Mam'selle, dit-il, pourrais-je savoir le sujet de? . . . "
> "Chut! Marguerite," dit le père. (46–47)

> [At the same time a burst of laughter, almost immediately suppressed, caused all eyes to turn to Marguerite, who had been trying for some time to contain herself.
> The notary looked at her, frowning slightly.
> "Miss, may I ask you what? . . . " he said.
> "Hush, Marguerite," the father said.]

Marguerite is the repressed subtext of the entire scene, representing as she does the risk of another speech emerging (she is no longer able to "contain herself" but overflows like a river). Just as they laughed at her maidenly confusion, she laughs at their absurd schemes for dividing the wealth from which she, as a daughter, is automatically excluded. Her laughter[11] is the voice of reason breaking in; unlike the abundant and silent tears she and her mother shed in other passages, it is dangerous and already half-articulate, implying, as it does, a judgment. But her father silences her before she can say a word, limiting her protest to the nonverbal realm. Marguerite lapses into silence until the end of the scene, at which point the notary remarks that she may not laugh so hard when the time comes to sign her marriage contract. The threat is clear, as is the silence imposed on women and the danger that their discourse presents. In this scene, both Marguerite's disruptive potential and its immediate suppression by male authority figures are powerfully underlined.

I have dealt with this scene at some length because it reveals a crack in the smooth surface of realistic, male-oriented representation. The harmonious passing on of land and power from father to son is disrupted by the momentary awakening of a woman's discourse. Only at the cost of Marguerite's exclusion can the narrative continue. In contrast, Houde has chosen to base her novel almost entirely on women's speech and women's silence. Even the titles of the two novels reveal the ideological distance between them: whereas La Terre paternelle emphasizes male possession of the (symbolically female) land and stresses mastery, ownership, and the continuation of male bloodlines, Houde shifts the focus from outside to inside, from male to female, from land to house. She is not interested in possession but in movement ("remous," whirlpool), inner tumult, and struggle. In her novel, the whole rigid edifice of values based on the possession of land and women crumbles as the story is told from the object's point of view:

> La terre n'est pas fiable. Elle peut déménager. Car les rivières coulent. Sûrement la terre ne demeure au même endroit qu'en apparence; elle coule ainsi que le font les rivières.[12]

> [The earth cannot be trusted. It can move. For rivers flow. Surely the earth only seems to stay in the same place; it flows like the rivers.]

If it is true that the structures of realistic representation, which claim to seize and harness the real, are linked to dominant ideology and to male mastery of women,[13] then the fragmented, nonlinear structure of *La Maison du remous* is another form of revolt against male possession and mastery. Indeed, one of the most striking aspects of the novel is its antirealism. In sharp contrast to detailed descriptions of the earth and the seasons in the traditional novel of the land, the first sentence of *La Maison du remous* reads: "The village seems improbable" (11). Houde has based her novel on a series of images that recur along generational lines, giving the book its open, flowing structure.

As we will see, Houde shifts emphasis away from the father-son relationships highlighted in the traditional novel of the land and toward the mother-daughter bond. In varying detail, her novel covers five generations of mothers and daughters at once closely bound together and unable to make contact. No sign here of the earthly paradise depicted by the novelists of the land: the doctrine of separate spheres — the man outside the home, the woman inside — creates insurmountable distance between the sexes, making him a stranger in the house and her a prisoner of it.

Before she is ten, Laetitia, the central figure of the novel, begins to replace her mother (exhausted by bearing too many children in too short a time) in everything from cooking and cleaning to beating her brothers and sisters when they disobey. Laetitia longs for one look from her mother, one word that will tell her she is loved, but every time, her hopes are shattered:

> Laetitia a osé la regarder, et leurs yeux se sont croisés. Cette lueur de surprise: Laetitia a cru un instant que sa mère la reconnaissait, comme après une longue absence. Laetitia lui a tendu la main droite. Et dans cette main, sa mère a déposé le balai. (14)

> [Laetitia dared to look at her, and their eyes met. That gleam of surprise: for a second Laetitia thought her mother had recognized her, as if after a

long absence. Laetitia held out her right hand. And in her hand, her mother
laid the broom.]

Because of her mother's silence (the mother will die without ever saying
what Laetitia needed to hear) and the female condition that separates them,
Laetitia is consumed by both love and hate for her, a pattern her own daughters will reproduce. Fear drives a wedge between mother and daughter:

> toutes deux pèlent les carottes, le navet, le chou en fixant attentivement leur
> couteau, leurs mains sur le couteau. Avoir si peur d'un regard.... Toutes
> deux ajustent les draps sur le lit; elles fixent attentivement les draps, ne se
> regardent pas. Avoir si peur. (13)

> [both peel carrots, turnip, cabbage, staring at their knife, their hands on the
> knife. Such fear of a glance.... Both fit the sheets to the bed; they stare at
> the sheets, don't look at each other. Such fear.]

Fear of violence, both violence against them and their own violence ("I'm
about to kill somebody," Laetitia's mother screams [15]), fear of sexuality
(the sheets, often covered with blood), fear of death and madness (Laetitia's
grandmother spent most of her adult life in a mental hospital), fear of speech
and closeness, all these keep Laetitia and her mother apart, as they will
separate Laetitia from her own children. The words neither woman dares
to speak stay inside them and fester there, like the laughing woman covered
with insects Laetitia imagines lives under the house. Laetitia realizes early
that the problem is one of speech: "dans le corps de sa mère, sa mère sans
parole, ce sera quand le moment de parler?" (47) (In the body of her mother,
her wordless mother, when will it be time to speak?). As was the case for
Marguerite in La Terre paternelle, women's lack of status and power is reflected in their inability to use referential language: "mots renversés comme
une marmite de ragoût" (11) (words spilled like a kettle of stew). Laetitia's
mother tells her to throw the clean clothes away and to put the soup on the
table to heat it up. Fortunately, Laetitia has learned to interpret her mother's
language, whereas one of her brothers follows the mother's garbled instructions to the letter and is beaten for it. His literal masculine reading does
not take into account the difficulty women have in gaining access to language, which Laetitia not only understands but shares.

Like her own mother, Laetitia as a parent becomes wordless, violent,
unreachable. Because her mother died shaken by terrible convulsions, Laetitia fears movement and has become extremely rigid, refusing even to let
one kitchen chair be moved to a new position. She beats her children out
of love and hate both and because she cannot speak to them. In fact, the

second half of the book, which focuses partly on Laetitia's daughters, is full of echoes of the first. Recurring images — the strap used to beat the children, the pregnant mother vomiting, her obsessive cleanliness — emphasize the links between generations of powerless, frustrated women unable to escape their house, which is as much a prison as the asylum where Laetitia, too, will end her life.

And yet, in this dark novel, there are moments of hope, moments where mother's and daughter's eyes and words meet, if only briefly. Even as Laetitia regrets that she and her mother did not have time to "go down to the river together" (55), she is expressing a wish that will one day be realized. Despite their enslavement, women have moments of rebellion, like Laetitia's sister Alvana, who makes love with many men and enjoys to the full her "disobedient body" (63). As a little girl, Laetitia bathes alone in the river one night:

> l'eau vient, repart, revient. Une sensation qu'elle n'arrive pas à nommer, calme, tendre.... La clarté s'est répandue dans ses jambes, ses bras, sa poitrine, et Laetitia l'a suivie ... suivre la clarté, palper sa gorge, reconnaître la vie de la rivière. (15)

> [the water flows in, flows out, back in. A feeling she cannot give a name to, calm and tender. Light has spread through her legs, her arms, her chest, and Laetitia follows the light ... follows the light, touches her throat, feels the life of the river beating there.]

This luminous sensuality is something Laetitia will cling to all her life, as she clings to memories of passionate love between her grandmother and a woman named Clarisse, between herself and her sister Marie. Even her madness can be read both as defeat and as an ultimate form of rebellion against patriarchal reason, as can Alvana's suicide. Madness is women's escape, their flight from referential language toward a new kind of speech that needs to be read differently.

Motherhood, too, both enslaves women and gives them great strength. Just after she is married, Laetitia runs away, and in a clearing in the forest, she finds a pregnant moose full of beauty and power, as "disobedient" as Laetitia herself. Laetitia defends Alvana's right to keep her illegitimate child; in fact, the children of desire are seen as miraculous, unlike the dutiful children of marriage: "Marie discovered more than one country with her ear on Alvana's belly" (69). Moments like this one, moments when mothers and daughters reach out for each other, are the only hope this difficult, often desperate novel offers.

In *La Maison du remous*, Houde shows in exhaustive — and exhausting — detail the suffering traditional ideology has caused women, whereas in the novel of the land, women's pain is at best a subtext. She rewrites the history of a genre by thinking its story through in terms of gender; her antirealism is a powerful example of what new women writers have achieved in terms of both literary form and groundbreaking subject matter.

Les Images: The Bible in the Feminine

Louise Bouchard's Les Images (Images), first published in 1985, is the brief but intense story of a young woman haunted by madness.[14] It takes the form of a long letter written to a friend, Théodore, during the narrator's stay in Denmark. Most of the story describes a terror so deep it resembles death: the narrator, who calls herself Isaac, is drawn to "les ponts, les rails, les tunnels sombres comme un désir" (12) (bridges, train tracks, tunnels dark as desire). As the title suggests, Isaac is unable to function because of the "images" that come between her and the world. The most powerful of these, which haunts her to the extent that she has chosen the name of its central character for herself, is Isaac on the altar as Abraham raises the knife:

> Oh! j'ai vu la mort! Et je suis éternellement Isaac dans ce temps arrêté, ce moment où le couteau, sa lame brillant sous le soleil, est suspendu au-dessus de ma gorge. . . . J'ai vu la mort dans la main d'Abrame. Je ne serai plus jamais vivante. (16)

> [Oh! I have seen death! And forever I am Isaac in this suspended time, this moment when the knife, its blade shining in the sun, hangs above my throat. . . . I have seen death in Abraham's hand. I will never be alive again.]

Throughout the text, Isaac obsessively asks: "Will an angel stay his hand?" This image — underlined by others such as the sacrificial Iphigenia and an infanticide by the Count of Foix — seems to be the source of her crippling fear of death and of the (symbolic) father's violence. But there is a terror worse than hers. The narrator contrasts the destiny of males and females in contemporary culture through the image of Isaac, who was saved from death by an angel, and that of Jephthah's daughter (Judges 11), who was not spared. Jephthah promised to sacrifice the first living creature to cross the threshold when he returned from battle. It was his daughter, and he kept his promise. She died, Bouchard suggests, because she was female:

> Isaac vit. La fille de Jephté est dans la mort. Elle n'a ni ange ni mère pour la garder de la mort. Elle est la fille de son père et son père l'offre en sacrifice. Elle n'a pas de mère, elle n'appelle pas. (55)

[Isaac is alive. Jephthah's daughter has entered into death. She has neither angel nor mother to keep her from death. She is her father's daughter and her father has offered her up as a sacrifice. She has no mother, she does not call out.]

In the same way, Isaac regrets that the mother's song of mourning she hears in her head is for the son, not for her; she even rents a room from an old woman who says she prefers male tenants. And when she opens Dante's *Vita nuova*, she reads: "Mon fils, il est temps d'abandonner nos fictions" (35) (My son, it is time to abandon our fictions). She longs for the spiritual nourishment of hearing herself addressed and valued as a woman: "Ma fille, il est temps..." (36) (Daughter, it is time...) But women were not "invited to the banquet"[15] of Western culture:

Tu n'es pas un fils.... Ferme le livre et attends à la porte. Il y aura des miettes pour toi quand le fils sera rassasié. (35)

[You are not a son.... Close the book and wait at the door. There will be crumbs for you when the son has eaten his fill.]

To escape spiritual neglect and death, the narrator chooses to identify with the male: "Je ne veux pas mourir. Je serai Isaac" (54) (I don't want to die. I will be Isaac). However, as Patricia Smart points out, Isaac's fear, her dependence, her lack of self-confidence, are perhaps specifically feminine.[16] If Bouchard's narrator uses male imagery, it is at once to rewrite her own narrative pattern in a more positive mode and to point to the lack of corresponding female figures in Western culture (unlike Isaac, Jephthah's daughter is obscure, nameless, and sacrificed). Fortunately, she has Dorothée, an older woman who plays a maternal role in saving her from death (unlike the absent mother of Jephthah's daughter). At one point, she even hears Dorothée say, "ma petite Isaac, il est temps d'oublier tes fictions" (36) (my little Isaac, it is time to forget your fictions). Dorothée thus offers Isaac a woman's voice and hope of a woman's culture.

Dorothée is seen as both a mother and a godlike figure able to protect Isaac from death. In her apartment, she has created a special room where Isaac can find refuge "comme si elle m'avait permis de m'abriter dans son ventre" (20) (as if she had allowed me to take shelter in her womb). But one day Dorothée pulls open the curtains and the sunlight pours in. Isaac is traumatized: "j'étais expulsée de la douce noirceur, livrée nue au soleil implacable" (21) (I was pushed out of the gentle darkness, given over naked to the implacable sun). In this birth trauma, Isaac thinks Dorothée is rejecting her, not helping her to move into the light. Here as elsewhere, Isaac's feelings toward Dorothée are ambivalent, like those of a small child for its mother: "Malgré l'intense besoin que j'avais d'elle...il me fallait souvent la fuir" (72) (Despite my intense need for her...I often needed to run away from her). When she travels to Denmark, Isaac suddenly feels herself "swallowed up" (27) by Dorothée as she imagines her at home waiting for a letter.

Isaac needs Dorothée to be a god who will save her from death; she is terrified and furious when she is forced to see her as a "femme sans divinité comme moi" (49) (a woman like me, ungodlike). She fears that Dorothée will no longer be able to protect her: "la nuit reste hostile autour de nous serrées l'une contre l'autre comme des enfants perdues, apeurées" (19) (the night remains hostile around us pressed together like lost, frightened children). Freudians would likely read this passage as an unmasking of the "phallic mother" that comes with the discovery of castration, whereas feminists would see it as a sign of women's lack of power and prestige in a male-dominated society. "Je ne pouvais risquer d'être à nouveau jetée dans la terreur, dans l'absence de Dorothée" (44) (I could not risk being plunged into fear again, into Dorothée's absence), Isaac writes. Throughout, Dorothée's presence/absence suggests Freud's game of Fort/Da, which the child plays to master its fear of the mother's absence. Here, writing itself is an elaborate game of present absence, of absent presence. Barthes's famous "a writer is someone who plays with his mother's body,"[17] if rewritten in the feminine ("her mother's body"), could change literary form. Les Images is a striking example of the difference this female perspective makes.

At the end of the novel, Dorothée falls ill, and out of concern for her, Isaac forgets her own terror: "Grâce à Dorothée, à sa douleur, la réalité l'emporta sur la fiction...Elle me donnait le jour" (90) (Thanks to Dorothée and her pain, reality triumphed over fiction.... She gave birth to me). Finally, Isaac has absorbed Dorothée's lessons and is able to play the maternal role to a young girl who is as afraid as Isaac once was: "Elle dit qu'elle s'appelle Isaac, mais son nom c'est Florence. Je sais. Elle habite à côté" (99) (She says she's called Isaac, but her name is Florence. I know. She lives next door). At the end of a very desperate story, this image of protection and tenderness, of generations of women helping each other, suggests a new female culture emerging.

"Quand je l'ai connue, je sortais d'une enfance passée dans la bible, je sortais tout droit du Livre" (82) (When I met her, I was emerging from a childhood in the Bible, I was just emerging from the Book), Isaac writes. The Bible gives Bouchard's novel not only its most striking images, as we have seen, but also important elements of its narrative form.[18] Significantly, in

Mimesis, Erich Auerbach uses the sacrifice of Isaac to illustrate Old Testament representation of reality. In Biblical narrative, according to Auerbach, place names are less important than characters' "moral position"; nothing is said of their appearance or thoughts. Isaac and Abraham travel for three days to reach Moriah, but we are told nothing of the journey; "it is as if, while he traveled on, Abraham had looked neither to the right nor to the left."[19] All these traits apply equally to *Les Images.* For example, Isaac's travels in Denmark are dealt with only in passing; the central aspect of her trip is her inability to write to Dorothée, which gradually becomes an obsession. In general, then, in *Les Images* as well as in Old Testament narrative, we see "the externalization of only so much of the phenomenon as is necessary for the purpose of the narrative, all else left in obscurity; time and place are undefined and call for interpretation."[20] The goal of such pared-down narrative is not "realism" but "truth": moral principles in Biblical narrative, inner experience in *Les Images.* For Isaac, too, writing is bound up with a spiritual quest: "J'écris toujours, je n'ai pas tué Dieu encore, cette idée, ce désir" (23) (I am still writing, I have not yet killed God, that idea, that desire).

Les Images is full of references to art and literature: Hamlet, Ophelia, Rembrandt angels, Dante, Ajax, and Iphigenia. But the other major subtext is Freudian. The novel does not follow chronological order, but rather a kind of inner logic based on dreams and on association of ideas. Isaac keeps a "book of dreams" (10) and constantly offers up dreams and her own interpretation of them in tribute to one of Freud's major works.[21] She constantly emphasizes both the centrality and the literarity of dreams: "le rêve était la seule langue que je pouvais encore comprendre et parler" (70) (dreams were the only language I could still understand and speak). Isaac's desire for interpretation also draws attention to the purely literary nature of her story. She shows everyone she meets an obscure drawing she hopes they will be able to interpret correctly, "like an enigma" (31), just as Freud compares the dream to a rebus. Failing that correct reading, she will remain "mad," outside of meaning.

Of course, Freud himself pointed out many resemblances between dreams and works of art, including the narrative techniques used.[22] In *Les Images,* Biblical and Freudian strands constantly reinforce each other. For example, the Freudian principle of condensation (one character in a dream representing several real-life figures, or vice versa) is illustrated by Biblical figures: Dorothée is at once herself, the angel, and Abraham raising the knife. Isaac's references to a dream related by Freud in which a dead son says to his father, "Ne vois-tu pas que je brûle?" (15, 57) (Don't you see that I am burning?)

also recall the image of Isaac and Abraham and the theme of fatherly neglect and cruelty. Thus, the various fibers of the text are woven together to suggest a culture in which women's place is limited and precarious.

In the Abraham-Isaac story, as Auerbach writes, "God appears without bodily form ... we only hear his voice."[23] Similarly, *Les Images* relies on the epistolary form to emphasize presence/absence and voice. Isaac claims to be writing not to Théodore but to "Someone behind [him]," whose absence terrifies her and who never comes. The capital letter and the overdetermined names of "Someone's" substitutes, *Théo*dore and Doro*thée*, suggest an absent and cruel divinity, as do the recurring images of Isaac and of Jephthah's daughter. Not surprisingly, writing is both a sign of illness (Isaac never writes until her condition becomes almost hopeless) and a way of warding it off: "Si j'écris, si je raconte tout, crois-tu qu'elle va s'éloigner, ma mort? (18) (If I write, if I tell everything, do you think my death will retreat?). Isaac says she is not a good storyteller, that she has never been able to finish a single story; Dorothée loses patience each time she stumbles over the passage "Will an angel stay his hand?" Yet the narrative act calms and reassures her. Ultimately, not finishing the story means not being forced to accept its unhappy ending:

> La fin c'était ma mort, et elle ne la voulait pas. Et jamais, jamais, elle ne m'a laissée finir mon histoire. (61)
>
> [The end was my death, and she didn't want that. And she never, never let me finish my story.]

By this simple means, Dorothée is able to subvert the closure of narrative and keep Isaac alive. Conversely, with her long letter to Théodore, Isaac fears that his silence will force her to finish it and, by implication, die. Finally, the arrival of Florence allows her to move out of the "terrible fiction" she has been a prisoner of and into life. The letter to Théodore is never sent; instead, Isaac will use language, as Dorothée did for her, to save Florence from despair and death. In a very brief space, Louise Bouchard has used biblical and Freudian images to question madness, writing, relationships between women, and the place of the feminine in culture, all without the word "feminism" ever being mentioned.

Maryse: The University in the Feminine

Maryse (1983) is a portrait of young Montreal intellectuals between 1968 and 1975, as they move up the ranks from students to professors.[24] Although

Francine Noël explores serious themes, her exuberant language play, elaborate puns, and zestful parodies make her work lighter and more amusing than the other novels studied here. Unlike Houde and Bouchard, she has written best-sellers that have also attracted critical attention.[25] Part of her books' popular appeal is probably their reassuring chronological structure, though this is offset by magical and fantastic elements, including an "evil spirit" called Fred and an archangel named Gabrielle.

The action begins in 1968, when Maryse falls in love with Michel Paradis, and ends in 1975, when she decides to leave him. Private concerns thus provide a frame for the political issues the novel raises. It is the era of macramé, happenings, and student uprisings: "Le monde était parfait et la vie, facile. Vivre, c'était parler, très tard la nuit, toutes les nuits" (14) (Life was perfect and living, easy. Living meant talking, far into the night, every night). Everyone dreams of changing the system, but because no one can agree on strategy, the debate goes on. At first, Maryse, who is from a poor family (her father has disappeared and her mother is on welfare), is delighted to be at university and eagerly struggles to master the unfamiliar theoretical language. She is made to feel ashamed of her ignorance (Michel and his friends are constantly discussing movements and theories she has never heard of) and of her "bourgeois" ideas about love and marriage (Michel wants to be "free" but gives Maryse a black eye after she spends the night with another man).

Although she admires Michel and his friends, Maryse cannot help noticing that all the young revolutionaries around her are the children of lawyers, doctors, professors; while they embrace the cause of the proletariat, they often neglect to tip their waiters. In the same way, Michel proclaims his solidarity with exploited third-world women but refuses to lift a finger around the house. In fact, these talkers and theoreticians never do reach the point of taking political action. Noël seems to be sketching out a male and a female vision of politics, one far removed from everyday life, the other based on daily action and commitment. Unlike Michel and the men (and male-identified women) who surround him, Maryse's friend Marité explains political questions in a language Maryse understands.[26] As a legal aid lawyer defending battered women, Marité has chosen a form of political action Michel does not understand or condone. He thinks Maryse's other friend, Marie-Lyre Flouée (whose initials, MLF, are those of the women's liberation movement in France), is crazy because she has chosen yet another kind of political action: she writes letters to the newspapers and telephones government officials and department stores to complain about racism, sexism, lack of French-language services, and other injustices. Little by little, Maryse's view of politics moves away from pure male-dominated theory toward the concrete, day-by-day struggle Marité and MLF embody. Their female world[27] of emotion, daily life, and small but committed acts is ultimately seen as more important and more rewarding.

As the novel progresses, Maryse gains confidence in her own ability to use critical language, while rejecting theories that do not fit her experience of reality: "Freud était un crosseur" (51) (Freud was a jerk-off artist), she says. She dreams of becoming a writer, but all her early texts deal obsessively with her unhappy love for Michel. She is also tormented by the spirit of the French language, a small creature who appears whenever she sits down to write, enjoining her to use "universal," that is, Parisian male, French. Eventually she drowns him in her ink pot, freeing herself to begin. Her focus will be on the silencing of women in male culture. Following her meetings with Adrien Oubedon, the great poet, and his "aspiring part-time muse," Elvire Légaré, Maryse plans to write her thesis on the "underground work" of muses and their contribution to the works of the Masters. But she is told the subject is trivial and overly referential, and she is forced to give up the idea. Still, despite the lack of institutional support, Maryse gradually moves toward women's issues.

Throughout the novel, Maryse identifies with Florentine Lacasse, the central character of Gabrielle Roy's *Bonheur d'occasion* (1945). Like Florentine, Maryse is a lower-class woman in love with an ambitious man who treats her badly; she waits passively for him or pursues him only to see him pull away. Similarly, she is obsessed with the film *My Fair Lady*, which she saw as a child with her father, and struggles to reject its image of men shaping and dominating women. As she frees herself from these cultural models and from her unhealthy love for Michel, as she moves closer to Marité and MLF, Maryse begins to find it easier to write. Finally she decides to co-write a women's show with MLF. It will be called: "Fragments des vies posthumes de Rosirène Tremblée, muette et morte-née" (Fragments of the posthumous lives of Rosirène Tremblée, mute and still-born), and as Maryse writes, "d'innombrables personnages de femmes se levaient sous sa plume, sortant de l'oubli et du silence" (441) (countless female characters took form under her pen, emerging from obscurity and silence). These include a waitress, a union activist, a nun, a hairdresser, and Rosa Luxembourg;[28] Maryse has moved from writing in isolation about her problems with her boyfriend to writing with others, about and for many women.

One of the most seductive aspects of Noël's work — and the hardest to render here — is her use of a mixture of standard French and Quebec slang, which uses many English words and turns of phrase. She joyously parodies academic language, among others. Some of the departments at the "new university" are radical logology, signology, and literology; François Ladouceur's thesis is on "the accumulation of denominative sememes on the left-hand side of the screen in Abel Gance's *Napoleon*." Various minor characters are named Lapsus Bérubé, Coco Ménard, Sigismond-Jacob, Litote Bergeron, all calling attention to language and knowledge, as do the long, exuberant lists of imaginary restaurants and nursery schools, for example.[29]

Borrowing a term originally applied to Isabel Allende, Georgiana Colvile speaks of "magic feminism" in Noël's work.[30] The expression illustrates how political and personal concerns merge in this ingenious novel, full of satire and exuberant wordplay. Throughout the novel, we move from an alienated Maryse in a male-dominated world to the affirmation of female values and female identification, confirmed by the novel's final scenes: in a parodic reworking of the Annunciation, the archangel Gabrielle returns, crashes into the window screen, and announces that the baby Marité is expecting will be a girl with extraordinary powers.[31] It seems an entirely fitting ending to a rich and inventive novel on women, power, knowledge, and language.

Conclusion: The Sex of the Stars

In the context of female language and culture, one last novel deserves mention. *Le Sexe des étoiles,* by Monique Proulx (1987),[32] is a literary romp that throws together a young girl in love with astronomy, an impotent novelist with writer's block, a struggling female researcher, and Marie-Pierre, a transsexual, raising fascinating questions about sexual identity, its ambiguities, and its mutations. Marie-Pierre (whose name alone speaks volumes) raises an intriguing question that is never answered:

> Où exactement, dans quelles cellules précises du cerveau l'identité sexuelle des individus s'imprime-t-elle? ... Qu'est-ce qui fait que l'on SAIT que l'on est un homme, ou une femme, les attributs physiques mis a part? (143)

> [Where exactly, in precisely what brain cells, is our gender identity imprinted? Our physical attributes aside, how do we KNOW we are a man, or a woman?]

The rest of the novel explores different polarities and attitudes, from the little girl who is too intelligent for the boy she likes to the new man who is enthusiastic about cooking and cleaning. Although the novel does not deal seriously with all the issues it raises, it does suggest some interesting questions, as do many metafeminist novels by new Quebec writers.

Different as they are, then, these new women writers share a common interest in the feminine. Compared to feminist writers of previous generations, though, their perspective has changed. As we have seen, their works abandon the search for a female language, returning to the novelistic form; feminism *as a movement* is rarely referred to, nor is there a call to solidarity or feminist action. In fact, the most important change of all is one of outlook. Although all these works illustrate in their own way the feminist principle that the personal is political, they approach it from the metafeminist angle — from the personal, rather than the political, perspective. The focus is collective only by implication. And yet, without feminism, the kind of questions these novels raise — questions about women, language, and society, mothers and daughters, sex and identity — could never have been asked. Between the lines, metafeminist works acknowledge their debt to feminism. Their authors rely on the foundations laid by feminist writers of the recent past to give their novels a broader meaning. It is in this sense of building on the work of "older" feminist writers — "thinking back through our mothers," to use Virginia Woolf's phrase — that these works are deeply metafeminist. My feeling is that women's writing in Quebec has reached a new stage and that many metafeminist voices are emerging to tell new stories in different ways, changing both the Quebec novel and our perception of women in culture.

Notes

1. For example, Suzanne Lamy, *d'elles* (Montreal: Hexagone, 1979) and *Quand je lis je m'invente* (Montreal: Hexagone, 1984); Suzanne Lamy and Irène Pagès, eds., *Féminité, subversion, écriture* (Montreal: Remue-ménage, 1983); Paula Gilbert Lewis, ed., *Traditionalism, Nationalism, and Feminism: Women Writers of Québec* (Westport: Greenwood Press, 1985); Louise Dupré, *Stratégies du vertige, trois poètes: Nicole Brossard, Madeleine Gagnon, France Théoret* (Montreal: Remue-ménage, 1989); Karen Gould, *Writing in the Feminine: Feminism and Experimental Writing in Québec* (Carbondale: Southern Illinois University Press, 1990).

2. Despite their differences, all these writers share a heightened awareness of the linked issues of language, gender, and power, and all inscribe a "self-consciously gender-marked writing" (Gould, *Writing in the Feminine*, xvi) that can be hermetic and is always dense, innovative, and demanding.

3. Carol Massé, "Entrevue," *Arcade* 16 (October 1988): 89–97. This passage and all other excerpts from Quebec authors quoted here are my translation.

4. See also Lori Saint-Martin, "Métaféminisme," *Spirale* 100 (October 1990): 12–13, and "Le métaféminisme et la prose féminine au Québec," *Voix et images* 18, no. 1 (fall 1992): 78–88.

5. As Suzanne Lamy (1990) has noted in *Textes, écrits et témoignages,* ed. Andrée Yanacopoulo (Montreal: Hexagone, 1990), many recent Quebec women writers have given in to what she calls "la tentation du récit," that is, the choice of the novel over more experimental forms. The writers I will be discussing here are representative of that trend.

6. Toril Moi, *French Feminist Thought* (New York: Basil Blackwell, 1987), 12.

7. Carole Massé, "La femme à l'écritoire," in *Qui a peur de l'écrivain?* André Beaudet Nicole Bédard, François Charron, Jean-Marc Desgent, and Carole Massé (Montreal: Herbes rouges, 1984), 77, translation mine.

8. Carole Massé, *Dieu* (Montreal: Herbes rouges, 1979).

9. Janine Boynard-Frot, *Un matriarcat en procès, analyse systématique de romans canadiens-français, 1860–1960* (Montreal: PUM, 1982). Patricia Smart, *Ecrire dans la maison du père, l'émergence du féminin dans la tradition littérature du Québec* (Montreal: Québec/Amérique, 1988).

10. Patrice Lacombe, *La Terre paternelle* (1846; reprint, Montreal: Fides, 1981). Translation mine. Page numbers will appear in parentheses.

11. For a modern feminist reader, intertextual play inevitably suggests Cixous's "The Laugh of the Medusa."

12. Nicole Houde, *La Maison du remous* (Montreal: Pleine lune, 1986), 37. All translations are mine.

13. Smart, *Ecrire dans la maison du père,* 90.

14. Louise Bouchard, *Les Images* (Montreal: Typo, 1985). All translations are mine. For reviews see Louise Milot, "Le refus du récit," *Lettres québécoises* 42 (summer 1986): 18–20; Lori Saint-Martin, "Au pied de la lettre," *Spirale* 64 (October 1986): 6; and Patricia Smart, "Prométhées au féminin: l'écriture d'une nouvelle génération de femmes," *Voix et images* 12, 1 (fall 1987): 145–50.

15. See also Louky Bersianik, *Le Pique-nique sur l'Acropole* (Montreal: VLB, 1979), a feminist and parodic version of Plato's *Banquet.*

16. Smart, *Ecrire dans la maison du père,* 146.

17. Roland Barthes, *Le plaisir du texte* (Paris: Éd. du Seuil, 1973), 60.

18. See Robert Alter, *The Art of Biblical Narrative* (New York: Basic Books, 1981), for principles of biblical narration such as repetition, scarcity of visual elements, recurrence, and analogy.

19. Erich Auerbach, *Mimesis: The Representation of Reality in Western Literature,* trans. Willard R. Trask (1946; Princeton: Princeton University Press, 1953), 8, 10.

20. Ibid., 10.

21. Bouchard's Ph.D. thesis dealt with parallels between dream-work and creative activity in Nerval's works.

22. For an overview, see Sarah Kofman, *L'enfance de l'art, une interprétation de l'esthétique freudienne* (Paris: Galilée, 1970).

23. Auerbach, *Mimesis,* 9.

24. Francine Noël, *Maryse* (Montreal: VLB, 1983). Translations are mine. Noël's second novel, *Myriam première* (1987), presents the same characters but largely from the point of view of Marité's daughter, eight-year-old Myriam. I have chosen to deal mainly with *Maryse,* which I find more enlightening.

25. See Anne Elaine Cliche, "Paradigme, palimpseste, pastiche, parodie dans *Maryse* de Francine Noël," *Voix et images* 12: 3 (spring 1987): 430–38; Georgiana Colvile, "L'univers de Francine Noël," *Québec Studies* 10 (spring/summer 1990): 99–105; Gilles Marcotte, "La poésie Oubedon," *Urgences* 28 (May 1990): 68–78.

26. Maryse has difficulty reading the newspapers and watching the news because they never seem real to her; the October Crisis seems to be happening *inside* the television set.

27. It is a vision shared by some men, such as François Ladouceur (whose last name means "gentleness"), Maryse's close friend and later Marité's lover.

28. In *Myriam première* Maryse will continue to write feminist theater about groups of women who have been silenced.

29. See Cliche, "Paradigme," for a study of language play in *Maryse*.

30. Colvile, "L'univers de Francine Noël."

31. Myriam will be able to see the future, as the novel that bears her name relates.

32. Monique Proulx, *Le Sexe des étoiles* (Montreal: Québec/Amérique, 1987). Translations are mine.

CHAPTER EIGHTEEN

Women's Space and Enabling Dialogue in Assia Djebar's *L'Amour, la fantasia*

JOHN ERICKSON

Assia Djebar's 1985 narrative, *L'Amour, la fantasia,* comprises three parts, titled respectively "The Capture of the City, or Love-letters," "The Cries of the *Fantasia,*" and "Voices from the Past."[1] The titles of these parts suggest the main story: the clash of aggressor and aggressed during the colonial period from the fall of Algiers to the French in 1830 through the Algerian Revolution; and a concomitant story: the shrouding of voices in opposition (the French title of part 3 is "Les voix ensevelies"). The military-political struggle between French and Algerians allegorizes the struggle of Algerian women to inscribe themselves in a space they can identify as theirs: for the woman whose story the narrator tells, social-sexual-historical space in a society gendered for men; for the narrator (and for Djebar herself), a space of writing inscribed in the written language of the adversary (*la langue adverse*).[2]

From the juxtaposition of nineteenth-century written commentaries of French military officers and soldiers, writers, and artists who described the taking of Algiers and the action of colonization following, and oral commentaries of Algerian women who participated in the Algerian Revolution of the 1950s and 1960s, arises a tension between the word of the oppressor and the oppressed, between the written (French) and the verbal (Arabic and Berber).

In *L'Amour, la fantasia* the narrator, an Algerian woman of the post-revolution generation, recounts how her experience in learning to speak and write French leads her to become the amanuensis for the collective voice of her Algerian sisters of the present day as well as of her women ancestors. She is especially mindful of the "révoltées" (rebels) among her veiled Algerian sisters, those who cried out: "La seule qui se marginalisait d'emblée était celle qui 'criait'" (228) ("The only one who put herself straight away beyond the pale was the [one who 'cried out']" [203]). For a woman to refuse to "veil" her voice as well as her physical aspect and to cry out left her accused of indecency and dissidence. Her cry, in fact, revealed the lie of other women's existences: "Car le silence de toutes les autres perdait brusquement son charme pour révéler sa vérité: celle d'être une prison irrémédiable" (229). ("For the silence of all the others suddenly lost its charm and revealed itself for what it was: a prison without reprieve" [204].)

She who cries out thus breaks the silence of all Arab women immersed in anonymity. The narrator likens her act of writing in French to that cry:

> Ecrire en langue étrangère, hors de l'oralité des deux langues de ma région natale—le berbère des montagnes du Dahra et l'arabe de ma ville—écrire m'a ramenée aux cris des femmes sourdement révoltées de mon enfance, à ma seule origine. Ecrire ne tue pas la voix, mais la réveille, surtout pour ressusciter tant de sœurs disparues. (229)

> [Writing in a foreign language, not in either of the tongues of my native country (mountain Berber and Arabic) . . . writing has brought me to the cries of the women silently rebelling in my youth, to my own true origins. Writing does not silence the voice, but awakens it, above all to resurrect so many vanished sisters. (204)]

Here, in crux, lies the generating principle of Djebar's narrative. Writing and vocalization hold the power to counter the aphasia that renders Algerian women silent. The space of writing so painfully carved out by the narrator offers to Algerian women the space of identity they seek.

Women in Algerian Society

How is the state of women in Algerian society represented by Djebar? After listening to stories of the brutal French occupation of Algeria, handed down by the ancestors of the old women who recount them to her, the narrator concludes: "Chaîne de souvenirs: n'est elle pas justement 'chaîne' qui entrave autant qu'elle enracine?" (201). ("Chains of memories: is it not indeed a 'chain,' for do not memories fetter us as well as forming our roots?" [178])

The past shackles as well as secures the women to their past. The stories whispered, while preserving a collective memory of the past, relate another side of the women's heritage, a collective state of bondage and submission in a society dominated by the male. The remark that follows in the text illustrates this negative side:

> Pour chaque passant, la parleuse stationne debout, dissimulée derrière le seuil. Il n'est pas séant de soulever le rideau et de s'exposer au soleil. (201)

> [For every passer-by, the story-teller stands hidden in the doorway. It is not seemly to raise the curtain and stand exposed in the sunlight. (178)]

The adverb "seemly" thrusts us into the shadow of another's discourse. "And in fact," as Jean-François Lyotard says, "we are always spoken by another's narrative, somebody has always already spoken our words to us, and we have always been already said."[3] The adverb here marks the umbrella presence of the male magisterial discourse that gives word to what is acceptable conduct for women.

The women are shackled to their past, incarcerated, out of sight of the male world, immured in their own private and invisible suffering.[4] In a traditional setting Algerian women spoke out only when they attained an advanced age. They never referred to themselves in the singular, "puisque ce serait dédaigner les formules-couvertures qui maintiennent le trajet individuel dans la résignation collective" (177) ("since that would be to scorn the blanket-formulae which ensure that each individual [woman] journeys through life in a collective resignation" [156]). The women to whom the narrator listens do not, moreover, speak aloud but whisper their stories: "Toute parole, trop éclairée, devient voix de forfanterie, et l'aphonie, résistance inentamée" (201). ("Words that are too explicit become such boastings as the braggard uses; and elected silence implies resistance still intact" [178].) The reverse side of the coin may lie in the fact that elected silence leaves resistance intact, but elected silence is still silence. Absence or loss of voice marks their existence, reduces them to whispers, broken only by the occasional cry of a *révoltée*.

The woman in traditional Maghrebian society is silenced and silent. The veil (*haïk*) folds her into a space of feminine enclosure.[5] "To be a female Mussulman is to live incognito."[6] The sole gaze permissible emanates from the male, whereas the woman's gaze is strictly legislated by religious belief. The Prophet called her gaze "the *zina* of the eye [*zina ul-ayni*]."[7] *Zina ul'ayni*, often translated as "the capital sin of the eye," literally means illicit sexual intercourse. An unabashedly direct translation might be "fornication of the eye."[8] Hence, despite the absence of a direct injunction against veiling in the Qur'an, the nature of the moral imperative for veiling lies in the fact that "the eye is undoubtedly [considered] an erogenous zone in the Muslim structure of reality..."[9] — even more apparently than the body.[10]

The women's position is entangled in oppositions that transcend their state, vis-à-vis the Arabo-Berber male, in Algerian society. The juxtaposition of the written accounts of the European colonizers with the oral accounts of the Algerian women projects these oppositions onto a screen: that of the relations of power obtaining, past and present, between France and the Maghreb. The former has historically served as the Sartrean "conscience néante" of the latter and has posited the latter as object and constituted itself as subject through the latter's negation. Such a process evinced itself in the phenomenon of colonial rule.

In its historical encounter with Maghrebian society, the West has often in fact tried to inflect and control the particular constitution of gender difference, of male/female being and relation.[11] Tahar ben Jelloun points out in his study of North African immigrant workers in France the special role of the mother in Muslim society: "Her body censored, her desire repressed, her word forbidden, her image veiled, her reality denied under the mask and by tradition: woman in the Maghreb generally ceases to undergo oppression by male society only when she becomes mother."[12]

He speaks of how the male immigrants are not only deprived of the figure of the mother but confront "a perpetual phallic aggression: it is the repressive and foreign father who imposes himself on his 'imaginaire' in the form of the police, the boss, the foreman, the unreadable technical manuals [*la technique illisible*]."[13] That same condition prevailed under colonial rule in the Maghreb, where the French male assumed the figure of male authority.

In the power relations existing between France and the Maghreb, the Maghrebian male resembles a boy child if not a eunuch, emasculated and shamed in face of the supreme male figure of Gallic authority. The campaign by French colonial authorities to unveil the Arab woman rested on the breaking down of traditional indigenous mores. Writing of the Algerian revolution, Frantz Fanon asserted that "To convert the woman, to win her from her [traditional] status, is at the same time to obtain a real power over the man and to possess practical and efficient means to destructure Algerian culture."[14]

However, women of the Maghreb face obstacles to self-affirmation infinitely more pronounced than that of their male confrères. They exist in a double bind, not only oppressed by Western aggression against the Maghreb that has used them as a weapon against the Algerian male, but also repressed by the male in Islam and by Islamic tradition. That same double bind confronts the Algerian woman writer seeking an alternate language in French, for her discourse faces repression as postcolonialist discourse by the Western magisterial discourse of power as well as repression by the Islamic discourse of the male and by Islamic tradition.

As Abdelwahab Bouhdiba remarks, "the great taboo of Islam is not so much the failure to respect a parental relationship as to violate the order of the world, the sexual division and the distinction between the feminine and the masculine."[15] In Islamic society, "The primacy of man over woman is in effect total and absolute. The woman proceeds from the man. [As the Qur'an asserts,] God 'has created us out of a single [*unique*] person (*nafs*) from whom he has drawn his female counterpart [*son épouse*].' The woman is chronologically second. It is in the man that she finds her finality."[16]

In a real sense, woman in traditional Arabo-Berber society occupies a non-state. Nor does the concept of the couple exist, for the woman is invisible, without name, without identity other than as chattel. The narrator describes her Algerian sisters as

> fantômes blancs, formes ensevelies à la verticale, justement pour ne pas hurler ainsi continûment: son de barbare, son de sauvage, résidu macabre d'un autre siècle! (131)
>
> [white walking wraiths, shrouded figures buried upright, ... to prevent them uttering such a constant howl: such a wild, barbaric cry, macabre residue of a former century! (115)]

Customarily Algerian women addressed their spouses in the third person, such that the men were "confondus dans l'anonymat du genre masculin" (47) (blended in the anonymity of the masculine gender [my translation]). The narrator describes how she marveled at a postcard sent by her father to her mother, addressing the mother by name: "Ainsi mon père avait 'écrit' à ma mère" (48) (Thus my father had actually written to my mother [my translation]), and the reader realizes what special power and significance the act of writing holds. Normally the father would address letters to the son, no matter how young he might be!

A Linguistic Abduction from the Seraglio

The first chapter of part 1 is preceded by an introductory section opening with a scene that will become a primal scene in the narrative: the narrator as a young Arab girl setting off for school for the first time, her hand in that of her father, who is a teacher at the French school in a village of the Algerian Sahel. The neighbors observe, thinking of the unhappiness ("malheur") that will befall the family: "Viendra l'heure pour elle où l'amour qui s'écrit est plus dangereux que l'amour séquestré (11). ("For her the time will come when there will be more danger in love that is committed to paper than love that languishes behind enclosing walls" [3].) This scene fixes the two poles of the narrative: setting forth into the outer world (learning to write) versus sequestration. The voice of male-dominated Algerian society speaks:

> Voilez le corps de la fille nubile. Rendez-la invisible. Transformez-la en être plus aveugle que l'aveugle, tuez en elle tout souvenir du dehors. (11)

> [wrap the nubile girl in veils. Make her invisible. Make her more unseeing then the sightless, destroy in her every memory of the world without. (3)]

The space traditionally designated for the female child is that of the inside. To go to the French school, to learn to write as an outside-directed activity constitutes an act of liberation from the inside.

Near the end of her narrative, the narrator returns to the scene of her father leading her by the hand. She speaks of the "voile-suaire" ("veil-shroud"), which she, unlike her cousins, escaped. When she had the occasion later to don a veil at a wedding, it became for her, unlike for the other Arab women, a mode of disguise. For the other women the veil signifies loss of identity. For her it merely hides from view an identity already affirmed by her exit from the enclosed space of sequestration, the harem.

When the mother was asked why her daughter, in her early teens, remained unveiled, she replied: " 'Elle lit,' c'est-à-dire, en langue arabe, 'elle étudie' " (203) (" 'She reads!' — which meant in Arabic, 'she studies' " [179–80]). The narrator understands by the verb to read, used by Gabriel in the Qur'an, that "writing to be read" is a source of revelation and liberation. Young girls of her generation, she says, used four languages: French for secret writing, Arabic for their "stifled aspirations" directed toward Allah, Libyco-Berber to revert to the mother-gods of pre-Islam, and that of the body, whose language society attempted to silence. The first "réalité-femme" for the Algerian woman is the voice; but writing in Arabic, likened because of its sinuous tracings to an act of sexuality, suggests woman even more than the voice.

The potential for liberation the narrator will discover in the act of writing, however, does not mean that writing in Djebar's narrative always conveys the prospect of liberation. Part 1, which describes her childhood summers spent with three young female Arab cousins, cloistered in a small village in the Sahel, compares the extensive correspondence of the young women with Arab males, contacted through the columns of a women's magazine, to the numerous writings of the French conquerors. The narrator speculates on the motives of the French chroniclers, who perhaps savored "the seducer's triumph, the rapist's intoxication" and for whom the written word became "their weapon" par excellence. She observes:

> Mes jeunes amies, mes complices du hameau de vacances, écrivaient la même langue inutile et opaque parce que cernées, parce que prisonnières; elles estampillaient leur marasme, pour en surmonter plus ou moins le tragique. Les comptes rendus de cette intrusion d'hier décèlent *a contrario* une nature identique: envahisseurs qui croient prendre la Ville Imprenable, mais qui tournoient dans le buissonnnement de leur mal d'être. (56–67)

> [The girls who were my friends and accomplices during my village holidays wrote in the same futile, cryptic language because they were confined, because they were prisoners; they mark their marasmus with their own identity in an attempt to rise above their pathetic plight. The accounts of this past invasion reveal *a contrario* an identical nature: invaders who imagine they are taking the Impregnable City, but who wander aimlessly in the undergrowth of their own disquiet. (45)]

The comparison exemplifies the failures of writing that establishes no praxis, effects no escape, does not allow one to enter into contact, true dialogue. With the confinement, the language of the prisoner written by both the girl cousins and the French occupiers is "[a] futile, cryptic language" because it opens no real relation, because each remain prisoners of language, confined by words that stand between the writer and the unpossessable object. What can the written language become on the other hand for someone who emerges from confinement?

Writing in the Language of the Adversary

The narrator concedes that the love letters of the young cousins, though providing no escape from confinement, are a means of affirming their self-identity: "Ecrire, n'est-ce pas 'me' dire?" (72) ("Is not writing a way of telling what 'I' am" [58]). Writing is, moreover, the equivalent of unveiling: "Le dévoilement, aussi contingent, devient, comme le souligne mon arabe dialectal du quotidien, vraiment 'se mettre à nu'" (178) ("Such incidental unveiling is tantamount to stripping oneself naked, as the demotic Arabic dialect emphasizes" [156–57]). In a somewhat cryptic passage, the narrator compares the act of unveiling/stripping-bare of the Algerian woman writing in the language of the former conqueror (who, she says, for more than a century possessed everything he desired except the bodies of Algerian women) to the sacking of Algeria in the previous century. We are left to surmise that, through the writing-unveiling of women, the magisterial discourse will be plundered and the Impregnable City of male-dominated society will fall as women come to repossess their own spiritual and physical being.

When the narrator receives her first letter from her classmate, written in French, she observes that French places her under a double and contradictory sign. She feels herself cut off from the words of her mother by "une mutilation de la mémoire" (12) ("a mutilation of memory" [4]). The danger of using the language of the oppressor is revealed in an anecdote concerning the French Commander De Bourmont, who gives letters to an old Algerian to carry to the Arab army, but the latter is assumed to be a spy and is put to death: "Toute écriture de l'Autre, transportée, devient fatale, puisque signe de compromission" (44). ("So, the first written words, even while promising a fallacious peace, condemn their bearer to death. Any document written by 'The Other' proves fatal, since it is a sign of compromise" [33].) Writing for Djebar, as for Duras, is touched with death: "To write, I believe, is actually an activity that puts us in the presence of death each day."[17]

The narrator's apprenticeship in French and Arabic in her youth, before her father chose for her the former over the latter ("light rather than darkness"), placed her, she says, in a "dichotomy of location," between two spaces (the closed space of the harem and the open space of writing), in which she does not comprehend the consequence of her father's option: "le dehors et le risque, au lieu de la prison de mes semblables" (208) ("the outdoors and the risk, instead of the prison of my peers" [184]). French, whose lexicon refers to objects not experienced by the narrator, objects existing in a country across the sea, offers her a vocabulary of absence, exoticism without mystery. Referentiality would be lost to her until she crossed the sea.

She calls French her stepmother language, as contrasted to her mother tongue, which she has lost except for Arabic love songs. She alludes to Spanish occupiers who, even before the French in the nineteenth century, established posts (*presidios*) and fought following the tactic of the *rebato*, which was a space, a no-man's-land, between the indigenous peoples and the aggressors from which the latter launched their attacks and to which they retreated during breaks in the fighting, either to seek refuge or to replenish their supplies. For the narrator a similar no-man's-land exists between

French and Arabo-berber languages. French has become for her a *presidio,* while the indigenous languages resist and attack: "Le rythme du 'rebato' en moi s'éperonnant, je suis à la fois l'assiégé étranger et l'autochtone partant à la mort par bravade, illusoire effervescence du dire et de l'écrit" (241) ("In time to the rhythm of the *rebato,* I am alternately the besieged and the native swaggering off to die, so there is seemingly endless strife between the spoken and written word" [215]). She describes the space to which writing in French relegates her:

> Sur les plages désertées du présent, amené par tout cessez-le-feu inévitable, mon écrit cherche encore son lieu d'échange et de fontaines, son commerce.
> Cette langue était autrefois sarcophage des miens; je la porte aujourd'hui comme un messager transporterait le pli fermé ordonnant sa condamnation au silence, ou au cachot.
> Me mettre à nu dans cette langue me fait entretenir un danger permanent de déflagration. De l'exercice de l'autobiographie dans la langue de l'adversaire d'hier...(241)

> [On the deserted beaches of the present, washed up by the inevitable cease-fire of all wars, my writing continues to seek its place of exchange, of fountains, of commerce.
> That language was formerly the sarcophagus of my people; I bear it today like a messenger bearing a sealed letter ordering his condemnation to death, to the dungeon.
> To strip myself bare in that language makes me chance a permanent danger of being consumed by fire. As a penalty for undertaking to write an autobiography in the language of yesterday's adversary...(my translation)].

A Dialogue of Sisters

At one point, the narrator compares her situation with that of Saint Augustine writing in Latin, the language of the conquerors, or Ibn Khaldun writing in Arabic, the language of those warriors who conquered the Maghrebian Berbers. Both languages imposed themselves as much by rape as by love, she remarks. Although she likens writing to unveiling, to being stripped bare, she also acknowledges that her writing rests on self-deception, for in believing that she was writing of herself, in choosing the language of the enemy, she was simply choosing another veil:

> Voulant à chaque pas, parvenir à la transparence, je m'engloutis davantage dans l'anonymat des aïeules! (243)

[While I intended every step forward to make me more clearly identifiable, I find myself progressively sucked down into the anonymity of those women of old—my ancestors! (217)]

In speaking of her childhood, the narrator switches from the third person to the first as she describes the penetration of her enclosed space by a letter written to her by a male classmate:

J'ai fait éclater l'espace en moi, un espace éperdu de cris sans voix, figés depuis longtemps dans une préhistoire de l'amour. (13)

[I blew the space within me to pieces, a space filled with . . . voiceless cries, frozen long ago in a prehistory of love. (4)]

The mention of "voiceless cries" calls to mind the distinction Maurice Blanchot makes between what he defines as the narrative voice and the narratorial voice.[18] Each, as virtual narrator, enunciates by means of (I quote Blanchot) "a neutral voice that utters [*dit*] the work from the placeless place where the work is silent" (143). In his essay "Living On," Jacques Derrida glosses Blanchot's words in this way: "The placeless place where the work is silent: a silent voice, then, withdrawn into its 'voicelessness' ['*aphonie*']. This 'voicelessness' distinguishes it from the 'narratorial voice,' the voice that literary criticism, or poetics or narratology strives to locate in the system of the narrative, of the novel, or of the narration. The narratorial voice is the voice of a subject recounting something, remembering an event or a historical sequence, knowing who he is, where he is, and what he is talking about."[19]

The narrator's words not only allude to the woman as excluded third in the dialogue of society ("To hold a dialogue is to suppose a third man and to seek to exclude him"[20]), buried within and by language and speech, but prefigure the role that writing will play in exploding the inner space of the Arab women who shriek voicelessly in a prehistory of love, that is, love never or not yet realized. Her narrative will externalize, give voice to those silent voices of her claustrated sisters.

The narrator recounts the events of 1842–43, when the French occupiers under their commandant, Saint-Arnaud, burned the *zaouia* (the center for Islamic brotherhood) of the Berkani, the tribe from which she descends. They drove out the women and children, who wandered the mountains in the winter. When the Berkani returned the next year, Saint-Arnaud decided to take as hostages members of the caliph's family. Saint-Arnaud wrote to his brother that he had seized eight leaders and their families. The women ancestors of the tribe (the "aïeules") passed their version of the story down to their children, and their children down to their grandchildren: there follows a description of the oral history transmitted from mouth to mouth (by what Djebar calls "chuchotements," whispers):

> L'héritage va chavirer — vague après vague, nuit après nuit, les murmures reprennent avant même que l'enfant comprenne, avant même qu'il trouve ses mots de lumière, avant de parler à son tour et pour ne point parler seul... (200)

> [The legacy will otherwise be lost — night after night, wave upon wave, the whispers take up the tale, even before the child can understand, even before she finds her words of life, before she speaks in her turn and so that she will not speak alone... (177)]

The women who whisper correct the details of the French version. Among these women is one who told the narrator of another story, from another war (the Algerian Revolution), of how she gave her fourteen-year-old son a silver jam spoon handed down to her from her father. When the French soldiers raided their house, her son fled with the maquisards, the resistance fighters, carrying away with him the spoon. Several years later, he returned safe and sound. For the narrator, the silver spoon, symbol of the heritage passed down, appears as a heraldic object:

> Les vergers brûlés par Saint-Arnaud voient enfin leur feu s'éteindre, parce que la vieille aujourd'hui parle et que je m'apprête à transcrire son récit. Faire le décompte des menus objets passés ainsi, de main fiévreuse à main de fugueur! (200–201)

> [The fires in the orchards gutted by Saint-Arnaud are finally extinguished, because the old lady talks today and I am preparing to transcribe her tale. To draw up the inventory of the tiny objects passed on thus, from febrile hand to fugitive hand! (177)]

The narrator surmises that she was born in 1842, the year Saint-Arnaud put fire to the *zaouia* of her tribe. That same fire lights her emergence from the harem (claustration) a century later, (en)lightens her and gives her the strength to speak. Her chant is accompanied by the sounds of all her Algerian sisters who suffered in the past.

> La langue encore coagulée des Autres m'a enveloppée, dès l'enfance, en tunique de Nessus, don d'amour de mon père qui, chaque matin, me tenait par la main sur le chemin de l'école. (243)

> [The language of the Others, in which I was enveloped from childhood, the gift my father lovingly bestowed on me, that language has adhered to me ever since like the tunic of Nessus, that gift from my father who, every morning, took me by the hand to accompany me to school. (217)]

The story of Nessus tells of how Hercules slew the centaur Nessus, who attempted to rape his wife, Deianira. The dying Nessus gives her a potion mixed with his blood under guise of it being a love potion. Later, Deianira, attempting to reclaim Hercules's affection, gives him a cloak soaked with the potion containing Nessus's blood. The cloak burns him horribly, giving him such agony that he causes himself to be immolated. The story of Nessus's cloak invoked the myth of the fire ritual associated with fertility. On one level we can analogize the narrator's own situation, in which writing at once produces agony and gives birth to her potential as amanuensis for her sisters. It is for the narrator simultaneously a gift of love from her father and the cause of her painful exile. We might further note, however, that the male-female relationship is reversed. It is this reversal that strikes us as most important, for it is paradigmatic of the reversal of the male-female role through women's writing.

As the narrator describes the hostages of Saint-Arnaud being put aboard a ship for transport to France in 1843, she addresses a *narrataire* in the second-person singular. The story of the "unknown woman," the "invisible woman," as she calls her, has been passed down among the women from storyteller to storyteller. She is one of the nameless hostages, the "ancestress of ancestresses," who holds special significance for the narrator, for she is on the one hand the prototype of the silent and invisible Algerian woman and on the other "the first expatriate" in whose footsteps she (the narrator) follows.

Paradox lies at the heart of the narrator's destiny as amanuensis for her silent sisters. To draw near to them in telling their story, she must exile herself in a foreign tongue. When she describes Chérifa, one of the Algerian women whose story of the revolution she recounts, she relates how the very words in French — " torch-words" ("mots torches") that bring light to the lives of the women whose story she tells — definitively separate her from her Algerian sisters: by the stigmata of foreign words she finds herself, like the nameless *narrataire*, expatriated from them.

Part 3 closes with a soliloquy where the narrator speaks of how she is called an exile, but "La différence est plus lourde: je suis expulsée de là-bas pour entendre et ramener à mes parentes les traces de la liberté" (244) ("It is more than that: I have been banished from my homeland to listen and bring back some traces of liberty to the women of my family" [218]). In attempting to execute this task, she flounders, as she says, "dans un marécage qui s'éclaire à peine" (244) ("in a murky bog" [218]). In writing, she creates a fiction, for the story of her past is unwritten in the mother tongue, and her imagination, like a woman beggar in the streets, crouches in absences and silences.

In speaking of veiling, the narrator says that during her childhood the women would don their veils whenever a male approached, unless he was a foreigner, a non-Arab, because, if a non-Arab looked at them, he did not really see them — he only imagined he saw them. And, at a distance, behind a hedge, his glance failed to touch them. The narrator cites a Westerner enslaved by the Algerians in the seventeenth century who spoke of how the women were indiscreet in the presence of a Western captive because they considered him blind, themselves "invisible," in contrast to the vilest of Arab males of the "dominant society," who felt himself to be their master. The narrator compares to this relation between the Algerian woman and the foreign captive her reaction to the French language, which served her as a recess from which she could spy on the world and into which she could withdraw from the unwanted attentions of a Western male. But she discovered that in so doing she became a veiled woman, "not so much disguised as anonymous," and that her imagined invisibility was an illusion. With the French language, she found herself unable to control her body presence — it signified more than she intended to signify. Moreover, with French she experienced an "aphasia of love" ("aphasie amoureuse"), an inability to express intimacy, which she could do only in her mother tongue. She had described herself earlier as seeking her mother tongue's "rich vocabulary of love," of which she had been deprived.

Such antimonies lying at the heart of writing, reflective of its force to destroy as much as to create, are paradigmatic of the intimate union of love and war signified in the original French title of Djebar's narrative: *L'Amour, la fantasia.* "Fantasia," deriving from the Arabic *fantaziya*, literally "ostentation," refers to the equestrian maneuver in which Arab or Berber horsemen gallop full tilt and at a given moment rein up and discharge their rifles in the midst of fearsome cries — a custom that has been recorded in a painting by another nineteenth-century artist-visitor to Algeria, Delacroix, in his "Fantasia" (1833).

In the closing part, titled "Tzarl-Rit (Finale)," an epigraph gives two definitions of the term "tzarl-rit," the women's cry that accompanies the *fantasia*: one denoting a cry of joy and the other a cry of unhappiness. Again, the act of breaking the silence, of crying out, betrays the mixed emotions attending liberation, writing, unveiling. In the last of three sections of this closing part, titled "Air de Nay" (a musical air played on a flute), the narrator brings together the time of the artist-novelist Eugène Fromentin's visit to Algeria in 1852–53 and the period twenty years earlier than the present moment of the narrative, at the end of the Algerian Revolution, when she visited the Algerian *diseuses,* who recounted stories of the war. Fromentin had described how, alongside the path, he found the severed hand of an unknown Algerian woman. The narrator remarks that she writes with that mutilated hand. She concludes her story by evoking the death of another young woman, Haoua, witnessed by Fromentin in 1852, as she was struck down by the hooves of a horse ridden in the *fantasia* by an angry lover she had spurned. The narrator envisages the threat against any woman who, like Haoua, dares to demand freedom:

> Oui, malgré le tumulte des miens alentour, j'entends déjà, avant même qu'il s'élève et transperce le ciel dur, j'entends le cri de la mort dans la fantasia. (256)

> [Yes, in spite of the tumult of my people all around, I already hear, even before it arises and pierces the harsh sky, I hear the death cry in the Fantasia. (227)]

Joy/suffering, love/war — antimonies of considerable importance to Djebar's narrative.

Early in her narrative, the narrator remarks on how the women prisoners of the French rendered the French victory a pseudo-triumph by refusing to look at the enemy, refusing to "recognize" him, to "name" him. She asks, "Qu'est-ce qu'une victoire si elle n'est pas nommée?" (69) ("What is a victory if it is not named" [56]). In describing letters sent by the French soldiers from bivouac in the nineteenth century, the narrator mingles the terms of love and war. The soldiers write home of an "Algérie femme" that is impossible to tame. And the narrator interjects: "Fantasme d'une Algérie domptée: chaque combat éloigne encore plus l'épuisement de la révolte" (69) ("A tamed Algeria is a pipe-dream, every battle drives further and further away the time when the insurgency will burn itself out" [57]). In the terms of the narrator's discourse, the French invaders are to Algeria what the man is to the woman in Algerian society — an *Algérie femme* ostensibly tamed to accord with the male phantasm but ultimately untamable.

Conclusion

The two perceptions of woman's space come together: the collective social-historical space in which Algerian women struggle to inscribe themselves and the personal-written space in the adversary's language in which the author struggles to inscribe herself—the plural chronicle and the singular autobiography. The tension between oppressor and oppressed, written and oral, is resolved through the narrator's assumption of the role of amanuensis in her writing, which renders written what was oral, vocal what was silent.

In traditional Algerian society, as we see in Djebar's narrative, women possess no enabling dialogue. Their speechlessness, their aphasia, presents an otherness that is characterized by a hermeneutical aporia (that inclines one to doubt the possibility of interpreting that otherness). To be without speech in its broadest sense (including body language) is to be without possibility of dialogue. In effect, writing permits the narrator to create an enabling dialogue between women, between present and past, between singular and collective, allowing the women to recuperate their historical consciousness, giving them a sense of common purpose. The narrator's initiation into writing and realization of its potential is tantamount to discovering the other in oneself as well as oneself in the other.

It is nonetheless true that by using the Euro-logo-phallocentric language of the adversary to recount the history of the Algerian women, the chronicle of their otherness, there is no unmediated access to what is passed down orally. Her telling manages, nevertheless, to transcend these ideological limitations through an allegorical process that operates as a distancing factor. Distancing or disengagement is advocated by most proponents of dialogical thinking "as a necessary precondition for the dialogical engagement."[21] But a cost is also exacted on the narrator, for she becomes alienated, exiled through her use of French.

Luce Irigaray, who speaks of how woman has been viewed negatively as a "place," a space that has been colonized, occupied by the aggressor, man, holds out the possibility of a third possible space, which woman and man may commonly share: "A world to be created or re-created so that man and woman may again or finally cohabit, meet each other and live sometimes in the same *place*."[22] This position seems overly optimistic, however, for it ignores the distance between Self and Other, the incommensurability between them. It repeats the ethnocentric tendency of ethnography, which functions as "an intertextual practice which, by means of an allegorizing identity, anaesthetizes us to the other's difference."[23] Woman's space, suggested in Djebar's scheme of things, will derive not from mere reversal or displacement of man's space but rather from the creation of a space that will express what Todorov calls "difference in equality" and Theodor Adorno "distinctiveness without domination."[24]

Notes

1. Assia Djebar, *L'Amour, la fantasia* (Paris: Ed. Jean-Claude Lattès, 1985). Dorothy Blair has rendered it into English, *Fantasia: An Algerian Calvacade* (London and New York: Quartet Books, 1989). I shall avail myself of her sensitive translation though my occasional modifications of it will be indicated in the text. Translations of other French texts referred to are mine unless otherwise noted.

2. For the notion of a "space of writing," see Abdelkebir Khatibi, "L'orientalisme désorienté" in Khatibi, *Maghreb pluriel* (Paris: Denoël, 1983), 141. Also, see my article, "Writing Double: Politics and the African Narrative of French Expression," *Studies in 20th Century Literature* (winter 1990): 101–22. The subject of writing in terms of space in Djebar's work has been treated rather extensively: see Djebar herself, "Du Français comme butin," *La Quinzaine littéraire*, 16–31 March 1985, 436, as well as her interview with Mildred Mortimer, "Entretien avec Assia Djebar, écrivain algérien," *Research in African Literature* 19, 2 (summer 1988): 197–205. Mortimer has approached the subject in several of her own works, notably "Language and Space in the Fiction of Assia Djebar and Leila Sebbar," *Research in African Literature* 19, 3 (fall 1988): 301–11; also *Assia Djebar* (Philadelphia: CELFAN Edition Monographs, 1988) and *Journeys: A Study of the Francophone Novel in Africa* (Portsmouth, N.H.: Heinemann, 1990). I must also mention the article by Marguerite Le Clézio, "Assia Djebar: Ecrire dans la langue adverse," *Contemporary French Civilization* 19, 2 (summer 1988): 230–44.

3. Jean-François Lyotard, *Instructions païennes* (Paris: Galilée, 1977), 2.

4. Harems were abolished in Turkey in 1909. The practice continued for several years in other Muslim countries. Although they do not exist as such in present-day Algeria, the social and psychological attitudes they expressed persist. The word harem (*haram* in Arabic) means "'unlawful,' 'protected' or 'forbidden.' The sacred area around Mecca and Medina is *haram*, closed to all but the Faithful. In its secular use, *haram* refers to the separate, protected part of a household where women, children, and servants live in maximum seclusion and privacy." Alev Lytle Croutier, *Harem: The World behind the Veil* (New York: Abbeville Press, 1989), 17. The author is a Turkish Muslim woman.

5. See Fatima Mernissi, *Beyond the Veil: Male-Female Dynamics in a Modern Muslim Society* (New York: Schenkman, 1975), esp. chapter 8, "The Meaning of Spatial Boundaries." Also see Mortimer, *Journeys*, and my essay, "Veiled Woman and Veiled Narrative in Tahar ben Jelloun's *Sandchild*," *boundary 2* 20, 1 (spring 1993): 47–64. It should be noted that the custom of veiling does not originate in the Islamic religion (the closest thing to a direct injunction against veiling in the Qur'an is Surah 24) but is secular in origin. As Germaine Tillion notes, "The harem and the veil are infinitely older than the revelation of the Qur'an." *Le Harem et les cousins* (Paris: Seuil, 1966), 22.

6. Abdelwahab Bouhdiba, *La Sexualité en Islam* (Paris: Presses Universitaires de France, 1975), 53. Also see Ghadah al-Samman, "The Sexual Revolution and the Total Revolution" in *Middle Eastern Muslim Women Speak*, ed. Elizabeth Warnock Fernea and Basima Qattan Bezirgan (Austin/London: University of Texas Press, 1977), 393–99.

7. Bouhdiba, *La Sexualité en Islam*, 53.

8. Mernissi, citing al-Ghazali, *Beyond the Veil*, 83.

9. Mernissi, citing al-Ghazali, *Beyond the Veil*, 83. Mernissi maintains that veiling the gaze is as much to protect men from themselves as from women, for the Qur'an bears out the notion that "seclusion in Islam is a device to protect the passive male who cannot control himself sexually in the presence of [the] lust-inducing female ..." (ibid.). See also Nawal El Saadawi, *The Hidden Face of Eve: Women in the Arab World* (London: Zed Press, 1988), 99–100.

10. "In traditional Islamic cultures, most women would sooner stand naked in a marketplace than uncover their faces. For the face is inviolate." Croutier, *Harem*, 77.

11. Mernissi asserts with reason that "the political and the sexual are closely linked: people's body image and self image are cards which the ruling classes have manipulated brilliantly throughout human history, which is unfortunately a history of exploitation. Seen in historical context, sexual relationships are a field which the class struggle appropriates and through which it expresses itself." "Virginity and Patriarchy" in *Women and Islam*, ed. Azizah al-Hibri (Oxford/New York: Pergamon Press, 1982), 191.

12. Tahar ben Jelloun, *La Plus Haute des solitudes: Misère affective et sexuelle d'émigrés nord-africains* (Paris: Editions du Seuil, 1977), 92.

13. Ibid., 64–65.

14. Frantz Fanon, *Sociologie d'une révolution (L'An V de la révolution algérienne)* (Paris: François Maspéro, 1972), 20. Ironically, the attempt by colonial authorities to unveil the Algerian woman miscarried, for the unveiling of women facilitated their assimilation into the revolution to work beside men. And eventually the strongest force for the eroding of role differentiation between the sexes in Algeria was not the French but the revolution itself. In fact, the veil or its absence became a revolutionary weapon: "The veil removed and then put on again, the instrumentalized veil, was transformed into a technique of camouflage, into a means of battle" (44).

15. Bouhdiba, *La Sexualité en Islam*, 45–46. The sexual exploitation of women in Islamic society has been described by several authors. See Fadela M'Rabet, *La Femme algérienne* (Paris: François Maspéro, 1954), and Evelyne Accad, *Veil of Shame* (Sherbrooke: Naaman, 1978). As Bouhdiba indicates, while the Qur'an speaks of a difference in degree between the sexes, the *fiqh* speaks of a difference in nature, such that "groups of facts institutionalize the repression [*l'écrasement*] of the woman, her derealization, her negation" (260). See also Ben Jelloun's chapter on "Une sexualité conçue par et pour l'homme," in *La Plus Haute des solitudes*, 57–97 (esp. 57–59).

16. Bouhdiba, *La Sexualité en Islam*, 20.

17. Marguerite Duras, "Ecrire," in *L'Esprit Créateur* 30, 1 (spring 1990): 6.

18. Maurice Blanchot, *L'Entretien infini* (Paris: Gallimard, 1969).

19. Jacques Derrida, "Living On: *Border Lines*," trans. James Hulbert, in Harold Bloom et al., *Deconstruction and Criticism* (New York: Seabury Press, 1979), 76.

20. Michel Serres, *Hermes: Literature, Science, Philosophy*, ed. J. V. Harari and D. F. Bell (Baltimore: Johns Hopkins University Press, 1982).

21. R. Lane Kauffmann, "The Other in Question: Dialogical Experiments in Montaigne, Kafka, and Cortázar," in *The Interpretation of Dialogue*, ed. T. Maranhão (Chicago: University of Chicago Press, 1990), 179–80. I am indebted to Kauffmann for certain terms and references I make in the following paragraph.

22. Luce Irigaray, *Ethique de la différence sexuelle* (Paris: Minuit, 1984).

23. Stephen A. Tyler, "Ethnography, Intertextuality and the End of Description," *American Journal of Semiotics* 3, 4 (1985): 83–98.

24. Cited by Kauffmann in "The Other in Question."

CHAPTER NINETEEN

"*Logiques métisses*"

Cultural Appropriation and Postcolonial Representations

FRANÇOISE LIONNET

If this weird, upside-down caricature of a country called America, if this
land of refugees and former indentured servants, religious heretics and
half-breeds, whoresons and fugitives — this cauldron of mongrels
from all points on the compass — was all I could rightly call
home, then aye: I was of it.
Charles Johnson, *Middle Passage*

Cependant, il n'y a pas de choix: il faut apprendre et avec ce dont on
dispose: un savoir colonisé et un langage truqué.
Claudine Herrmann, *Les Voleuses de langue*

Francophone women writers in Africa, the Caribbean, the Indian Ocean,
as well as *within* France, to where they or their families immigrate for various personal or economic reasons, have given us unique insights into what
Renato Rosaldo has called the "border zones" of culture.[1] In those areas on
the periphery of stable metropolitan cultural discourses, Rosaldo explains,
there is an incessant and playful heteroglossia, a bilingual speech or hybrid
language that is a site of creative resistance to the dominant conceptual paradigms. In border zones, all of our academic preconceptions about cultural,
linguistic, or stylistic norms are constantly being put to the test by creative
practices that make visible and set off the processes of adaptation, appropri-

ation, and contestation that govern the construction of identity in colonial and postcolonial contexts.

These processes are the ground upon which contemporary global culture can begin to be understood, defined, and represented, and postcolonial writers encode the everyday realities and subjective perceptions of a numerical majority whose cultural contributions are still considered to be the products of minority voices. By reproducing the changing cultural practices of this majority as it negotiates the conflicts between tradition and modernity, writers create a space for themselves within the dominant discourses while simultaneously articulating a problematic that is increasingly becoming accepted as a quasi-universal process. The global mongrelization or métissage of cultural forms creates hybrid identities, and interrelated, if not overlapping, spaces. In those spaces, struggles for the control of means of representation and self-identification are mediated by a single and immensely powerful symbolic system: the colonial language and the variations to which it is subjected under the pen of ("francophone") writers who enrich, transform, and creolize it.

Writers such as Maryse Condé, from Guadeloupe, Assia Djebar, from Algeria, and Leïla Sebbar, a Franco-Algerian, share one important characteristic: they belong to an increasing number of astute interpreters of the postcolonial condition whose works, published in the 1970s and 1980s, have been redefining francophone history and literature. They create new paradigms that represent, through innovative and self-reflexive literary techniques, both linguistic and geographic exile, displacements from the margins to a metropolitan center, and intercultural exchanges.[2]

To understand the cultural and literary praxis of these writers, I want to make a brief incursion into the field of cultural anthropology, a field that has established some of the parameters within which we commonly understand negatively coded terms such as "acculturation" and "assimilation." My purpose in this essay is to develop, first of all, a theoretical argument about postcolonial culture. This argument is an eminently political one, and on one level it does address the current academic polemics about various forms of cultural fundamentalism. But my approach tends to be an indirect one. I want to raise some of these issues by way of the voices of postcolonial women *writers* from non-English-speaking contexts whose perspectives on multiculturalism differ from the ones we are most familiar with in the United States, mostly because a term like "multiculturalism" takes on different valences in different linguistic and geopolitical contexts, that is, in countries where the relative power of hegemonic and subaltern groups shifts according to factors altogether different from the ones that obtain in this country. That is why, in the second part of the paper, I draw my examples from the works of contemporary francophone women. I thus suggest that these writers' concerns and perspectives are an important contribution to such debates because they echo and often predate those of cultural anthropologists, whose theoretical approaches are nonetheless very useful for analyzing the processes at work in the women's novels.[3] My interest in using these novels to understand cultural configurations studied by social scientists is grounded in my belief that literature allows us to enter into the subjective processes of writers and their characters, and thus allows us to better understand the unique perspectives of subjects who are agents of transformation and hybridization in their own narratives, as opposed to being the objects of knowledge as in the discourse of social science.

Let me start with some simple, common sense definitions: "acculturation," *Webster's Dictionary* tells us, is "the transfer of culture from one ethnic group to another," whereas "assimilation" is "the act of bringing or coming to a resemblance; the merging of diverse cultural elements," or, as the Oxford English Dictionary would have it, to assimilate is "to make like, to cause to resemble, to incorporate...To become conformed to." Already, we can see some contradictions in the semantic fields of these terms: is the "transfer...from one ethnic group to another" only a one-way process that causes one culture to erase another? Or could we infer that the transformation of both — or all — of the cultures in contact is extremely likely, if not inevitable, through this process of "acculturation" of one (or several) culture(s) to the other(s)? Is "the merging of diverse cultural elements" to be understood as the inevitable erasure of one element by another? Might it not also suggest that a more intricate and complex phenomenon is in fact taking place, as in those "border zones" where a complex syncretic cultural system comes to replace two or more ostensibly simpler cultures? In such a case, acculturation would not simply be the means of making one element conform to another, assimilate to it, in order to become *like* that other, but it would more truly be a process whereby all elements involved in the interaction would be changed by that encounter. Dominant systems are more likely to absorb and make like them numerically or culturally "weaker" elements. But even then, these "inferior" or subaltern elements contribute to the evolution and transformation of the hegemonic system by producing resistances and counterdiscourses.[4]

It has of course been ideologically and politically convenient for the dominant cultures to entertain the fiction of "assimilation" as a means of incorporating—"civilizing"—those cultures viewed as too different and "inferior" to be comfortably accepted and integrated into their norms.[5] But in the long run, the more powerful system does incorporate elements of the weaker one, often to the point where certain of its patterns and practices become indistinguishable from those of the imported or inferior culture. Kwame Anthony Appiah has recently said, "there is, of course, no American culture without African roots," but this fact is not—yet—a commonly accepted premise when couched in those terms.[6] It is commonly accepted that African Americans are "more or less" assimilated and acculturated to "white" American culture, but rarely do we hear the reciprocal formulation being discussed in academic or popular circles.[7] As Toni Morrison forcefully puts it in her essay on "Unspeakable Things Unspoken: The Afro-American Presence in American Literature": "Afro-American culture exists and though it is clear (and becoming clearer) how it has responded to Western culture, the instances where and means by which it has shaped Western culture are poorly recognized or understood."[8] Similarly, South African anthropologists study the Westernization of blacks in Southern Africa but not the Africanization of whites who adopt the culinary or musical tastes of blacks. Singer Johnny Clegg, the "White Zulu," and the white Southern African youths who have assimilated (into) black culture have not yet, to my knowledge, become the object of the anthropologist's scrutiny.[9] Here in the United States, a white rap singer named Vanilla Ice has been called "the Elvis of rap," whereas the black rap singer named L. D. Shore rose to fame as "the Black Elvis." But, as Patricia J. Williams recently pointed out, this is "divinely parodic: Elvis, the white black man of a generation ago, reborn in a black man imitating Elvis" (and one might add, reborn in Vanilla Ice, a white man imitating the black rapper imitating Elvis: a dizzying thought).[10] What is interesting in all of these cases is that the point of reference remains "white culture," even if it is an already "mongrelized" white culture, to use Charles Johnson's formulation used as an epigraph to this essay.[11]

My quarrel, then, with terms such as "assimilation" and "acculturation" when used in the (post)colonial context is a quarrel with history: the terms have acquired through use a negative connotation because they underscore the relation of subjugation that exists between the colonized culture and the hegemonic system. Rosaldo points out that "metropolitan typifications suppress, exclude, even repress border zones, "those areas of shifting practices, located in the orbits of established discourses.[12] This, he suggests, is because

> the model for cross-cultural understanding that produces immigration as a site of cultural stripping away is the academic version of the melting pot: theories of acculturation and assimilation. In this view, immigrants, or at any rate their children and grandchildren, are absorbed into the national culture. Above all, the process involves the loss of one's past — autobiography, history, heritage, language, and all the rest of the so-called cultural baggage . . . The theory of assimilation appears to have the inevitability of a law of history. If it doesn't catch up with you this generation, it will in the next. (82)

Thus, in this view, the "assimilated" are seen as existing passively and not as creative agents capable of transforming the practices that they come to adopt. The message proclaimed by contemporary art and literature from Africa and the Caribbean, however, is quite different: it is not assimilation that appears inevitable when Western technology and education are adopted by the colonized, or when immigration to the metropole severs some of the migrants' ties to a particular birthplace. Rather, the move forces individuals to stand in relation to the past and the present at the same time, to look for creative means of incorporating useful "western" tools, techniques, or strategies into their own cosmology or weltanschauung.[13]

What is needed, then, is a new vocabulary for describing patterns of influence that are never unidirectional. Because the influence is usually mutual and reciprocal, however much that fact might have been occluded from the political consciousness and modes of self-representation of metropolitan cultures, a more appropriate term for describing this contact of cultures would be the word "transculturation." The Cuban poet Nancy Morejón has used this neologism (*transculturación*) to describe a process of cultural intercourse and exchange, a circulation of practices that creates a constant interweaving of symbolic forms and empirical activities among the different cultures that interact with one another. As she puts it, "*reciprocal* influence is the determining factor here, for no single element superimposes itself on another; on the contrary, each one changes into the other so that both can be transformed into a third."[14] Rejecting the binarism of self and other, nationalism and internationalism, Africa and Europe, women writers like Morejón point to a third way, to the métissage of forms and identities that is the result of cross-cultural encounters and that forms the basis for their self-portrayals and their representations of cultural diversity.

Cross- or transcultural exchange has always been "an absolute fact" of life everywhere, even if, as Edouard Glissant has pointed out, "the human imagination, in Western tradition, has always wished to deny or disguise" it.[15] The realization that the theory of the melting pot did not correspond to a reality but was a necessary myth, or perhaps an enabling metaphor in the construction of an American national identity, is opening the way for a more cautious understanding of the dialectical and complex phenomena of ethnic interactions that have existed in this country since the beginning of colonial times. Similarly, French theories of cultural assimilation that aimed at turning colonized peoples — or, at any rate, the educated elites of the colonies — into acculturated *évolués* who could speak perfect French corresponds only to one aspect of a complex colonial picture: although the colonial linguistic enterprise is alive and well in the "départements d'outre-mer," it now coexists with a strong movement in favor of *créolité*, a movement that does not aim at the outright rejection of French but at valorizing the multilingual and multiethnic character of Creole cultures.[16]

That is why the concept of transculturation proves so useful: the prefix "trans-" suggests the act of traversing, of going through existing cultural territories. Its specifically spatial connotations demarcate a pattern of movement, across cultural arenas and physical topographies, that corresponds more accurately to the notion of "appropriation," a concept more promising than those of acculturation and assimilation, and one that implies active intervention rather than passive victimization. It is easy to establish how useful this concept can be for our analysis. Abdelkebir Khatibi has shown, in his novel *Amour bilingue* and his collected essays titled *Maghreb pluriel,* that for francophone writers whose mother tongue may be Arabic, Berber, Wolof, or Creole, the use of the French language is a means of translating into the colonizer's language a different sensibility, a different vision of the world, a means therefore of transforming the dominant conceptions circulated by the more standard idiom.[17] To write in French is thus also to transform French into a language that becomes the writer's own: French is appropriated, made into a vehicle for expressing a hybrid, heteroglot universe. This creative act of "taking possession" of a language gives rise to the kind of linguistic métissage visible in many contemporary francophone works.[18]

Acts of appropriation will produce a greater degree of cultural complexity than the standard anthropological categories (metropolitan vs. colonial, developed vs. primitive, or civilized vs. aboriginal) would tend to suggest. Indeed, the notion of culture has itself become quite controversial among some anthropologists, and in his essay titled "Ideology, Place, and People

without Culture," from which I have already quoted, Rosaldo contextual-
izes and summarizes the issues:

> Anthropologists hold contradictory notions of culture. The discipline's
> official view holds that all human conduct is culturally mediated. In other
> words, people act in relation, not to brute reality, but to culture-specific
> modes of perceiving and organizing the world ... No domain of culture is
> more or less culturally mediated than any other. Indeed the quantitative
> notion of "more" or "less" culture appears to be a throwback to the days
> when high culture" was (and, in certain sectors of the academy, still is)
> measured in terms of opera houses, museums, and literary salons.
>
> If official [anthropological] view holds that all cultures are equal, an
> informal filing system, more often found in corridor talk than in published
> writings, classifies cultures in quantitative terms, from a lot to a little, from
> thick to thin, from elaborate to simple ...
>
> Culture in this view is defined by difference. Difference ... makes
> culture visible to observers. (78)

If "difference" is what makes culture visible to observers, then the emphasis
on difference has the merit of underscoring specificities that would be muted
and ignored otherwise. But an overemphasis on dissimilarities is likely to
lead from racial and biographical determinism into an essentialist impasse.
In this erroneous view of culture wherein difference is rigidly valorized for
its own sake, or for the sake of identifying authentic and "pure products,"[19]
any process of acculturation or transculturation (however real, inevitable,
and reciprocal it may have been) is automatically labeled as merely assimi-
lationist. Hence, assimilation is (mis)construed by the dominant system as
the elusive means of retaining or creating a fictive purity and authenticity
within which the colonized "people without culture" can be absorbed; in
opposition to this tendency, the subaltern group, on the other hand, will
seek to retain a sense of its own cultural authenticity by advocating a return to precolonial traditions, thus contrasting the past to the present and
mythifying its own original ethnic or cultural purity. Difference then becomes — on both sides of this binary system — the reason for exoticizing,
"othering," groups that do not share in this mythic cultural purity.

The issue of defining identity in a colonial context has always been a
highly charged one: the first generation, represented by Aimé Césaire, Frantz
Fanon, Albert Memmi, and Edouard Glissant, has examined with some anxiety the processes through which the colonized internalize a vision of themselves projected by the colonizer, a vision that promotes a form of mimetic
idealization of, and identification with, the colonizer.[20] To a degree, these
formulations remained dependent on a Hegelian view of the master-slave

dialectic and of the importance of recognition as the means of self-valida-
tion for both colonizer and colonized. By contrast, during the last two
decades, writers have largely engaged in a painstaking redefinition of the
paradigms of decolonization, thus seeking to undermine any simplistic
understanding of the process of assimilation and the concurrent presup-
positions regarding the existence of authenticity in either the dominant or
native cultures. As Rosaldo points out,

> the view of an authentic culture as an autonomous internally coherent
> universe no longer seems tenable in a postcolonial world. Neither "we" nor
> "they" are as self-contained and homogeneous as we/they once appeared.
> All of us inhabit an interdependent late 20th century world, which is at
> once marked by borrowing and lending across porous cultural boundaries,
> and saturated with inequality, power, and domination. (87)

Hence, I would suggest our task, as critics, is to describe the complex inter-
weavings of traditions that the texts and voices of francophone women map
out and interpret for us, and that philosophers and anthropologists are beginning to theorize and propound in their own disciplines. As Appiah puts
it, "if there is a lesson in the broad shape of this circulation of cultures, it is
surely that we are already contaminated by each other, that there is no
longer a fully autochthonous *echt*-African culture awaiting salvage by our
artists."[21] He is echoed by Swedish anthropologist Ulf Hannerz, who has
pointed out that "the world system, rather than creating massive cultural
homogeneity on a global scale, is replacing one diversity with another; and
the new diversity is based relatively more on interrelations and less on autonomy."[22] What these writers and thinkers — "from all points on the compass" — increasingly underline is the dialectical tension that exists between
local variations and a worldwide system of interdependent cultures, between
diversity and resemblance, between relativism and universalism.

In a controversial book, *Logiques métisses: Anthropologie de l'identité en
Afrique et ailleurs*, French anthropologist Jean-Loup Amselle echoes some
of the statements made earlier and goes a step farther in arguing that even
before colonial times, the interrelations of cultures were the norm, and
that it is the Western anthropologist who has "invented" separate ethnic
groups as his objects of study. Arguing against ethnological reason and in
favor of a form of originary indistinction or syncretism, he critiques the
anthropological bias in favor of cultural relativism and attempts to define
a universalist "logique métisse":

> Les anthropologues culturalistes américains tout comme Lévi-Strauss ont
> eu raison, face à toutes les philosophies de l'histoire et autres sagas du

progrès de mettre l'accent sur les spécificités et le caractère relatif des valeurs promues par chaque société; mais le corollaire de cette attitude généreuse est l'érection de barrières culturelles étanches qui enferment chaque groupe dans sa singularité.

N'est-ce pas dans le droit fil de l'anthropologie culturelle américaine que se situe la notion de société multiculturelle dont on a déjà souligné les ambiguïtés? Loin d'être un instrument de tolérance et de libération des minorités comme l'affirment ses partisans, cette expression manifeste au contraire tous les travers de la raison ethnologique et c'est à ce titre qu'elle a été revendiquée en France par la "nouvelle droite." Isoler une communauté par la définition d'un certain nombre de "différences" conduit à la possibilité de son confinement territorial sinon de son expulsion. L'assignation de différences ou l'étiquetage ethnique, prophéties autocréatrices, ne traduisent pas seulement la reconnaissance de spécificités culturelles, ils sont également corrélatifs de l'affirmation forcenée d'une identité, celle de l'ethnie française. De la sorte, la problématique de la société multiculturelle conduit tout droit, si l'on n'y prend garde, à un développement séparé analogue à l'Apartheid sud-africain — qui lui-même procède en partie de l'application dévoyée de la notion de culture.

A ce fondamentalisme ethnique ou culturel que certains assimilent à la "défaite de la pensée," il ne s'agit pas d'opposer de façon abstraite les droits de l'homme, ces principes dont personne ne sait au juste de quoi ils sont faits. Il faut plutôt mettre en avant l'idée d'un mélange ou d'un métissage originaire des différents groupes qui se sont formés tout au long de l'histoire de l'humanité.[23]

[Given all the philosophies of history and other sagas of human progress, American culturalist anthropologists along with Levi-Strauss were right to stress the particularist nature and the relative character of the values promoted by different societies. But the flip side of this generous attitude is the erection of impermeable cultural barriers that imprison each group in its own singularity.

Doesn't the notion of multicultural society, the ambiguities of which have already been emphasized, follow directly from the concepts put forth by American cultural anthropology? Far from being an instrument of tolerance toward, and liberation of, minorities as its proponents like to claim, this notion reveals instead all the wrongs of ethnological reason, and that is why it has been claimed by the "new right" in France. To isolate a community by defining a set of characteristic "differences" can lead to the possibility of its territorial confinement, and its eventual expulsion. Ethnic labeling, and the assignation of differences, are self-fulfilling prophecies. They do not just correspond to the acceptance of cultural specificities, but are also correlative with the coercive affirmation of one identity, that of French ethnicity. This is why, if we are not mindful of it, the problematic of the multicultural society can lead straight into a state of separate development analogous to South African apartheid — itself a consequence of the misapplication of the notion of culture.

To this ethnic or cultural fundamentalism that some would like to assimilate to the "defeat of thought," one does not need to oppose the abstract notion of human rights, these principles that no one can truly define. Rather, one must support and articulate the idea of an originary mixing or métissage of the different groups that were formed all through human history.]

Amselle's remarks force us to rethink some of the fundamental notions that we are beginning to take for granted as literary and cultural critics: the respect for multiculturalism, the vexing questions of separatism and cultural autonomy, and the need for contemporary societies to respect difference without falling into a situation of apartheid. It is thus interesting to note that postcolonial women writers implicitly address identical issues in their recent essays and fictional works: they depict characters whose originality stems from the fact that the authors give them universal appeal, letting them live their métissage in the most original, ingenious, and beneficial ways. These hybrid characters exemplify the inevitability as well as the benefits and disadvantages of intercultural exchange. For, as Amselle goes on to add:

> Les cultures ne sont pas situées les unes à côté des autres comme des monades leibniziennes sans porte ni fenêtre: elles prennent place dans un ensemble mouvant qui est lui-même *un champ structuré de relations.* . . .
> *La définition d'une culture donnée est en fait la résultante d'un rapport de forces interculturel* . . . La modification du rapport des forces . . . ainsi que l'éclosion et la disparition des cultures rendent compte des changements qui interviennent dans chaque système sous-culturel pris isolément. (55, my emphasis)

> [Cultures are not located next to one another, without doors or windows, like the monads of Leibnitz: they are situated in a fluctuating context which is *a structured field of relations.* . . .
> *The definition of a given culture is in fact the resultant of a ratio of intercultural forces* . . . The modification of the ratio of forces . . . along with the appearance and disappearance of cultures explain the changes that occur in each subcultural system when one looks at them in isolation.]

To follow Amselle is to come to the conclusion that it is not the existence of *different* cultures that induces a comparative (ethnographical) approach, but rather that it is the critic's (or anthropologist's) stance as comparatist that creates an arbitrary and singular object (be it "Bambara culture" or "francophone studies") — and thus imposes the constraints of a determinate set of particularisms. Although Amselle does not deny the specificities inherent in certain cultural manifestations, he is in fact arguing against all theories of culture that would locate singularity within a restrained space, an enclosed geographical area, a "nation" or a "tradition."[24] Based on Amselle's extensive field research in Africa, *Logiques métisses* opposes his own theorizing of a sociological and historical "*espace métissé*" to the traditional culturalist approach of anthropology that, according to him, is just another form of fundamentalism, itself the breeding ground for many contemporary forms of fascisms, and essentialist tendencies, as witnessed by the pre–civil rights Southern ideology of "separate but equal" and the various other forms of apartheid promoted in recent years by Enoch Powell in Britain, Jean-Marie Le Pen in France, and David Duke in Louisiana.

There is a very real sense in which the works of Maryse Condé, Assia Djebar, and Leïla Sebbar make concretely visible the dialectical tensions present in Amselle's and Appiah's theorizing, and shed new light on what previous generations of francophone critics had taught us to regard as an "alienating" contact between cultures, one in which the dominant group names and circumscribes the subjected one, instilling a colonized or victim mentality into the latter. What these writers illustrate instead is the dynamic and creative processes mobilized by subgroups as means of resistance to the "victim" syndrome. They use their transformative and performative energies on the language and narrative strategies they borrow from the cultures of the West. To represent their regional cultural realities, they make use of appropriative techniques that interweave traditions and languages. The way they portray characters transforms the way that *they* themselves see the realities of their worlds, as well as the way *we*—readers who are outsiders to the region or culture—will in turn perceive those worlds, that is, no longer as a radically "other" realm, so different and alien that it could only alienate itself more through contact with the West but rather as a microcosm of the globe. In other words, these recent works point the way back to a new/old concept: humanism, a word that feminists of different stripes are beginning to revalorize; or to borrow Evelyne Accad's more precise formulation, a "femihumanism," a nonseparatist feminism committed to bringing about a pluralistic society based on the rejection of oppression and domination, whether globally or locally.[25] It is this ethical imperative that governs their search for new cultural forms and hybrid languages that better represent the particularisms of the communities about which they write without locking them into idiosyncratic dead ends.

Thus, for Assia Djebar, the use of the French language leads to an ambiguous situation, because it is the only means through which she can acquire a measure of freedom from the confinement of the harem. Yet, it is also a language in which she suffers from a form of "aphasie amoureuse" (142) ("aphasia of love" [125]), that is, from the complete inability to express "le moindre élan de mon coeur" (145) ("the slightest heart-felt emotion" [128]) because it is a language that necessarily creates distance and artificiality. Hence, emancipation is a way of breaking ties that bind but also ties that create a loving, caring community. For Djebar, then, there is this constant tension between individual emancipation and collective female bonding, autobiography and history, writing and orality, as well as between verbal self-unveiling and the quiet dialogues of bodies and words that the ancient traditions of the harem and the hammam make possible among Islamic women. As she explains:

> Comment dire "je," puisque ce serait dédaigner les formules-couvertures qui maintiennent le trajet individuel dans la résignation collective? ... (177)
> Laminage de ma culture orale en perdition: expulsée à onze, douze ans de ce théâtre des aveux féminins, ai-je par là même été épargnée du silence de la mortification? Ecrire les plus anodins des souvenirs d'enfance renvoie donc au corps dépouillé de voix. Tenter l'autobiographie par les seuls mots français, c'est, sous le lent scalpel de l'autopsie à vif, montrer plus que sa peau. Sa chair se desquame, semble-t-il, en lambeaux du parler d'enfance qui ne s'écrit plus. (177–78)

> [How could she say "I," since that would be to scorn the blanket-formulae which ensure that each individual journeys through life in a collective resignation? ...
> My oral tradition has gradually been overlaid and is in danger of vanishing: at the age of eleven or twelve I was abruptly ejected from the theatre of feminine confidences—was I thereby spared from having to silence my humbled pride? In writing of my childhood memories I am taken back to those bodies bereft of voices. To attempt an autobiography using French words alone is to lend oneself to the vivisector's scalpel, revealing what lies beneath the skin. The flesh flakes off and with it, seemingly, the last shreds of the unwritten language of my childhood. (156)]

Caught between the urgent need to speak of herself as woman and the age-old restrictions on self-unveiling, the narrator of *L'Amour, la fantasia* (*Fantasia, An Algerian Cavalcade*) faces a dilemma that is crystallized by the use of French: "L'autobiographie pratiquée dans la langue adverse se tisse comme fiction" (243) ("Autobiography practised in the enemy's language has the texture of fiction" [216]). Djebar can chart the complexities inherent in the problem of domination by suggesting that the construction of self and other, of conqueror and conquered, of France and Algeria, and of the woman as mother/sister/daughter is always mediated by an intricate set of images, words, and spaces that are never univocal. The construction of subjectivity is made possible by means of a complex interweaving of metaphors of imprisonment and liberation that are not set in opposition to one another but rather as alternating patterns in the fabric of self-portraiture, as well as in the evocation of national and/or female liberation:

> Parler de soi-même hors de la langue des aïeules, c'est se dévoiler certes, mais pas seulement pour sortir de l'enfance, pour s'en exiler définitivement. Le dévoilement, aussi contingent, devient, comme le souligne mon arabe dialectal du quotidien, vraiment "se mettre à nu." (178)

> [Speaking of oneself in a language other than that of the elders is indeed to unveil oneself, not only to emerge from childhood but to leave it, never to return. Such incidental unveiling is tantamount to stripping oneself naked, as the demotic Arabic dialect emphasizes. (156–57)]

To bare one's self in the language of the conqueror is at once a form of betrayal and the inescapable consequence of any gesture of female emancipation:

> Or cette mise à nu, déployée dans la langue de l'ancien conquérant, lui qui, plus d'un siècle durant, a pu s'emparer de tout, sauf précisément des corps féminins, cette mise à nu renvoie étrangement à la mise à sac du siècle précédent. (178)

> [But this stripping naked, when expressed in the language of the former conqueror (who for more than a century could lay his hands on everything save women's bodies), this stripping naked takes us back oddly enough to the plundering of the preceding century. (156–57)]

To unveil this elusive female self thus complicates all relations of power and domination, because the female had come to represent the land itself and the difficulties of conquest and appropriation. But here, emancipation and unveiling come to be the alternating patterns in the palimpsest of history, whereas in *Ombre sultane* (*A Sister to Scheherazade*), the second volume of Djebar's projected quartet, betrayal and liberation again become intertwined as Hajila and Isma are made to represent two facets of a single female destiny that is emblematic of the same dialectic of seclusion and dispersion, confinement and liberation, individuality and collective integrity that forms the basis of Djebar's continuing reflections on the process of othering and the problems of being other in one's own culture.[26]

Within the Caribbean context, the focus has been somewhat different, given that writers, ever since Jacques Roumain's *Gouverneurs de la rosée* (*Masters of the Dew*) or Aimé Césaire's *Cahier d'un retour au pays natal* (*Notebook of a Return to the Native Land*), had been engaged in an enterprise of "creolization" of the French language. Among women writers, Simone Schwarz-Bart and Maryse Condé represent the most interesting examples of this phenomenon, although their respective use of language differs considerably. When it was published in 1972 to great critical and popular acclaim, *Pluie et vent sur Télumée Miracle* (*The Bridge of Beyond*) did much to revitalize the genre of the Caribbean novel by harmonizing the Creole vernacular and a rich and subtle metropolitan syntax. But that was in large part because, unlike Condé's *Traversée de la mangrove* (1989), it did not *need* to contain a glossary of Creole terms: the French language is appropriated and enriched without apparent syntaxic or semantic dislocation. The French reader can approach this text and enjoy its exoticism without feeling too disoriented: s/he can entertain the illusion that the protagonists are from a completely different cultural sphere but that they are knowable, and the language of the text perpetuates this illusion. The originality of Schwarz-Bart is to have succeeded in translating into French a uniquely Caribbean way of perceiving the world: proverbs and oral tales communicate an ancient wisdom. Her use of narrative devices common to the tradition of oral storytelling and her deft mixture of genres (fable, legend, historical chronicle, and realist descriptions) give this novel a richness of tone and a depth of meaning that make it a major landmark in Caribbean women's writing. But in many ways, this novel is also a transitional one. Thematically it is linked, as critic Roger Toumson holds, to the "mythe idéologique de la quête identitaire" (ideological myth of the identitary quest) by its portrayal of male revolt (Amboise) and its emphasis on the painful history of slavery, which continues to have a profound impact on the life of its female characters (Toussine, Victoire, Télumée).[27] *Pluie et vent* thus corresponds to certain expectations that the non-Caribbean reader has about "traditional" Antillean culture and that the French have about the natural and timeless beauty of the tropics. The novel also satisfies the convention of the Caribbean "roman paysan," a genre that begins with Roumain's *Gouverneurs de la rosée*.

Condé's *Traversée de la mangrove* also belongs in that tradition of peasant novels, but it is a resolutely contemporary work, without the mythic atemporality of Schwarz-Bart's earlier work, *Pluie et vent sur Télumée Miracle*. Condé's characters are multifaceted and live in the present, going about their daily lives, self-possessed, and speaking Creole. They do not live under the gaze of the colonizer, they are self-assured in their difference, and they do not—it seems to me—correspond to any existing metropolitan stereotypes about the Antilles. The text does not mythify them, nor does it reveal traces of nostalgia or discontent about the (pre)colonial past, although the past is present in the person of Xantippe, the former slave and "nèg mawon" (255) (runaway black), and in the figure of Francis Sancher, the former revolutionary and disillusioned intellectual. As Xantippe says, "le temps de la vengeance est passé" (259) (the time for vengeance is now passed).

This is indeed the first time that Condé has a truly Caribbean audience in mind: although published in Paris, like her previous books, *Traversée* is not written for a French public. Creole words and expressions are translated at the bottom of each page, but this was done after the fact, as a favor to the French reader and on the recommendation of Condé's editor. Aside from this linguistic *dépaysement*, the text offers no major cultural surprises: the cast of characters is a familiar one for a rural community, with its conflicts among families, its storytellers and teachers, its village idiot and its healer, its migrant workers and other outsiders who bear the brunt of xenophobic reactions on the part of longtime residents. These characters live, love, and die in Rivière au Sel as do humans everywhere. Because the village is isolated, it is possible to identify particularisms that have disappeared from more urban settings in other parts of the Caribbean—but by the same token, these rural characteristics are not unlike those that might be shared by a similarly isolated village in the heart of France's Berry, for example.[28]

One might surmise, then, that an anthropologist looking for "culture" and difference in Rivière au Sel would initially be disappointed, as were Renato and Michelle Rosaldo when they did their field work among Filipinos, who are generally viewed by anthropologists as "people without culture" because, having been "acculturated" by three and a half centuries of (Spanish then American) colonial rule, they are not all that "different": they are "rational, not cultural," and "to the ethnographic gaze, these civilized people appear too transparent for study; they seem *just like us*: materialistic, greedy, and prejudiced."[29] The point, of course, as Rosaldo suggests, is that it is precisely those "zones of cultural invisibility" (78) that pose the most compelling questions for contemporary critics and theorists because that is where the transcultural process, through appropriation and contestation, manifests itself with clarity. It is because "they" appear to be like "us" (Western readers), because "they" are involved in "universal" human problems that the characters of *Traversée* are subversive: they undo that opposition between "us" and "them" that is indispensable to the representation of the exotic other in art, literature, or ethnography.[30] The villagers of *Traversée*, like Rosaldo's Filipinos, are human beings whose cultural production and consumption defy the West's attempt to exoticize them.

To refute the paradigm of exoticism and/or victimization, Condé skill-fully depicts a self-sufficient community unburdened by crises of identity. She gives voice to each one of a series of characters with a unique perspec-tive on the events that have caused them all to assemble at the wake for Francis Sancher, the stranger whose presence in Rivière au Sel caused some major changes in the relations among the villagers. As a figure that allego-rizes both the colonial process and the fate of nomadic intellectuals such as Condé herself, he is a cleverly drawn character who enters into a com-plicated relationship with the local *habitants*. He allows Condé to be self-reflexive about her writing and about the role of writing in her own cul-tural context (203). Condé appropriates the technique of the novel within the novel to reflect on the role of the writer as outsider and of the outsider as catalyst or *pharmakon,* as both poison and antidote, dangerous supple-ment, chronicler, and *aide-mémoire* of the community.[31]

The organization of the story follows the classic dramatic technique of the three unities: unity of time, unity of place, and unity of plot. Condé borrows from classical and modernist aesthetics to create a novel that rep-resents "créolité" in all of its complexity. The Creole and Indian characters voice their own unique perspectives, and it is through them that Condé the writer achieves a sense of her own humility as a recorder and transcriber of reality, a role very much unlike the heroic and prophetic ones that male writers such as Césaire or Glissant espoused as poets and leaders of the community.

For Leïla Sebbar, who writes from within France, the postcolonial con-dition is synonymous with exile and nomadism, literary métissage, and bi-cultural identity. The theme of immigration is central to all her works, and she focuses on the *Beurs,* the second generation descendents of Algerian immigrants, on "marginal" types of all sorts (runaways, drug addicts) who live in the "border zones" of French cities, on regional peasant culture, and also on historical or literary characters whose mythic lives as nomads and eccentrics fascinate her: Rimbaud, Flora Tristan, Isabelle Eberhardt, V. S. Nai-paul, Jeanne d'Arc, Phoolan Devi, and the Dahoman amazons of the eigh-teenth century. Her characters are from nowhere and everywhere, they are emblematic of the shock of societies resulting from the major upheavals of (de)colonization. It is the very concept of the French "Hexagon" and the notion of "francité" that is questioned in her novels and essays. She belongs, it seems to me, both to French and francophone literature, and her writing undermines our academic distinction between "French" and "francophone" areas.[32]

Her *Shérazade* trilogy consists of a geographic and symbolic journey through the signifying system of French orientalisms.[33] A seventeen-year-old runaway who knows very little about her Algerian heritage, Shérazade embarks on a hitchhiking trip through the Hexagon that will allow her to discover the Orient and the meeting of East and West, through the paintings of nineteenth- and early twentieth-century artists. She writes in a set of notebooks, the title of which is the same as the one Sebbar gives to the second book in the trilogy: here, too, self-reflexive devices allow Sebbar to comment both on the status of writing and on the social problems faced by her characters. If, as Michel Foucault has argued, "we are in the epoch of simultaneity... of juxtaposition... of the near and far, of the side-by-side, of the dispersed... [an] epoch... in which space takes for us the form of relations among sites," then Sebbar's narratives are exemplary of a condition of hybridity that allows different historical and spatial configurations to coexist.[34] By reading texts and images of the past in order to understand her own situation as a postcolonial nomad, Shérazade uses all the means at her disposal to survive and contest the negative representations of Oriental women that are embedded in the dominant culture. Sebbar gives her character the opportunity to refuse to be made into an "other": although subjected to the male gaze of Julien or Gilles who can only perceive her through Orientalist codes, Shérazade is able to manipulate those codes, to historicize them, and to point to the historical Arab or Saracen influences on southern France, to the always already hybrid nature of French culture: "Tu sais que les guerriers musulmans arrivaient en Gaule avec leurs familles? Ils venaient de loin, depuis l'Arabie en passant par l'Égypte, l'Afrique, l'Atlas. Il y avaient des Mozarabes, des Juifs, des captifs chrétiens ralliés à l'islamisme, des Berbères islamisés" (264). (Do you know that Muslim warriors would arrive in Gaul with their families? They came from far away, from Arabia, via Egypt, Africa, the Atlas mountains. There were Mozarabs, Jews, Christian prisoners who had become allies of Islam, and Islamized Berbers.)

In contrast to popular views that hold that "la France profonde" of the provinces is the purer, more authentic France (unlike cosmopolitan urban centers), Sebbar stages heterogeneity among rural people as well. There, regional patois reinforce difference and plurality:

> "Je ne sais pas leur langue," dit Shérazade.
> "Moi, je sais parler l'alsacien," dit Marie, "mais c'est pas le patois d'ici. L'alsacien c'est une langue; mon père m'a toujours dit ça et il m'interdit de dire que les paysans parlent en patois; il dit que c'est aussi une langue et qu'on doit pas les mépriser." (168)

"I can't speak their language," Shérazade said.

"I can speak Alsatian," Marie said, "but that's not the same dialect as the one spoken here. Alsatian is a language; my father always tells me this, and he forbids me from saying that peasants speak patois; he says that it is a language, and that they should not be despised.]

Sebbar's emphasis on regional minorities mirrors the postcolonial thematics of diversity. Here, as in *Traversée,* peasant culture is represented in all of its complexity, while it is implicitly contrasted to the appropriative gestures of the young urban *Beurs* whose dress codes reflect their postcoloniality:

"Bon, alors ils disent que c'est leur look à eux, leur style, que personne peut leur piquer parce qu'ils sont les seuls à oser mettre en même temps une chéchia, tu sais ce que c'est? comme leurs ancêtres de là-bas et un jean comme tous les jeunes de partout, ou un battle dress des stocks américains ou une veste de smoking qu'ils trouvent aux Puces, ou un boléro brodé... Tu comprends... les habits traditionnels de leurs grand-pères turcs, arabes, berbères, africains sont à eux et les habits européens sont à tout le monde et eux, leur look, c'est de tout mélanger, mais pas n'importe comment, c'est très étudié..." (159)

["Well, they say that this look is theirs alone. It is a unique style, and nobody can steal it from them because they are the only ones who dare to wear a *chechia*, you know what that is? like their ancestors from overthere, along with a pair of blue jeans like young people everywhere, or an American army battle dress, or a smoking jacket found at the flea market, and an embroidered bolero... You see... the traditional clothes of their Turkish, Arab, Berber, African grandfathers are theirs, and European clothes belong to everybody, and their look, well, it is to mix everything, but not just any old way, it is a very carefully studied way..."]

Dress is a signifying system that denotes not just the global process of neocolonialism and assimilation ("un jean comme tous les jeunes de partout"), but the *Beurs'* own rich construction of their lives and transcultural identitites, their sense of how the past and the present, the near and the far come together in the material things that they use, in the practices that they adopt. Their control over their sense of personal identity is evident in this creative use of the means of self-representation, in the "logique métisse" of their sense of self.

Nor surprisingly, Sebbar's text reveals the same conscious control of the means of representation. *Les Carnets* draws a new geography of France from Marseille to the Ile de Ré, from Narbonne to Nantes. In its formal organization, the text integrates the voices and the idioms of regional or immigrant minorities, numerous intertextual references to eighteenth- and nineteenth-century travel narratives as well as to traditional and classical Arabic texts, to film, operatic music, and popular culture represented both by *Carte de séjour* ("un groupe rockarabe, rockmétèque" [148]) and by a group of female rappers ("rap arabe" [253]) who perform at a Moroccan country wedding near the southern town of Castres. Like the *Beurs*, Sebbar weaves her own tapestry using an aesthetics of *bricolage* that carries over into her style of writing and into the way she actually puts words on paper, because she often writes in cafés, using bits and pieces of paper, "un morceau de nappe, des papiers-sucre, le dos de la note" (a piece of paper tablecloth, sugarcube wrappings, the back of the bill).[35] This image of the unassuming nomad or bohemian writer is also in stark contrast to the heroic and angry voices of Maghrebian male writers of the immediate postcolonial and nationalist periods, whose sense of self and seriousness of purpose are derived from an oppositional nativist ideology and not from the studied ("C'est très étudié") appropriation of such objects and techniques that can transform the relations of "inequality, power and domination" that saturate the social and cultural field but cannot succeed in preventing intercultural exchanges.

Although politically and socially peripheral, francophone women writers share with the *Beurs* this ability to suggest alternative paradigms that maintain discrete *moments* of opposition (translated in dress codes, music, idioms, etc.) without necessarily becoming a counter-ideology. Such moments are not part of a rigid system, because each context will generate different practices (the metaphoric link between territorial conquest and the rape of women in Algeria, the use of Creole in the Caribbean, and rap music in France) that make visible both the dominant culture's power to impose meaning and the social actors' power of agency over configurations that will ultimately undermine those meanings. The practices thus serve to delegitimate the cultural hegemony of "French" culture over "francophone" realities.

What the writings I have briefly surveyed suggest, then, is that the old dichotomies are no longer tenable, that the local and the global are increasingly interrelated, and that one cannot be fully understood without reference to the other. But, at the same time, it becomes clear that universality would be an empty proposition without the gendered specificities offered by particular writers representing different cultural configurations. Francophone women novelists offer us rich and varied ways of understanding this contemporary dialectic — and the ways in which it reweaves the problematics of classical European humanism into a new tapestry in which there can be no room for the normative approaches of the past.

Notes

1. Renato Rosaldo, "Ideology, Place, and People without Culture," *Cultural Anthropology* 3 (February 1988): 85; and "Politics, Patriarchs, and Laughter," *Cultural Critique* 6 (spring 1987): 67. Rosaldo uses this term in reference to areas of Hispanic influence in the United States.

2. I will be making reference to the following works: Maryse Condé, *Traversée de la mangrove* (Paris: Mercure de France, 1989); Assia Djebar, *L'Amour, la fantasia* (Paris: Lattès, 1985), trans. Dorothy S. Blair, *Fantasia: An Algerian Cavalcade* (London: Quartet, 1985); Simone Schwarz-Bart, *Pluie et vent sur Télumée Miracle* (Paris: Seuil, 1972), trans. Barbara Bray, *The Bridge of Beyond* (London: Heinemann, 1974); and Leïla Sebbar, *Les Carnets de Shérazade* (Paris: Stock, 1985).

3. For a more developed analysis of the narrative strategies used in the novels discussed here, see Françoise Lionnet, "*Traversée de la mangrove* de Maryse Condé: Vers un nouvel humanisme antillais?" *French Review* (February 1993): 475–86; and "Parcours narratif/Itinéraire culturel," in *Etudes romanesques 2*, ed. Jean Bessière (Paris: Lettres modernes-Minard, 1994), 137–58.

4. I use the term discourse in the Foucauldian sense. See Michel Foucault, *The Archeology of Knowledge*, trans. Alan M. Sheridan Smith (New York: Pantheon, 1972).

5. As Albert Memmi has indeed pointed out in *The Colonizer and the Colonized* (Boston: Beacon Press, 1967), "it is the colonized who is the first to desire assimilation, and it is the colonizer who refuses it to him" (125), because to assume "that the colonizer could or should accept assimilation and, hence, the colonized's emancipation, means to topple the colonial relationship" (126). Assimilation is thus a fiction uneasily perpetuated by a hegemonic system that simultaneously fears what it wrongly perceives to be its inevitability.

6. Kwame Anthony Appiah, "Is the Post- in Postmodernism the Post- in Postcolonial,"*Critical Inquiry* 17 (winter 1991): 354.

7. One notable recent exception is the work of historian Mechal Sobel. In *The World They Made Together: Black and White Values in Eighteenth-Century Virginia* (Princeton: Princeton University Press, 1987), she analyzes the contributions that African notions of time and space made to the slave owner's weltanschauung, thus becoming part and parcel of the Southerner's perception of reality.

8. Toni Morrison, *Michigan Quarterly Review* 28 (winter 1989): 3.

9. In a 1990 talk at the Program of African Studies at Northwestern University, Jean Comaroff gave a fascinating account of late nineteenth-century practices of South African blacks who were adopting Western clothing, including Victorian wedding gowns and suits. See *Of Revelation and Revolution: Christianity, Colonialism, and Consciousness in South Africa* (Chicago: University of Chicago Press, 1991), chapter 2.

10. See James Bernard, "Why the World Is After Vanilla Ice," *New York Times,* February 3, 1991, section 2, 1 and 26. Also, Patricia J. Williams, "Pre-Old Law, Post New-Man and the Adventures of Everywoman," unpublished paper, presented at Northwestern University, Cultural Studies Working Group, February 5, 1991.

11. Charles Johnson, *Middle Passage* (New York: Atheneum, 1990), 179.

12. Rosaldo, "Ideology," 87.

13. One stunning example of such creative incorporation is the sculpture of a *Man with a Bicycle* exhibited at the Center for African Art in New York in 1987 in the show "Perspectives: Angles on African Art." K. A. Appiah has discussed that exhibit in his article "Is the Post- in Postmodernism" This piece was chosen by James Baldwin, one of the co-curators of the exhibit, and Appiah writes: "I am grateful to James Baldwin for his introduction to the *Man with a Bicycle*, a figure who is, as Baldwin so rightly saw, polyglot — speaking Yoruba

and English, probably some Hausa and a little French for trips to Cotonou or Cameroon . . . *Man with a Bicycle* is produced by someone who does not care that the bicycle is the white man's invention: it is not there to be Other to the Yoruba Self; it is there because someone cared for its solidity; it is there because it will take us further than our feet will take us; it is there because machines are now as African as novelists" (357).

14. Nancy Morejón, *Nación y mestizaje en Nicolás Guillén* (Havana: Union, 1982), 23. My emphasis and my translation. See also my discussion of this phenomenon of "transculturation" and its relationship to métissage in my *Autobiographical Voices: Race, Gender, Self-Portraiture* (Ithaca, N.Y.: Cornell University Press, 1989), 16. The concept of transculturation was first advanced by Fernando Ortiz, as Morejón explains. However, Ortiz's view of culture promotes a form of transculturation that implies the assimilation of Afro-Cuban culture *into* Hispanic culture. Morejón's view of *transculturación* is a more dialectic phenomenon, as is my use of the term *métissage*. I should add that this essay was written before the publication of Mary Louise Pratt, *Arts of the Contact Zone* (New York: MLA, 1991), an essay excerpted from the book *Imperial Eyes: Travel Writing and Transculturation* (New York: Routledge, 1992). In her essay, Pratt makes use of the term "autoethnography" much in the same way that I have used the term in *Autobiographical Voices*, although the corpus she studies, and her approach, are different from mine.

15. See Edouard Glissant, *Caribbean Discourse* (Charlottesville: University Press of Virginia, 1989), 251. See also my discussion in *Autobiographical Voices*, 9.

16. This is true both in the Caribbean: see Jean Bernabé, Patrick Chamoiseau, and Raphael Confiant, *Eloge de la créolité* (Paris: Gallimard, 1989), and in the Indian Ocean: see J-F. Sam-Long "Créolie: Les premiers problèmes . . . ," *Expressions: Revue culturelle réunionaise* 1 (October 1988): 11–24.

17. Abdelkebir Khatibi, *Amour bilingue* (Paris: Fata Morgana, 1983), *Love in Two Languages*, trans. Richard Howard (Minneapolis: University of Minnesota Press, 1990); and *Maghreb pluriel* (Paris: Denoël, 1983). See also my discussion of this phenomenon in "Of Mangoes and Maroons," in *De/Colonizing the Subject: The Politics of Gender in Women's Autobiography*, ed. S. Smith and J. Watson (Minneapolis: University of Minnesota Press, 1992), 321–45.

18. For a discussion of the linguistic originality of some of these works, see for example, Jean Bernabé, "Le travail de l'écriture chez Simone Schwarz-Bart," *Présence africaine* 121–22 (1er et 2e trimestres 1982): 166–79; Lionnet, "*Traversée*"; Clarisse Zimra, "Writing Woman: The Novels of Assia Djebar," *Substance* 69 (1992): 68–84, and "In Her Own Write: Circular Structures of Linguistic Alienation in Assia Djebar's early Novels," *Research in African Literatures* 11 (summer 1980): 206–23; Marguerite LeClézio, "Assia Djebar: Ecrire dans la langue adverse," *Contemporary French Civilization* (spring 1985): 230–44.

19. See James Clifford, *The Predicament of Culture: Twentieth Century Ethnography, Literature, and Art* (Cambridge: Harvard University Press, 1988), Introduction, 1–17.

20. Frantz Fanon, *Peau noire, masques blancs* (Paris: Seuil, 1952), Albert Memmi, *Portrait du colonisé* (Paris: Buchet/Chastel, 1957), Edouard Glissant, *Le Discours antillais* (Paris: Seuil, 1980).

21. Appiah, "Is the Post- in Postmodernism," 354.

22. Quoted by Clifford in *The Predicament of Culture*, 17.

23. Jean-Loup Amselle, *Logiques métisses: Anthropologie de l'identité en Afrique et ailleurs* (Paris: Payot, 1990), 35.

24. Amselle's work thus intersects with Benedict Anderson, *Imagined Communities* (London: Verso, 1983); Eric Hobsbawm and Terence Ranger, *The Invention of Tradition* (Cambridge: Cambridge University Press, 1983); and Roy Wagner, *The Invention of Culture* (Chicago: University of Chicago Press, 1975). For a detailed and thorough examination of some of these

issues from a different perspective, one that emphasizes the importance of relativism as a mode of intercultural critique, see Christopher Miller, *Theories of Africans: Francophone Literature and Anthropology in Africa* (Chicago: University of Chicago Press, 1990), chapters 1 and 2 especially.

25. For a brief philosophical and personal approach to the question of humanism and the holocaust, see Sarah Kofman, *Paroles suffoquées* (Paris: Gallilée, 1987). Evelyne Accad's formulation appears in her recent manifesto, *Sexuality and War: Literary Masks of the Middle East* (New York: New York University Press, 1990), 25–26.

26. Assia Djebar, *Ombre sultane* (Paris: Lattès, 1987), trans. Dorothy S. Blair, *A Sister to Scheherazade* (London: Quartet, 1986).

27. Roger Toumson, *La Transgression des couleurs: Littérature et langage des Antilles* (Paris: Ed. Caribéennes, 1989), vol. 2, 497.

28. I mention the Berry because it is a mostly agricultural region of France, noted for its healers and storytellers. In an interview published in 1984, Marie-Blandine Ouedraogo, discussing the shortcomings of ethnographic representations and the problems of the women's movement in Upper Volta, makes a similar point: "On a parfois l'impression que les ethnologues ne s'intéressent pas beaucoup à la vie des femmes ... qu'elles cherchent à tout prix à découvrir un autre système tout à fait étranger au leur, qu'elles tiennent à se démarquer de nous.

Moi, je trouve que tu mettrais une Africaine devant une paysanne européenne et tu ne verrais pas tellement de différence. De la même manière, une Blanche urbaine ne me paraît pas très différente d'une Africaine des villes. Quand celle-ci veut entrer en contact avec les femmes villageoises, elle rencontre les mêmes difficultés, la même méfiance que l'européenne."

[Sometimes it seems that female ethnologists are not very interested in women's lives ... that they try, at all cost, to discover a system completely foreign to their own, that they insist on differentiating themselves from us.

I think that if you were to compare an African woman with a European peasant woman, you would not see a whole lot of differences. Similarly, a white urban woman does not seem to me to be that different from an urban African woman. When the latter wants to communicate with a village woman, she encounters the same difficulties, the same level of suspicion as a European woman does.] See "Paroles de Haute-Volta," interview conducted by Joele Meerstx in "L'Africaine: Sexes et signes," *Les Cahiers du Grif* 29 (autumn 1984): 33.

29. See "Ideology," 77–80, my emphasis. The Rosaldos were studying the Ilongots, who "lacked the ethnographic staples of the day: lineages, villages, men's houses, elaborate rituals ... " (77).

30. Hence, these characters are the counterpart of the *Man with a Bicycle*, as described by Appiah (see note 14). For an interesting discussion of the issue of cultural and historical relativism, see Satya P. Mohanty, "Us and Them: On the Philosophical Bases of Political Criticism," *Yale Journal of Criticism* 2 (spring 1989): 1–31.

31. I use the term in the Greek sense made familiar by Jacques Derrida in "La Pharmacie de Platon," in *La Dissemination* (Paris: Seuil, 1972), 71–197: "Le *pharmakon* est ce supplément dangereux qui entre par effraction dans cela même qui voudrait avoir pu s'en passer" (126) (The *pharmakon* is this dangerous supplement that enters forcibly where one would prefer to have been able to do without it).

32. A few recent critical essays on Sebbar and the *Beurs* include: Michel Laronde, "Leïla Sebbar et le roman 'croisé': Histoire, mémoire et identité," *Celfan* 7: 1–2 (1987–88), and "La 'Mouvance beure': émergence médiatique," *French Review* 61 (April 1988); Mildred Mortimer, *Journeys through the French African Novel* (Portsmouth, N.H.: Heinemann Educational Books, 1990), chapter 6; and Winifred Woodhull, "Exile," in *Post/Colonial Conditions*, ed. Françoise Lionnet and Ronnie Scharfman, *Yale French Studies* 82 (1993).

33. *Shérazade, 17 ans, brune, frisée, les yeux verts* (Paris: Stock, 1982) is the first volume; *Les Carnets,* the second; and *Le Fou de Shérazade* (Paris: Stock, 1991), the third.

34. Michel Foucault, "Of Other Spaces," *Diacritics* 16 (spring 1986): 22–23.

35. Nancy Huston and Leïla Sebbar, *Lettres parisiennes: Autopsie de l'exil* (Paris: Barrault, 1986), 9.

~

Contributors

Irène Assiba d'Almeida is associate professor of French and Francophone African Literature at the University of Arizona. Her most recent publications include "Echoes of Orpheus in Werewere Liking's *Orphée-Dafric* and Wole Soyinka's *Season of Anomy*," "Femmes? Féministe? Misovire? Les romancières africaines face au féminisme," and *Francophone African Women Writers: Destroying the Emptiness of Silence* (1994).

Eloise A. Brière is associate professor of French studies at the University of Albany. Her research focuses on French language-based communities in Africa and the Americas. Her publications include *Le Roman camerounais et ses discours*. Her last article appeared in *Notre Librairie Les Nouvelles Ecritures Féminines* (no. 117), which she coedited.

Miriam Cooke is professor of Arabic at Duke University. She is the author of *Anatomy of an Egyptian Intellectual: Yahya Haqqi* (1984) and *War's Other Voices: Women Writers on the Lebanese Civil War* (1988). She is coeditor with Margot Badran of *Opening the Gates: A Century of Arab Feminist Writing* (1990); with Angela Woollacott of *Gendering War Talk* (1993); and with Roshni Rustomji-Kerns of *Blood into Ink: South Asian and Middle Eastern Women Write War* (1994).

345

Joan Dayan writes on the Caribbean and on "romance" and "race" in the Americas. She is author of *A Rainbow for the Christian West*, *Fables of Mind: An Inquiry into Poe's Fiction*, and most recently, *Haiti, History, and the Gods* (forthcoming).

John D. Erickson is professor of French at the University of Kentucky. He has taught and lectured at Louisiana State University, the Université de Provence, Rice University, the University of Morocco, and the Sorbonne. He is founder and editor of *L'Esprit Créateur*. He has coedited three volumes of critical essays and authored two books: *Nommo: African Fiction in French* and *Dada: Performance, Poetry and Art*. He is completing a book on postcolonial writing.

Karen Gould is associate dean of the graduate college and professor of French at Bowling Green State University. She has authored or coedited four books, including *Writing in the Feminine: Feminism and Experimental Writing in Québec*, and numerous essays on Quebec women writers. She is the former editor of *Québec Studies* and has also served as president of the Association for Canadian Studies in the United States.

Mary Jean Green is currently associate dean of the faculty for the humanities and professor of French at Dartmouth College, where she also teaches in women's studies and comparative literature. The author of numerous articles on Quebec fiction and film, she has published a book on the contemporary Quebec novelist Marie-Claire Blais and is completing a collection of essays on women's writing in Quebec entitled *Writing in the Mother Tongue*. In addition to her work in francophone literature, she continues to explore the intersection of history, politics, and literature in modern France, which provided the subject matter of her first two books, *Fiction in the Historical Present: French Writers and the Thirties* and *Louis Guilloux: An Artisan of Letters*.

Françoise Lionnet teaches French and comparative literature at Northwestern University. She is the author of *Autobiographical Voices: Race, Gender, Self-Portraiture* (1989) and *Postcolonial Representations: Women, Literature, Identity* (1995), and is one of the coeditors of a special issue of *Signs* on "Postcolonial, Emergent, and Indigenous Feminisms" (1995).

Christiane Makward teaches contemporary French literature, criticism, gender theory, and francophone women writers at Pennsylvania State University. Her publications include the autobiography of Corinna Bille, *La Vrai Conte de ma vie*, and *Plays by French and Francophone Women: A Critical Anthology*, with Judith Miller. She served for seven years as the chief editor of the Research Bulletin in Francophone Feminist Studies (BREFF) and is now coordinator of the Bulletin Franco-Femmes (BFF) for *Présence Francophone*. She is the principal author and general editor of *De Marie de France à Marie DNiaye: A Literary Dictionary and Bibliographical Repertory of Women Writers in French* (forthcoming). She is also writing a monograph on Mayotte Capecia and editing Corinna Bille's complete dramatic works.

Kitzie McKinney is professor of modern languages at Bentley College in Waltham, Massachusetts. She teaches French and Spanish language, interdisciplinary cross-cultural studies, and courses in francophone and Caribbean cultures and literatures.

Christopher L. Miller is professor of French and of African and African-American studies at Yale University. He is the author of *Blank Darkness: Africanist Discourse in French, Theories of Africans: Francophone Literature and Anthropology in Africa,* and essays on francophone African literature.

Mary-Kay Miller is an assistant professor of French at Vanderbilt University. She is currently working on a book titled *(Re)productions of Self: Autobiography, Colonialism, and Infanticide.*

Jane Moss is the Robert E. Diamond Professor of women's studies and French at Colby College. She has served on the executive board of the American Council for Québec Studies since 1984, most recently as president. Her numerous articles on Quebec and French theater have appeared in *Signs, Canadian Literature, French Review, American Review of Canadian Studies, Québec Studies, Women and Performance, Atlantis, Journal of Canadian Studies,* and *Modern Language Studies,* among others.

Elisabeth Mudimbe-Boyi is an associate professor in the departments of French and Italian and Comparative Literature at Stanford University. She teaches twentieth-century French literature and francophone literature from Africa and the Caribbean. Her publications include numerous articles on francophone literature from Africa and the Carribbean and *L'Oeuvre romanesque de Jacques-Stephen Alexis: une écriture poétique, un engage-*

ment politique (1993). She is particularly interested in cultures in contact and in the question of literature and history, representation, and francophone women writers.

Micheline Rice-Maximin, a native of Guadeloupe and a specialist in French and francophone studies, teaches at Swarthmore College. She has published on African-American and Caribbean historical, cultural, and literary questions. She is currently working on the representation of history through literature in contemporary Caribbean texts and also on woman writing in French in Africa and the Caribbean. Her manuscript on Guadeloupean literature is soon to be published.

Lori Saint-Martin is a faculty member at Université du Québec à Montréal, where she teaches Quebec literature, women's writing, and feminist theory. She has published widely in scholarly journals in Quebec, the United States, and Europe. Her books include *Malaise et révolte des femmes dans la littérature québécoise depuis 1945, Lettre imaginaire à la femme de mon amant,* and, with Paul Gagné, a French translation of Daphne Marlatt's novel *Ana Historic.* She has also edited a two-volume anthology on women's writing in Quebec, *l'Autre lecture.* Her latest book, *Le Nom de la mère: Maternité et textualité dans l'écriture des femmes au Québec,* will appear shortly.

Ronnie Scharfman is professor of French at Purchase College, State University of New York. Her book *Engagement and the Language of the Subject in the Poetry of Aimé Césaire* won a Gilbert Chinard Literary Prize. She has published widely on francophone authors of the Antilles, the Maghreb, and Sub-Saharan Africa and, most recently, coedited two special volumes of *Yale French Studies* with Françoise Lionnet, *Post/Colonial Conditions.* She is currently coediting an anthology, *Ecritures de femmes: nouvelles cartographies,* with Mary Ann Caws, Mary Jean Green, and Marianne Hirsch (forthcoming).

Keith L. Walker is a modernist specializing in nineteenth- and twentieth-century French literature and francophone literature. He is primarily known as a Césaire scholar. Walker is the author of *La cohésion poétique de l'oeuvre césairienne* and the forthcoming *Counter-modernism and Francophone Literary Culture: The Game of Slipknot.*

Jack A. Yeager is professor of French and women's studies and former director of the Center for International Education at the University of New

Hampshire. He has published *The Vietnamese Novel in French: A Literary Response to Colonialism* as well as articles on this literature in such journals as *Québec Studies, L'Esprit Créateur, Présence francophone,* the *Revue Francophone de Louisiane, Notebooks in Cultural Analysis,* and *Vietnam Forum.* His *Vietnamese Literature in French* will appear in 1996.

Index

Compiled by Eileen Quam and Theresa Wolner

Bakhtin, Mikhail, 25, 40n6, 266
Baldwin, James, 340–41n13
Barthes, Roland, 266
Bastide, Roger, 48
Battle of Algiers, The (film), 249
Baudelaire, Charles, 45
Bauer, Dale, 151
Bazile, Dédée, 53
Beauvoir, Simone de, 68–69
Belair, Sanite, 53
Bellegarde, Windsor, 53
Benveniste, Emile: *Problems in General
    Linguistics,* 128, 138n7
Berber language, 141
Bernabé, Jean, 41n15
Bersianik, Louky: *L'Euguélionne,* 201; *Pique-
    nique sur l'Acropole,* 201
Béti, Mongo, 281
Beyala, Calixte, 118, 134, 139n10; *C'est le
    soleil qui m'a brûlée,* 135
Bille, Edmond, 123
Bille, S. Corrina, 118–19, 120, 122–23; *La
    Chemise soufrée,* 121, 122; *Deux
    Passions,* 122–23
Biographie des regrets éternels, 39
Biraciality. See *Métissage*
Black women: history of, 35–38; unification
    of, 247; voice of, 22, 27–31
Blackburn, Marthe, 80
Blais, Marie-Claire, xvi, xviii, 61, 62, 64–67,
    70–76; *L'Ange de la solitude,* 75; *La
    Belle Bête,* 64, 64–65, 70–73;
    Manuscrits de Pauline Archange, 73;
    Les Nuits de l'Underground, 74; *Une
    Saison dans la vie d'Emmanuel,* 64–65,
    66, 71–73, 74; *Le Sourd dans la ville,*
    74–75, 117; *Visions d'Anna,* 75, 188;
    and women's theater, 80
Blanchot, Maurice, 313
Bogart, Humphrey, 205
Border crossings, xiv–xv, xviii–xx; and
    cultural exchange, xix; and physical
    displacement, xix; Quebec-U.S., 187
Bouchard, Louise: *Les Images,* 293–97
Boucher, Denise: *Les Fées ont soif,* 80
Bouhdiba, Abdelwahab, 308
Boynard-Frot, Janine, 65–66
Brathwaite, Kamau, 42
Breeze, Jean Binta, 52
Brière, Eloise, xvii

Brock, Renée, 116
Brodber, Erna, 52; *Jane and Louisa Will
    Soon Come Home,* 51
Brontë, Charlotte, 52
Brossard, Nicole, xix; on American culture,
    188–89, 196–201; *Le Désert mauve,*
    188, 196–201, 207; on Quebec women
    writers, 61; and women's theater, 80,
    81
Brouard, Carl, 45
Brutus, Timoléon, 48
Bugul, Ken, 100, 101, 139n10, 157
Butler, Judith, xiv

Caldwell, Erskine, 39
Camaroon women's writing, 265, 266
Canadian national identity, 4–5
Capécia, Mayotte, 52
Carbet, M.-Magdeleine, 118
Cardinal, Marie, 134, 139n10
Catherine of Siena, 116
Centre d'essai des femmes, 80
Césaire, Aimé, 233, 327; *Cahier d'un retour
    au pays natal,* 38, 40n7, 60n23, 333
Charrière, Isabelle de, 118, 253
Chassay, Jean-François, 187, 206–7
Chauvet, Marie, xvi, xx, 52, 54, 55–58, 118;
    Amour Colère Folie, 58, 229–44; *Fille
    d'Haiti,* 55, 230; *Fonds des Nègres,*
    55–58, 230; reception of novels of, 230
Chedid, Andrée: *L'Etroite peau,* 121; *La
    Maison sans racines,* 117; *Le Sixième
    Jour,* 117; *Le Sommeil délivré,* 121, 143,
    145–48, 153
Chekhov, Anton, 38
Chesler, Phyllis: *Women and Madness,* 136
Chodorow, Nancy: *The Reproduction of
    Mothering,* 68, 69, 77n21, 134
Christian, Barbara, xiv
Christophe, Henri, 53
Cinéas, Jean-Baptiste, 54
Cixous, Hélène, xv, 121
Clegg, Johnny, 324
Cliff, Michelle, 52; *Abeng,* 47
Colère (Chauvet). See *Amour Colère Folie*
    (Chauvet)
Comaroff, Jean, 340n9
Commune à Marie, 80
Conan, Laure, 118; *Angéline de Montbrun,*
    66

Nasrallah, Emily: *Those Memories*, 143,
 149–50
National literature, 54
Nationalism: and loss, 54–55
N'Diaye, Catherine, 157
NDiaye, Marie, 120
Nef des sorcières, La, 80
Negritude, 270–71, 283n9
Nickrosz, John, 10
Noël, Francine: *Maryse*, 297–300
Nova Scotia: naming of, 3. *See also* Acadians

Oanh, Trinh Thuc, 210, 222
Oppenheimer, Robert, 199–200
Oppression: and despair, 24; of
 enslavement, 30; and gender, xiv;
 internalized, 23, 175; maternal, 68, 76;
 patriarchal, xviii, xix–xx, 134; social,
 xvi, 151; of working class, 82
Oral tradition, 22, 23; Acadian, xvii, 3–5, 14,
 16, 20n2, 20n6; adaptations of, 40n13;
 and aesthetic representation, 54; of
 Africa, xix; in *Pélagie-la-charrette*, 3,
 13, 14–16; of women, xii, xviii, xxi, 3,
 122–23, 165–66, 171. *See also*
 Storytelling
Other: francophone women writers as, 120,
 123; respect for, 137; and self, 24
Oulette-Michalska, Madeleine, 188
Oyono, Ferdinand, 281; *The Old Man and
 the Medal*, 275

Paradis, Suzanne, 66, 71, 77n17
Partridge, Colin, 12–13
Patriarchy: and alienation of women, 80;
 and gender roles, 79, 124–25; neo-,
 148; oppression of, xviii, xix–xx, 134;
 questioning, 119–21, 123; tradition of,
 65–66
Paul, Emmanuel, 47, 59n4, 59n9
Pélagie-la-charrette (Maillet): as Acadian
 epic, 7; and Acadian women, 6; and
 ethnic consciousness, 8; as feminine
 epic, 17; French folksong in, 11; and
 Grand Dérangement, 4, 9, 18; and
 linguistic decolonization, 10; male
 voice in, 18–19; narration in, 14–19;
 and national culture, 12–14, 16; oral
 tradition in, 3, 13, 14–16; revisionism
 in, 18; women characters in, 6, 10, 13

Pépin, Ernest, 136–37
Petites Violences (Monette), 188, 189–96,
 207; on sexism, 190; on violence,
 190–94
Pisan, Christine de, 116, 117
Pivot, Bernard: *Apostrophes*, 211, 224n14–15
Plat de porc aux bananes vertes, Un
 (Schwarz-Bart), 32, 38, 39n3; madness
 in, 135; narrative in, 24; West Indian
 experience in, 23–26
Polletier, Pol, 80
Poulin, Jacques, 187
Powell, Enoch, 331
Prince, mon jour viendra, Un, 80
Probyn, Elspeth, 193
Proulx, Monique: *Le Sexe des étoiles*,
 300–301

Quebec: francophone women's writings,
 xvi, xviii, xix, xx, 61–76, 285–301; and
 French language, xi–xii; image of
 America in, 186–89; Patriots Rebellion
 (1837–38), 62–63; Révolution
 tranquille (1960s), 62–63, 71, 82;
 romans de la terre in, 288; women's
 theater in, xviii, 79–95
Québécois, 62, 67–68, 70–71, 75–76, 82, 119
Queen of Sheba, 123

Ranavalona(s) (queens), 115
Rape: in *Amour Colère Folie*, 241–42
Rhys, Jean, 52
Rice-Maximin, Micheline, xix
Rich, Adrienne, 74
Riffaterre, Michael, 266
Rimbaud, Arthur, 116, 128, 229
Ringuet: *Trente Arpents*, 65, 66, 67
Rivard, Jean, 65
Robichaud, Louis, 11
Rochefort, Christiane, 119
Rollet, Marie, 76
Romans de la terre, 288
Romans du terroir, 186
Rosaldo, Renato, 321, 327, 328, 335
Rosenblum, Mort: *Mission to Civilize*, x
Rossignol, Michelle, 81
Roumain, Jacques, 54; *Gouverneurs de la
 rosée*, 54, 55–56, 333; *The Masters
 of the Dew*, 41n20; *Montagne
 ensorcelée*, 54

POSTCOLONIAL SUBJECTS

POSTCOLONIAL SUBJECTS

Francophone Women Writers

MARY JEAN GREEN
KAREN GOULD
MICHELINE RICE-MAXIMIN
KEITH L. WALKER
JACK A. YEAGER

EDITORS

UNIVERSITY OF MINNESOTA PRESS

Minneapolis / London

Grateful acknowledgment is made for permission to reprint excerpts from
the following: Antonine Maillet, *Pélagie-la-charrette* (Montreal: Leméac, 1979);
Marie Laberge, *Jocelyne Trudelle trouvée morte dans ses larmes*.

Chapter 3 first appeared in *Research in African Literatures*, 25, no. 2 (1994), reprinted
by permission of Indiana University Press; the original French version of chapter 14
was published in *Violence, Théorie, Surréalisme*, ed. J. Chenieux-Gendron and
T. Mathews (Paris: Collection Pleine Marge, Lachenal & Ritter, 1994),
copyright 1994 Association des Amis de Pleine Marge, translated into English
by permission of the editors; chapter 19 first appeared in *College Literature* 19.3/20.1
(1992/1993), reprinted by permission.

Published by the University of Minnesota Press
111 Third Avenue South, Suite 290, Minneapolis, MN 55401-2520
Printed in the United States of America on acid-free paper

Library of Congress Cataloging-in-Publication Data

Postcolonial subjects : francophone women writers / Mary Jean Green
... [et al.], editors.
p.   cm.
Includes index.
ISBN 0-8166-2628-6 (hc)
ISBN 0-8166-2629-4 (pbk.)
1. French literature—Women authors—History and criticism.
2. French literature—French-speaking countries—History and
criticism.   3. Women and literature—French-speaking countries.
I. Green, Mary Jean Matthews.
PQ149.P57   1996
840.9'9287—dc20
95-43890

The University of Minnesota is an
equal-opportunity educator and employer.

Contents

Part II. Border Crossings

Part III. Engendering the Postcolonial Subject